NAKAM

STANFORD STUDIES IN JEWISH HISTORY AND CULTURE

Edited by David Biale and Sarah Abrevaya Stein

NAKAM

THE HOLOCAUST SURVIVORS
WHO SOUGHT
FULL-SCALE REVENGE

DINA PORAT

Translated by
Mark L. Levinson

STANFORD UNIVERSITY PRESS
Stanford, California

Stanford University Press
Stanford, California

English translation © 2023 by Dina Porat. All rights reserved.

Nakam was originally published in Hebrew in 2019 under the title *Li Nakam v'Shilem* © 2019 Pardes Publishing with support from Dr. Axel Stawski, New York, and Dr. Michael (Micky) Margalit, Tel Aviv.

The publication of this volume was supported by a generous contribution made by Orna and Behzad Kianmahd.

Documentation and testimony were collected with the kind assistance of Hava Zexer.

Printed in the United States of America on acid-free, archival-quality paper

Library of Congress Cataloging-in-Publication Data

Names: Porat, Dina, author.

Title: Nakam : the Holocaust survivors who sought full-scale revenge / Dina Porat ; translated by Mark L. Levinson.

Other titles: Li naḳam ye-shilem. English | Stanford studies in Jewish history and culture.

Description: Stanford, California : Stanford University Press, [2023] | Series: Stanford studies in Jewish history and culture | "Originally published in Hebrew in 2019 under the title Li Nakam v'Shilem." | Includes bibliographical references and index.

Identifiers: LCCN 2022022185 (print) | LCCN 2022022186 (ebook) | ISBN 9781503630314 (cloth) | ISBN 9781503633773 (epub)

Subjects: LCSH: Nakam (Organization)—History. | Nazi hunters—Germany—History. | Holocaust survivors—Israel—Interviews. | Holocaust, Jewish (1939-1945)—Influence. | Revenge—Moral and ethical aspects.

Classification: LCC D804.195 .P6713 2023 (print) | LCC D804.195 (ebook) | DDC 940.53/18—dc23/eng/20220518

LC record available at https://lccn.loc.gov/2022022185
LC ebook record available at https://lccn.loc.gov/2022022186

Designed by Elliott Beard
Typeset by Motto Publishing Services in 11/15 Garamond Premier Pro
Cover design and illustration: Derek Thornton | Notch Design

"Before us lies only one path to life—constructive vengeance."

From the passage read on the summit of Masada during the Chanukah 1943 hike of the youth movement Hamahanot Ha‘olim, led by Nahum Sarig and Azaria Alon. On his back, Alon carried a large rock inscribed with the words "If I forget thee, Diaspora, let my right hand forget her cunning." The reading was published in the December 1943 issue of *Bamivhan*, the movement's periodical, and republished in Yitzhak Kafkafi's book *Shnot Hamahanot Ha‘olim*, volume 2, Hakibbutz Hameuchad Publishing House, Tel Aviv, 1995, p. 314.

"Your pure blood will forever be a mark of shame on Hitler's Germany. Rest peacefully where you lie. We the surviving remnant will avenge your blood—our blood."

From the writings in Yiddish, Russian, and Hebrew placed by survivors in 1944 on the mass grave of the 23,500 Jews of Rovno who were tortured and murdered on November 7 and 8, 1941. Quoted in *Rowno, a Memorial to the Jewish Community of Rowno, Wolyn*, ed. Arye Avatihi, Association of Rovno Jews in Israel, Tel Aviv, 1956, p. 562.

Contents

Preface and Acknowledgments　　　　　ix

Introduction　　　　　1

PART I

CONCEPTION AND PREPARATION

1　Lublin, January–March 1945　　　　　31
The Idea of Vengeance

2　Bucharest, March–June 1945　　　　　71
From Conception to Preparation

3　Italy, July–August 1945　　　　　99
The Jewish Brigade

PART II

ATTEMPTED VENGEANCE

4　Palestine and Europe, August 1945–March 1946　　　　　145
Kovner and the Yishuv

5　Paris, February–June 1946　　　　　195
The Haganah and the Avengers

6 Germany, August 1945–June 1946 225
Life Apart from Life

Conclusion 275

APPENDIXES

Chronology 309

List of the Avengers 313

Notes 317

Sources 329

Index 347

Photographs appear after page 142.

Preface and Acknowledgments

THIS BOOK HAD ITS BIRTH in a promise. After the book I wrote about the poet and wartime partisan Abba Kovner was published,[1] Yitzhak "Pasha" Avidov (born Reichman) called me to his house for a talk and scolded me: "You've written a whole thick biography with only one page about the group of Avengers that Abba commanded and led, rest his soul. One page for an entire year!" In vain I explained that the focus of the book was Kovner, who for most of that year—between the summer of 1945 and the summer of 1946—was a leader isolated from his followers. Avidov had served as commander of the group, filling in for Kovner from the moment Kovner left.

His complaints subsided a little only once I gave my word, accompanied with a handshake, that there would be a future book exclusively about the Avengers—the *Nokmim,* as they called themselves in Hebrew—with descriptions and analysis of the group's experiences and dilemmas as they actually occurred, and chronicling, to the best of my ability, its members' activities as they actually unfolded. I carried that obligation onward as much as I could. I thank him deeply, and I am very sorry that it has come to fruition only after his passing.

There were also misgivings among other members of the Nokmim, with whom I had remained in close contact since the days of my work on Kovner's biography. They had kept their secret for forty years, from the end of World War II until the mid-1980s, when they began apprehensively agreeing to be interviewed and photographed, and to respond to accusations, meet together and record their experiences. This occurred only after great hesitation. They feared then, and still do, that neither the idea guiding their attempted operation nor the methods they wanted to employ will be understood; that instead of being remembered as moral people with Jewish and humanitarian values, they will go down in history the way Shaul Meirov (subsequently Avigur) described them: "rife with a spirit of rebellion [. . .] that derived from deep feelings of inferiority" and eager for revenge without restraint.[2] At the time, he headed the Mossad for Aliyah B (a clandestine infrastructure for illegal immigration, to circumvent British limitations), and these words are quoted in *History of the Haganah*: The Haganah was the major Jewish underground force in British-ruled Palestine, and it operated the Mossad for Aliyah B.

Until now, the story of the Nokmim has been told primarily by journalists and on television. It has been covered in brief chapters in two books of research, as well as a comprehensive article in a periodical,[3] but it has never been the sole focus of thorough research. Today, aged ninety and over, the Nokmim want to see their story told in full. From their shelves and drawers, they have brought out previously hidden diaries, letters, and writings in small notebooks, yellowing pages written in Polish and Lithuanian, German and Russian, Yiddish and Hebrew, and they have graciously opened their homes for lengthy interview sessions. Abba Kovner's widow, Vitka Kempner-Kovner, handed me a file from a metal closet in his workroom and said, with characteristic plainness, "Here—take it." It holds documents and correspondence from the Nokmim group, and she had been keeping them undisturbed, ever since he died, the way he left them. It sends a flutter through the historian's heart to hold decades-old papers that speak out across the years.

This book, then, is the fulfillment of my promise to record the story of the young men and women who gave of their strength and will and intended to give their lives, if necessary, for vengeance against the Germans after the Holocaust. At the same time, it is an attempt to answer the question that gnaws at them to this day: Why did such vengeance fail to come about on the scale that they desired? What—or who—thwarted them? They'd invested months and months of planning under difficult conditions. They'd come with the initiative, skill, and persistence that they'd already demonstrated in the years of the Holocaust and war. And yet they didn't manage to carry out the task that they'd set for themselves. This mystery does have answers, and they become clearer, sharper, when the participants' memories are juxtaposed with the evidence preserved at their homes, archival material, and interviews with people outside the participants' own tight circle.

And the book has a third purpose, besides the pledge I gave and the attempt to tackle previously unanswered questions. There was also the desire to understand how the personalities of the Nokmim, individually and collectively, could square with the incongruously terrifying deed that they planned. During the meetings, each and every one of them gained my ever-increasing marvel and admiration for their strength and determination, vividness of memory and depth of emotion despite the years since the events, and commitment to the mission that they undertook—and then, having left it unfinished, to the memory of that commitment and of their departed friends and families; and for their inexhaustible humor and joie de vivre, as well as the friendship that still bonds them despite their differences. Above all, however, I noted their sense of concern about the fate of the Jewish people in the absence of a clear warning against harming Jews again. Some of the Nokmim live near one another and help one another out as needed. All are frequently in touch by phone, and all are constantly aware of the news from the others. They immediately tell the others about whom they've met with and what was said, they warn about journalists and photographers who may be coming while lacking previous background or knowledge, and they coordinate strategies for dealing with potential sensation-mongers.

My deep and heartfelt thanks to Hava Zexer, formerly my student and today my friend. Together we jounced along Israel's roads, Hava with her camera and tripod, and I with the file of testimonies we'd collected so far. Hava would drive, and I would consult the map on my knees and misdirect her around Haifa and Jerusalem, Michmoret and Shoham, Ein HaHoresh, and especially Ramat Gan and Givatayim. Hava, gifted with a pleasant manner and an astute and assertive mind, asked incisive questions at the interviews with the Nokmim and advanced fruitful theories afterward. Together, we put order into the swarm of confusingly similar-sounding names—Poldek, Yulek, Manek, Yashek, Kazhik, Idek. They insisted on more interviews, particularly in order to commemorate the comrades who had already gone to their reward, such as Bartek, Willek, and Shimek. And of course there were the "girls," Lenka, Vitka, Mirka, and Tzeska, rest their souls, and Hashkah and Rochkeh. Long may they and their surviving comrades live.

I am greatly indebted to that fascinating circle for the many hours they devoted to the telling of their story; for their trust and hospitality; for the wealth of material that they searched out, retained, and entrusted us with; and for the privilege of gaining their close acquaintance. A particularly large amount of material was collected at the home of Rachel (Rochkeh) Galperin-Gliksman, the "historian" among the Nokmim. For years she collected books, testimonies, pamphlets, and letters, and she organized them with care and love. Thanks to her for graciously, cheerfully providing access to the material. A great deal more material was found in archives, particularly in the Moreshet archive at Givat Haviva where Kovner's family deposited most of his papers. I am appreciative also for Yosepha Pecher, who cataloged the papers; to Daniella Ossatski-Lazar, who, on her own initiative, searched for and found treasures; and to Ariella Carmi for elucidating the recordings of the first reunion of the Nokmim. Thankful good wishes for their kind help also go to the archive staff at the Ghetto Fighters' House, particularly Yossi Shavit, the director; to Roni Azati, the director of the Yad Tabenkin Archives; to Eldad Haruvi, the director of the Palmach House Archive; to Michael Laks, of the IDF Archive; and to Boaz Tal, the archive manager at Massuah. I am grateful to the late Levi Arieh Sarid for much valuable material that he generously gave us; and to Shlomo Nakdimon, the first to interview the Nokmim and publish press reportage about this story, for the seventy-year-old material that he found in his files and provided to me; to Orly Levy and Dorit Hermann, of the Haganah Archives; and especially to Neri Arieli, of kibbutz Ein Gedi, who tracked down important material there; to my student Rachel Hadaio for tape-cassette copies of her interviews; to Louise Fisher, of the Israel State Archives; to Devorah Stavi, of the Gnazim Institute; to Adi Portughes, of the Ben-Gurion Heritage Institute at Sde Boker; to Yarin Kimor, who interviewed the group for a film that he produced; to Aron Heller, an Associated Press correspondent in Israel, and to researcher Randy Herschaft for material from the US government's National Archives in Washington, DC; to Merav Segal, the director of the Weizmann Archive; to Sima Borkovski for the photos of the Nokmim; and to Yitzik Nir for the transcripts of testimony from Yitzhak "Antek" Zuckerman. Avidov's son Avi provided several boxes brimming with surprises and encouraged us to keep going. Yonat Rotbein, daughter of Ruzka Korczak, helped with good advice and pointed out material contained in recordings of Nokmim meetings from the 1980s and particularly from the 1990s. I am especially thankful to the late poet Elisha Porat (no relation) of Ein HaHoresh, who accumulated many, many hours of "face time" with Kovner. He wanted very much for this book to be published, he provided guidance and material, and his loss is deeply felt.

The archives contain testimony given by thirty-four of the Nokmim, including several who spoke a number of times over the years, which includes a majority of the group's most central and active members, a total of fifty men and women. I thank them for their testimonies, and I also thank the sons and daughters of the Nokmim, the second generation—and the third generation as well—for the material that they sought and found in the homes of their parents and in their own homes, and for the great interest that they showed in the book.

Special thanks to Dr. Axel Stawski, of New York, to Dr. Michael (Micky) Margalit, of Tel Aviv, and to Orna and Bezhad Kianmahd, of Los Angeles, for their generous support in advancing the work of research and publication.

Thanks to my student Dr. Shlomo Kron for collecting and analyzing materials from Judaic sources; to my dedicated student Tal Cohen, who helped me assemble the material during the phase of the book's writing; and to Talia Naamat, whose help is always invaluable.

Many thanks to Professor Daphna Erdinast-Vulcan, editor in chief of the Haifa University Press, and to the staff of the press: Sharon Hanuka Ben-Shimol, the director, and Shoshi Leber, the secretary, who cooperate with David Gotesman, the head of Pardes Publishing, and his staff, and to the Bahat Prize committee members and the reviewers who recommended the manuscript as worthy of their distinguished prize. I am deeply honored.

Many thanks go to the team at Stanford University Press: Profs. David Biale and Sara Abrevaya Stein, editors of the series; Margo Irvin, the acquisitions editor; Cindy Lim, the editorial assistant; and Gigi Mark, production editor; as well as to Gretchen Otto of Motto Publishing Services; Sarah Rutledge, the copyeditor; and to Mark L. Levinson, the translator, for all their excellent work.

Some of the meetings with the Nokmim, as a group and as individuals, were photographed and recorded, but it may be said—after reading the dozens of testimonies from the interviews, watching the films, and listening to the recordings—that despite the media options at the researcher's disposal, even including photography and sound recording, there is no substitute for meeting one on one, researcher and witness, face to face, without the intrusion of a camera or microphone. Only the trust that is built between two people, and the silence between the words, can beget the most sincere and detailed of interviews, and such interviews were an inexhaustible source of information and insight. In very rare moments, however, the testimonies contradicted one another. There, the profession meets its limits, since a definitive assessment was impossible. Those stories are presented in their full scope, but without definitive conclusions.

Direct quotations from the interviewees, whether or not they were members of the group, appear, of course, in quotation marks and with references. In some cases, for the sake of brevity and to reduce repetition, the quotations are paraphrased, with the speaker's attitude and tone preserved, and presented without quotation marks but still with references provided. The speakers used their nicknames from their days as Nokmim, but with one exception, the first time they appear in the book they are referenced with their full names. Those who have changed their names, in most cases to Hebraize them, appear under their Hebrew names because those are better known to the public, and certainly to the generation born after the war. These speakers too, of course, are presented with their full original names the first time they appear.

Dina Porat

RAMAT HASHARON, MAY 2022

NAKAM

Introduction

"NO ONE HAS SPOKEN the whole truth about this business, and no one knows everything about it. I don't envy the person who has to research all the details. I think that by now, with so many stories still circulating, some of us are beginning to believe them, partly because there are so many legends that we've told and heard, and they carry all kinds of symbols and ideas." These are the words of a person who was tasked with keeping a close watch on the Avengers (the *Nokmim* group) of Abba Kovner. The task was assigned to him by the leaders of the Yishuv, the Jewish establishment in the Land of Israel (the official name used by the British Mandate over the land, 1919–48, was Palestina/E.I., Eretz Israel, the Land of Israel).[1] Nevertheless, despite such an admonition, a historian who knows that a certain event occurred, and that certain people were involved in it, must ponder whether the event should be ignored on the simple grounds that in light of today's values, the story may not be understood; because it might, heaven forbid, have harmful effects; because it touches on a topic that Jewish tradition may have prohibited or surrounded with a hundred barricades; or because certain legends and symbols may be damaged in its telling. Or the outcome may be the opposite: convinced that the event did occur, the historian may feel not only that there is no retreat or returning the material to obscurity, but that he or she rather has an obligation to press on, to examine the event, to retell and analyze it, to bring it to public attention. Regarding the Hebrew word for "truth," from the quotation that opened this introduction, the Midrash notes that it begins with aleph, the first letter of the Hebrew alphabet; its middle letter is mem, the middle letter of the alphabet, and its final letter is tav, the last. Thus the search for truth requires a full journey from beginning to end—investigating all the stories, all the symbols, and all the legends.

This book deals with the Nokmim group, which was founded by the poet and partisan Abba Kovner after World War II, when nearly six million Jews were murdered in the Holocaust and an entire culture was nearly wiped out. Some fifty young women and men decided to take vengeance against the German nation and kill six million of them. The book will concentrate on the Nokmim in particular and not on the various other acts of vengeance carried out primarily by non-Jews against Germans, both before and after the end of the war. In contrast to those acts, the Nokmim wished their revenge to be public and on a scale that, in the view of the planners, would be commensurate with the Holocaust. They wanted vengeance that would stand as the overt response of the victimized nation against the murderers, vengeance to be recounted around the world, visited on millions, vengeance that would strike the Germans in specific but warn the rest of the world that Jewish blood would never again be forfeited as it had throughout history and, above all, during the Holocaust. Kovner's name for the group was an acronym spelling *Din*, the Hebrew word for justice, and standing for "The Blood of Israel Remembers." The name also echoed *Dayan*, the Hebrew word for a judge, signaling that anyone attempting to kill Jews would now risk judgment and execution.

The question of punishment after the Holocaust, as understood by the Nokmim, had metaphysical aspects touching on the basis of the world's existence and functioning. The world had reached a dead end in the form of moral bankruptcy, and the punishment would settle the account and return order as is written in our scripture. The Lord commands Moses to take revenge on behalf of the Israelites after their slaughter by the army of Midian: "Avenge the children of Israel of the Midianites: afterward shalt thou be gathered unto thy people" (Numbers 31:2). And the Yom Kippur prayers say,

"Our Father, our King, avenge before our eyes the spilled blood of Your servants." The phrase "before our eyes" implies "for all the world to see."

The vengeance that the Nokmim had in mind, that burned in their very bones and gave them no rest, was intended to repay the Germans in their own coin, duplicating the scope of the disaster that they had wreaked against the Jewish nation: an eye for an eye and a tooth for a tooth (as in Exodus 21:24): vengeance with no warning, arrest, or trial; vengeance direct and immediate. In their view, vengeance without trial was the fitting and proper course because the laws prevailing at the time, both in the various countries and internationally, were incapable of responding properly to the terrible deeds that had been committed. Existing law, which had never known crimes on such a scale, had no adequate answer. Therefore, a new law—and a new court of judgment—was required. It was clear to the Nokmim that there would be a long wait before any such legislation would be enacted, and even before it was decided who would pass the legislation, much less conduct the trials. There was no telling who the judges would be, what attitudes they would bring to this unprecedented task, or when they would hand down sentencing (although it would surely be based on their previous experience). The Nokmim had already seen with their own eyes what certain laws were worth and where they were liable to lead—especially in their recollections of Nazi legislation. Moreover, they had no doubt that the presumably non-Jewish judges, convening after the war but without having personally experienced what had happened in those years, would lack understanding. The judges would be unable to envision the situations that the witnesses described to them and therefore incapable of rendering just rulings.

"When I close my eyes and think of what was," said Kovner, "I ask myself: Was that reality a reality?"[2] Many survivors, including the Nokmim, had little interest in the later search for an official and systematic definition of the Holocaust, although they knew well that over the years many researchers and thinkers concerned themselves with defining the nature of the Holocaust and in delineating "that reality." Still, let us try our hand:

The Holocaust was an unprecedented event in human history that included the methodical murder—by bullets, gas chambers, and unsurvivable conditions—of nearly six million Jews: men, women, and children. Thousands of Jewish communities, with their material and spiritual treasures, were eradicated by Nazi Germany and its accomplices. Between the Nazi Party's ascension to power in 1933 and the surrender of Germany in May 1945, the Germans and their collaborators murdered several million more people from across various cultures and sectors. However, the Holocaust visited on the Jews differs from other genocides in history because of the unique stance of the Nazis regarding Jews. The uniqueness of the Holocaust lies in its generality (the desire to murder every single Jew), in its borderlessness (targeting Jews everywhere), in a racial, antisemitic ideology that was totally divorced from reality, in the absence of pretext in the form of already established conflict between Jews and Germans, in the industrialization of murder, and in the depiction of the Jewish people as the symbol of absolute evil.[3]

For many survivors, including the Nokmim, the traumatic event was a lengthy span of years during which their lives were reduced to rubble. It was a personal existential disaster, resulting in the loss of family, home, community, town, and property. Life as it had been was replaced by forced relocation, torture, hunger, physical exhaustion, and disease. Surviving from moment to moment was a struggle involving impossible choices, and, most of all, it left behind the worst of gnawing feelings—humiliation—caused by the sharp transition from being recognized as a person, with all the characteristics of a self-reliant identity, to being a hunted creature, dispossessed and above all helpless, unable to rescue your most beloved, being thrown aside and tossed about with senseless cruelty by forces and processes susceptible to neither understanding nor influence. The humiliation was both personal and national, wreaked by the attempt to stigmatize everyone who belonged to a supposedly unclean and dangerous race. Finding the strength to respond was very difficult. Later, Kovner would repeatedly stress in his speeches that what happened before the genocide, what laid the groundwork for it, was worse than death. When you understand the scope of the Holocaust, he said during his first days in the Land of Israel, "you will know the numbers destroyed, but you still will have no grasp of the fathomless depths of *what came before* [. . .]. The horror was in the life that preceded the death, in the humiliation of a people as we were witness to how the nation and the individual are turned to dust, how all sacredness is smashed and crumbled."[4]

The constant humiliation and helplessness drove the blaze of passion for revenge. It was intended to pay back the vandals, robbers, and murderers, to prove that they could be defeated, that helplessness was not incurable, that the Nokmim, in levying punishment upon them, were not only their equals but their superiors. It is impossible to understand that passion, which burned in the hearts of both Jews and non-Jews, without understanding what the Germans wreaked during the Holocaust and the war. This understanding is critical, even if it is painful to read full, accurate accounts of the Holocaust and to analyze its evolvement—indeed, recent decades have seen a trending away from grisly descriptions of evil and merciless cruelty in favor of penning descriptions and creating artworks that are easier to digest. The horrors of the World War are fading and blurring in global memory as well. Because they are drifting away from the terrible reality, they are being conceived as cinematic entertainment and escapist reading.[5] It is impossible to deeply understand the feelings of those who lived then, Jewish and non-Jewish, without considering that their souls were branded with the images of a baby whose head was repeatedly pounded against a wall, of human beings buried alive, of entire towns and villages being torched along with their inhabitants, of brothers and friends who turned to walking skeletons—all while being helpless to prevent any of it.

VENGEANCE BY NON-JEWS

In January 1945, Marshal Georgy K. Zhukov, the acclaimed and decorated Soviet military leader, declared in an order of the day: "Woe to the land of the murderers. We will get our terrible revenge for everything."[6] In his book *Year Zero: A History of 1945*, historian Ian Buruma devotes a long and comprehensive chapter to the grim deeds of vengeance carried out in many countries that year. He tells of the Soviet soldiers who fulfilled Zhukov's order assiduously, as the loss and destruction suffered in the Soviet Union was beyond understanding. More than eight million Soviet soldiers were killed. Of the five and a half million soldiers who were imprisoned by the Germans, more than three million were murdered using the cruelest of methods. The Germans also abused the civilian population, having created a delusional hierarchy of races and ranking the Slavs as an inferior race near the bottom. Following not only hunger, scorched earth, extended siege, and humiliation but also the murder of sixteen million civilians, Zhukov's formula for revenge was clear: the Red Army soldiers were explicitly instructed to inflict the harshest cruelty immediately upon entering German territory. Road signs at the border commanded in Russian: "Soldier, you are now in Germany. Take revenge against the Hitlerites!"[7] And indeed the acts of looting, of murder, and especially of incessant brutal rape by Soviet soldiers—until, after some weeks, the order came to cease the rampage—were seared into the memory of Europe, and especially Germany, for years.[8]

But not only the Soviets took revenge. Buruma describes a concentration camp for German prisoners in Czechoslovakia in 1945 where an inscription above the main gate read, "Eye for Eye, Tooth for Tooth." The Czech officers treated their prisoners the way the Germans treated concentration camp inmates, and worse. Czech president Edvard Benes declared, "Fate will be three times as harsh and bitter for the Germans; we will destroy them!"; subsequently, three million Germans were deported by the Czechs from the Sudetenland, with some thirty thousand dying during the travails of that deportation.[9] In Poland, similar camps were set up for some two hundred thousand Germans, and roughly thirty thousand died there. A book about these camps entitled *An Eye for an Eye*, raises the question of what role Jews, placed in charge of Polish camps by the Communist regime, played in the acts of vengeance that occurred there and in other severe acts of violence.[10] In at least one camp, thousands of Germans were murdered, including hundreds of children.[11]

American foot soldiers and officers, "shocked by the visual evidence of German depravity," according to Buruma, stood by as liberated prisoners at Dachau cruelly lynched one SS guard after another. After seeing the corpses of prisoners ready for burning at the front of the crematorium, an American officer had three hundred German guards executed by gunfire.[12] Nonetheless, even among the administrators of the American zone in conquered Germany, as among the Soviets, there were those who had second thoughts. The Americans began implementing the Morgenthau Plan, which represented a policy of punishing Germany for the collective malfeasance of the German people and aimed to prevent the country from starting a third world war by destroying its industry and de-Nazifying its society. But those plans were difficult to carry out, and there was concern that as a result Germany could become an economic burden on the United States.[13]

"It is difficult to imagine how a war of such shocking brutality could conclude without brutal revenge," writes historian Antony Beevor at the end of his monumental book *The Second World War*. He too describes a number of cruel acts of vengeance, as does historian Timothy Snyder in his book *Bloodlands*. Ethnic cleansing proceeded at full tilt, as Stalin had desired from the start, and troops of the First and Second Armies of Poland forced Germans from their homes, herded them across the Oder River, loaded them onto cattle cars, and looted the property left behind. Of the more than two million Germans in eastern Prussia, for example, fewer than two hundred thousand remained, and six hundred thousand were sent to the Soviet Union for forced labor. Women marched toward Germany, sometimes for hundreds of miles, with babes in arms.[14] More description could be added regarding the hair-raising deeds of vengeance carried out in many countries, particularly on German soil, as well as the deportations and ethnic cleansing. There were Greek, Ukrainian, Slovak, French, Italian, Hungarian, and other citizens who, after being freed from the camps, refused to return home until they enacted their revenge.[15]

VENGEANCE BY JEWS

Granted, non-Jews vented their emotions on a large scale through acts of vengeance directed against the Germans, but as Buruma tells it, "while vengeance was being taken all over Europe [. . .] the people who had suffered most showed extraordinary restraint." However, this generalization is not completely accurate. Jews in the Red Army and in partisan militias joined with their comrades in arms to commit acts of revenge, particularly the murder of collaborators—individuals and groups identified among the Ukrainians, Lithuanians, and Poles—which they undertook immediately upon emerging from forests and other hiding places while the Soviets were advancing westward. In Rovno, for example, those who emerged from the forests swore upon the mass grave of the city's Jews that their blood would be avenged. To that end, the justice-seekers dedicated themselves to bringing hundreds of collaborators to trial from among the Ukrainian population: they prepared solid cases against them and ultimately had six hundred of those defendants executed.[16] Even Jews who had not served in the armies organized death squads comprising individual disparate Jews, to carry out executions of their own. They wandered from place to place and carried out executions. Obtaining weapons was no problem in the days of disorder that followed the end of wartime.[17]

Jewish revenge groups were founded in not only Eastern Europe but also Central Europe. *Nasza Grupa*, a group of Zionist Youth members from Będzin, Poland, aimed to exact vengeance in Germany. Emil Brigg, later a hero in Israel's War of Independence, recounted: "We had nothing to lose [. . .]. We wanted only revenge. Young men and women burning for vengeance, with nothing in their world but a mighty urge to kill Germans and to destroy whoever was collaborating with Germans."[18] Some members of Nasza Grupa, who had volunteered for the Red Army, succeeded in acts of vengeance, but not as much as they had wished: not as Jews, and not as representatives of the entire Jewish nation against the entire German nation. One of them, Manos Diamant, visited Auschwitz as soon as the war ended, and he saw this command written on one of the walls of the torture chambers: "Jews, take vengeance!" These words guided his future. He and Alex Gatmon, a fellow member of the group, headed a squad in Austria that executed those who had been found guilty. Most of the members felt as if they were judges without robes, judges of a special kind who together delivered and immediately carried out their sentences. They bound and gagged suspects, held a few minutes of trial proceedings for each, and read an indictment. They prosecuted murderers who had been active in the ghettos and concentration camps—those who had killed with their own hands and could be reliably identified, in the group's opinion, by at least two witnesses. "No court of true justice in the world would have handed down a different verdict if he confessed on his own without being interrogated," said Diamant. These killers were mostly, but not always, SS troops. The group then killed the suspect. They made a practice of leaving a note on the murderer's body so that the world would know that this was vengeance by Jews; they concentrated primarily on eliminating war criminals who had been released by the Allied nations' judges, a particularly galling lack of justice: "We had been sure that all Europe would be swept up in a wave of vengeance," Diamant recounted.[19]

Near the end of 1945, Asher Ben-Natan arrived in Vienna. He was among the leaders of the *Bricha*—a clandestine exodus of survivors out of

Europe and bound for Palestine—through Austria and Italy. In later years, he would serve as Israel's first ambassador to Germany. Members of Nasza Grupa, including Gatmon and Diamant, joined him as activists in the Bricha, and they became a self-styled documentation center, compiling a long, detailed list of the war criminals they discovered. "My instructions were clear," Ben-Natan wrote, referring to instructions from the Zionist leadership of the Yishuv. "We aren't judges, and we are not to personally harm the criminals but to turn them over to the allied or Austrian authorities for punishment."[20] But he noted the severity of such punishment: in those days, in several countries, war criminals delivered to the authorities were typically either sentenced to death or given long prison terms, most often in Siberia. For that reason, Ben-Natan instructed the Nasza Grupa members not to continue their previous methods of revenge.

Many of those who left for Israel returned to Europe in 1949 because they disagreed with Ben-Natan's course of operations and had decided to renew the acts of vengeance, but despite punctilious preparations and great effort, they failed to achieve their goal. Some of the group's members persisted until the Israeli embassy was opened in Vienna. In 1950 they received an order to cease their activities, an order they obeyed because they were already Israeli passport-holders. However, from that point until their deaths, they expressed disappointment in the leadership of the newborn country for not adequately investing time and effort into the matter and for preventing them from carrying out what they believed was called for.[21]

There were survivors who spent months finding the killers of their loved ones and enacting deadly revenge; still other survivors took revenge, whenever conditions permitted, on whomever they came across. For example, four young men who had been freed from the Landsberg/Kaufering concentration camp, near Munich, stole British jeeps and drove into a neighboring town, where they mounted a pogrom of their own for four or five hours, punching and beating. Soldiers of the Jewish Brigade who arrived at the scene "stood there stunned. They couldn't agree with this [and sent us away]. We broke everything around—we broke windows, we hit children and old people too. The hatred inside us was terrible, a heavy burden of rage." It is difficult to determine how many such incidents occurred, with survivors taking action either independently or with a few comrades; there has not yet been a study on this individual vengeance.[22]

Aside from one chapter, devoted partly to acts of vengeance by the Jewish Brigade (a five-thousand-strong Eretz-Israeli volunteer unit within the ranks of the British army who fought against Nazi Germany), this book will not detail the above matters: not the acts of vengeance by non-Jews, partisan militias, Jewish soldiers in Eastern Europe, spontaneously self-organized groups, individuals at their own initiative, or even concentration camp survivors. It will not inquire whether the survivors, who had passed through seven departments of hell, summoned their strength to initiate or join in on these acts of vengeance. But although none of those stories will be discussed here, they do testify to the scope of the desire for vengeance that prevailed among Jews and non-Jews across Europe during the war and for some years afterward. In other words, Kovner and his group were not alone in their desire for revenge. On the contrary, they gave expression to a feeling common to many—even if, indeed, it remained a mere wish for most Jews. Only occasionally was this translated into action—and those rare events have faded from memory over the years.

WHAT IS VENGEANCE?

The Nokmim took their name from the Hebrew word for vengeance, *nakam*, which relates—as virtually any Hebrew dictionary will explain—to retribution for a foul deed, to retaliation, to the principle of measure for measure, an eye for an eye, a harm for a harm. The avenger nurses a grudge, gives the inflictors of harm, of hatred, and of harassment their due in return, deals defeat in return for suffering defeat, wreaks vengeance, responds to the evildoer according to the evil, fights back and maintains the feud, claims recompense for humiliation, is zealous for justice that has yet to be done, and (according to one dictionary) takes or exacts revenge for the people of Israel, envisions vengeance, or stands as a witness to the harm that befalls the enemy. Punishment too, and particularly the principle of reward and punishment, are mentioned in this context, but briefly and at a remove—as a separate issue, and especially as presenting the possibility of compensating the wronged party financially, as suggested in the interpretation of the "eye for an eye" commandment of Exodus (21:24). Dictionary definitions of nakam are accompanied by a variety of examples from the scripture. These examples

span the entire Jewish canon and its extensions, from Genesis 4:15 ("Therefore whoever kills Cain, vengeance will be taken on him sevenfold"); to Hebrew poet laurate Chaim Nachman Bialik's "On the Slaughter" ("Cursed be
he who says: 'Avenge!' / [...] For the blood of a small child, / The vengeance
has not yet been devised by Satan").[23] Dictionary definitions in other languages are not dissimilar from those in Hebrew. Aside from the basic definition common to them all, certain aspects are often emphasized, particularly those linked with the emotions accompanying vengeance—"the fury
of vengeance," as Bialik called it. Vengeance is born of fury; it spares no one
and satisfies the vengeful urge, according to an English-language dictionary.
Another dictionary notes that vengeance is carried out, with great power
and finality, on an extreme scale. A Spanish-language dictionary too attests
to strength, violence, and disproportion. Vengeance becomes sinful when it
strays from the norms of justice because anger is tinged with envy, pride, hatred, ambition, and cruelty, according to a French Catholic dictionary. And
a German-language dictionary notes that whether or not it is justified, vengeance—unlike punishment—is always the result of personal decisions and
judgment.[24]

The famous scholar and thinker Yeshayahu Leibowitz wrote a detailed
analysis of how the Bible speaks of vengeance (nakam)—the term appears in
various forms some eighty times in the Biblical text—and he drew a number of conclusions about the concept in general. He dwells on expressions
that include the word "blood" and that refer to deeds of revenge in response
to murder. Such a deed, he writes, not only settles the account between the
avenger and the murderer but also upholds the law, which is an objective
principle: "Whoso sheddeth man's blood, by man shall his blood be shed"
(Genesis 9:6). However, the word "nakam" connotes not just the act of retribution but also the subjective fulfillment of the urge to avenge, an urge that
awakens outbursts of destructive emotion and cruelty; in scripture, nakam
is contextually related to such concepts as rage, wrath, and ferocious zeal. It
implies excessive cruelty, evil, and uncalled-for hatred (in Hebrew, *sinat hi-
nam*). The results of real or threatened vengeance in the Bible may be harm
to the individual, community, or entire nation, involving destruction and
death-dealing ruin even to the point of extinction for nations and kingdoms,
sometimes without distinguishing between innocent and guilty. Revenge

can exhibit retribution that extends beyond a reasonable response to a single occurrence or to a continuing situation that causes the avenger suffering or humiliation, or causes distinct harm to someone close. Accordingly, vengeance is forbidden between individuals and certainly between Jews: "Thou shalt not avenge, nor bear any grudge against the children of thy people" (Leviticus 19:18). In contrast, vengeance of the nation against its enemies, particularly in wartime, is called for, as is divine vengeance.

The Jealous God avenges the blood of the faithful. "May God avenge their blood" is a phrase repeatedly spoken, and abbreviated in writing, after the names of unavenged victims. In the Bible, such vengeance is always presented favorably, whereas vengeance against another suggests blameworthiness. How is it that this behavior can be questionable among the people, and even forbidden to them, but be invoked in praise for the Creator? Leibowitz pondered the question and answered: Divine vengeance against the enemies of the nation, as presented in scripture, is generally future vengeance, not yet realized. It is part of a vision of apocalyptic salvation, the dawn of redemption, to be led by God in full majesty and awesomeness. The faithful nation prays to God and expects God to fight its battles and inflict its revenge, to expunge its humiliation as tantamount to a humiliation of God.[25]

It would take many studies to properly cover all the contexts in which Jewish sources mention vengeance, because it connects with every aspect of the relationship between individuals and between the community and its God. This is not the place for such a discussion, but the words of Leibowitz could serve as a suitable foundation for one—both because they expand and clarify the dictionary definition of vengeance and because Abba Kovner, the leader of the Nokmim, was immersed in Jewish sources and studied them throughout his life, citing them in his conversation and in his works. Kovner and his comrades, who were essentially secular Zionists, were filled with a sense of mission that included answerability to the Jewish people and their history. That history was the point of reference for their activities and must be the point of reference for understanding them as young people who grew up in a Jewish educational system before the war. The words of Leibowitz also raise the same issues that the Nokmim struggled with and that they tried to answer, such as the obligation to enact revenge to restore order, determining reasonable retribution, facing the possibility that innocent people will be harmed, and accepting the duty imposed on them by the Holocaust—predicaments that stand at the heart of our topic.

LITERATURE AND STUDIES

Can the definitions and their commentary be helpful in assessing the studies that deal with vengeance, in examining the various attitudes toward it, and in answering the central questions that they suggest? The first such question arises from a look through the existing material, and it immediately arouses puzzlement: Why is so little research literature devoted to the topic? The second question regards morality, law, and punishment: Does vengeance, as defined, stand in opposition to the principles of law and punishment, and if so, is vengeance justified despite such opposition? The third question is whether, by a broader definition, vengeance can include certain given actions and courses that those who embrace them, or who research them, consider to be forms of vengeance.

"It is strange that the research studies do not deal much with revenge; because after all the indescribable suffering justifies a collective bitter cry for revenge," writes historian Walter Zvi Bacharach, referring to the Holocaust period. Philosopher Berel Lang agrees: "The most notable aspect of the place of revenge in the aftermath of the Shoah is its absence, both as a topic of discussion and, before that, in its occurrence [. . .] still less has been said about this absence itself. [. . .] The role of revenge should be and should have been more visible."[26] Indeed, how can so few studies, and so few works of literature, have been written about an emotion that is so basic to the Jewish people, a small nation who suffered a host of wrongs and who extensively considered that emotion, as noted above, in their scripture? The definition of the term helps us understand that the reason for the scarcity of writing on the subject may be because it is not an emotion to be proud of, and that the inhibitions and principles that advise communities to seek out the ways of orderly justice and punishment are reinforced by law. The paucity of writing about vengeance may derive from the practice, among the Jewish people, of following the approach that "a law exists and a judge exists" and that "the law of the land rules the land," and refusing to join an environment of anarchy. Or perhaps the reason there is little research into vengeful feelings is historical: With a past that abounds in suffering, a small nation may weave dreams of vengeance but refrain from putting them into practice, both because of its weakness and because of its culture's prohibition of vengeance. Vengeance is absent from the Jewish DNA, from the Jewish mentality; according to author Aharon Appelfeld, a survivor of Transnistria, a region of terrible suffering, the collective Jewish ethos is ignorant of vengeance. "The concept of vengeance, or blood vengeance, is not to be found in the practical Jewish lexicon; blood vengeance is not, and must not be, exacted by human beings," wrote Rabbi Moshe-Zvi Neria, a leader of Zionist religious youth. His unambiguous statement rules out anyone who claims to interpret divine vengeance, or to have been chosen to implement it, and it rules out the cruel acts of vengeance committed over the course of history by those who marshalled their followers in the name of God.[27]

As to the question of why vengeance is rarely considered by researchers and authors, one possible answer is apparent in the differences between the versions of Elie Wiesel's memoir *Night*, a global bestseller and one of the best known and most quoted books about the Holocaust, through which Wiesel became an international voice for survivors. In it, the author describes his time at Auschwitz. The first edition of the book was written and published in Yiddish in Buenos Aires in the mid-1950s. Its title was *Un' die Welt Hot Geschwigen*, "And the World Kept Silent," and it harshly blamed God, humanity, and the nations of the world for allowing a place such as Auschwitz to exist. Near the end of the book, Wiesel describes the day of liberation. First, everyone searched for something to ease their pangs of hunger; even after eating their fill, no one considered the idea of vengeance. But the next day, several young Jewish men ran to Weimar, where they stole potatoes and clothing and raped German women. The paragraph nonetheless ends with these words: "The historical obligation of vengeance was not discharged."[28] Near the close of the decade, a shortened and edited version of the book was published in Paris, in French of course, and with the addition of an enthusiastic preface from one of the greatest writers of the time, François Mauriac. The accusation against God, the God of the Jewish people in particular, remained in place for this edition, but the rest was omitted, as was the reference to the historical obligation of vengeance. The title was changed, and so *Night* (or *La Nuit*) stepped forth to welcome a global readership—without blaming the non-Jewish world and the non-Jewish God for the tragedy, and without sharing vengeful feelings toward the perpetrators. In this way, Wiesel could provide readers with an acceptable version of the story of a Jewish boy at Auschwitz, one that didn't induce feelings of guilt; indeed, *Night* remains one of the most read, most translated books about the Holocaust. In fact, revered poet Haim Gouri translated the memoir into Hebrew.[29]

But a third version was found in Wiesel's rich personal archive even before his death—an unpublished version that Gouri had never known about. Written in Hebrew, it was more coarse, outspoken, and condemning than either of the others. It expressed terrible anger against God; against the Jews who were still tempted to believe they had a chance of being saved; against those who could have warned the Jews but did not; against the leaders of the Jews in the free countries and in the Land of Israel; against the voiceless world; against Wiesel's Hungarian neighbors, who stood in the road and gloated about the deportations; against the "true face of the Hungarian, a merciless animal's face"; against Wiesel himself for not returning home to enact revenge on those neighbors while it was still possible; and against the fierce hatred he learned to direct at the Germans while in the camps. At the same time, his heart went out to the young couples who embraced in the unlit railway car that was taking them to their death. None of those details appear in the French edition or in the subsequent translated editions that use that version; if any of the above are hinted at, the hint is vague and made en passant.[30] Wiesel refused to explain what readership he was intending for that Hebrew version, apparently written at the end of the 1950s, or why he had consigned it to his archive. In response to a question regarding the vengeful details that had been deleted from the French and subsequent versions, he answered that he had come to the conclusion that vengeance was not a worthy path for Jews. He said that Jews, time and again, despite sharing a ferocious urge for vengeance, had failed to act on it, and that he considered this inaction not a failure but a moral victory. He claimed that many Jews had spoken not infrequently with one another about revenge, particularly in the first years after the war, but that they said nothing about this to outsiders, as they had to continue living among non-Jews, or at least in a world controlled by non-Jews. It may be worth mentioning how influential the element of time was here: As the days passed, one's internal dialogue regarding vengeance underwent a gradual change, shifting to focus on its practical aspects and how it squared with Jewish morality. "Were hatred a solution, the survivors, when they came out of the camps, would have had to burn down the whole world," Wiesel wrote.[31]

Bacharach was, like Wiesel and Appelfeld, a survivor. He differentiated between the act of vengeance itself and the call for vengeance. Although in Jewish tradition, and in human society overall, the act of vengeance is considered unlawful and wrong, if victims facing death call angrily for vengeance, they are not blamed. First of all, there is the scope of the Nazi atrocities; they fall outside the norms of familiar human behavior, and so the call for vengeance, also outside the norms of typical behavior, is not for us to condemn. Secondly, the greater the harm inflicted, the greater the pain. When the pain exceeds what humans can endure, Bacharach asks, who dares to pass judgment on those who demand vengeance?[32] And yet, as early as June 1942, the popular Eretz-Israeli newspaper *Davar* published an article, titled "No to Vengeance," which contained a warning against revenge seekers. "The paramount European Jewish morality," it said, considered revenge "a despicable instinct that must be uprooted from the heart." That definition is more severe than Bacharach's. Not only is the act of vengeance despicable, but so is the desire for vengeance, and it must be uprooted. Still, the writer of the piece, Falk Heilperin, a senior journalist at *Davar* and a prolific author, goes on to distinguish between the call for vengeance in response to a fleeting event, which is an urge that should be quashed, and the vengeance for a wrong "that never ceases from day to day, from moment to moment, into eternity" because its ramifications are ineradicable and because its cruelty is greater in magnitude than all the teachings of paramount human morality. He points to a quandary: on the one hand, the urge for vengeance may be seen as a despicable emotion, whereas on the other, it may be seen as justified because of a terrible, eternal wrongdoing.[33]

Researcher Mark Roseman notes the contrast between the paralyzing trepidation that gripped Germany after the war, the fear of terrible vengeance from the Jews for their crimes, and the reality: the absence both of large-scale postwar acts of vengeance and of attention to the matter. Israeli historians—including Israel Gutman, a pillar of Holocaust research—have warned for years, Roseman says, about other researchers greatly understating the strength of the call for vengeance that Jews raised even during the Holocaust itself. And here the journals and letters written at the time of the events—and particularly those final ones, which constitute a kind of last testament, clearly and forcefully expressing the hope for revenge—must be differentiated from the testimonies of survivors and the memoirs that were written later and that more rarely mention vengeance. In those texts, vengeance is mentioned primarily in terms of an emotion or a recollection at the time of the interview or writing, not as a motivator for actual deeds. In survivors' memoirs and testimonies, the balance of accounts was considered primarily internal, among the Jews; the Germans, while generally described as a factor causing the events, remain out of focus, remote and indistinct, a sort of deus ex machina, "only an element in the vista of suffering and destruction." And in the years after the war, obviously, Nazism disappeared from the scene, and the Allied forces governed instead. Were there further thoughts of vengeance, concealed in the postwar world? Was the paucity of vengeance really because the survivors were too weak to inflict it? Or did they fail to immediately understand the scope of the crime, in all its horror? Did the Jews perhaps hesitate to frankly describe the abominations because they feared disbelief, particularly from non-Jews? If the deeds described are not horrifying enough, though, will calls for vengeance have any effect? Perhaps the idea of an honorable moral standing—which abstaining from seeking revenge bestowed on these victims of appalling deeds, who might accordingly be seen as displaying restraint—was also a factor preventing action. Roseman's conclusion is that if so, the nature of the crime—the crime of the Holocaust—aroused vengeful emotions and then impeded them, limiting the desire for vengeance and the likelihood of its implementation.[34]

The writings of Appelfeld and Neria on the Jewish mentality's opposition to vengeance, the revision of Wiesel's book to exclude revenge and accusations, the distinction drawn by Bacharach and Heilperin between the wish for vengeance and the actual deed (the word and the action are always separated by "five hundred leagues," according to a Jewish proverb), and Roseman's insight regarding how the nature of the Holocaust kept vengeance from being wreaked or even discussed—each of those is an attempt, in its way, to clarify why there was so little vengeance exacted on Germany, certainly in proportion to the scale of the Holocaust; why there was no sufficient attempt to investigate why vengeance was not exacted; and why a sort of taboo was leveled against such action, and even against the discussions of such action, when it was apparently the most natural response on the part of those who suffered the most extreme of injustices. All those issues will be reviewed later.

As to the second question, regarding the discussion of the contrast between vengeance on the one hand and law and punishment on the other: Why are there so few books of research approaching that issue from a universal point of view, and why do those who write about vengeance feel the need to appear apologetic about even dealing with the topic? One example is researcher Susan Jacoby, who took the title of her book *Wild Justice* from the late sixteenth-century essay "Of Revenge," by the British polymath Sir Francis Bacon. Jacoby's publication touches on the concern with revenge in all areas of life, but in the first chapter, "Taboo," she relates to the inhibitions that all human societies, not just Jewish culture, have developed regarding vengeful feelings: "We are more comfortable with the notion of forgiving and forgetting, however unrealistic it may be, than with the private and public reality of vengeance, with its unsettling echoes of the primitive and its inescapable reminder of the fragility of human order. Justice is a legitimate concept in the modern code of civilized behaviour; vengeance is not. [. . .] Justice and vengeance have nothing [. . .] to do with each other." She goes on to contend that those who desire vengeance are disruptive to the public welfare and that the very word "vengeance" carries negative connotations. Nonetheless, Jacoby raises a fundamental question: Are justice and vengeance really two separate issues? In her answer, she invokes the balance between restraint, which enables people to live together, and the unrestrainable urge for retaliation against a wrong committed. She sees such restraint as one of the vital functions of civilization. The victim wants to see the attacker punished, not only for the sake of deterrence but also in order to repair the sense of public order and of personal identity. If a society is unable to convince its members that it can resolve a wrong that has been done, there is danger that those members will pursue more savage ways of obtaining what they consider justice. No one has the right to blood vengeance, but everyone has the right to expect the guilty person to be punished as befits the severity of the harm inflicted. Jacoby contends that if those conditions are not met, if order is not repaired and the punishment is not suitable, then the taboo imposed on vengeance is likely to pave the way for a retreat from public order so that a "legalized revenge" will be desired: a vengeance that is not wild and unrestrained but is accompanied by controlled acts; such legalized vengeance can be an integral part of justice.[35]

Thus Jacoby again follows the lead of Bacon, who rejected vengeance for a series of reasons and doubted the possibility of legally or morally defending the act. He suggested that Shakespeare's vengeful Hamlet would have done better to turn the other cheek, in the spirit of Jesus, and leave vengeance to God. Bacon clearly distinguished between law and vengeance, terming the latter "a kind of wild justice," but nonetheless, he added: "The most tolerable sort of revenge is for those wrongs which there is no law to remedy."[36] Another distinction is made by philosopher and sociologist Hannah Arendt in her book *The Human Condition*: the contrast between vengeance and forgiveness, two states that are opposed to each other. Vengeance is an act that follows naturally from the original act of offense, but it does not end the ramifications. Rather, it initiates a chain reaction that repeats itself endlessly. Forgiveness, in contrast, releases the forgiver and the forgiven from the ramifications of the offense, and this freedom offered by forgiveness is freedom from vengeance too—in accordance with the teachings of Jesus, which Arendt quotes at length. But even Arendt, like Bacon in his day, stresses that people are unable to forgive what they cannot punish and they cannot punish what they find unforgivable.[37] In other words, the offended party will be content only after measure has been returned for measure.

Berel Lang, who wondered why revenge was absent from Holocaust discourse, is another who continues this approach of considering vengeance in opposition to law and forgiveness. Vengeance, in contrast to the other two, disturbs tranquility and deviates in its path, and avengers act on their own, outside the social norm. However, like Bacon and Jacoby, Lang believes that vengeance is justified and even compulsory only if there is no chance of obtaining justice, if the avengers set limits for themselves, and if the vengeance fits the crime. And here, Lang finds that vengeance has a surprising advantage over forgiveness: Forgiveness expunges the past and puts an end to it, whereas vengeance preserves it because the consequences continue to exist (especially if a chain reaction is created) and because it repeatedly reminds one of the pain caused by past events. Thus it contains an element of remembrance, and even of identity-building—a covenant that is not commonly found, he grants. In a world of ideal justice, in which wrongdoers are punished and everyone knows punishment can be expected, there is no place for vengeance. Vengeance is justifiable only if no alternative exists—law and its implementation, if available, are de rigueur. Yet even without justifying vengeance, much less recommending it, recognition can be afforded to its role in history.[38]

Some decades after Jacoby's book was published, another comprehensive book was released, titled *Payback: The Case for Revenge*. Its author, Thane Rosenbaum, comes to the same conclusion as his predecessors but further clarifies and pinpoints why and when vengeance is necessary, as well as the role it plays in society. He writes that justice and vengeance "are not polar opposites" but rather "mirror images of one another. There is no justice unless victims feel avenged; and vengeance that is disproportionately taken is not just." Furthermore, "justice is not as dispassionate as the legal system has instructed us to accept. And vengeance is not as irrational as we have been taught to believe." The title of his book's first chapter is "Running Away from Revenge"; he points out multiple examples of what he deems socially mandated hypocrisy, including the pretense that standing up for one's honor is dishonorable, and the pressure that victims, even Holocaust survivors, experience to publicly state that they hope for justice and not revenge. Justice and revenge arouse the same feelings and derive from the same moral compulsion. Thus, righteous vengeance performed righteously produces the feeling of morally righteousness, because vengeance is one of the ways in which people demonstrate their commitment to moral order and to righteous behavior—here, the emphatic repetition of the word "righteous" is no coincidence. Vengeance has marched through history together with humankind, as past generations well understood. Vengeance is part of the human DNA. However, even Rosenbaum seeks out the "righteous avenger" who can act with restraint and within self-imposed limits, who knows when to stop, who avenges to the proper degree and no further, and who operates only when the legal system has failed and the debt can be paid no other way. Only then can the vengeance be termed righteous.[39]

From among those who experienced the events of the Holocaust personally, or who witnessed the results, several thinkers and authors write that
they have been torn between the urge to take action and the feeling that it
is not the proper, righteous course, and they claim that the issue has continued to eat at them. In his book *The Truce*, Primo Levi, a survivor of Auschwitz, chronicles his arduous eight-month journey, after the liberation
of Auschwitz on January 27, 1945, until his return home to Turin in mid-
October with some other travelers. In the conclusion of the book, he recalls
that before the journey ended, they stopped at the devastated city of Munich, and he felt as if all the Germans he saw owed him a debt that they were
refusing to pay. He looked among them for the faces of "those who could
not know, not remember, not respond; of those who had not ordered and
obeyed, killed, humiliated, corrupted." But the German faces did not accept the challenge. They were "deaf, blind, and mute [. . .] in a fortress of de-
liberate ignorance [. . .] still capable of hatred and contempt, still prisoners
of [. . .] pride and fault."[40] In his book *The Periodic Table*, he asserted that
"every German must answer for Auschwitz."[41] Nonetheless, in his book *The
Drowned and the Saved*, he said, addressing his German publisher, "I have
never harbored any hatred toward the German people, and, if I had, I would
be cured of it now that I have come to know you. I cannot understand, I cannot bear to see a man judged not for who he is but for the group he happens
to belong to."[42] Is there no contradiction in those statements? On the one
hand, the Germans are seen in their totality—each encased in pride and indifference, and each bearing liability for Auschwitz—but on the other hand,
there is the demand that within the German totality, each person must be
judged as an individual actor, without collective guilt.

Michael Elkins was a Jewish American journalist who immigrated to
Israel, befriended Kovner, and transcribed some remarks of his in a mystical tone; he believed that the Nokmim, knowing that those who had killed
their loved ones had also killed many others, saw themselves as representing
the entire Jewish people. Thus, personal vengeance was identical to the justice the Jewish people required, and therefore the vengeance was not limited to those who had personally harmed them. "The German people themselves had expelled the concept of personal guilt," as hundreds of thousands

of Germans participated directly in the murder of European Jews, and therefore the weight of their guilt was so heavy as to require redress not inferior in magnitude to the evil that was done. Moreover, since the Germans had left not a single Jewish family without a victim, not one German family must remain whole. Elkins does note the implications of this attitude, however; in this way, killing can follow killing and never end, as Arendt noted, and it will still be comparable to throwing stones into an endless sea of guilt accompanied by indifference—the same indifference of which Levi took note, and to which there is no effective response.[43]

Officer Haim Ben-Asher was one of the Jewish Brigade's intellectual leaders and among the editors of its periodicals, and when the group crossed the border into Germany in July 1945, he wrote to his wife about the dilemma that continually beset the soldiers:

> For us, no vengeance will suffice. The legendary command of vengeance against Amalek, in God's war against Amalek from generation to generation, is not for us to carry out [. . .]. Such vengeance, for the blood of a small child, has not yet been devised by Satan, Bialik prophesied without realizing. The mythological responsibility, the collective responsibility of Amalek for the seed of his seed, which the fathers ate sour, setting the children's teeth on edge—the practical terms of that burden of responsibility have allowed me no rest [. . .]. Are babies to be murdered for the crimes of all Hitler's nation, who sentenced our babies to gas and fire? [. . .] It is not easy to practice humanism. [. . .] Is this not a weakening of the urge to avenge a million children, the seed of our patriarch Abraham? What would the English or the Americans do if a million of their babies had been dealt such a fate? Is "a child for a child" an obligation or a barbaric need? [. . .] I find it a question of personal conscience for myself whether confronting action or inaction. [. . .] I truly don't know where the truth is. And since the truth—the obligatory act of redemption through shedding blood, and specifically the blood of babies—is very difficult to find for a man raised on the sanctity of life, on the individual's responsibility for every action, on resistance against capital punishment, and on Bialik's divine blood redemption through productive love, I have no basis and no reliable scale of measurement in my heart for a decision of conscience.[44]

Simon Wiesenthal was one of those who firmly resolved the quandaries surrounding vengeance. He titled his book *Justice, Not Vengeance*. Wiesenthal was a survivor who passed through seven circles of hell in multiple concentration camps and who devoted his life to exposing and bringing to trial war criminals; he spent most of his postwar life in Austria where he was viewed there as a merciless avenger. However, he makes clear in the book that he acted not out of vengeful emotion and vengeance-seeking but was instead impelled by the concept of justice, which admits no absolution for the sin but provides atonement through a clemency that requires suitable restitution. He does not easily forgive, but because two Nazis once saved his life, he opposes collective punishment.[45] Immediately upon the end of the war, many groups of young Jews or former partisans approached him, and among them were members of the Gatmon/Diamant group mentioned earlier. They tried to convince him to provide names and addresses for the purpose of vengeance operations, assuring him they would handle the rest. Wiesenthal declined. He did not agree to take "eye for eye, tooth for tooth." He believed that only a court of law is entitled to pass sentence and that its verdict must be respected, even by those who disagree. In his opinion, the meaning of the term "vengeance" implies the possibility of acting like the Nazis, who arrogated to themselves the right to kill. Accordingly, Wiesenthal continued to rebuff the groups who approached him, even when they insisted that they meant to kill only a few hundred guilty people, in contrast to the Nazis' murder of millions of innocents.[46]

The third question that thinkers and researchers discuss in their writings regarding the matter of vengeance against the Germans and their accomplices is whether, when vengeance appeared impossible, and certainly impossible on a scale appropriate to the crime, the survivors settled on various other forms of action and alternative attitudes instead—whether they found a route into alternative channels or, as it is called by researchers, a "model of displacement."[47] To the traditional 613 Jewish commandments, theologian Emil Fackenheim adds a 614th, which is that Jews must survive as Jews in order for the Jewish people to survive. Otherwise, Hitler—may his name be obliterated—will have enjoyed another victory. Fackenheim does not use the word "vengeance," but he indicates a worthy method of depriving Hitler of another triumph: a course that all Jews, those who lived through the

Holocaust as well as those born after it, are commanded to follow.[48] Historian Atina Grossmann, author of a comprehensive study of close Jewish-German-Allied encounters in occupied Germany after the war, echoes the 614th commandment in this expression: "Find revenge in existence." She presents a number of equivalents to vengeance: the presence of Jews, albeit mainly in displaced-person camps, on German soil, in complete opposition to the German aspiration for a *judenrein* country (one "clean" of Jews); the Zionist flags and placards on official buildings that were once strongholds of the Nazi Party; the events held by displaced persons in the very locations that were symbolic to the Germans, such as the Munich beer cellar where Hitler began his career; the Zionist demonstrations held in the city streets, during which participants cried out, "Not only have we survived, but we will also have a future of our own"; the stunning pace of Jewish weddings and births, creating families as a recommencement after loss and continuing a people that had been marked for annihilation; the collection of material, including in the form of many testimonies, as precise as possible, that served to bring the criminals to trial; and the satisfaction of seeing the Germans' anger toward the Americans' sympathetic policies toward the Jews and negative attitude toward the Germans. To the German population, it was obvious that vengeful Jews were behind that attitude. "Revenge did not mean only killing Germans. We had revenge when we saw the Germans acting as hewers of wood and drawers of water . . . when we saw them cleaning Jewish houses, the Jewish school I attended, buying cigarettes and paying for them in gold—gold that had undoubtedly been taken from Jews. We sold them bread and coffee, and they gave everything they had. . . . Revenge also meant living with German women."[49]

Lang, who, as aforementioned, searched for an explanation of why there was a paucity of vengeance in response to the Holocaust, as well as why that very question isn't more extensively discussed, came to the conclusion that vengeance takes various indirect forms and that the reason for this may be the moral problem involved: morality does not admit direct physical vengeance, but it points to other avenues. He shows indirect vengeance in a variety of examples. There was international vengeance against Germany: in turning it into a nation of farmland that lacked industry and an army, incapable of harm and empty of Nazism but nonetheless subject to the supervision of the

Allies, and in dividing Germany into East and West, a split that many Germans considered vengeful on the Allies' part. There was the activity of Nazi-hunters, such as Wiesenthal and the couple Beate and Serge Klarsfeld, who wanted nothing more than to expose Nazis and bring them to trial; though these individuals did not enact direct vengeance, their activity forced the war criminals to live in a state of constant flight and concealment—an existence that in itself amounts to vengeance. There was the avoidance of travel to Germany and of purchasing German products, a personal vengeance on a small scale, and there was the ban on publicly performing the works of Richard Wagner, whom Hitler had considered his guiding light. In Israel, a trenchant debate raged over the acceptance of reparations, which meant laying collective responsibility on today's Germany for the acts of yesterday's Germany, and over Germany's permanent moral obligation toward Israel and the rest of the Jewish world. The reparations were punishment unlimited in time and extent, says Lang. They were an expression of everlasting blame. The trial and execution in Jerusalem in 1961–62 of Adolf Eichmann, chief orchestrator of the deportations of Jews to the death camps, also reduced the need for direct vengeance. Lang raises the question of whether the urge for revenge against Germany has been replaced with the struggle against the Arab world, also a form of indirect vengeance: he asserts that particularly because Jewish helplessness had spanned centuries and reached its apex with the Holocaust, Jews' desire to leave it behind found satisfaction in standing up to the Arabs.[50]

And to conclude the discussion of those three questions—Jean Améry, another survivor known for his incisive and anguished accounts of experiences in several camps, wrote decisively: "I cannot prove this, but I am certain [. . .] that none of us [survivors] who is sound of mind would embrace the morally impossible notion of forcibly leading four to six million Germans out of life into death. Never has *jus talionis* [the right of retaliation] been more senseless historically and morally than in this case. Neither revenge by one side, nor atonement by the other side, is for discussion."[51]

Although Améry has ruled out the idea as impossible historically and morally, his words make it clear that among survivors, there were those who did raise the idea. Otherwise, he would not have addressed it. This book will describe a group of survivors who believed that six million Germans should indeed be led forcibly to death, as both a historical and a moral obligation. The means at the disposal of the national and international institutions following the war, in the view of those survivors, were incapable of dealing appropriate punishment. Without such punishment, the world could not be righted, and until the world be righted, life could not recommence. The absence of punishment constituted an offense against the social order. Let us end with the words of the philosopher Friedrich Nietzsche, who combined revenge and justice, when writing about attempts "to sanctify revenge under the name of justice."[52]

Vow

AVRAHAM SHLONSKY

Ha'aretz, April 30, 1943

My eyes have seen desolation and grief
And heaped anguish upon my heart;
My goodness begged and urged to forgive
But the infinite horror forbade a new start.
I vow to remember as long as I live.
[Remember—and forget nothing.]

To the tenth generation not to forget
Until the offense has abated and also the vow
And my wrath has faded and finally set
I promise to carry in me all I know.
I promise not to unlearn and later regret
But to inscribe and remember all that I saw.

Translated by S. J. Goldsmith, published in *the Jewish Book Annual*
34, 1976/7, p. 75, the Center for Jewish History and the Jewish
Book Council. Courtesy of Sigal Eshel and Ruth Eshel-Shlonsky.
   The change in the brackets is mine. —D.P.

PART I

CONCEPTION AND PREPARATION

1

Lublin, January–March 1945
The Idea of Vengeance

THE WAR IN EUROPE ended officially at the start of May 1945. As the end approached, and increasingly in the months that followed, throngs of humanity extended along the continent's roads, including sons and daughters of all the nations that populated the disaster-stricken countries: refugees and displaced persons who hoped to return to their homes, to parents and children, to wives and husbands, but who had no idea what had befallen their families during almost six years of war. Among the throngs were many freed from the camps and prisons, together with refugees and former soldiers. There were the penniless, clad in their only shirt, and there were also those who had already managed to enrich themselves. Borders were not yet clear. Money had lost its value. Bread, scarce as it was, had become a currency. Transport was managed chaotically. Identities were switched and certificates were forged. The black market flourished. A hodgepodge of languages was heard all around. Governments in exile tried to return to their states. The Red Cross, meanwhile, was dispensing hot soup. The Allied forces were standing at one end of the country and the Soviet forces at the other.

This ungodly chaos was described by Primo Levi in his disturbing book *The Truce* (also published as *The Reawakening*). In it he recalls the hardships he suffered over eight months of cold, hungry wandering back from Auschwitz to his home in Turin. The journey, which at one time would have taken an hour by train, extended day after day without supplies. A dead horse meant the rare luxury of meat. There was no one to be found who had responsibility for the travelers, or who even cared about them—particularly not among the Russians, who liberated the camps and then sent what remained of their inmates, including Italians (whom they considered enemy citizens), eastward instead of westward. "Poland is a sad country," he was told, and he was promised, "Tonight all Germans kaput" by someone "with an eloquent gesture, passing his index and middle fingers, like a knife, between chin and larynx." Thousands of Russian soldiers were returning joyfully home in freight cars repurposed as troop trains and resembling whole villages on the move: "soldiers and civilians, men and women, former prisoners, Germans now prisoners themselves, and in addition, freight, furniture, animals, dismantled industrial installations...." Cars full of Ukrainian women returned homeward carrying the burden of shame and remorse. Wehrmacht soldiers, abandoned and exhausted, begged for bread, and a Jew whose entire family had been murdered at Auschwitz agreed to give them some, on the condition that they crawl to him on all fours—which they submissively did.[1]

The scene of destruction is powerfully depicted by Anglo-Jewish historian Tony Judt in the opening of his wide-ranging book *Postwar: A History of Europe Since 1945*: "pitiful streams of helpless civilians trekking through a blasted landscape of broken cities and barren fields [. . .] dying of starvation and disease." More than thirty-six million Europeans had been killed, including nineteen million civilians; millions had been tortured and annihilated in unimaginable ways; cultures had been demolished; languages had been wiped out; cultural and political elites had disappeared; priceless art had been stolen; entire villages had been erased; great cities were bombed to the ground or beyond recognition; infrastructures were wrecked; millions of people were uprooted from their homes; and tens of homeless millions were on the roads, walking or using any vehicle available. There was little food, and diseases that had long ago been eradicated broke out once more. With men killed by the millions, women left alive were attempting to survive. In Germany alone, there were at least six million freed inmates from the camps, refugees, and displaced persons.[2]

Among all the wanderers, the remnants of Jewry were also present but were unaccounted for. Their world had been demolished, and they had no home to go to, no land to build on. The desire for revenge against the destroyers was shared by all, remarked Yitzhak Zuckerman, one of the leaders of the Warsaw Ghetto uprising: "I didn't know one Jew who wasn't vengeance sick."[3] Among the survivors who had started seeking out a path after the war, a group came together that felt vengeance was the one fierce and burning ambition that outweighed all else for them. That group numbered roughly fifty men and women in their early twenties. Those young people encountered one another after years in the ghettos and in the forests, in the camps and in hiding places. Each and every one of them was scarred by hardship and grief, and they had brought their heavy burdens and personal stories into Lublin. There the group began to coalesce.

Some of the members came from Vilna in December 1944, following Abba Kovner. Fearing that the Soviets were about to arrest him for Zionist activity, Kovner had hurriedly left his hometown. He fled south to Lublin, which was already liberated and where a provisional Polish government had been established. A handful of close friends arrived on his heels, from among the remaining veterans of the ghetto underground, and of the partisans in the forests. Additional groups continued to arrive, mostly members of youth movements and underground members who had become partisans. Some of them did not go directly into Lublin but stayed at the way stations that were set up north and south of the city, particularly in Lvov and Bialystok, in order to show other arrivals the route.[4]

Following Kovner and his comrades' wake, several dozen more began to gather, and they quickly turned into hundreds—survivors who found one another and decided they had no future where their homes had been. Thus began the project known as the *Bricha* (Hebrew for "escape"), aiming to leave the continent of Europe, which had become a graveyard for the Jewish people; there was movement south and west of the places where Jews had begun to assemble, such as Lublin, and where there were representatives of Jewish organizations, particularly from Palestine and the US. And there was movement toward the coast, where passage might be available to a safe destination, especially to Palestine. All this movement was spontaneous. It began along the route from Vilna to Lublin, but it was joined by streams originating in other places unrelated to one another and unrelated to the central flow. It lasted roughly four years, between 1944 and 1948, and it brought at least a quarter million people into Palestine, including 140,000 from Poland.[5] Directions for travel passed on the wings of rumor among those who were tramping along the roads, those who found a corner on the top of a freight car, and those who crossed borders with counterfeit papers. The rumor said *Partisanen geyen* ("Partisans are walking"), and they were the leaders to follow.

The Holocaust discredited most of the great ideologies, in a failure that was tragic for the Jewish people: the Communist "brotherhood of nations," the *Bund* Yiddishist workers' party, definitely the principles of Jewish territorialism and Jewish autonomism, and the Messiah who did not turn up in time. Thus, for many people, the Land of Israel became the only remaining option—even if many of the survivors had no idea where that land was in fact located. Many thought of it as a faraway place beyond the blue horizon and never saw immigrating there as a practical possibility. But now Jews of all ideological backgrounds chose "post-catastrophic Zionism," if the term may be coined, and it stood as the foundation for the Bricha movement. However, two aspects of their motivation must be stressed: First, those heading south for the sea did not all have the Land of Israel in mind as a destination. Primarily, they sought an opportunity to leave the European continent turned graveyard and find sanctuary. Second, it was the surviving members of the youth movements, the partisans, and the ghetto combatants who started and directed the Bricha movement and saw to the needs of journeyers on the roads. The soldiers of the Jewish Brigade also joined the project after the end of the fighting, warmly and readily, and in a third stage, in the fall of 1945, emissaries came from the Mossad for Aliyah B, the organization managing clandestine immigration into Palestine.[6]

As leaders of the effort, the partisans and the youth movement veterans established way stations on the roads and waited for arrivals; they obtained forged documents that appeared appropriate; they raised funds and saw to a rudimentary supply of food; they provided instructions and pointed the way. The Soviets, who were taking over in Eastern Europe, imposed difficulties and saw every homeless refugee as a potential smuggler or a profiteer in currencies or merchandise—at the very least a former collaborator with the enemy. For the first line of migration southward from Eastern Europe and Lithuania, Kovner was the leader. However, he believed that the migration was instigated neither by his leadership nor his ideas but by the necessities of the time—that it gave birth to itself—thus proving itself inevitable. Still, activists saw him as their guiding figure:

> No Jewish life could be built in that cemetery—from all our hearts, Abba Kovner mined forth the words of reason. It would be dishonoring the memory of the victims and disdaining the lessons of the Holocaust [. . .]. It appeared as if fate had assigned him to express the wishes of the souls who had not been privileged to survive this far [. . .]. A shiver would pass through those who listened to his words, which expressed the pain and the heavy responsibility that rested on those who had remained alive.[7]

Kovner, who would become the leader of the *Nokmim,* had a strong influence on others. Those around him saw him as a true prophet, leader, and commander. He exhibited captivating rhetoric, an ability to observe processes and see ahead, and a complete lack of self-indulgence and power seeking. Additionally, he boasted ample credentials: as the head of a thousand-member chapter of the Hashomer Hatzair (the Young Guard, a movement of a leftist Socialist-Zionist inclination) in Vilna before the war; as the leader of an underground during the time of Soviet annexation; and as the author of the first Holocaust-era manifesto, which demanded, "Jews, let us not go like sheep to the slaughter!" and called for self-defense to the last breath because all Jews are doomed to death. When the Nazis ruled the ghetto, Kovner was among those who founded the United Partisan Organization, a formidable underground that smuggled its members out into the forest through the sewer system. In the forests, he became the commander of four Jewish regiments—an uncommon occurrence in the *Partizanka,* the partisans sponsored by the Red Army. He and a handful of remaining fighters helped liberate Vina, hoping to find and assemble the remains of the community and its cultural treasures.[8] Pasha Avidov, who was Kovner's right-hand man among the Nokmim, first met him in Lublin, and he put into words the feeling that Kovner immediately inspired: "We all sensed that the man before us had the ability to navigate our craft to far destinations; we had never before encountered wisdom like his."[9]

TRAITS OF THE NOKMIM GROUP

Who were those fifty men and women who coalesced around the quest for vengeance, those Nokmim led by Abba Kovner? Where did they come from, and what had they undergone during the war years? Did they have a name they had chosen? Was there a common denominator in their collective biography, a sort of shared profile belonging to a certain generation or personality type, that brought them together into this particular group? Did they come from other groups, movements, or towns that contributed to the making of an aggregation?

Those questions have a number of possible answers. It was not until 1985, forty years after the war, that a meeting in Israel first reassembled the Nokmim to clarify the group's history. On that occasion, Kovner set forth an in-depth analysis for his listeners regarding how the plight of the Jews in the ghettos and forests inclined them to vengeance. It was a sort of retrospective portrait in summary: a group that has something very special about it, he said, one with members who persisted in their identification with it. One that left a deep, lifelong mark on them like no other previous allegiance its members had had to any movement or community. Should his remarks be understood to imply that these people represented a certain type who began their development in a youth group or political party, devoting themselves utterly to it, as was customary in the 1930s and 1940s, and later joined an underground that aimed, sometimes successfully, to fight the Germans? Was one key factor in common a background in the Eastern European cities that had a ghetto, an underground, and a fighting spirit—the "fighting cities," as they are called in *The Book of the Ghettos' Wars*?[10] If members had not fought in the ghettos, they had fought as partisans in the forests of Lithuania, Ukraine, and Russia. Each of them, said Kovner, had a "fighting past; that is, we assumed an active stance during the period of destruction," regardless of the practical results of that stance. Each individual and each localized group decided on that path without being directed to; there were "no lords, no king, no radio, no government, no generals, no accepted leader." Kovner thus depicted the program of vengeance as a continuation of the path that had been charted in the ghetto—with an active stance on the part of a minority that believes it represents the broader community, and with an insistence on Jewish honor, which the ghetto witnessed in the will to fight—before the escape into the forests. When she arrived in Palestine in late 1944, Ruzka Korczak, a ghetto Vilna fighter and a partisan, wrote to her close friend Vitka about vengeance: "I see it as a direct continuation of the course, of *our course.*"[11]

Vitka Kempner-Kovner, Abba Kovner's life partner, who excelled in self-restraint and courage, participated in the first derailing of a German train before they had even left the ghetto and commanded a patrol squad in the forest. She also tried to define what the Nokmim had in common: they had not been injured by the Germans, not tortured or broken. They had actively resisted previously, and they had violated the limits that the Nazi system imposed on the Jews.[12]

The reason that the Nokmim consisted mostly of former partisans and former fighters might be traceable to the years of the war and to the subsequent fighting in the forests, which had demonstrated to them the worth of legal codes and procedures, whether Soviet or German, and turned them against any system of law except what they devised for themselves. In that spirit, they adopted vengeance as an indispensable stage in their rehabilitation, without which they could not return to life, society, and the social order. Kovner attested, and Vitka agreed, that this consciousness of the duty to avenge ran particularly deep among those who had physically fought. Kovner said that to the best of his knowledge there were no Nokmim who had not actively responded to the situation. By this he included those members of the underground who had been caught and sent to the camps, such as Poldek (Yehuda Wasserman, later Maimon), a veteran of the "Fighting Pioneer" underground in Krakow who, while being imprisoned at Auschwitz for twenty-two months, contacted the international underground and managed to escape the death march; or Arie (Leib or "Leibke") Distel, a member of the underground in the Vilna Ghetto who was caught but escaped from a camp in Estonia. They were of course considered fighters. To Kovner's remarks, it should be added that it was a fighting spirit, and not necessarily the experience of fighting, that characterized the Nokmim. Thus, Moshe (Manek) L. from Będzin, for example, was apparently not a member of a ghetto underground before he was imprisoned at Auschwitz and Günthergrube, one of Auschwitz's auxiliary camps; similarly, Rachel

Galperin-Gliksman was not accepted into the underground in Vilna, where she grew up. However, they both insisted and were accepted into the Nokmim on account of other activities.[13]

Vengeance, which had been part of the battle against the Germans, was also a continuation of it. Therefore, fighters were chosen for the Nokmim who had accumulated certain experience during the time of the Holocaust and who were "cunning, quick, resourceful, able to improvise solutions, unwilling to give up, and so on," Kovner enumerated. They had to understand that this was national vengeance, the vengeance of a people against a people, rather than personal vengeance for what was inflicted on oneself—in the view of the Nokmim, most of the German nation not only knew about the atrocities but were also complicit. The selection of certain young men and women, Kovner continued, was on a personal basis rather than according to affiliation. They had previously belonged to various political parties and party youth movements, and they represented a broad political spectrum that had no remaining significance after the war. Moreover, they came from a number of previous groups in various places, each with its own character, and therefore what they formed together was a "confederation," later to meld into a single unit. Kovner clarified that he had needed to choose youngsters who would not break down when, at a time of distress and emergency, they were obliged to suddenly part from the friends who had shared their wanderings since the Holocaust, and from the surviving remnants of their families, in order to blend in among the Germans—an intolerable undertaking in itself; to speak neither Hebrew nor Yiddish; to become unidentifiable as Jewish; to become part of a conspiracy; to live in suffering and loneliness; to be devoted to an idea that, in the context of a normal world, is madness or worse than madness, as Kovner put it.[14] People were chosen who were willing to give themselves over to the idea of vengeance and recompense and to pay the full price—that is to say, to give up all other priorities, to be aware in advance that what awaits them is hardship, and to be willing to sacrifice their lives. Those chosen had already stood on the brink of death more than once.

A feeling of despair, seeing no point in surviving, had beset those young people after liberation, and it underlay their readiness to die, like Samson with the Philistines. It must be noted, however, that this feeling was common to many survivors. It appeared, counterintuitively, after liberation. "Instead of suicide, after you arrived home and found that no one was left and the scope of the disaster was unbearable, came vengeance. Vengeance was a kind of suicide, because afterward there would certainly be no sense staying alive," Poldek attested to Natan Beirak, a researcher who collected in-depth testimonies from some of the Nokmim. A number of them told Beirak that the intent was to complete the mission and then kill themselves. Many recalled that belonging to the Nokmim gave them the strength to overcome the guilt of having survived. "My life was spared for the purpose of avenging all those who are gone and who wished for vengeance—vengeance." The quest for vengeance forestalled suicide. It was clear to the Nokmim that if they carried out the avenging operation and were captured before they managed to kill themselves, they would be tried and sentenced to death. But if they were not captured, they would not manage to live with the burden of their deed despite their belief in its justifiability.[15] Furthermore, after they emerged from the forest and after the liberation of Vilna, in the summer of 1944, Kovner had suggested that they continue the fight by joining a unit of the Red Army that would parachute into Berlin; however, his suggestion was quickly rejected both by the Soviets, who feared that the unit would take vengeance into its own hands, and by Vitka and Ruzka, who understood that Kovner, unable to cope with the overwhelming disaster, was seeking out another form of suicide.[16]

Another common trait among the Nokmim inconsistent with their ambitions was a lack of ability, training, and mentality required for killing human beings. The idea that extrajudicial execution was crucial completely violated the upbringing of the group's members, who were mostly from the political left. They were educated in humanitarian values, aspiring to a solidarity between people and nations familiar with the universalist struggle for a just tomorrow across the world. Gusta Draenger, a member of the Akiva youth movement in Krakow—and also the wife of Shimshon (Szymek) Draenger, who led the Fighting Pioneer underground in that city—wrote in her diary that she and her comrades did not know how to be a military organization because they were wholly a youth movement. And in their periodical, the movement's members wrote: "We do not know how to kill—and that's it [. . .]. Bloodshed repels us." Manos Diamant said that "the thought of vengeance was always present," but he knew the members were not professional.[17] One more example is that of Shimon Lavee, the son of Anna and Mundek Lukawiecki, who learned about the story of his family and asked himself, "Was my father a born assassin? Was my mother a born assassin? The answer is no. The correct question is whether at a certain moment they were able to become assassins, and the answer to that is affirmative. Each of them experienced a formative moment like that." For his mother, that formative event was her rape by the Ukrainian commander of the ghetto. That night, she knifed him to death. For his father, it was watching from a distance as the Ukrainians killed his family and kicked their bodies into a pit.[18] Thus, even after the events of the Holocaust, the minds of the Nokmim were a barrier, an outcome of their prewar upbringing that they needed to transcend in order to participate in acts of vengeance.

With their background as members of a movement, an underground, or a political party, the Nokmim always felt an obligation and an allegiance to the mission. Thus, for example, when Ruzka, en route from Bucharest to Vilna, met emissaries from the Yishuv who instructed that she go to Palestine, she did so, despite the desire to go back to her friends and tell them that the route to Romania had been opened: "*Az menn darft geyen—geit menn.*" (When you should go, get going.") When an order, command, or instruction reaches you, you obey. The Nokmim were soldiers, operatives of the movement, trained to do their duty. Yosef (Yulek) Harmatz, a former member of the Komsomol (the All-Union Leninist Young Communist League) who had accumulated a great deal of face time with Kovner in the ghetto and forest, said: "If Abba had told us to kill a Jew, we certainly would have done the killing. It's not even a question." Shlomo Kless, one of the Hashomer Hatzair members who escaped eastward into the Soviet Union and returned after liberation, contended that the youth movement background was decisive. Inside the movement during the Holocaust years, there developed what he called "leading clusters," which applied themselves to labor for the movement and the public and which militated for an active response to events; a member of the movement was obliged to remain faithful to the imperative of personal ideological fulfillment within the framework that he or she occupied—obliged to achieve. There were norms of comradeship and mutual trustworthiness, of internal solidarity. It was a "relatively hard-nosed ideal of activists and activism."[19]

To conclude the matter of commonality among the Nokmim, I will once more emphasize the factor of continuity, which includes the leader's decisions: some members had been following Kovner since the days of the ghetto and the forest. At that time, he had given meaning and direction to their lives—indeed, that may have been the secret of his authority—as he read them the manifesto, calling for self-defense and enlistment in the underground. According to Galperin-Gliksman, the way Abba chose people in the ghetto for the underground, for the forest, and for other missions was the way he chose them for the Nokmim. Zelda Treger (later Nissanilevich), a partisan known for her bravery, recalled that it seemed natural to take instructions from Kovner after the war; she said he was still a source of authority in a world where there was no other authority left to respect. Thus, she stressed continuity as a common factor among the Nokmim. When the Soviets entered Vilna in June 1940, Kovner split the most dedicated members of the youth movement—after having tested their loyalty and ability to maintain secrecy—into squads of five that went underground. The ghetto underground, founded in 1942, also featured loyal five-person squads that were compartmentalized to the point where a member, such as Yulek Harmatz, was often unaware that his own brother was also a member.[20]

The idea of a compartmentalized underground was so ingrained in them that it became a way of life—for both them and Kovner. Later, during the forest era, they fought the Germans, and Kovner commanded a regiment called Hanokem ("the Avenger," the singular form of "Nokmim"). Another regiment was named "Death to Fascism," after the tradition of the Red Army. Yet another was named "Nekamah," meaning "vengeance." Kovner told Levi Arieh Sarid, the historian who later took down the history of the Nokmim from Kovner's spoken recollections, that "vengeance was, at that time, the most legitimate element" in the culture of politics. And not only of politics—in the area controlled by the Soviet Union. "There was nothing more natural in those days than 'hunting Nazis' [. . .] and many people turned their energies to those activities."[21] There were vengeance operations initiated by the authorities, and participants even before the war ended included military units in the field and Jewish soldiers of the Red Army. These Jewish soldiers advanced with the Red Army toward Germany and Berlin, and the revenge operations fulfilled a heartfelt wish of theirs. When the war ended, many Jews volunteered for the militias in order to be able to enact vengeance against the murderers of their families and communities. Members of the Nokmim group also included some who had already been wreaking vengeance, such as former partisans from Rovno, who had taken revenge against murderers among the local population before heading southward toward Lublin from their town and elsewhere.[22]

THE REASONS FOR VENGEANCE

The primary motivators for the Nokmim were, then, the Holocaust, the loss it inflicted, and the burning resolution to justly retaliate against the authors of that disaster, the Germans and their collaborators. Those who emerged from the Holocaust—who understood the profound meaning of the helplessness and defenselessness that enabled the Germans to eradicate almost one-third of the Jewish people, a nation that numbered 16.8 million before the war and 11 million when it ended—wished for vengeance in order to ensure that the Jewish people would never be harmed again. Michael Kovner, the son of Abba Kovner, his firstborn, said that Jewish existence and the imperative of security were like fire in his father's bones.[23] Pasha told his son Avi that the main motivation for vengeance was not what the Germans had done but what they had made their victims do. That had been the true humiliation. According to Avi, before his father lost his memory in old age, he recounted the "most truthful story he'd ever told"—about an elderly Jew whom the underground had not taken with them when they left the ghetto for the forest. That glare of accusation haunted Pasha until his memories faded.[24]

But in addition to the major reasons, ghastly and self-evident as they were, the idea of vengeance drew associations with other reasons, circumstances, and factors in the minds of the Nokmim and other revenge seekers after the war and the Holocaust, foremost being a sense of mission and duty: to fulfill the final behest of their parents, brothers, and sisters whose last words, in the face of death, revolved around vengeance. If we move on with our lives, it is as if nothing happened; then we insult the memories of our loved ones who died and whose call for vengeance was their last will and testament, they kept saying. The call for vengeance was written in blood on the walls everywhere survivors walked on the roads to Lublin—ignoring it was an insult to those who were lost, as if to say that their anguish and deaths were not worth bothering about. "Within vengeance, there lies the elemental factor of remembrance. Vengeance is required as a remembrance of the loved ones who went to their death," wrote historian Walter Zvi Bacharach.[25]

After the most horrible event that had ever happened to this people in their long history, it was unthinkable to return to everyday life as if it had not occurred, as if there were no reward and punishment in the world and no such thing as justice or judges, as if the Jews were not part of history, as if history continued to unfold without them. During the war, the Nokmim had listened to the admired leaders of their movements, and now the Nokmim considered those former leaders' words an inherited obligation that Kovner was continuing to carry out. Zippora Birmann, who belonged to the Dror movement in Bialystok, demanded in a "Letter to the Comrades" that she sent to Palestine "vengeance without mercy, without sentiment, without 'good Germans' [. . .]. For good Germans, death without suffering [. . .]. Our shattered bones will find no consolation [. . .]. Remember that, and do as we ask."[26] In the periodical *The Fighting Pioneer,* the members of the Akiva movement in Krakow—from which a subgroup joined the Nokmim—wrote: "We shall forever remember that the spilt blood [of fallen comrades] shouts for vengeance, and blood will have blood, in order that the world remember forever that innocent blood shall not be spilt without punishment."[27]

A second reason behind the urge to avenge was the nearness in time and location: "In 1945, we were standing beside a fresh grave, right after the war, with the screams still echoing in our ears. It's hard to understand that after fifty years," Manos Diamant remarked.[28] The distressing memories that had not faded, the family and friends who were, in most cases, gone with no chance for farewells—the loss was difficult to comprehend. Each moment was, again and again, the moment that the disaster came.

A third reason was the question of having the right to return to everyday life after the Holocaust. Kovner's testimony to historian Anita Shapira in 1982, a few years before his death, was a sort of summation. In it, he said that they had not imagined themselves able, or entitled, to return to life, come to the Land of Israel, establish families. They knew that most of them would then have set up kibbutzim, gotten up and gone to work every morning, and

settled accounts with Germany that way. Germany had not yet been liberated when the idea of vengeance was raised, but one day it would be, by
which time they would be on a boat (imagined ironically, of course), traveling over the Mediterranean to the Land of Israel.[29] Zila (Cesia) Rosenberg
(later Rosenberg-Amit), a member of the Vilna Ghetto underground who
had carried out several dangerous missions, wrote:

> Would I be able to live a "normal" everyday life like everyone else? To shoul-
> der the yoke of routine [...] to enjoy life's little enjoyments, to laugh and cry
> about trivialities, to adore a baby's smile, to give birth to children, to set up
> a household as if nothing had happened, as if I hadn't been at the bottom of
> hell and it didn't still live on inside me, as if my dead had stopped shadow-
> ing me wherever I go? Would I want to? Would I be able? By what right?[30]

The question of having that right, which comes up repeatedly in the testimony of many survivors, is what disturbs their tranquility. The survivors
had nagging doubts about why they had been spared, about their right to
be spared, about why it applied to them and not to others whom they considered better and more deserving. And having received the privilege, how
could they turn their back on the past and start a new life as if indeed nothing had happened?

A fourth reason was the awareness of the Holocaust's scope, an awareness
that developed incrementally but within a short time. The survivors, no matter where they were emerging from at the time of liberation—the camps, the
forests, or other hiding places—met on the roads and at the assembly points
that began to develop, and they told one another the story of the ghetto, the
town, the group that made its way to the forest or was sent to the camp. With
the exchange of more and more stories and descriptions, a terrible picture
came into focus: Entire areas and cities all across Europe emptied of their
Jewish inhabitants. Murder in industrial forms resembling nothing ever
known before. Acts of merciless, senseless cruelty. A crime steadily revealing
itself as too enormous and unprecedented to be seen in its entirely. It is unclear how six million became the understood figure—there was still no possibility of surveying all the remaining Jews to determine just how many had
come through the disaster—but the number was already circulating in late
1944, as Eastern European territories were progressively liberated. It came to

be regarded as an indisputable reckoning, and afterward, when all the data was collected, it proved very close to the actual figure: 5,860,149 souls. This enormous number contributed to the understanding that the episode had no precedent in all time and could not be casually left behind. However, according to historian Israel Gutman (he and Yehuda Bauer were close friends and together the two main pillars of Holocaust research), after the war the very discovery of the crime's enormity underscored the inconceivability of any suitable revenge and dispelled the thought of retaliating against the Nazis as they deserved.[31]

A fifth factor behind the urge to avenge was visits to the recent killing sites and death camps. After Vilna was liberated in July 1944, a group of partisans and other survivors went to see the killing field outside the city, at Ponar, where most of the esteemed community that resided in "the Jerusalem of Lithuania" were murdered together with Jews from nearby towns and with Soviet prisoners of war—some seventy thousand to a hundred thousand in all. The visitors returned stunned and tense from the blunt reality bespeaking widescale slaughter into gigantic round pits, and from the bestial brutality of those who would aim deadly gunfire face to face at living creatures. Evidence of that brutality was still visible; scattered bodies remained that had not yet received proper burial. And the visitors knew very well who had been killed there at the edge of the pits: "Their parents, and all of their neighbors, acquaintances [...] well-to-do and proletarian, pious, assimilated, and baptized, communal leaders, synagogue functionaries, pedlars and drawers of water, Communists and Zionists, intellectuals, artists, and village idiots, and some four thousand babies [. . .]. All of them," as writer Amos Oz described the end of a Jewish community.[32] When the visit was over, Kovner composed a detailed questionnaire, and the survivors, who had begun to gather, filled it out. The copies were collected with a view to preparing for future trials, punishment, and vengeance. Immediately after the visit to Ponar, Kovner suggested that the front-line command headquarters of the Red Army, which was to continue on its way westward from Vilna, organize the remaining veterans from the Jewish regiments of the Lithuanian forests into a unit on German soil to carry out sabotage and revenge. As previously noted, he also wanted to volunteer for parachuting; however, the military accepted neither suggestion. Vitka and Ruzka were firmly opposed as

well, on the grounds that the handful of surviving Jewish fighters would also
be killed, that those fighters had already done their part and contributed to
the general victory, and that at this point the immediate welfare of the Jewish people must take priority. In agreement with Vitka and Ruzka was General Ivan Chernyakhovsky, a decorated hero of the Soviet Union and a commander who had led the forces that liberated Lithuania and were on their
way to Germany—and who may himself have been Jewish.[33]

In December of the same year, and in the first months of 1945, survivors
who had reached Lublin went out to see the forced-labor camp of Majdanek, which was five miles from the city. Inside the camp, there was a space
allocated for extermination. Because the Soviets closed the site to the public shortly after liberating the city, not everyone managed to visit it, but the
ones who did returned even more stunned than from Ponar. The Jews of
Vilna and of Lithuania had been unaware, while shut inside the ghetto for
two years and surviving in the forest for ten months, that killing was underway not only at the nearby pits and ravines but also at death camps, where
three million souls or more were being murdered, including most of the Jews
of Poland—the country where the survivors themselves had recently arrived.
The visit to Majdanek "kindled the fire of vengeance," according to Gavriel
(Gabi) Sedlis (Schedlitz), who went out to the forest as a member of the underground and was noted as an expert forger of certificates and documents.
His mother was killed at Majdanek, and to this day, when he tells his story,
he is agitated by rage at her murder. Seeing Majdanek "spurred me to go personally to Romania" in order to let the world know, Menashe Gewissar testified as well. He was the treasurer for the Bricha, the exodus out of Europe,
and one of its primary leaders. "Here I first learned of the death camps and
gas chambers," wrote Rosenberg-Amit, who immediately described how she
joined the Nokmim. Mira (Mirka) Verbin-Shabetzky, a member of the Vilna
underground and a partisan in the forest, said similarly: "When I saw how
Majdanek operated, I thought to myself that being a partisan was a small
thing compared with what the Jews went through there." Yulek Harmatz
testified that when the Avengers saw what had happened in Majdanek, that
human beings had been burned, "we said we were not leaving Europe before taking revenge against the Germans [. . .]. We were shocked, particularly as former fighters. We couldn't imagine anything worse." And Vitka

testified: "Until we went there, we thought that the very worst had happened in Vilna." Ben Meiri too, who had returned from the Soviet Union, having fled there when the Germans invaded Lithuania, said that when they came back from Majdanek they started to think about what should be done.[34]

As the Red Army neared Germany, tens of thousands of Soviet troops were brought to visit Majdanek and Treblinka as mental preparation for an uncompromising assault. The tragedy of the Jews was clearly being used for internal Soviet purposes, since the commanders felt that nothing else could arouse a passion for vengeance like a visit to the camps. It could well be that the soldiers were told not that in the death camps it was principally Jews and Poles who were murdered there but rather that the victims were "Soviet citizens," in keeping with the accepted Soviet terminology.[35]

The structures, including the gas chambers and the round hatch through which the cans of Zyklon B were emptied, remained intact. They stand to this day at Majdanek just as they did when they were used. A visitor may shudder and glance backward, lest the metal door close behind them and remember the industrialization of killing, the cold and efficient planning that drove it, the calculated operation of turning people to ash in a given amount of time. According to others who had come from Polish cities, the survivors from Vilna also heard of Treblinka and Chelmo, and they were astonished to meet Auschwitz survivors still clad in striped uniforms. In retrospect, as described by survivors, the visit to Majdanek mingled with the visit to Ponar and the other death camps—and these experiences all demanded a response. Kovner, distressed, could find no rest. The idea of vengeance, terrible vengeance, against the German nation, increasingly took hold of him and his comrades after they saw and understood the system of mass killing. With increasing intensity, they viewed vengeance as an insistence on Jewish honor, which had been violated, and as retaliation for the victims' continued humiliation and helplessness, details of which were now more graphically evident.

The sixth is *a fundamental reason*, and its importance cannot be overstated: it was the resurgence of antisemitism in full force, even though the war was over. Fear now gnawed at Kovner and his comrades every day, not because of the Germans in their defeat but because of the Soviets, who were advancing westward and taking control of territory after territory, country after country, and who controlled Majdanek as well. Granted, the war had ended. But had the Holocaust? Could it be that the "devouring turnabout in the fields of Treblinka"[36] would continue? When Jews returned in July 1944 to Kiev and hoped to reoccupy their houses, they discovered Ukrainian squatters who refused to vacate. The Ukrainians started throwing Jews from moving train cars and beating random Jews. The feeling was of an impending pogrom. There was no one to turn to with an alert. In July 1944, upon the liberation of Lithuania, Jews who returned to their homes from the forests and hideouts attempting to find relatives and perhaps a small fraction of their properties, were murdered on their doorsteps by neighbors and local Lithuanian gangs, who had hidden in the forests and elsewhere in order not to be conscripted by the Germans. In the pockets of five Jews, who had survived the Holocaust but were then murdered in the Lithuanian town of Eišiškės, a note was found in Polish saying, "This will be the fate of all the Jews left alive."[37]

In an interview with poet Haim Gouri, Kovner spoke of how important it is to understand what confronted the partisans who returned from the forests: the "depth of hostility from the world around them," a hostility that persisted after the ghetto days and even in the forest days, when Polish nationalist partisans had attacked them murderously and Soviet soldiers had harassed them, disarmed them, and left them to die. And after the liberation, Lithuanians murdered the survivors, and right-wing Polish partisans halted trains and killed any Jews they could identify by the dozens and hundreds. Not only did the previous woes continue after the ghettos and the forests, but a new dimension was added to antisemitism. As the Soviet regime took hold in the countries of Eastern Europe, the remaining Jews there were identified with it—the Poles even called it the *żydokomuna,* the Judeo-Communist regime, as if the Soviets were trying to take control by means of the Jews. Whether that was the reason, above and beyond the traditional Catholic antisemitism that had not dulled over time, or whether, as Polish researcher Jan Gross contends, these were only pretexts for the wartime deeds of the Poles against the Jews—deeds that precluded the possibility of Jewish reintegration into Poland—deadly antisemitism continued with all its might.[38] Local nationalists, particularly those of the right-wing Polish underground group *Armia Krajowa* (AK), the "Army of the Homeland," which had not yet lost hope in leading a free Poland, tried to perpetrate terror operations against the Soviet regime that had recently seized their country, and they included the Jews as targets. "Jew-killing suited them perfectly [. . .]. For them, in short, killing Jews was fun [. . .]. Victim after victim from among the few surviving Jews" was murdered, Kovner told Gouri. But harder yet than the encounter with the blatant Jew haters, with the bone-deep antisemites, was the encounter with the feckless majority that expressed "shock and sorrow, apparent in their words or behavior toward us survivors, that Hitler had not finished the work for them." When Kovner returned to liberated Vilna, so he told Gouri, and saw his family's home bereft of any signs of life, he sat on the sidewalk with his head in his hands. A neighbor happened by and asked in astonishment, "Are you still alive?"[39]

Thus it happened later, in 1945, then in other places that were subsequently liberated, such as eastern Poland. The worst was the Kielce Pogrom, at the start of July 1946, when forty-two Jews were murdered, but there were other pogroms in Poland before it: in Krakow, for example, and in Radom, in Częstochowa, in and around Warsaw, and in and around Łódź. Less than two weeks after the Kielce Pogrom, the press in the Land of Israel reported thirty-three Jews murdered on a train in Poland, twenty-eight more forced off another train and murdered on the spot, and the bodies of further victims found. "We are living on top of a volcano. In Krakow there was a flagrant pogrom; there are people dead and people injured. The antisemitism is growing, the pogroms are increasing [. . .]. Help us!" came a plea to the Jews of Palestine. Afterward, a detailed report arrived about incitement that before the pogrom had used the old blood libel and hung posters accusing "Jewish murderers" of slaughtering Christian children at the synagogue.[40]

In practice, the Soviets already controlled the Baltic nations and Poland, and they had set up and were running what would become the Eastern Bloc; they neither stopped those murders nor punished their perpetrators, though they also failed to reprimand Jews who took revenge against local collaborators. One Polish woman had informed on 112 Jews who had managed to hide out in Vilna during the German occupation, and they underwent exceptionally brutal, twisted torture. On their way to Ponar, they succeeded in flinging out a letter that contained a detailed description of their torture. When Kovner and his group returned to Vilna from the forest, he planned to kill the Polish woman, and he consulted with someone close to the author and journalist Ilya Ehrenburg, asking through him about the reaction of the authorities. The answer was "Being the partisan you are, use your own judgment"—but carefully, and not publicly. According to data that the Haganah collected in Europe and passed onward to Palestine, at least a thousand Jews were murdered in the second half of 1945 and early 1946, mostly in Poland, but researchers believe that in Poland the actual figure was closer to 1,500 (with the exception of one researcher, who believes the death toll was in the hundreds).[41]

In addition, gangs of former Nazis, together with criminal elements and wartime collaborators, continued killing Jews, especially in Germany and Austria, and they banded together as if their mandate had never ended. Indeed, at the command posts of the Allies, there was a perceptible suspicion that even after the defeat, extreme Nazi elements would continue operations against them, including guerilla and terror operations, from bases prepared in advance among the mountains of southern Germany and Austria. Intelligence reports spoke of the recruitment of several thousand young Germans into the Werewolf unit for that purpose, and the Jewish Brigade began to train for the appropriate manner of fighting in case the occasion arose. In a booklet prepared during the 1950s in New York titled "West Germany Prepares War of Revenge: Facts on the Rebirth of German Militarism in the Bonn State," hundreds of groups of former soldiers are listed, as well as tens of publishing houses that distributed Nazi literature. In January 1946, for example, half a year after the war ended, leaders of a political group that called itself the Democratic Party were—according to a radio report in the British occupied zone—found to possess "National Socialist literature and weapons." Antisemitism roiled not only among members of extreme groups but also among the general population of Germany in response to an influx of Jews into their country for housing in displaced persons camps. Occasionally, violence broke out between survivors and local residents.[42]

With its many aspects and many locations, the phenomenon had an unmistakable implication: the further killing of Jews as if it were a fact of nature. "All that, together, implanted in the survivors a feeling of hostility doubled and redoubled against them," Kovner summarized to Gouri, speaking to him as one poet to another, peer to peer; that feeling was part of the "terrible void that yawned in the heart of every person whose lot was to be a survivor."

Talking to his friend Shlomo Kless, Kovner said further that the murderous antisemitism after the war, springing up "like a brushfire," pushed him to the breaking point, after which only deep pessimism remained regarding staying even one more moment in Europe.[43] The Haganah organization in Europe, aware of the situation, decided that one of its tasks was to physically protect the surviving Jews. It requested and received emissaries from the Land of Israel who would train young survivors to wield weapons and fight to protect the survivor community against attempts to renew pogroms.[44]

Thus there were two fears: fear that the murder of Jews would continue, and fear that the Soviets would dominate Eastern Europe. Regarding the Soviets, ambivalence was apparent, especially among those who had absorbed the principles of the Socialist movement.

On the one hand, there was the possible influence of the Soviets' saber-rattling propaganda sheets (their so-called battle pages calling for uncompromising vengeance), and the attitude of the Red Army soldiers and the partisans toward Germans, on the Jews' desire for vengeance and on the view of vengeance as a possibility. The Soviets' battle pages were not the fundamental inspiration for Jewish vengeance, but they served as a model for emulation, as did the writings of the much-admired Ehrenburg, whom the partisans encountered when they emerged from the forest and he approached them with a photography unit of the Red Army. To the Red Army soldiers, Ehrenburg was a journalistic superstar. They read his articles every day during the war, and it was said that his writing could give you goosebumps. Newspapers were dropped from planes wherever there was fighting. They were eagerly awaited, and not for rolling cigarettes—they were read out to soldiers and officers. Ehrenburg unequivocally promoted vengeance. In summer 1942, during the second wave of German conquest, when the Germans seemed unstoppable, he wrote a particularly fiery article headlined "Let's Kill":

> The Germans are not human. The word "German" has become the foulest of obscenities. Let's not talk. Let's kill [...]. If you don't kill the German, the German will kill you. He will seize your family and torture them on the accursed soil of Germany [...]. If you've killed a German, kill another. There is nothing more exhilarating for us than German corpses.

Ehrenburg was not the only one writing in this vein during that summer and afterward.[45] Two years later, in spring 1944, Ehrenburg and Abraham Sutzkever, who was the greatest of the Yiddish poets—and who had been with Kovner in the ghetto and in the forest—spoke to thousands of people at an event organized by the Jewish Anti-Fascist Committee operating in the Soviet Union. Sutzkever ended his speech not with the traditional invocation of Stalin's name but with an impassioned call for vengeance.[46] Ehrenburg went on to write that the fighters were motivated not only by vengeance but also by the quest for justice that would punish the murderers of six million Jews—a matter that was scarcely mentioned with such directness in the Soviet Union.[47]

On the other hand, Kovner and his comrades had seen the Soviet regime up close in Lithuania and in the forest, and their conclusions were clear and categorical: there was no future for Jews under that regime, and action must be taken to ensure that it would not continue the deeds of its predecessor. Kovner's concept of vengeance was influenced by the regime's attitude toward the Jews whose neighbors had informed on them and who were attacked everywhere, by the attitude of the Partizanka to the Jewish fighters who came to the forest—allowing them to fight only as individuals rather than in Jewish units—and by the death of thirty-five members of the Vilna Ghetto underground, including Kovner's younger brother Michael, who were sent by the Partizanka command straight into a German ambush. Also influential were the abuse and humiliation, the confiscation of weapons, and the misogynistic attitude of the Soviet commanders in the forests of Narocz when the Vilna underground sent in a coed battalion. All those were strong influences on Kovner and on his concept of vengeance as a warning, legitimately following the anti-Soviet rage aroused by the antisemitism that prevailed in the Soviet Union during and after the war.[48]

Even previously, in Vilna after liberation and before setting out southward, partisans and other survivors met Jews who served in the Red Army, including some who had held high ranks and many who were still in uniform, and the survivors were impressed with the awakening of nationalism that was evident among those veterans. The Jews whom the survivors met were convinced that legal emigration to Palestine from the Soviet Union would commence, and they urged the survivors—the partisans in

particular—to wait rather than endanger themselves by roaming and border jumping. But the partisans and other survivors were instilled, by the very
hardships that had endangered them, with a restlessness and an urge to leave.
Their experience with the Soviet authorities left them no cause for optimism
regarding legal emigration;[49] on the contrary, Kovner believed that the urgent question was what fate the Soviets were planning for the Jewish people,
starting with the Jews of the Soviet Union and perhaps extending to all who
remained in the territories where the Soviets were progressively entrenching themselves. Kovner was prophetic in this respect, without knowing how
prophetic. Indeed, the years between 1946 and Stalin's death, in spring 1953,
were the darkest years for the Jews of the Soviet Union. There were murders
of doctors, poets, writers, actors, dozens of cultural figures and public activists, and members of the Jewish Anti-Fascist Committee, together constituting the unofficial leadership of Soviet Jewry. There were closures of theaters,
newspapers, and publishers. There were arrests, torture, deportations, and libel, and perhaps even a plan of overall exile to Siberia. The worst was the fab-
ricated Doctors' Plot, with trials beginning at the start of 1953, shortly before Stalin's death.[50] Kovner could not have known all that in 1945, but the
distress that beset him, and his analytical forecast relating to Soviet intentions and to the likelihood of new and Kremlin-inspired savagery against
the Jews, later proved justified. His analysis of the situation was set out in his
"Missive to Hashomer Hatzair Partisans," which he wrote as early as 1944 in
the Rudniki Forest. In it, he made several political predictions that did indeed come to pass, among them the Cold War and the Soviet Union's attitude toward the Jews.[51]

Kovner's fears must be considered, then, to have been solidly founded,
and they continued to arise. He was not the only person losing sleep over
such apprehensions in the months and years to come. A striking example is
the testimony provided at Kibbutz Yagur in June 1946, a year after the war's
end, by Zivia Lubetkin, who was one of the leaders of the Warsaw Ghetto
uprising. She reinforced the reports, already echoing in Palestine, that the
days immediately following liberation were harder even than the days of war.
She and her friends were seized by "the certainty that this was only a pause
between one *aktzia* and the next, and that the lesson from this period is: Prepare for the next *aktzia,* which is about to come whether after a shorter or

a longer pause." In other words, she did not doubt that on the streets of Europe, the return of the *aktzia*—an organized roundup of Jews to be sent to death—was only a matter of time. And, two years after liberation, standing there at Yagur, in the Land of Israel's blooming Jezreel Valley, she said at the very start of her remarks, in present tense like Kovner before her, "We are all living with a deep feeling of anxiety. Who knows what more awaits us? Who knows what the coming days will bring?"[52]

Thus, although the endeavors of Kovner and his group arose for a number of reasons, the underlying basis, the foundation, was the fear that the Holocaust would continue. And such fears were supported by the antisemitism that continued in every form, even open and murderous forms, after the war.

THREE AVENUES OF ACTION

From the fear of a rekindled and persistent Holocaust, three conclusions arose, which inspired three avenues of action: one was the *Bricha* movement, in recognition that the Jews no longer had a home in Europe and, since new graves were still being dug there, must leave immediately. And indeed a stream of refugees, which had begun trickling southward at the end of 1944, strengthened progressively into the hundreds, thousands, and tens of thousands, an odyssey that has been much discussed over the years. Kovner compared the journey toward the Land of Israel, which came to include two-thirds of those who left, to "the motion of a people, of a nation of shadows [...] a certain spontaneous event, a certain great ambition to transpose themselves from the land of Holocaust into the land of life."[53] The Bricha developed into a rare phenomenon, an entirely improvised organization whereby the war refugees, who had nothing but the shirts on their backs, were helped along and led forward by volunteers.

The second avenue of action was the establishment of the *Hativa* (brigade), the East European Survivors' Brigade. The idea was conceived in Lublin and was implemented in Bucharest in 1945. The purpose was to bring together all willing survivors, irrespective of past political movements or parties, to form an association separate from and above political parties. With the Holocaust expected to continue, the survivors had a lesson to learn from the divisiveness in which they had wallowed before and even during the Holocaust: to close ranks and bring a message of unity to the Jews of Palestine. It was likely thanks to the impetus of unity from the Hativa that the Bricha became a magnetic popular movement without party affiliation. "The *Hativa*, when it arose, had an immediate influence on the Bricha, and it inspired increased pressure favoring all forms of legal and illegal emigration to our destination."[54]

The third avenue of action was *vengeance*, and it aimed to prevent the Holocaust from continuing. For that purpose, those toying with the idea of further genocide were to receive—along with all the rest of the world—a warning that no one would forget. Such a warning could be achieved only by punishing the previous murderers. Therefore Kovner sought a "unique operation of organized vengeance" that would not resemble the other operations already carried out at the end of the war by Jews who returned from the forests and emerged out of hiding. The idea taking shape in Lublin was

> to pay the Germans back in a way that only the survivors of such a massacre can. An idea which the man on the omnibus, to use a figure of speech, could only consider deranged. But I will not claim that our thinking was far from deranged in those days [. . .]. Maybe worse than deranged. A terrifying idea, made wholly from despair and carrying a sort of suicide within it [. . .] a mental inferno [. . .]: an eye for an eye. In other words, wiping out six million Germans.[55]

Their goal was not, and could not be, to kill individual Nazis, not even the most prominent ones, because in their view the German nation, a nation of murderers, must receive in return as a nation what they inflicted on the Jewish nation. The entire German nation, at least one generation of it, must pay—it was unthinkable that the murder of six million people go unpunished. If no punishment was provided by heaven, then the source would be earthly. When justice is visited on the Germans, the world must shudder at "the wildness and cruelty practiced by the last of the survivors. And even if only a dozen Jews survive—Jewish blood shall not be forfeit." To that end, an inhuman weapon must be found, severe and cruel, a weapon "that none of us, with our upbringing, our tradition, our intellectual environment, was ever able previously to conceive of [. . .]. Horror in return for horror." This shock would serve as a warning for the future, because if the nations that joined in the massacre or watched with tranquil dispassion as butchery traversed the fields of Treblinka understood that murder was permissible and worthwhile, they would join in again. The Western world was already reconciling with the murderers and rehabilitating their country, while the de-Nazification of Germany remained on paper. Already, the murderers had returned to their villages and cities by the thousands and tens of thousands, and their neighbors welcomed them. Any political or military disturbance could restart the Holocaust, and the danger to the Jewish people's existence still loomed.[56] Shimon Avidan (Koch), who commanded the Givati Brigade in the War of Independence, remarked that since the Allies showed almost no interest in the fate of the Jewish people and preferred not to devote resources to saving Jewish lives lest the war effort suffer, "I believed we owed nothing to anyone, no obligation whether morally or otherwise, as to the means we chose for saving the surviving remnant or for vengeance against the Germans."[57]

There was one more argument for vengeance as deterrence: "If we want to build there, then we need to meet our obligation here," said Pasha (Avidov) in his testimony. He had entered the war as a communist and came out of the forests a committed Zionist—by historical necessity, in his words. He and his friends, in discussions revolving around the reason they remained alive and the purpose of their mission, heard from Kovner that there was an additional need, a deep one, that must be answered by deterrence against further harm to the Jewish people: In the Land of Israel, those who have already arrived are building and creating, but a constant threat hovers over their endeavor. There are fatalities, and there is fear of a future that may see such countries as Britain siding with the Arabs. Therefore the Avengers, although Zionists who desire to reach Israel, cannot immediately go there because they see Jewish survival from a broad perspective extending into future generations. Having survived the Holocaust, they must retaliate against the Germans so that all the world, including the Arabs and the British, will realize that the wheels of justice are turning and that nations are best advised to abandon any plots against the Jewish people. Thus the obligation must be met before they leave Europe. If it goes unmet, then the Jewish people will not be considered entitled to build themselves a home, and—even more to the point—they will not be left in peace to build one.[58]

It could be said, without overdramatizing, that the nascent group considered itself responsible for the future of the much-buffeted Jewish people, setting itself a comprehensive historical purpose: "We wanted, by our great act of vengeance, to admonish and warn those who hate the nation of Israel, in our generation and in generations to come; we wanted to sunder, once and for all, the chain of murders and abuses, to break the cycle of persecution and humiliation that had been our lot during the history of our exile"—to break it for the long term and overall. In the short term, regarding those matters confronting the Jewish people at the time, Pasha and Poldek testified, "We all were aware that the struggle to reach Palestine and establish the state was the priority, and we believed that our efforts were contributing to the security of Jews and of the future Jewish population in the Land of Israel."[59]

In Lublin, partisans who had survived in the Lithuanian forests met partisans from Rovno; they met those they called "Asians" or "Tashkenters," whose flight from the German invasion extended into the Soviet Union as far as the Asian republics and who returned after the liberation; they met groups of fighters and survivors from the ghettos, such as those from Częstochowa; they met former inmates of concentration camps and survivors of the Warsaw Ghetto uprising. They met with all those in approximately that order. In these meetings, they identified and discussed three avenues of action: *the Bricha,* leaving Europe's giant graveyard behind for the Land of Israel; *the Hativa,* an organization where all the survivors could find their place irrespective of party affiliation; and *the Nokmim.* The members of the Avengers' group took part in the day-to-day activities of the other two avenues of action. Thanks to the Bricha, the Hativa was able to fulfill its obligation to the survivors and put into action the feeling, formed during the Holocaust, of a fate in common, a concept they wished to bring with them to the Land of Israel. At the same time, the Bricha and the Hativa served to camouflage the underground activities of the Nokmim and helped them more easily operate on the roads of Europe. Moreover, during the first half of 1945 the three avenues of action were in practice under a single leadership, headed by Kovner.

THE MEETING IN LUBLIN

Lublin was flooded with refugees. As early as July 1944, the provisional Polish government moved from Moscow to the already liberated city. Living conditions there were harsh, and refugees of various nationalities came and went. Everything was fluid and inchoate. Cesia Rosenberg-Amit wrote that Lublin was swamped by thousands of refugees, some Jewish: inmates freed from the camps, underground fighters, partisans, youth group members back from Central Asia, the remnants of the Warsaw Ghetto resistance. Some stayed longer in the city, hoping that other acquaintances and relatives would follow. Others stayed only a week or two and moved onward in order to set up the next way station, in Romania, or in order to give encouragement to the Bricha movement at the stations already operating on the borders. In "the great tract of refugees named Lublin,"[60] it was clear from the start that the power was held by the Soviets, not by the provisional government. That government could not manage to overcome the city's chaotic atmosphere and its lack of basic security. Nonetheless, civic activity was able to recommence, Jewish political parties reawakened and were deemed legal by the authorities, and a Jewish Central Committee was established. It was constituted according to the size of the parties in the Jewish community, and it operated under the government's patronage.[61]

Yet in the opinion of Kovner and his comrades, committee members could not be considered leaders if they had not shown hardiness and a civic backbone before and during the war. "We couldn't be reconciled with having those people, in either their personal or their public capacity, representing us again in the Jewish community and to the outside world. And it would make no sense for anyone who calls himself a Zionist and behaved as they did to stand at the head of the survivors."[62] And because the leadership reverted to dealmakers dependent on foreign rulers, without proper lessons learned and without deep consideration of what had happened, "at that building in Lublin, in the winter [. . .] my life may have hit its biggest void. A sort of chill [. . .] suddenly seemed to leave our future without desirability." The Jewish people were no more, but their institutions were being put in place, he said ironically. Kovner may have been hasty in passing judgment on the heads of the committee, and it may be that as a Lithuanian Jew he was alienated from Polish Jews, some of whom did not speak Yiddish. Be that as it may, a further factor in vengeance appears here, born after the arrival at Lublin: to perform a deed that would prevent Jewish public life from returning to its previous rut and prevent Jews from resettling in Poland.[63]

Kovner began looking for those who shared his idea of vengeance among the varied and growing throng of Jews assembling in Lublin. Before long, he discovered that he was not the only Jew in whom deep anxiety combined with an urge to avenge the crimes of the past and issue a warning to the future. The Nokmim who began to gravitate around Kovner were, to begin with, Jews who already knew him from his days in the Vilna Ghetto and the forest of Rudniki, or as a leader of youth before the war. He had no need to exert himself in persuasion; everyone who approached him reported that Kovner seemed to express exactly the aspiration that beat in his listeners' hearts, an aspiration that he clothed in words that would ripen into deeds. There were a few who declined, a disinclination that was hard to absorb since a firm majority did favor vengeance.[64] When Gabi Sedlis was undecided, Kovner told him: "You remained alive not because you're better than other people, and not because you deserved it. You were just lucky. So your life isn't important in itself, and you should volunteer to sacrifice it for the common good." In other words, even at the start of membership in the Nokmim, it was clear to participants that the avenging operation could be fatal. In fact, they considered that prospect a given: they would not live on afterward.[65] "I was stirred," Cesia attests, recalling the occasion of her initiation by Kovner into the secret of the Nokmim. From that moment, she was "like a different person—someone who has regained the right to be alive [. . .] I felt the change occurring inside me." Vengeance provided not only a purpose for life but also a framework for it.[66] "A fear we held in common joined us to one another the way a flame welds metal," Kovner said later—the fear that the world, the Jewish world included, would return to its bad habits and wonted course with no repentance, and no recompense for spilling Jewish blood. That feeling gave them no rest. "The desire to participate was boundless," Yulek said. "*And for that they remained alive.*" (Emphasis in original.)[67]

The first who responded positively to the Vilnaites were from Rovno. They had arrived in Lublin shortly before the Vilnaites and settled on Lubratovska Street. Pasha Reichman (later Avidov) and his wife, Dorka; the brothers Eliczer and Avraham Lidovski and Avraham's wife, Vita, who were originally from Baranowice and had come to Rovno with the partisans; Bezalel Kek-Michaeli, from Rokitno; and others for a total of roughly forty. They included partisans and members of various political parties—Zionists, communists, and the unaffiliated—an assemblage of individuals who had met in the forests and had spun out many conversations about a future that might follow the lucky possibility of their liberation. Most of the communists among them suffered deep and terrible disappointment from the Soviets and from their Ukrainian neighbors, and hewed closer to the Zionist point of view. "When we heard the idea of a Jewish state, we were drunk with it," said Pasha.[68] When the Rovno fighters emerged from the forest and immediately began a vengeance campaign against the locals, they were already convinced that the former political movements could not be revived after the Holocaust. Their goal was the Land of Israel: a quick departure from the valley of death, without even marching onward toward Berlin with the Red Army, although they were still in uniform. In Rovno, they were already contemplating more widespread vengeance, as many throughout Europe had been complicit in the crime.

When they met, those from Vilna and from Rovno spoke with one voice, as if they had already shared a partnership for years. They lived in the same building, in the same apartment, bunking on three different levels. "The arrival of the Vilna group in Lublin, with Abba Kovner heading it, had the standing of an event," wrote Eliezer Lidovski, who had led fighters in the ghetto and in the forest. "His name went before him."[69] Lidovski and Kovner met one on one for a frank discussion, a conversation Lidovski saw as historic. They exchanged the Holocaust histories of Vilna and Rovno, and this private exchange begat cooperation in operational projects: in the Bricha, in establishing the Hativa, and in vengeance. They spoke of a prompt mass migration, an "exodus from Europe" to the Land of Israel, an exodus which would emerge spontaneously "from the ground up" to join and complement the foremost movements and the "top-down" leadership. Pasha too repeatedly recalls the enormous impression the first meeting of the Rovno partisans with Kovner made on him. It was a moving, unforgettable evening. Abba embraced and kissed them. Pasha immediately recognized Kovner's singular greatness, and to the end of his days he loved and praised Kovner unreservedly. He considered Lidovski a tribune of the people, in the full sense. And indeed, Lidovski and Kovner included Pasha and Bezalel Kek-Michaeli in their subsequent conversations, as they all agreed on the plan that was being formulated. According to historian Levi Arieh Sarid, it may be said that when Kovner, Lidovski, and Pasha met, they were establishing the future of Zionism, because if the survivors had not organized to immigrate to the Land of Israel, the alternative would have brought Zionism to an end. Pasha recounted more than once that in conversations between the Rovno Jews and the Vilna Jews, the idea of vengeance came up "by itself. By itself, vengeance entered the discussion." It united everyone, and no one could take credit for introducing it. The leadership for vengeance was assigned in Lublin as a result of those discussions, and at first it included Kovner, Lidovski, Pasha, and Bezalel (Kek-Michaeli.) Each of them began recruiting members from among his own circles.[70]

In January 1945, the refugees from Tashkent (dubbed "Asians" by the other refugees) arrived, led by Mordechai Roseman. Originally they numbered a few hundred members of pioneer movements—mostly Hashomer Hatzair, and a minority from Dror—and had been in Vilna when it was a hub of a growing number of youth movements. They had fled to Central Asia at the start of the war, but they had managed to stay in touch with one another. In Lublin, their numbers quickly grew to twenty, all of whom resided together in a small apartment. They reestablished ties with the Hashomer Hatzair members who had come from Vilna to Lublin. It must be remembered that they remained Hashomer Hatzair members; because they did not experience the Holocaust, the ideas of the Hativa, which was without party affiliation, were new to them if not outright foreign.

These young people enlisted primarily and enthusiastically in the Bricha movement, staffing key locations along the way. Ben Meiri, one of the "Asians," told Sarid that Kovner was the prophet of the Bricha concept—a poet who was a greater realist than those he recruited and who imbued them with an emotional sense of history.[71] As for vengeance, the "Asians" had never actually met a German before. They had set off for the east as soon as the Germans invaded the Soviet Union. It was only on their way back to Lublin, when they stopped in the abandoned city of Kovel, that they saw a message written in blood on the wall of a desolate synagogue: *Nemmt Nekama!* ("Take revenge!")[72] In Lublin, Roseman, Kless, Ben Meiri, and their "Asian" friends encountered the concept of vengeance, and they waited for Kovner to approach them as future members of the revenge group, but he did not seem eager to do so. They were not asked to participate or to express an opinion because they were not among those who had spent recent years under the heel of the Germans. Roseman testified that he could not say that the "Asians" were in favor of the ambitious plan, but he saw no possibility of their opposing it. "We were in our own sight as grasshoppers, next to the fighters." Kovner said that the "Asians" came from the other side of the moon, and therefore he "opted for the partisans and fighters" who had nothing but a gigantic graveyard behind them. The "Asians" felt that with hundreds of friends and tens of thousands of refugees yet to return from the far reaches of the Soviet Union, they should wait for more arrivals and help the Bricha movement before considering leaving Europe.

Therefore, the "Asians" immediately applied themselves to handling the new arrivals and to rekindling hope and belief among despairing people. And though the ideas of the Hativa, immediate leaving and revenge, were strange to them, the group—Asians and partisans altogether—was a close one. Friends returned into the arms of friends, living in close quarters, sleeping on wooden tiers in the same house on Leszczyńska Street. According to Ben Meiri, they had been less crowded in the ghetto. And if later the Nokmim asked for assistance in traveling onward—be it in the form of money, documents, escorts—they could not refuse. Kless recalled: "We completely identified with him [Kovner], and we followed him heart and soul. We carried an eternal stain of not having been in the ghetto, and not in the forest, and therefore we weren't included in the vengeance." Friendship continued, however, as if there were no distinction. It was to Kless, an "Asian," that Kovner—after both had settled in Israel—afforded one of his deepest and most important sessions of testimony with respect to memory and to building the nation's history.[73]

After the "Asians," further groups arrived, each from a different ghetto. One memorable group included, among others, Dov (Bolek) Gewirzman (later Ben-Ya'akov) and Pinchas (Yashek) Bencelowicz (later Ben-Zur), who had been fellow fighters in Częstochowa.[74]

However, the most emotional meeting in Lublin was with the survivors of the Warsaw Ghetto uprising. Antek Zuckerman saw that encounter as the greatest of events: "The experience of that meeting . . . let us know there are living Jews, living friends, living pioneers." Antek had arrived in Lublin from Warsaw with his life companion Zivia Lubetkin, as well as Tuvia Bozikowski and Stephen Grajek, all known Warsaw ghetto fighters. For many days and nights, they sat together with other arrivals from the various ghettos, telling their stories, weeping, "and giving soul-deep accounts." Afterward, when the inclusive meetings ended, and with the feeling that there had been a reunion of brothers and sisters from the two movements that had worked together during the Holocaust, Dror and Hashomer Hatzair, Kovner, and Antek sat down for a long conversation. It ended without agreement, despite Antek's esteem for the Hashomer Hatzair members from Vilna that he met (and who even knew Hebrew!) and for Kovner, who he hadn't known was "writing poems of powerful, trenchant expression."[75] Antek announced that he would be returning to Warsaw to care for those still emerging from the forest and other hiding places, and Kovner announced that there would be no lingering in the vast cemetery. Antek had in mind the revival of his Dror movement. Kovner was thinking of the Hativa, which had no room for the factionalized prewar movements. Antek believed that the new Communist regime in Poland would provide help because it was composed of leftists who had shown solidarity with Poland's Jews, whereas Kovner believed this was a misconception that would result in disillusionment. Antek was friendly with several members of the Jewish Central Committee and was in fact a member of the committee's presidium. Unlike Kovner, he had a solid understanding of the Polish Jewish leadership; and his disagreements with Kovner were all the more bitter for it, as Kovner completely ruled out any participation in a new Communist regime and showed little respect toward committee members. "This was the beginning of the big argument between us," Antek said. This argument between these two leaders would resurface more sharply in later years. In his testimonies, Antek said several times that "I kept it to myself"— that in Lublin he had heard from a Jewish minister of the provisional Polish government that negotiations were underway between the Polish and Soviet authorities for a repatriation of Jewish and non-Jewish citizens from the Soviet Union back to Poland. The repatriation was intended to begin quickly and would perhaps include tens of thousands of Jews.[76] There is no knowing if, had Antek given him that information, Kovner would have changed his mind regarding the urgent need to leave the accursed burial ground immediately and switched his focus to registering and caring for the expatriates. It could well be that, on the contrary, Kovner would have remained committed to his own path. But the fact stands: Antek did not tell Kovner, and Kovner remained unaware.[77]

In Lublin, Kovner spoke with Antek and Zivia about vengeance—but apparently not in detail, insofar as the idea was still germinating, despite the stories they told of Treblinka and Chelmno and of the loss of the largest ghetto of all, amounting to some 450,000 souls. Yudke Hellman, a close friend of Zuckerman who recorded the history of the Dror movement, attested later that according to Antek, who had spoken to him about it, Kovner and Antek first exchanged their differing views regarding vengeance in Lublin and that as soon as they did, their paths diverged. According to Hellman, neither Antek nor Zivia opposed vengeance, but they prioritized it differently, attaching more importance to caring for the survivors. "If it had been raised as a single idea [including both vengeance and caring for the survivors], we might well have turned our energies to it." Zuckerman himself said: "In Lublin, there was no arguing over vengeance,"[78] meaning that the disagreement was over not the idea itself but the manner of achieving it. At the end of the meeting, having decided upon their division of labor, Antek returned to Warsaw, and Zivia stayed with the partisans.

LEADERSHIP FOR THE BRICHA AND THE NOKMIM BEGINS TAKING SHAPE

Solidarity developed among the members of the various groups, and they felt responsible for providing the growing throng of refugees with leadership. Moreover, they enjoyed acceptance, and even preference, from the Soviet authorities because they were former partisans. Nonetheless, they had a definite motivation: immigration to the Land of Israel. In order to be able to pursue not only the Bricha project (an effort that was the closest to their hearts because it was their obligation to the survivors) but also the project of vengeance, they allocated responsibilities. According to Lidovski, a new member, Reuven Feldschuh, provided the ideological foundation and was the first to propose the idea of poisoning millions of Germans, while Pasha headed the operational force tasked with undertaking concrete steps. The three leaders (Lidovski, Pasha, and Kovner) decided to recruit several dozen former partisans; Kovner was designated as the contact in this effort responsible for communicating with representatives of the Jewish leadership in the Land of Israel and elsewhere and arranging for assistance through those leaders. The idea of obtaining support from the worldwide Jewish community was mentioned for the first time, a feat they took for granted.

Opinions on how to proceed were not unanimous. Nisan Reznik, a member of the Vilna Ghetto underground's leadership on behalf of *Hanoar Hatzioni* ("Zionist Youth"), was asked by Feldschuh to join, and he replied that without the support of the appropriate Jewish institutions, the vengeance operation would lack weight, significance, and even positive results. He declined to join.[79] Yulek Harmatz, who was more emphatically in favor of vengeance, said that there was work to be done for the sake of the nation's honor, and Lidovski, who considered the Bricha no less important than revenge—perhaps even more so—replied that for the sake of the dead, the necessity was to live rather than die. But Roseman says that the Nokmim were always surrounded by a circle of supporters and enablers, despite the differences of opinion.[80]

The Vilnaites, living at 10 Leszczyńska Street, immediately made the place the first headquarters of the Bricha. The commanders included several of the Nokmim leadership: Kovner, Pasha, Bezalel, and Eliezer Lidovski. Also included were certain other leading activists, such as Avraham Perchik, Roseman, and Grajek. However, these were not official appointments; additional leaders joined and participated prominently later on, while others chose different paths. Because of the Nokmim's compartmentalization with respect to membership, not everyone knew who the other members were. Lidovski wrote that as far back as Lublin, the leadership of the Nokmim was already "an underground within an underground." Senka Nissanilevich, who would later marry Zelda Treger, testified that he was with Zelda in Krosno, Czechoslovakia, both ostensibly as representatives of the Red Cross, in order to set up a way station for refugees on their way to jumping the border. At the same time, they were there to serve as camouflage for future revenge operations.[81] Thus, the Bricha functioned as cover for the Nokmim based on the presence of the Nokmim in the broader leadership of the Bricha. Moreover, Nokmim leaders later featured in the Hativa leadership as well. They thought day and night about how to exact vengeance, while at the same time also advancing in the two other directions.[82]

FUNDING THE OPERATIONS

As the Bricha began to expand and the refugees passed through at an increasing pace, particularly from the Soviet Union—even before repatriation began—the most urgent matter facing them was funding the operations. Crowded communal residences were set up, and every day there were new mouths to feed. Assistance came from the Joint Distribution Committee (JDC), headed by Joseph Schwartz, which saw to lodgings and food, and from the United Nations Relief and Rehabilitation Administration (UNRRA). Jews who worked for the UNRRA were very helpful.[83] Still, there were many additional expenses, such as paying smugglers and guides, bribing officials, finding transport, forging documents without which nothing could be done (since the great majority of refugees could not provide a single valid document), not to mention temporary lodging, hot meals, and medical treatment, a necessity after years of deprivation and physical and psychological torture. The help from the JDC and UNRRA proved insufficient, and in any case, neither of those bodies could fund illegal activity without endangering their own status.

In response, the group turned to a popular method of obtaining funding during this period, in the months after the liberation of Eastern Europe but before the end of the war in Western Europe. Activists from Lublin were sent eastward, mostly to Moscow, and they inexpensively bought gold rubles (which, for some reason, were nicknamed "pigs"). Then they returned west and sold the rubles for a good profit on the black market. It goes without saying that the Soviet authorities took a stern view of currency smuggling and of black-marketing in general, particularly in Russia and Poland—lengthy imprisonment awaited anyone suspected of such activities.

An additional method was developed, which the Bricha activists and the Nokmim called "expropriation." Put simply, it was extortion of money by means of threat from Jewish speculators who were trying to profit by the same methods of buying and selling gold but who refused to answer the call of their people.[84] Appeals to Zionists from the Jewish Central Committee in Lublin were refused because the Bricha operation itself was considered illegal by the Soviets and assistance to it from the JCC could endanger all the committee members. Some families of the youth movements' members contributed sums of money from stashes that had previously been hidden and then recovered after the war. In addition, there were large sums of money that the Nazis had stowed away or counterfeited in an attempt to ruin the economies of the Allies, Britain in particular. According to testimony from the counterfeiters, who were imprisoned in a special camp under strict German supervision, the Nazis distributed no less than ten million counterfeit pounds sterling. Some of it found its way to the activists. There were also people who agreed to make loans to the activists against a written commitment to return the money; the commitment was generally honored later by the emissaries, when they received money from the Land of Israel and channeled it to the needs of the Bricha.[85] Money had lost its value, and the members of the movement carried suitcases and rucksacks full of paper currency, recalling the days of great economic crisis that closed the 1920s.

While the Bricha was being run, and particularly after the Nokmim split off from the other groups and began operating separately but using the same methods that the Bricha had developed, there was a recurring question: Were the activists who were securing funding, those who were a separate "financial department" within the Nokmim, entitled to receive a certain small amount of funding against their own expenses? The question was never formally discussed, and matters were administered on the basis of perfect trust and frugal living. No one received a salary, and all work was volunteered. "Nothing stuck to the fingers of the activists," Lidovski wrote. From time to time, when members returned with booty, they would empty their pockets and set hundreds of thousands of rubles on the table as a matter of course; they would then request and receive a small sum for themselves from Lidovski and Kovner. Roseman, a close friend of the Nokmim though not a member himself, testified that among all the border crossings and all the journeys, "no embezzlement was ever reported, and no missing money. It was a temple, with priests and Levites and an altar for sacrifices. No one pocketed a penny."[86] Menashe Gewissar, who served as treasurer for the Bricha for ten months, recounted: "I'd received money from [Moshe] Auerbach [later Agami], the emissary from the Land of Israel, and he trusted me completely. I never had to give him a report." And Ben Meiri added: "Purity and integrity governed the flow of money [...]. A system of codes was established between us and Moshe Agami [Auerbach] for numbers and quantities, and they [the refugees] would receive money against a note that I signed." The money obtained was intended both for the Bricha and for vengeance. It granted them independence. If it had come from another source, they would have been answerable to that source; since they did not want to depend on others, their only choice was to continue these same methods.[87] Nahum Shadmi (formerly Kremer), the commander of the Haganah in Europe, distinguished between "smugglers and moneychangers"—innate black marketers who retained that quality after the war, and members of the Avengers, about whom he wrote that most were "fine young guys, among the best of Jewish youth."[88]

Just as the departure in December 1944 from Vilna to Lublin was a hasty one, with Kovner dogged by the danger of arrest, so was the departure from Lublin. At the end of February, one of the town's central activists from among the Jewish communists on the Jewish Central Committee warned Kovner and Lidovski that under the new regime their activity was considered subversive. They took the hint: on March 1, 1945, relocation from Lublin south to Bucharest began. Way stations, which had been set up for the Bricha, were already in place, and the members passed from one station to the next: through the Carpathians; through Krosno and Sanok into Czechoslovakia; and into Romania, along a route prepared by activists and partisans who had been tasked with finding ways to cross the southern borders.

Manek testified that in Lublin the Avengers had believed time was abundant. The war was by no means over yet, but there actually was no time to spare. In retrospect, he believed that they should have set out at once for Germany, where the SS camps were, and taken action there as soon as the war ended—in June and July 1945, not 1946. Thinking back, Gewissar questioned their reasoning for moving south from Lublin to Romania. It was a mistake, he concluded, because it didn't fulfill the purpose of vengeance. In order to take revenge, they could have set their sights on Poland, which was already being liberated and which was home to many Germans. Yehuda Arazi (code name "Alon"), who headed the activity of legal and illegal immigration, believed that vengeance should target not only the Germans but also their Polish accomplices. He was in touch with several of the Nokmim concerning that matter.[89] It should be remembered that Gewissar was a member of Dror, Antek's movement, which favored resettling in Poland. However, most of the refugees' leaders were convinced that staying in Poland would mean remaining under a Communist regime that was steadily entrenching itself—after all, Poland was a graveyard of Jews, and Jews were still being murdered there. Moving southward meant drawing nearer to the Land of Israel, and so their hearts were pulled in that direction, toward the shore where they would someday embark. Those already recruited to the Nokmim moved south in military trucks, on trains, and in every chance vehicle available, and they carried papers indicating that they were Greek refugees returning home. The hope was that in the ears of the Soviets, Hebrew and Yiddish could pass for Greek. The papers were embellished with the stamp of the Red Cross. The travelers were detained, were released, forged new papers, continued onward, were detained again, and so on.[90]

In Lublin their idea had begun to crystallize, in the light of all the reasons mentioned above. The Nokmim had begun to aggregate and already numbered some tens of men and women. In Bucharest, they began the phase of practical organization and of establishing principles.

Accursed be the Jew who is not horrified upon hearing of the murder of an entire people; who does not search into the manner of the killing of seven million of his brothers; who does not desire, does not dream of, does not constantly speak of avenging the blood of his martyred brothers, the blood of seven million souls of Israel [. . .]. Every single German deserves death; the hand of every German is stained with Jewish blood: the blood of a child, an old man, or a woman. German children who have not yet killed a Jew are raised to do so, educated to it, dedicated to it by murderous parents and murderous teachers. Accursed be the Jew who does not destroy them in the bud when he is able [. . .]. I curse all those so-called Jews who, at the loss of seven million of their best and truest in Europe, will turn back to their contemptible daily affairs. I curse them because I am unable to kill them.

Itzhak Katzenelson, *Last Writings: Hebrew Years 5700–5704 (1940–1944)*; translated from Yiddish into Hebrew by M. Z. Wolfovsky, Tel Aviv, Hakibbutz Hameuchad, 1956, p. 22. Translated into English by Mark L. Levinson. Courtesy of Hakibbutz Hameuchad publication house.

2

Bucharest, March–June 1945
From Conception to Preparation

ON MARCH 1, 1945, the group that had begun to coalesce in Lublin left for Romania. It included Rachel and Eliezer Lidovski, Dorka and Pasha Reichman, Abba Kovner and Vitka Kempner, Zelda Treger and Netanel (Senka) Nissanilevich, Shlomo Kless, and Gabi Sedlis—who was toting a rucksack with the forgery equipment that had provided documents in the ghetto and in the forest. Zivia Lubetkin also left with them, whereas her life companion Yitzhak (Antek) Zuckerman returned from Lublin to Warsaw to wait for other Holocaust survivors and refugees from the Soviet Union to arrive. In Warsaw he hoped to revive the remains of his Dror movement.

On their way from Lublin and elsewhere, Jewish refugees were heading to Bucharest in hopes that from there they could reach the Land of Israel or reestablish contact with, and receive support from, representatives of the free world's Jewish organizations, such as the Joint Distribution Committee, whom they had met in Lublin. They followed no single organized migration route, but rather a primary stream with other separate streams. The "Asians" and the partisans managed way stations like the ones they had previously managed on the way to Lublin. Millions had yet to return home, and the number of Jews on the roads grew from hundreds to an avalanche of thousands. "We hadn't imagined that we were poking our finger at one grain in a mountain of sand," said Kovner.[1] In Bucharest, they met for the first time with emissaries from the Land of Israel. It was a very emotional meeting, but a disappointing one too, since the two sides were on different pages regarding what could and could not be done. There was only one ship waiting at the port to sail to Palestine. The emissaries told the activists about the existence of the Jewish Brigade in Italy, and activists sent messengers there to make contact.[2]

As in Lublin, but even more so in Bucharest, they were struck by the throng of Jews who had assembled in the city. Bucharest was "crowded, multi-faced, multi-active, mumbling and thundering: refugees from Poland, repatriating Soviets, dealers in currency and in UNRRA aid packages alongside disparate youth groups," according to author Yonat Sened.[3] Once more, comrades lodged together, according to hometown, in crowded quarters with fourteen bunk beds to a room. The primary center was Vitorului Street, an area that was mostly Jewish. The beautiful city of Bucharest had been spared by the war, and it was verdant, bustling, and teeming with restaurants and movie theaters. Who remembered that such things existed? Everything seemed to be falling into place.[4]

KA-TZETNIK AND THE AUSCHWITZ GROUP

Among the many various faces and personalities that continued to flow into Bucharest and assemble there, an outstanding figure was Yehiel Feiner (later De-Nur), better known by his nom de plume Ka-tzetnik and remembered for his dramatic testimony at the Eichmann trial, during which he fainted on the witness stand. He switched names and documents in the Bricha, but he primarily carried a passport issued to Kalman Tsitinski or Tsetinski; it is under that name that he appears in sources appertaining to the time in Bucharest.[5] He was one of a group of five Auschwitz survivors there, and the Bricha activists bluntly referred to them as "the Auschwitz group." The five had come to Romania along with a group of six Warsaw Ghetto fighters they had encountered along the way and whom—as recorded by one of the fighters, Pnina Greenspan (later Greenspan-Frimer)—they clung to admiringly, excessively, and embarrassingly. They insisted on occupying the same room as the fighters, who also included Zivia—"a human angel; she understood us," Ka-tzetnik said years later—and there they would hold an *appel*, lining up as if for roll call at the concentration camp. They would tell and retell the abominations of Auschwitz and sing prisoner songs, dressed always in their striped uniforms. Ka-tzetnik declared from time to time that he was, in any case, no longer a living man and that they "were possessed by a kind of abandon."[6] Their Auschwitz stories intensified the feeling with which the fighters had ended their visit to the Majdanek camp near Lublin, and the meeting with the Auschwitz survivors in Bucharest deeply shocked the fighters—especially the Lithuanians, who had known nothing about the extermination camps. Their descriptions impressed on them the unprecedented monstrosity of the Holocaust: "Suddenly, an incomprehensible tragedy became clear to us."[7] Manek L., also part of the Auschwitz group, later joined the Nokmim. After Auschwitz, he had been imprisoned in another camp with his brother, with Ka-tzetnik, and with several other comrades. One night in January 1945 they all jumped from a train that had left the camp and was on its way to Germany, and they continued together to Bucharest. It was the natural thing to do, Manek said: the rumor had spread that from Bucharest, there was a route to Palestine.[8]

In 1945, the Passover holiday fell at the start of April, and tens of comrades, from among some 1,300 who had already arrived in Bucharest and the vicinity, gathered in the dining room of one of the Bucharest kibbutzim. The division into a dozen kibbutzim had largely corresponded with the members' towns of origin, but representation at the Passover gathering aligned with wartime experiences—the partisans, the "Asians," the members of undergrounds, and the survivors of camps (with Auschwitz foremost)—or membership in the various movements. This was apparently the first post-Holocaust gathering of any large and varied Jewish public, and it opened with a minute of silence for all those who had perished. The speakers at the gathering expressed painful feelings: of loneliness in a hostile world, of guilt for having survived. They noted the large numbers of non-Jews who were also murdered by the German enemy and its accomplices, and they protested against Jews who themselves accused the Jewish people of having failed to resist the genocide. They angrily demanded punishment for those Jews, whom they believed had betrayed the Jewish people. For the first time, what had happened in the Holocaust was spelled out in bitter public debates, which served as the basis for future debates. Kovner, who delivered the major address, warned that the Holocaust might not be over and that the factionalism that preceded the war could continue to ravage the world. Accordingly, he proposed the creation of a survivors' *Hativa* as part of a unification of survivors that would supersede the old, politicized frameworks. He also expressed the fear that everyday life, and certainly life in the Land of Israel, could sideline any political agenda.

The members of the Auschwitz group also spoke. Ka-tzetnik—cited in the protocols as Tsitinski, his Bricha pseudonym—invoked "the oath that we swore," and in so doing he may have meant he was speaking for all members of the group. According to him,

> Those who came away from the smokestacks of the crematoria know what they want. We want tanks demolishing city streets. Rebuilding comes later. Our job now is destruction [. . .]. Who dares deny it to us? We are Frankensteins. We, who came away from the ruins, will show the world. We will snatch up the name "Jew" in every language and uplift it [. . .]. Words of vengeance will light our way. For as long as one member of this nation remains, we shall not rest.

In contrast, another speaker from the Auschwitz group focused on the need to clearly inform the Yishuv of what had happened, but he continued in the same prophetic tone as Ka-tzetnik: "Such is the power driven into us by Hitler."[9] Their words made a powerful impression on the attendees, and although the Auschwitz group was not among the partisans, they had the ear of the Bricha leadership—Ka-tzetnik even appears in their photo. Yulek Harmatz testified that "Ka-tzetnik was in our group [the Nokmim], and he was intended to write about our deeds." Ka-tzetnik and Manek did not feel that vengeance was the task of partisans in particular. On the contrary, they thought, the partisans had already done their part, whereas the ex-prisoners from the camps (Ka-tzetnik refers to this group not as "survivors" but as "ex-prisoners"), who had not yet gotten the opportunity, should be the ones to take the lead.[10]

Despite having unambiguously asserted the necessity of vengeance, Ka-tzetnik also swore the "Auschwitz oath":[11] to record the world of Auschwitz, the "other planet," on paper. In conversations with Ka-tzetnik in Bucharest, Abba Kovner—who had been an author since his youth—expressed an understanding of the fire that burned in Ka-tzetnik's bones and that impelled him to write. It was decided that Ka-tzetnik would receive a space of his own, and a small room was allotted to him (a rare luxury).[12] Apparently it was there that he wrote the poem "Salamandra," a forerunner of his next novels. It was Ka-tzetnik's first postwar literary work. He presented it to friends as a work in progress, recalled Manek, who remained a close friend of his after they moved to Israel. The poem is full of the urge for vengeance— the vengeance of a salamander. This creature of fire burns for seven years, an amount of time that roughly corresponds to the length of the war. The salamander, thirsting for vengeance, crosses continents, and it levels an eternal curse "as long as vengeance has not quenched the fire in my bowels"—meaning that vengeance will never be fully achieved.[13] Afterward, Ka-tzetnik traveled with the Bricha members and the Auschwitz group from Bucharest to Italy. He reached Naples, and there he again received a small room, one with just three walls remaining after a shelling. There, while the Jewish Brigade soldiers saw to his needs and the Nokmim supported him financially, he wrote his first book "without respite. Without cease. He had shed his here and now. Passed into the planet Auschwitz, which moves in orbits beyond the boundaries of time."[14]

The Organizing Continues

In Bucharest, Kovner continued organizing the Nokmim. He told Manek that a group was forming that would exact large-scale vengeance. "It didn't take me a second to decide," Manek recalled later. "I was glad." The calm of Bucharest, the preparations surrounding immigration to the Land of Israel— those very things made him feel uneasy, as if he were about to jump from one important phase of his life to the next without bridging the gap between them. Taking a leap without knowing the fate of his sisters, without personally witnessing the collapse of the Nazi regime. Immigration to the Land of Israel presented the aspect of another uprooting, something akin to knowing one's home is on fire but not even glancing back to see what has become of it. So, to be bound for the Land of Israel already?[15] In Bucharest he joined the Nokmim, at Kovner's invitation. So did Yulek, even though his mother had already arrived there and he had an emotional reunion with her, an event that brought tears to the eyes of everyone who had not been so lucky—the majority who were present. Yulek had particular difficulty accepting Kovner's invitation: it would mean he would have to leave his mother a second time, after she had lost her other two sons. After the war, Yulek was hounded by the death of his younger brother, who had not escaped with the other members of the underground through the sewer system into the forest.[16]

A group of Akiva movement members from Krakow also reached Bucharest: Yehuda (Poldek) Wasserman (later Maimon), Yehuda (Idek) Friedman, Ze'ev (Willek) Shutzreich (later Shenar), Theodore (Dzhunek) Hershderfer (later Dan Arad), Shimek (Shimon) Lustgarten, Yitzhak Hammel, and Joseph Wolf. Most had fled the death march from Auschwitz in January 1945. They set up a kibbutz of their own at the suggestion of Zivia, who had welcomed them warmly at Bucharest just as she had welcomed the Auschwitz group. They sat together with other survivors and recalled the terrible experiences they had endured; they called themselves "members of the ghetto undergrounds," particularly those from Krakow. (Poldek, for example, had participated in the first-ever armed attack against German officers by a Jewish underground in occupied Europe, at the Cyganeria café in Krakow in December 1942.) Meanwhile, the group from Częstochowa also arrived, having passed through Lublin as aforementioned, and it joined the Krakow group.

In exchanges between and within the groups, the idea of vengeance would come up. Vitka, who was sharply discerning and apparently more alert to individual character than Kovner was, would occasionally rule that one person or another was ill suited for the mission.[17] As word of the Nokmim's existence spread, friends recruited friends, and the group's membership expanded. Dan Arad, for example, who had a perfectly legal certificate for immigration to Palestine and made a good income sewing women's shoes in Bucharest, knew nothing about the Nokmim until a fellow member of the Krakow group, fearing that the walls had ears, approached him on the street and recruited him. Arad said later that he was interested in joining a group that to him seemed a small, secret underground elite with a high-quality membership. He also found it appealing that the group gathered together almost every evening and that most of its members had fought in the cities, in the underground, or among the partisans. As mentioned earlier, Kovner also used such criteria.

Pasha recruited Mira (Mirka) Verbin-Shabetzky; after he swore her to secrecy, she replied that she was alone in the world, that no one was going to seek her out, and that she would stay quiet. "When I heard about the Nokmim, I was in seventh heaven," Mira recalls today, "because they deserved it—we'd seen Majdanek—and because it gave us something to do. It provided a structure." Because this underground was carefully organized and compartmentalized, she was unaware that Kovner had already recruited Cesia Rosenberg in Lublin. Mira and Cesia were good friends, having been together in the Vilna Ghetto, where they had been members of the FPO underground (the United Partisan Organization); later, they had fought in the forests of Narocz, where the Soviet command harassed the Jewish partisans. However, they never spoke with each other about being recruited into the Nokmim. Cesia was a natural choice. She had successfully carried out extraordinary missions that Kovner assigned her in the ghetto, such as crossing the front lines in order to pass information about the ghetto to Soviet authorities. Kovner told her repeatedly that the Nazis must be called to account by a powerful act of vengeance that would warn and deter all the enemies of the People of Israel. Each time, she said, his words "cried out inside me, whirling madly." In Bucharest, he repeated his message in private recruitment conversations and on public platforms: The Holocaust could recur anywhere in the foreseeable future. The sword is still hanging over the heads of all Jews. But Jewish blood must no longer be forfeit.[18]

Then one evening they found themselves, at Kovner's invitation, in a room filled with young people. Word had spread that this would be an unusual evening. Kovner, the verbal magician, "using his mesmerizing power of expression [. . .] clad our feelings in words. The hatred against the Germans burnt in our bones [. . .]. We needed no persuasion—we knew that this was our duty." It was an evening worthy of ceremony indeed, as it marked the start of operations.[19]

Again, as in Lublin and as in the ghettos and forests, in Bucharest everyone, all Kovner's followers, lived in the same house—a very nice house, as Mira remembers it, and with a kitchen of their own. They even received a little money for clothing, as well as free tickets to performances of the Red Army Chorus. It appeared that after some years of inadequate conditions, things were looking better. The Joint Distribution Committee saw to the group's needs; otherwise they would have been scrounging for bread. By their accounts, the "setters of the tone" (*Tongiber*, in their Yiddish parlance) and those who stood out as leaders in Bucharest, aside from Kovner, were Pasha as number two—"I would stand in for him"—and Bezalel Kek-Michaeli, as well as Yulek and Eliezer Lidovski, of course. Avraham Perchik was in charge of finances, and Bolek Ben-Ya'akov of the Częstochowa group, a man who strongly felt the flame of vengeance, remembering every minute the murder of his beloved wife and only son, relates how he was recruited into the extended leadership. To the astonishment of the emissaries from the Land of Israel, this leadership and its close followers declined to set off on the ship that was waiting at the port; they waived the rare immigration certificates that had been approved for them. They preferred to continue onward, heading the camp in the missions of the Avengers and the Bricha. Their sacrifice won them a firm moral standing in the eyes of those they led.[20]

If the group of coalescing Avengers is analyzed by affiliation with Jewish movements rather than just by hometown, we find that members joined from Hashomer Hatzair, Akiva, and Hanoar Hatzioni. Members of the Dror did not, and their nonparticipation may be viewed in light of the stand taken by Antek and Zivia, to be discussed below. It also bears noting that among the emissaries sent to Romania from the Land of Israel, Moshe Agami and paratrooper Yitzhak (Mano) Ben-Ephraim of Kibbutz Shamir were not deemed suitable to share the secret of the Nokmim despite the great respect felt for them as representatives of the Land of Israel.[21] Stated plainly, they were representatives of a place where the Holocaust had not occurred, and vengeance was a matter for those who had personally experienced it.

The members of Beitar, the youth movement affiliated with the rightist Revisionist Party, coming from Vilna and elsewhere, were excluded despite their eagerness: "Our dream was that if we were privileged to stay alive, we would do everything we could to exact vengeance for the spilt blood of our people so that all would see and know," Haim Lazar wrote later. He was a Beitar member in his youth, a member of the Vilna Ghetto underground, a partisan in the forests of Lithuania, and later an Israeli writer and chronicler. He knew that no vengeance would reduce their pain; even in the forest and in battle, when they took revenge against the Germans and collaborators, they had no sense that such "accursed blood" redeemed the innocent blood that had already been spilled. They saw the entire German nation as responsible for the genocide against them, he said. That nation had raised Hitler to power, the murderers had sent home the property they had robbed from the Jews, and all Germans had benefited.[22] In other words, the attitude among the Beitar members—particularly those from the Vilna Ghetto who had helped organize the underground and then escaped into the forest to fight—matched that of the other groups that joined together for vengeance. And as Lazar recounted later, although they learned in Bucharest that an avenging group was being organized, they were not recruited and were not entrusted with inside knowledge. Even years later, Lazar was full of rage about this. He described the succession of events with anger if not always accuracy. He was scornful of the Nokmim and believed that they had excluded the Beitar members on the opinion of Palestine's Jewish leadership, which was in bitter conflict with the Beitar's affiliated underground there, the IZL (military fighting organization).[23] Still, it was not a few emissaries that turned the group's leadership against admitting the Beitar members; it was a difference in objectives. Years later, Konver told Lazar he could not admit Beitar members who wished the British targeted for even harsher revenge. They were considering blowing up a representative office that the British had established a short while before in liberated Poland, an act that was out of the question: only Germans should be targeted. "We are not terrorists"—that is to say, the Nokmim saw themselves as agents of a unique national mission arising from the Holocaust not at all comparable to the terrorist operations in Palestine.[24]

In fact, despite his complaints, Lazar noted that when surviving Beitar members met Jewish Brigade soldiers who were also Beitar members and tried to inspire them to join in inflicting vengeance, they were told that the means were insufficient and that it was necessary to wait for experienced IZL fighters to come from Palestine. But when those experienced Beitar fighters reached Italy, they claimed that all-out war was underway against British rule, for the fate of the Land of Israel, of the survivors, and of the entire Jewish people hanging in the balance and demanding all resources and energy. Victory was near, they said, and afterward the matter of vengeance could be handled. Lazar said sadly in summation that their participation in the project of vengeance never did come about, and that "that was the tragedy for us; that was a failure that cannot be absolved."[25] But beyond that, looking at the membership of the Nokmim and noting what members (such as Vitka or Leibke Distel) said without reference to Lazar, it is apparent that the Nokmim came from different worlds, different movements in different places, and different backgrounds. According to Vitka, the group consisted of "people whom, in normal life, I couldn't have convinced myself to join."[26] Membership was afforded on a personal basis, not based on one's political party, as Kovner emphasized, and the idea of revenge was what bound everyone together.

The Stances of Antek and Zivia

Kazhik Rathajzer (later Simcha Rotem) joined the Nokmim after arriving in Bucharest from Warsaw, where he had participated in the uprising and had helped tens of surviving fighters escape through the sewage canals. On his arrival, apparently at the end of February 1945, he met Vitka in the street and through her he connected with Kovner. Kazhik immediately found common ground with them. In his memoirs, he briefly mentioned that he did not see immigrating to Palestine as an urgent objective since, like them, he believed that there was a prior duty to fulfill in Europe: "things concerning our unsettled score with the Germans." To author Yonat Sened he said that the matter was clear as day (or as darkness, Sened adds): those who remained alive had the task, and the obligation, of vengeance. "Otherwise, what? A clean slate, just like that, as if nothing happened?"[27] He tried to raise the subject with Zivia, who, it may be remembered, came to Bucharest at the same time, but she did not share his view on the obligation to avenge; and Kazhik, a reserved and taciturn person, writes: "Our ways thus parted."[28] There is no doubt that the rebuff from Zivia, who had come a long, difficult way with him in the Warsaw Ghetto before, during, and after the uprising, was painful to Kazhik and created at least a separation, if not a division, between them. Later, he recounted that when they were together on the Aryan side of Warsaw after the uprising and beginning to consider what they would do after the war, he had already mentioned vengeance to her. He believed that just as they had organized to rebel against the Germans in the ghetto, they must also organize to take revenge against them; however, Zivia immediately rejected the idea.[29] Kazhik, despite his respect for Zivia, was convinced that vengeance was necessary, and when the plans were presented to him, he was ready "to pitch in for everything it implies"; if exposed, he would stand trial, not run away. A trial would be their only chance at a platform from which they could describe what the Holocaust had been. A platform from which to address the world was, according to Kazhik, part of the plan.[30]

Zivia had come to Bucharest with the Bricha activists, because, as Antek said, "we divided the work. I helped with rehabilitation and she helped with the Bricha." Zivia helped pave the way and set up exit points for Jews, Antek explained, and there was no contradiction between the two projects. Kovner said that she stayed with him and his group in order to serve as the commissar, that is, to stay alert and keep Antek informed regarding how Kovner was proceeding, especially since the meeting between Antek and Kovner in Lublin had ended in disagreement on most topics.[31] In addition to Kazhik, others in Bucharest revealed to Zivia their intentions to avenge, but she continued her outright rejection of it. She tried to have conversations with those who were central to the Bricha operations and in establishing the Hativa— those who, in her view, appeared to have been most attracted to the idea of vengeance. She wanted to provide a counterweight to Kovner's compelling power. "What are you? Little boys?" she scolded Senka Nissanilevich. "You'll wind up killing each other." Zivia was also concerned that the preoccupation with vengeance would debase the minds of the movement's junior followers. In her opinion, not all the Germans deserved vengeance, only those who had been involved in actions against Jews.[32] Poldek Maimon, alone among the Nokmim, believed that at heart Zivia did support vengeance. Poldek had fled the death march that started in Auschwitz and reached Warsaw, where he met Zivia and Antek. Their preference was to stay in the city, but he proceeded to Bucharest.[33]

Antek recounts in his memoirs, quoting Zivia, that her relations with the Hashomer Hatzair members in Bucharest deteriorated and she sank into a depression after she was excluded from their circle. But one should keep in mind that the idea of vengeance was not the purview of any particular party or movement; the opposite was the case. Again, Zivia was on warm terms with everyone who came to Bucharest, including adherents of Hashomer Hatzair. The Nokmim would sit and argue for entire days, according to Antek, who himself must have heard this from Zivia, since he was not there at the time. They lived in a self-made atmosphere that was mystical, messianic, and murky, and they atrophied from inactivity as they waited for the miracle to arrive from the sea. "It was actually a cult, a sect, of avengers," he said.[34] In Antek's opinion, they came to Bucharest feeling stymied because the emissaries from the Land of Israel had failed to prepare more than one ship. So the arguments continued over what to do next, over the founding and the future of the Hativa, and over the vengefulness that burned in their bones. They "stewed in their own juice," and they "sat, ate, drank, and swapped yarns."[35]

However, other remarks by Zivia and Antek indicate that in Bucharest vengeance was not a black-and-white issue. In her well-known testimony at Kibbutz Yagur in the summer of 1946, following her arrival in the Land of Israel, Zivia briefly noted that after liberation, everyone seethed with a desire for revenge: "We knew only one thing: If we find the people we need and the power we need, the one thing to accomplish is *vengeance*! At that time, we were not feeling constructive; we wanted to bring destruction, all the destruction possible, all that we could!" To Zivia's thinking, the driving force was the conviction that they, the survivors from among the movements, must first meet with the Jews of Palestine and convince them that the next pogrom was impending.[36] As mentioned, she and Kovner, with one voice, also expressed the same deep fear that the blade could still swing again in the fields of Treblinka, but they chose a different path. Bella Gutterman, Zivia's biographer, writes that as a clearheaded and practical person who assessed priorities and followed them, Zivia could not join vengeance operations because they were based on an emotional component that outweighed all else.[37] As her first priority, she chose—alongside and in agreement with Antek—rehabilitating the survivors from among her movement, as well as taking in refugees returning to Poland and providing for them in preparation for their immigration to the Land of Israel. And as she labored, her view was always to the future, not to unsettled accounts of the past. While all that may be true, to dwell on the contradiction between the logic underlying her activities and the vengeful emotion that gave Kovner no rest is to undervalue Kovner's thinking and that of his fellow Nokmim, which exhibited a broad, principled, national-historical approach to judgment, justice, and the world order.

Antek's stand was much more complex. He described himself as having been "mad with vengefulness" like every other Jew, but firmly opposed to indiscriminate punishment.[38] In candid testimony twice, once in 1964 and once at the start of the 1980s, Antek tried to clarify his stance to Zvika Dror, who was a member of his kibbutz and a major participant in the work of documentation and memorialization. So frankly did Antek speak that Dror was asked to make a number of deletions, even after Antek's words were ready to be published in *Pages of Testimony*, a comprehensive collection of accounts from the members of the ghetto fighters' kibbutz, Kibbutz Lohamei Hagetaot.[39]

As noted, Antek and Zivia had come to Lublin in the third week of January 1945, immediately after the liberation of Warsaw. As early as that time, Antek was gaining an understanding of the anti-Soviet hatred that flamed in Kovner and his friends, the "Asians" included. In long conversations with them extending over multiple days and nights, he heard about the antisemitism, both overt and concealed; about life in the Soviet Union as they saw it; and about the comrades who had been humiliated and killed in the forests. They described the Jewish experience acidly, Antek told his interviewer, and they expressed the conclusion "that all the world murders us, all the world hates us," and all the Jews are the slain. These emotional words strongly affected him, even as he considered them spoken in despair. He could understand the conclusions that the group drew: that all the available forces, without exception, must be unified into an organized Jewish force with the goal of immediate immigration to the Land of Israel. And from such conclusions, the Hativa, Bricha, and vengeance against the Germans emerged.[40]

However, Antek came from a different world; he believed that relations were respectful between the Jewish Combat Organization, which had fought in the Warsaw Ghetto, and the Polish communists. Among the left-wing Polish underground, the *Armia Ludowa*, he and Zivia had friends who had begun assuming key positions in the new regime after the war and who could be of help to them. He contended that the entire Polish nation had not been slaughterers; there were also Poles, albeit a meager minority, who had risked their lives to save Jews; therefore, he did not believe that the other nations were wholly murderous. And so his attitude toward an urgent departure from Europe, and toward vengeance, was different. "It's wrong to have nothing but vengeance in mind," he said. While not ruling out vengeance, he saw it as one of a series of tasks incumbent on the youth movements' survivors after the war.

> The same movement that will organize the young people and the adults toward their constructive path will also be the movement responsible for the campaign of vengeance—not merely vengeance, but also education. Not as one item divorced from the overall developments in the ruined, despoiled Jewish streets, but as a part of them, as a function of them, as one aspect of them.[41]

In his view, one of the tasks incumbent on the movement was to head the postwar rehabilitation; and since he was determined that the movement be the Dror movement that he headed at the time, and since Kovner and his associates were determined to move onward, vengeance was accordingly also seen as a task that he must take upon himself.[42]

Thus Antek, by his own account, saw no contradiction between the Bricha and vengeance, nor between vengeance and getting organized in Poland. "There was no need at all to hold such an argument with Zuckerman and with Zivia Lubetkin over vengeance," he said to Dror, speaking of himself in the third person. It was also not a question of whether to avenge. The question was who would avenge, under what auspices, and how. First of all, vengeance would not be the assignment of all the forces. Second, vengeance, although a given, would be visited only on the guilty ones known by name and who had a "pedigree" as participants in murdering Jews. It would not be indiscriminate mass vengeance. "We are not setting out to kill millions [. . .] by poisoning," he said—although such a project would become known to him later. If he had been given the choice, he certainly would not have dropped the abundant work that awaited him in Poland and devoted himself only to vengeance. Still, he said to Dror on a different occasion: "If I'd thought then that we were able to wipe out the German nation, I would have joined in. Then I would have known: they annihilated us, we annihilated them. Nation for nation."[43]

Antek's final testimony, given shortly before his memoirs were to be published, contains the harshest criticism he ever voiced against Kovner,

Hashomer Hatzair, the partisans, and the Nokmim. He used expressions such as "false messianism" and "stooping to the enemy's level." He argued that Jewish humanism was not extinct and that it forbade blind vengeance. In Antek's criticism, there is much settling of accounts between the movements, especially in a chapter in his memoirs titled "Debating Our Image." There, in a repetitive, unfocused fashion, he reiterates what he said in his testimony regarding vengeance. In that testimony, Antek claimed the opposite of what he had told Dror about annihilating the German nation. "That issue had me sleepless [...] but my thinking was far from theirs, which bordered on insanity. Could a nation of sixty million Germans really be liquidated? And if you managed to kill a thousand Germans, then would you sleep soundly? Would you then think that you really avenged your nation?" However, he said, the matter never stopped troubling him and that even in the Land of Israel he was burdened by it.[44] Accordingly, by his account, after he returned from Lublin to Warsaw, he was informed that the Nokmim wanted him to lead their efforts in Germany, and he did not refuse. Who put that proposal to him, when and why did it happen, how did Antek ultimately respond, and what was the evolving context—all that will be discussed later.

Chaika Grossman, a member of Hashomer Hatzair in the Vilna Ghetto and one of the underground fighters in the Bialystok Ghetto, did not arrive in Lublin among the streams of refugees who assembled there and continued southward; she did not reach Bucharest either. In the months after the war, she had formed a strong aversion to vengeance. Although she met Kovner briefly while he was on his way from Vilna to Lublin, they apparently did not touch on the subject and she did not hear of the idea from him— nor from the friends with whom she passed through the long travails of the Holocaust. During those first few months, she remained in Poland, spending most of her time in Bialystok. She worked at the Polish Department of Security, known as the Uzrad Bezpieczenstwa (UB), which was established after the war, under Soviet influence. In that way, she said, she could have worked toward vengeance but differently—by submitting files against those who had murdered Jews during the war and against those who were about to do the same thing at that very time, after the war, in Poland.[45]

A messenger came to Chaika as well, just as one had come to Antek, apparently during her stay in Lodz, at the beginning of 1946. "A special messenger [. . .] someone from the Jewish Brigade"—she didn't remember exactly who the man was—had been sent to persuade her to join the Nokmim. The conversation was extremely short, since she immediately and firmly answered *nyet*, neither asking for time to consider nor changing her opinion later. Chaika was opposed to blind vengeance, and to her, even the plans for action against the captive SS men who were being held in camps, in the British and American occupied zones of Germany, amounted to blind vengeance. Later, during her testimony, she said that on the basis of such grounds for killing, "we would have had to kill half the nation of Germany." She did not see that as the correct course, as a solution, or as realistic, but she admitted that she did not know the exact details. Chaika was also opposed to personal vengeance: "Strange though it may seem, in my heart there was no flame burning for vengeance." She felt that she was something of an exception. Why did she refuse with such intensity? Possibly because she had begun to recover, as she put it, the hope that after the Holocaust the world would run properly and perpetrators would be held accountable for their actions, whereas vengeance, in her opinion, violated the accepted moral code.[46] In the same testimony, in which she looked back at the period from the age of nearly seventy, after having been an active political leader in Israel, she stated and restated that when, years later, she followed the trials of the Nazi war criminals in Germany, with the distortions of justice and the obfuscations that prevailed, as well as the humiliation of Jewish witnesses, and when she read of the Nazi war criminals who had fled to the USA and were welcomed there, she thought, more than once, "Maybe Abba Kovner was right and I wasn't." It was important to her, in her final years, to write and publish that reconsideration in order that history not consign her to a single side. Chaika emphasized repeatedly that despite their different opinions and conclusions, she did not utter a word of condemnation against Kovner; she maintained that her friendship with him, dating from the ghetto, only deepened as they met with each other during their lives in Israel, because she knew the man and recognized his greatness.[47]

FOUNDING THE EAST EUROPEAN SURVIVORS' BRIGADE

Meanwhile, discussions had been continuing, since beginning in Bucharest in April 1945, regarding the founding of the survivors' Hativa. Being founded at a level above politics, such an organization would mean, in practical terms, the abandonment of the previous political frameworks that had provided a home. The proposal engendered arguments, perplexity, and resistance as well, directed at Kovner as the leader of the campaign. Despite the disagreement, the members' discussions did produce a set of principles, and on April 26, 1945, in Bucharest, an ebullient ceremonial meeting established the East European Survivors' Brigade, that is, the Hativa. The agreed-upon principles were legal and illegal immigration to Israel, self-defense as a nation, Hebrew culture, the dissolution of the Diaspora, and the struggle for unity in a Jewish state. At the end of the meeting, everyone stood up and sang "Hatikva," the national anthem.[48] The principles were summarized later in a dramatic Order of the Day that was written in Hebrew—there was of course also a version in Yiddish. Central to the order was the unification of the survivors on their way to Israel, not as the dust of humanity and not as pitiable survivors of slaughter but as the bringers of new blood and new meaning into the Yishuv. In addition to the Order of the Day, an oath was formulated:

> I, a child of the Jewish people, do hereby swear, in full awareness, by the earth that is soaked with the blood of my dear ones, and by the memory of the millions of martyrs who were slaughtered, burnt, tortured, and raped, that I will fulfill all the commands that I receive, safeguard all the secrets, and follow any path in order to reach the Land of Israel.[49]

At that time there were 1,300 Jewish refugees amassed in Bucharest, and two questions may well be asked: First, did they actually all take the oath, or was it an oath primarily of the core that supported the Hativa and its ideas? On that question, opinions are divided. And the phrasing of the oath raises the second question: Do the words "I will fulfill all the commands that I receive" and "I will safeguard all the secrets" already extend to the plans for vengeance? After all, the Hativa—a body established openly and publicly with the intention of including as many people as possible—had no need to issue commands to its membership, nor to preserve secrets. What's more, the original text for the oath, in Kovner's handwriting, is included inside the file labeled "Vengeance" in Kovner's archive at his home in Ein HaHoresh. Thus, could it be theorized that only the Nokmim were sworn in, while the Hativa served as cover for the assembling of the Nokmim? In support, there

is also the fact that two men, Kovner and Lidovski, headed the founding of
the Hativa and were also leaders of the nascent Nokmim group. But most of
the members have no memory today of any swearing-in ceremony. Manek
believes that there was no need for an oath, as they were all so dedicated
to the idea. According to Lidovski, the authors both of the Hativa's decisions and of the oath were the members of the council that had taken form:
Kovner, Zivia, Nissan Reznik, Haim Lazar, and Lidovski himself; and apparently only new members, not founding members, were sworn in. When
the new ones were sworn in, said Pasha, "the criteria were the person's moral
record and our assessment of his fortitude," not politics and not ideology.
The central activists of the movements, who were partners in the Hativa and
the Bricha, knew vaguely "that something separate was brewing among the
partisans," and they called it "the undercover." Kovner said, "The big thing,
more deeply undercover, was the matter of the Nokmim." In Romania "our
really double-sided operations" had already begun, Kovner attested later,
and the forces were divided into two: for the Bricha and for the Nokmim.[50]

There was an additional oath, however, that was similar but broader.
Members of the Organization of Partisans, Soldiers, and Pioneers, established in Poland and known by its Hebrew acronym *Pakhakh*, were sworn in
before leaving Poland on their way to Palestine as part of the Bricha. Their
oath was written in Yiddish by Baruch Levin, a well-known partisan who received many decorations of high distinction. He was among the founders of
the Pakhakh, and the essentials of the oath read were very similar to those
formulated in Bucharest.[51] Thus it appears that there was a shared sentiment
not only in Bucharest but also in Poland, where the Pakhakh were concentrated, and among the survivors in general: the wish to reach Palestine, the
dedication to looking after the needs of the Jewish people, inflicting vengeance unto death to whoever, wherever perpetuated antisemitic hatred, and
the commitment to fulfill every command and safeguard every secret. This
feeling was not confined to a single group.

But despite the oaths, the principles, the euphoria, the singing of "Hatikva," and the power of Kovner's uplifting rhetoric, the story of the Hativa—that rare phenomenon of unity among the Jewish people—was short-
lived, though it did become a sort of magic word among the Holocaust
survivors. At the start of June, exhausting deliberations wore on, indicating

the difficulty of implementing unity among such a diverse public. The emissaries from the Land of Israel, Zivia among them, opposed the founding of the Hativa because it stood in contradiction to Antek's efforts to revive the Dror movement on the one hand, and to the party politics in the Land of Israel on the other. Indeed, the protocols of the Bricha meetings do not cite Zivia even once.[52] Her resistance to the idea, along with resistance from the emissaries, contributed to the lessening of the excitement—as did, presumably, the time and energy that Kovner was increasingly devoting to the project of vengeance.

DEFINING THE GOALS OF THE NOKMIM AND FORMULATING THEIR METHODS OF ACTION

In Bucharest, in April or May 1945, Kovner set down the premises and the essential goals of the Nokmim, along with the broad background of their revenge idea, in seven clauses, which he called "fundamentals."

A. The danger that the Jewish people will suffer an additional, final destruction did not disappear upon the military defeat of Hitlerism.

B. Many nations joined in the murder of the six million, and many of them are ready to continue it further, each in its own way.

C. [*Kovner wrote this clause illegibly.*]

D. Humanity must not retain the impression that Jewish blood is forfeit.

E. We are bitterly disappointed in the world not only because we received no proper answer and no suitable restitution for the destruction; reconciliation with the murderers, which is the norm today, means nourishing the plan for a new slaughter of the Jewish people, which could break out and thrive during some new military and political upheaval in the world.

F. [*Kovner deleted this clause.*]

G. Therefore we assume the duty to make forgetting impossible, and will do so by means of the necessary deed: reprisal [in Yiddish, "payment"]. This will be more than vengeance. It must be the law of the murdered Jewish people! And therefore our name shall be "Din," which stands [in Hebrew] for "The Blood of Israel Remembers," so that coming generations will know that in this pitiless world, there is justice and there is a judge.[53]

As noted in the introduction, the Hebrew acronym "Din" spells out "justice" and, when pronounced differently, also spells out "judge."

Besides those seven fundamentals, or principles, there was also the desire to respond to the Holocaust with a shock not only to the world at large but also to the Jewish people. In the extremity of that desire, Lidovski for example proclaimed that after accomplishing vengeance, they would proceed through the "peaceful, well-fed, rich" lands of the Jewish Diaspora "which did not know war, and we will be missionaries haranguing the Diaspora Jews to leave because everything that happened to us will happen to them." Someone else said, "We'll use terrorist methods, we'll burn buildings, we'll wreck Jewish businesses in America and all over the West to get the Jews out and make them move to the Land of Israel so that what happened won't repeat itself."[54]

Those principles provide the background and the justification for Plan A, the large-scale objective that took shape: a mass killing of Germans in a way that would echo around the world and openly avenge the Jewish people for what had been inflicted on them. Gradually the plan took on the specific form of killing six million Germans by poisoning the water system in three or four major cities. The intention, as early as the Bucharest days, was to infiltrate members of the group into the municipal waterworks and then, when the appropriate chemical means were obtained, to time a simultaneous operation in all those large cities. Kovner wrote notes to himself on slips of paper, splitting the force into a number of subgroups and drafting general instructions: infiltrate the center of the waterworks; establish contact with influential Jewish activists; remain in touch with the group commander and with the center (that is to say, headquarters); remember the code names, the general password, the rendezvous site, and the address in Palestine—in Tel Aviv. The existence of a Tel Aviv address is mentioned only on those slips of paper, which were written in small print, in Yiddish, and there is no knowing what Kovner meant by it. The code names of the group's officers and of most of the members are listed on the slips. A seventh subgroup had received the task of obtaining money in Italy. It had departed from Bucharest in the middle of June, and the notes referred to it as the "financial department." Its specified rendezvous site was the office of the Jewish Committee in Milan, at 5 Via Unione, which was also the focal point of the Diaspora Center, which the Jewish Brigade had set up for survivors. This was an additional indication of the involvement of the Nokmim in more general activities.[55]

But it must be emphasized that this was not the only plan. Along with it, others were floated, plans that had been cultivated in Bucharest; they were part of the discussions that Kovner and his associates had with the Jewish Brigade members while they were in Italy, and that Kovner had later with the Haganah leadership after he arrived in Palestine. According to Kless, who discussed the issue with Kovner, a number of operational ideas arose as early as Bucharest for dealing massive harm to large numbers of prisoners of war from the SS who were being held at camps in Germany; these aims were termed "Plan B." Certainly Plan A was clearly preferred, being intended as the ultimate vengeance, but the group was obliged to take into account the circumstances that might require resorting to Plan B. In fact, according to Kazhik, in Bucharest he was already spoken with both about the large-scale plan—which, it was emphasized, required finding a method of attacking a very large number of Germans while leaving both refugees and Allied forces unharmed—and about attacking imprisoned SS veterans. The latter plan was smaller in scale but not in its foreseen strength as a public message. Both plans were discussed in parallel in Bucharest prior to the question of whether, and how, Plan A could be carried out.[56]

With those plans in mind, arrangements and agreements began for deploying the group's members as small units inside Germany, where most would arrive by indirect routes. Kazhik and Kovner agreed, for example, that in order to camouflage the operation that was planned for Germany, Kazhik would return to Poland (which he had left not long ago) on behalf of the Bricha organization and would smuggle some tens of Jews from there to Czechoslovakia and Hungary across the Polish border, which was already well guarded on both sides by the Soviets. He accomplished that task by carrying a forged document identifying him as a representative of the International Red Cross. Even so, those being smuggled across the border were stopped for interrogation by the Soviets for the traditional search and seizure of watches and other valuables, generally the last remaining objects from their homes or their parents' homes—treasured reminders of a normal life that was gone. Afterward, Kazhik continued to Italy as agreed, and then he left for Germany.[57] Also discussed as early as the Bucharest days was the matter of how the subgroups in Germany would be commanded and would communicate. "You will receive your instructions from Bolek [Ben-Ya'akov]; he will be your liaison," Kovner told Cesia Rosenberg. She was beside herself with excitement, understanding that the idea was becoming a reality. Pasha told Mira (Mirka) Verbin-Shabetzky her destination in Germany, and in her testimony she emphasized that there had indeed been a division into subgroups in advance but that because they were always moving from place to place while in Germany, it was difficult to point to stable subgroups. That topic will be discussed further in chapter 6, which is devoted to the time in Germany.[58]

As noted, in Lublin the idea arose out of a variety of postwar causes and feelings, whereas in Bucharest the stage of committing the consensus to words was reached—and with it the more practical work of organizing. The group took definite form, with roughly fifty members, and they began to divide into subgroups and select the locations for activity. Everyone had, and knew, an assignment that was exact or almost exact. "In Bucharest, the big team came together," said Mira, although not everyone knew all the other members of the group; in Bucharest, the compartmentalization was already beginning as separate subgroups were formed.[59]

ALONG THE PATHS OF THE BRICHA:
ON THE WAY FROM BUCHAREST TO ITALY

Toward the end of May 1945, after roughly three months in Bucharest, the leadership of the Hativa and Bricha set out for Italy through Hungary and Austria, riding in trains and sometimes, for lack of room, on the roofs of train cars. On the car roofs they were at risk of falling onto the tracks below, and they continually witnessed Soviet troops robbing, extorting, and raping travelers, particularly women. The behavior of the Soviet soldiers reinforced the leaders' feeling that they had chosen the right course: to leave increasingly Soviet-conquered Europe as quickly as possible. Only in the city of Graz, Austria, did they cross into territory that the Allies controlled. By then, they had been robbed of the last of their watches. Once across the border, Kovner turned back and spat as an expression of the hostility that had built up in him toward the homeland of the "Sun of the Nations."

Other subgroups set out in advance of the leaders, or immediately after them. In their wake, the Bricha continued; emissaries from the Land of Israel had reported that the Soviets would be ruling Romania as soon as September, and so the Bricha leaders hired, by bribery and subterfuge, a train from Romania through Bucharest and Cluj. Two cars set out every day from Romania to Budapest, where Mordechai Roseman had set up a way station, and in that way 1,300 people crossed into Italy—in addition to the truck that traveled to and from the places that had no railroad line. "A mass of humanity—how the uprooted rose and marched, station after station, to the evanescent sound of a command, to the voice of the nameless pioneers who led them along their way, to a voice from us," Kovner remarked, amazed at the ever-growing phenomenon.[60]

Not all the Nokmim left immediately for Italy—some were busy with important Bricha tasks they'd been assigned. They had opened the first route for the Bricha, as will be recalled, and as the original leaders there, they were still running it. At this point, however, leadership of the Bricha passed from their hands to the emissaries from the Land of Israel. Nahum Shadmi, the commander of the Haganah in Europe, recalled, "I took over their people," a move that was a great help to the Bricha. Yashek Ben-Zur testified that Yehuda Arazi (code-named "Alon" as the representative of the Mossad for Aliyah B handling clandestine immigration from Italy) examined and interviewed the activists and then sent each on a large number of missions. Dan Arad recounted that when he reached Graz, he immediately volunteered to return to Budapest and lead a group of 150 Jewish refugees to Graz. From Graz, they were sent onward to various displaced persons camps. Senka Nissanilevich, for his part, went back and forth across the Polish border four times on behalf of the Bricha and to smuggle heavy communications equipment on his back, as tasked by the European command of the Haganah. He had joined the Nokmim despite already holding a desirable job in the Polish NKVD, the Soviet-inspired secret police. Lena Satz-Hammel used suitcases with false bottoms to pass money to the emissaries in Bucharest, including various activists of the Bricha, such as Roseman and Israel (Srulik) Shklar, who was the treasurer for the Bricha in Poland. The money came from the Jewish Agency in Palestine. The first three thousand dollars sent to Lublin by the emissaries in Bucharest arrived in the keeping of Ze'ev (Velveleh) Rabinovich, the youngest of the partisans.[61]

Poldek related that they were "the commandos of the Bricha," the ones assigned to tasks that required courage, trickery, and sangfroid. Hasya Taubes (later Warchavchik), one of the Hashomer Hatzair members in the Vilna Ghetto who escaped to become a partisan in the Rudniki forests, came to Bucharest, where Kovner recruited her into the group. She recalled that she had felt unable to settle down, and enlisting in the Bricha was exactly what she wanted. The Bricha leadership sent her immediately to Poland. She crossed Czech territory first, equipped with *komandirovka* papers—travel documents that a Jewish officer in the Russian military provided to the group—and, being short and thin, disguised herself as a little girl in order to pass money and instructions to the survivors. After she returned to Bucharest, she was ordered to go to Italy to meet the Jewish Brigade; from there, she was sent back to Poland by delegates from the Yishuv at the Diaspora Center whom she had befriended. Dressed in a Jewish Brigade uniform and carrying watches with which to bribe Soviet soldiers, she reached her destination in Lodz carrying large sums of funding, documents, and instructions, and when she again returned to Bucharest, she received orders to continue to Germany. Ben-Zur and Shlomo Kantarowicz (later Kenet; a member of Kibbutz Beit Zera) were sent to Bari, in southern Italy ("We reached Italy long before Kovner's people!") to pack up tommy guns and a radio kit; they stayed a month or two, then they were taken, with all their baggage, to the Haifa coast on two ships, each carrying 150–160 refugees. When they returned, accompanied by emissaries from the Land of Israel, they reported once more to Arazi at Via Unione in Milan.[62]

Yehuda (Idek) Friedman complied with a request from the Joint Distribution Committee to shepherd thirty children to Hungary. He received a little money and an assistant, a Romanian woman, for the job. When he returned, he set out again, with Bolek Ben-Ya'akov, to Hamburg with instructions. Rachel Galperin, later to marry Zygmunt (Zygi) Gliksman, wandered southward at the end of the war, and when she came to Budapest she heard that a group of Avengers was forming. After trying to figure out how to join it, she succeeded by way of activity in the Bricha. Roseman, who ran the way station in Budapest, left her there and assigned her some tasks—for the most part transferring money. The money was principally sums sent by the delegate of the Yishuv, Moshe Agami, for distribution to the way stations, where it supported the refugees who were waiting to continue onward to the Land of Israel. The refugees received food, clothing, and blankets, while the Bricha activists who operated the way station under Roseman's command made do with the minimum for themselves. Rachel renewed her contacts with friends from the Vilna Ghetto as they traveled on the Warsaw–Lodz–Częstochowa route and the Bucharest–Budapest route. On those missions, besides the transfer of money, there was the transfer of documents, particularly documents attesting that the holder was returning home to Greece. As mentioned, members of the group who were detained spoke Hebrew and pretended it was Greek, assuming Soviet guards at the border would not know the difference. Pasha eventually recruited Rachel to the group, "almost despite himself."[63]

When the travelers entered Northern Italy and met the Jewish Brigade soldiers posted there, a sort of legend was born that appears in most of the testimonies: the Brigade sent messengers to them, and they sent messengers to the Brigade. Thus, the messengers from both directions met along the way in the mountains of Austria, in a symbolic and historic encounter. According to legend, both contingents had been singing Hebrew songs while walking, and they met when they heard each other. Testimony from Zygi Gliksman, a Hashomer Hatzair member imprisoned in the Częstochowa Ghetto who endured the camps and forests, illustrates the relations that had been established between the Bricha activists and the soldiers even before they met: "I was in a group of eight people that left Bucharest for Italy to meet up with the Jewish Brigade and commence operations." In Budapest, Roseman was in charge of taking care of them. Appropriate documents were prepared for the group, and they continued through Vienna to Graz, where they boarded Jewish Brigade trucks. The trucks took them through the Alps to Pontebba, near the Brigade's location. Gliksman gave this account matter-of-factly: to his delegation, it was obvious that soldiers of the Jewish Brigade would come for them, and the travelers never stopped to think how the military truck had located them and why such a truck was transporting refugees. For them, it went without saying that the Jewish Brigade troops would welcome them with open arms and conduct them to safety.[64]

And Ka-tzetnik? By the time he finished writing his first novel in Naples, there were no Nokmim left in Italy; they had moved onward, and he remained apart from them and their activity—even though, according to Manek, he was "committed to the idea; and he was very disappointed afterward that it didn't work out." But Ka-tzetnik might have had another reason for not participating. He might have developed doubts about the rightness of vengeance in actual practice. In his book *Phoenix over the Galilee* (republished in part under the Hebrew title *Nakam*, meaning "vengeance"), the protagonist, who is based on the author, feels during the act of vengeance that he is "excruciatingly alien here. Belonging to no one here, no one here belonging to him. He felt no sense in the victory, no sense in the revenge" that he had previously dreamed of. A different vengeance presents itself to him: "Through him, the world would hear the dying cry of the burning ghetto." He would write in Israel of the Holocaust and the war so that they would not be shunted behind the screen of forgetfulness, and would fight the underground battle for the resurrection of the nation. On that understanding, he turns to God, the God of vengeance, and asks, "If not now, when?" To his beloved, he has said that in his body nothing is alive but ashes and vengefulness, but she insists that their future children will be the real vengeance.[65] Nonetheless, revenge became a central motif in Ka-tzetnik's writings over the years, starting with the poem "Salamandra," and it returned in various forms as an axis around which the characters of his books revolve. They each find unique forms of revenge. And thus he fulfilled his vow: to avenge by means of writings that make forgetting impossible—as he put it at the meeting of the East European Survivors' Brigade, writings that would elevate the standing of the Jewish people. He wished to do so by infusing his works with basic elements from traditional Jewish sources, ranging from the Bible to Zionism, so that the murdered nation, with all its symbols and their long-standing historical significance, would stand on its own feet facing the murderers and those who collaborated with them worldwide.[66]

On July 5, 1945, a week and a half before the Nokmim members reached Italy, Kovner sent ahead a small, brief handwritten note to the members of the Jewish Brigade and the emissaries of Aliyah B and the Bricha. The note included a sentence indicating that he still feared additional pogroms against the Jews: "Regarding the release of hundreds of Lithuanian Jews from the camps [Dachau and the Landsberg/Kaufering camps, where the surviving Jews of Kovno were imprisoned, and the other camps in Germany that were liberated toward the end of the war], we would like you to take *particular* interest in the matter of the Lithuanian Jews and arrange that they not return to their places of residence."[67] Kovner warned against returning survivors to their homes, lest they be murdered on their own doorsteps, as had happened in July 1944, a year earlier.

Oath

I, a child of the Jewish people,
do hereby swear, in full awareness,
by the blood of my dear ones which has soaked the earth,
and by the memory of the millions of martyrs killed, burnt,
   tortured, and slaughtered,
that I will fulfill every order and keep secrecy,
I will not betray the ranks of the pioneers and partisans,
I will follow every path and reach the Land of Israel,
I will take my place in the front line among the builders of our
   homeland, the Land of Israel, for our downcast people,
my foremost concern will be the welfare of my people and of
   my Land,
I will live by my own labor and protect my Land from every enemy
   whether foreign or internal.
I will continue in the tradition of the partisans,
avenge the spilt blood of my brothers,
and strike dead those who hate us wheresoever I find them.
I will obey the authority of the Zionist institutions, the General
   Federation of Hebrew Workers, and the Haganah,
and should I violate my oath,
I shall be pursued by my conscience and subdued by the hands, and
   the justice, of my comrades.

From *The Book of the Ghettos' Wars: Inside the Walls, Camps, and Forests* (in Hebrew), 3rd edition, edited by Yitzhak Zuckerman and Moshe Basok, published by Hakibbutz Hameuchad Publication House and the Ghetto Fighters' Kibbutz, Tel Aviv, 1956, p. 692 (hereafter *The Book of the Ghettos' Wars*). This oath was sworn by the members of the *Pakhakh*—the Organization of Partisans, Soldiers, and Pioneers—when they left Poland to make their way to the Land of Israel. Written in Yiddish by partisan Baruch Levin. Translated from the Hebrew by Mark L. Levinson. Courtesy of the Ghetto Fighters' House and Hakibbutz Hameuchad publication house.

3

Italy, July–August 1945
The Jewish Brigade

ON APRIL 3, 1945, while soldiers of the Jewish Brigade were fighting on the Senio front as a unit of the British Army in the battle to liberate Northern Italy, Moshe Shertok paid them a visit. Shertok, at that time the head of the Political Department at the Jewish Agency, brought a flag from the Land of Israel as a gift of the Yishuv and of the World Zionist Organization. It featured a gold Star of David in the center against vertical stripes of white and light blue, and it became the flag of the Jewish Brigade.

At a festive and emotional assembly that the Brigade organized in Shertok's honor, the flag was raised "high and lofty for the eyes of the sun," in Shertok's words. He had invested much effort in establishing the Jewish Brigade, despite the reluctance of the British. And now he emphasized the meaning of this moment in the life of each person present and of the Jewish people: The flag, anointed with the blood of five million Jews—of the ghetto resistance and of those who died defending the Land of Israel (thus he linked together the Holocaust and the homeland)—was being raised "as the banner of our vengeance against the enemy, as a symbol of the redeemed honor of our slaughtered brothers who could not turn back the battle at the gate" and as a symbol of the resurgence of the nation on its land.[1] This was the first time that vengeance against the German enemy of the Jewish people had been mentioned in a speech by a senior representative of the institutions of the Yishuv as a matter of honor owed to the slain, with legal immigration, clandestine immigration, and resurgence mentioned only afterward. Shertok clearly meant that the presence of the Jewish Brigade, with its flag, was in itself vengeance against those who had thought to erase the Jewish people from the land of the living, and that the war, still ongoing at the time, was the correct way to achieve it.

The Jewish Brigade was founded in July 1944. It consisted of five thousand Jewish soldiers from the Land of Israel, and it fought in the British Army under Brigadier Levi (Ernest Frank) Benjamin, a Canadian-born Jew. Its first commander representing the Haganah and the institutions of the Yishuv was Shlomo Rabinovitch (later General Shamir), and it had three regiments. A considerable number of the Brigade's soldiers had come to Palestine from German-occupied countries; in the Second Regiment, for example, many were born in Germany, Austria, and Czechoslovakia, and they had lost their families and friends in Europe. Some of them had lived in German-occupied countries before fleeing, and they knew what this regime meant. They were convinced that the German population not only knew what was happening but actively took part in it—or at least consented through its silence, as had the populations of other countries.

In mid-April 1945, the Jewish Brigade left the areas it had been holding north of the Senio river and continued northward. On April 28, a cease-fire was declared in Italy, and hundreds of thousands of German troops surrendered to the Allies on all their fronts. On May 7, Germany and Italy unconditionally surrendered after Mussolini was hanged and Hitler died by suicide. The Jewish Brigade soldiers found it difficult to rejoice and participate in the celebration that swept the Allied soldiers; they were mourning the terrible loss that the Jewish people had endured, and they feared that they would not receive proper recognition for their participation in the war. There were more than one and a half million Jews among the Allied forces, the partisans, and the undergrounds; of those, about half a million Jews had fought in the Red Army, and more than half a million had served in the American Army. That fear was accompanied by doubt that the political reward for fighting would be forthcoming. "Moreover," wrote Dr. Ya'akov

Lipschitz, who served as the Jewish Brigade's chief rabbi, "in the very days of victory, the Jewish heart also felt a bitter droplet of poison sinking in: Was this in fact the last deathly nightmare of our generation? Was there not another cup of suffering yet to come?"[2] Despite the Holocaust, the Jewish people still remained unrecognized as a political entity. Thus, the soldiers shared the fear that beset Abba Kovner and his comrades, even before the soldiers met and conversed with them. The Holocaust left behind a fear for the very future of the Jews, a fear that started sinking in immediately after victory.

The soldiers were concerned about not only the future of the Jewish people. The soldiers also wondered how they themselves would continue their activity on European soil. The answer became evident: in the form of all possible assistance to the survivors. The soldiers' extensive and dedicated work in this regard is already a widely discussed topic in itself. Another question concerned the contribution of the Jewish Brigade to the founding of a defense force in the Land of Israel upon its arrival there. The soldiers would be able to put their experience at the service of the Yishuv, in anticipation of postwar conflicts. That matter will not be discussed here either, but it bears emphasizing that in the institutions of the Yishuv, the opinion was common that with the war over, the prompt return of the Jewish Brigade was vital.[3]

UNCERTAINTIES AND DECISIONS

Another decision with significant implications was the issue of vengeance. According to Rabbi Lipschitz, matters during battle had been simple: kill as many Germans as possible, without mercy. There was an element of vengeance to the intensity of the fighting and to the taunts of the Palestinian Jewish soldiers against the German soldiers. But with the end of the war and the surrender of Germany, the Jewish Brigade's soldiers faced a keen new question regarding their proper attitude, as Jews and as an organized body, toward the Germans who were prisoners, civilians, and former agents of the regime. "It was a hatred fierce as death, and the soul craved to take revenge on every German for the blood of millions of Jews. But how could we carry out such revenge?"[4] International law protected prisoners of war, so that avenue was closed. Even previously, during the fighting, the soldiers received a special order forbidding abuse of captured and wounded German soldiers.

Indeed, a brigade soldier related, "We treated the prisoners according to all the laws and regulations." The book published by the Second Regiment—many of whose soldiers, it will be recalled, had lost their families—attests that they behaved according to the rules, to the extent that even the German commander expressed his satisfaction to the commander of the regiment. Apparently he had expected "something more acute" and had been pleasantly surprised.[5]

Above and beyond that, while the division was en route from the battleground to its next assigned location, Shamir assembled a "broad forum of decision-makers"—that is to say, the soldiers who were listened to in the Jewish Brigade, irrespective of rank or official title—in order to determine whether to support a policy of vengeance or to concentrate on saving Jews. The forum decided unequivocally on the motto "Yes to rescue, no to vengeance," and Shamir proudly counted that decision as one of the most important achievements of the Jewish Brigade's internal echelons. However, he added, the decision was made before the group knew whether they would have the opportunity for vengeance.[6]

That was not the only decision the group weighed on the complicated issue of how to treat civilians, prisoners, and those who surrendered. A few soldiers spoke in favor of "an eye for an eye" in order to immediately gratify their feelings of vengefulness, but most spurned such behavior even if they already knew about the fate of their families. In that spirit, according to Rabbi Lipschitz, two basic decisions were made. He did not specify how these decisions were made— it may be that they emerged from general consensus. In any case, one decision was to search every city and village along the way for SS personnel and Nazi Party members who were either directly responsible for or the actual perpetrators of war crimes against Jews; the group would then collectively determine, in a considered fashion, what to do with them. And the second decision—with reference to the entire German nation as aware of what was happening and as, by a definite majority, abetting the crime, even indirectly—was to completely boycott the nation and its land: "To us, that land is anathema" and "That land is under a ban from us," expressing contempt and repulsion without even naming that land. The decision was not merely theoretical; the soldiers were hoping for the fulfillment of British prime minister Winston Churchill's promise, in his September

1944 speech to Parliament announcing the Jewish Brigade's establishment, that the Brigade would take an active part in the fighting and in the occupation of Germany.[7] Within the heart of every soldier of the Jewish Brigade, and within many hearts in the Land of Israel, pulsed the hope that the Brigade would march through the streets of Berlin behind an upraised blue-and-white flag with the Star of David in the middle. "I want each German man, each German boy, and each German Nazi to see the Jews as Hebrew soldiers from the Land of Israel, and part of the very army that conquers their country. If that's vengeance, then it's the vengeance that I want," said Golda Myerson (later Prime Minister Meir), who supported a ban against Germany.[8]

As a conquering army, and as an army likely soon to be stationed in Germany, the Jewish Brigade needed to decide on its compulsory procedures in advance. It goes without saying that the Brigade faced the same temptations that have beckoned to every conquering army and army of occupation in every generation and location, from women to looting to black-marketing, violence, and the breakdown of discipline, especially during a time when Brigade members were consumed with vengefulness. Indeed, the hope of marching proudly in the streets of Berlin was accompanied by internal debates, since an army of occupation, by its presence, was in contradiction of the ban everyone felt should be imposed on any contact with Germany and could be vulnerable to imbroglios and moral degeneration. Golda, along with Shertok, who sympathized with the soldiers, held the minority opinion in discussions at the institutions of the Yishuv. Shertok wanted the Hebrew soldier to feel gratification, like the Russian soldier who, remembering Stalingrad, would be able to tell his grandchildren about being part of the army that occupied Germany. "It is moral," said Shertok. "It is uplifting and empowering."[9]

It quickly became clear that even before the end of the war, the Germans expected to suffer terrible vengeance. There were many indications of this. The fear of vengeance drove the Germans to fight with desperation and discipline during the last stage of the war; although German units could have surrendered and saved their soldiers' lives, their commanders responded categorically that the fight would continue to the bitter end because the alternative was the coming of vengeance.[10] As the years passed and more documentation was revealed, the depth of that fear only became clearer, especially among those who believed the propaganda that the Jews are a cruel, vengeful race that abides by the commandment to remember (*zachor*), who, as written in its holy scripture, neither forgives nor forgets. Here, a deep gap is evident between the weakness of the Jews during the war and Holocaust on the one hand and on the other, the fear of many Germans that the Jews would rise up and seek vengeance. That fear only increased when the consequences of Jewish helplessness came to light. In his book *Guilt, Suffering, and Memory*, in a chapter entitled "The Crystallization of Germany's Consciousness of Guilt," researcher Gilad Margalit provides multiple examples of German apprehension. One Jewish officer in the American Army who was stationed in the city of Aachen wrote of "guilt about the Jews, an uneasy feeling and frequently an open admission that a great wrong has been committed. There is also a fear of revenge and a dread of hearing the worst about the horrors that have been inflicted on the Jews in Poland." And Antony Beevor writes: "The rumors [. . .] stoked the Germans' worst fears."[11] Elie Wiesel, who crossed the American-occupied zones a number of times in order to visit his sister in a displaced persons camp, met Germans and even slept among them. "The Germans were afraid of us. The mere sight of a free Jew must have filled them with terror. They must have been afraid that the camp survivors and underground partisans would return as avengers and make them pay for the torments they had inflicted," he wrote after a German girl offered herself to him in self-defense, in an attempt to calm his Jewish rage.[12]

At the start of November 1945, as the seventh anniversary of Kristallnacht neared, panicky rumors spread around Germany that the Jews were preparing an organized attack on German homes in revenge. The American occupation army promised to intervene if any flare-ups of hostility occurred from the Jewish refugee side, and the German population breathed more easily when the nights of the ninth and tenth of the month passed quietly. When German citizens heard of the speech by Churchill establishing the Jewish Brigade, a radio broadcast warned that he

> intends to allow the Jews, a pack of wild dogs, to descend on the German masses if we are defeated. Such bloodthirsty behavior befits the Jews more

than fighting at the front [. . .]. Now every effort must be made in order to save Europe from falling into the hands of the Jewish anarchists and their accomplices.[13]

Author Hanoch Bartov, who was a young soldier in the Jewish Brigade at the time, wrote that soldiers from other nations who had joined the British Army were also unable to imagine that Jewish soldiers would not exact vengeance—they understood the feeling. Antisemitic statements even after the war were understandable, in the bitter opinion of Bolek Ben-Ya'akov of the Częstochowa Avengers, with a burning vengefulness: If a mass murder like the Holocaust passes without reaction and the Germans believe that we no longer feel upset, maybe the genocide was justified and can be acceptable.[14]

The soldiers' officers and opinion makers tried to encourage a sense of moderation, knowing that "this discussion will not be silenced and will not silence itself among us, among the people, whether we rage or whether we are 'cool and collected.'" Everyone would be looking to retaliate, and therefore "why should the Jewish people's vengeance not be openly positioned under the flag of the Jewish Brigade," at least by virtue of the presence of the Brigade's flag and symbols in Germany as an occupying force, and perhaps in other ways as well? In any case, the matter would be handled in an orderly manner, in cooperation, with each fighter under the proper flag and not with each deciding individually and inflicting individual vengeance. The campaign should be dignified and respectful of everyone. Motke Hadash, a member of the Kinneret Kvutza (close to a kibbutz) who joined the Jewish Brigade with his son Shmulik, was one of those voices of moderation. But even he, after hearing a soldier musing aloud that vengeance would constitute "for us a luxury," decided that every day he would reread the booklet *A Year in Treblinka*, a Treblinka survivor's account that was printed and distributed by the Histadrut, the Yishuv's workers union, in order to strengthen the feeling of vengefulness and to realize anew what they were fighting for. Hadash spoke of the personal and national urge for vengeance along with the stubborn urge for survival despite the extermination and obliteration.[15]

On their way north to Tarvisio in Italy, the soldiers of the Jewish Brigade passed near the Austrian border and saw columns of German prisoners being led south by British guards. In preparation, they had hung messages prominently on their trucks for the Germans to see, such as *"Kein Volk, kein Reich, kein Führer"* ("No nation, No Reich, No Führer"), "Jerusalem–Berlin," *"Deutschland kaputt,"* and *"Jehuda erwacht, Deutschland zerkracht"* ("Judah has awakened, and Germany has shattered"), all reversals of Nazi slogans. On both sides of their vehicles' headlights, they wrote in Hebrew so that survivors they came across could see and make contact: "Going Home." They had been ordered to exercise restraint, but when a large column of prisoners from the SS approached them, they flared up spontaneously for the first time. Many threw stones, cans, and tent pegs, as well as cursed and spat, and the British were constrained to stop the column. "Spontaneous and unauthorized gestures of vengeance were carried out by the Jewish soldiers, without permission and without instructions, against the captive Germans" who fell into their hands just days after the German Army surrendered in Northern Italy, the editors of *The History of the Haganah* conceded. Hadash was worried: "There's a need to get the soldiers' feelings under control, to stamp out lawlessness, to impose restraint, to provide direction."[16]

James (Michael) Rabinovitch (later Ben-Gal), who briefly replaced Shlomo Rabinovitch (no relation; later Shamir) as the Jewish Brigade commander representing the Haganah, declared: "It is lack of discipline and it is hooliganism, not vengeance. When a military unit is on the road, it does not throw stones." Ben-Gal added in his testimony: "I suppose that the seceders [in Hebrew, *porshim*: those who did not accept the authority of the Yishuv leadership] encouraged it," accusing, among the soldiers, members of the IZL and Lehi (two small, militant ardently anti-British underground groups in Palestine) of being behind the disturbances. That parallel between those who seceded from the Yishuv and those seeking active vengeance returns in several more testimonies and recollections that depict them as an opposing formation standing against the formation that favors restraint and responsibility. That depiction begs further assessment.

After several such incidents, it was clear that protection for all trucks containing prisoners was a necessity. Subsequently, whenever soldiers from the Jewish Brigade traveled with prisoners, a detachment of British military police accompanied them—the Germans had expressed apprehension about traveling with Jewish soldiers. The soldiers of the Jewish Brigade expressed their wishes: "When soldiers from the Land of Israel go by, the Germans should be afraid to breathe." And "To them, the bright colors of our flag looked like the colors of dark vengeance [. . .]. Soldiers from an army of murder [. . .] came face to face with fighting volunteers whose clothes bore the Star of David and whose hearts bore a vow of revenge."[17]

A short while after the war ended, three Brigade soldiers entered an Austrian village, beat two women, and took, at gunpoint, a considerable sum of money for the refugees' needs. Hadash immediately demanded that the soldiers of the unit assemble, and he gave a speech warning that such deeds would not only bring shame but also halt the progress of the plan to enter Germany, degenerate into behavior that violated morality and national dignity, and defame the division. Immediately, a heated debate erupted. Years later, Bartov, who was present at Hadash's speech, would describe the incident, the lineup, and the debate among the soldiers in his book *The Brigade*. His highly detailed account reveals the complexity and sensitivity of the problem as the soldiers saw it: On the one hand, they wished for "a single wild Jewish revenge. Just once, like the Tatars. Like the Ukrainians. Like the Germans. All of us, all the bleeding hearts, [. . .] we'll all go into one city and burn it, street by street, house by house, German after German." At the same time, in a letter to his girlfriend, he wrote, "Spilt German blood—blood of the men, women, and children of Germany—will cleanse the spilt Jewish blood, the blood of the millions, and will end the shouts for vengeance that fill the blood of living Jews." Only then, he said, would the soldiers be able to return home with their heads held high, having done their duty. On the other hand, "From the tragedy that we occupy, there is no way out [. . .]. Woe to us if our vengeance can come about only with our descent to the level of thinking and operating as if we were Nazis. That would be not merely ironic but the curse of history." And without vengeance,

> We would never be able to forget the vengeance which was not exacted, never attain peace and reconciliation. [. . .] That is the tragedy, because woe to us if we waive vengeance, and seven times the bitterness for us if we do not reach the Jews for whom we are the only dream remaining. And we shall not be released from that tragedy, neither now nor in years to come. [. . .] We are those people condemned to walk the earth with the image of G-d on our forehead like a mark of Cain. Unable, incapable of seeing a girl raped.

Incapable—a pure Jewish soul. [. . .] Obviously we will go mad if we continue the same way [. . .] groaning under the cross of vengeance.[18]

At war's end they arrived in Pontebba, a village west of Tarvisio. Some units of the Jewish Brigade had reached the place already and started establishing lodging for survivors. One day, a unique kind of German unit arrived: two hundred prisoners from among the troops of Andrey Vlasov, a Ukrainian general who had defected with his units to the German side and fought with them until almost the end of the war. His soldiers were said to be not merely worse than the Nazis but worse than predatory beasts. Along with the announcement of their arrival, a specific plan gained ground: to blow them up together in the building where they were staying. All the Jews—survivors and Brigade soldiers alike—agreed that Vlasov's men deserved no less. Hadash describes the conundrum: vengeance would provide great satisfaction, but the next day the Jewish Brigade would be transferred away. Who then would take care of the Holocaust refugees who were just beginning to arrive? Of the women, the children? Who would guide them to the Land of Israel? That had been the Brigade's task all along, its purpose! Quiet prevailed, and that act of vengeance was dropped from consideration.[19] If the Jewish Brigade were to be transferred out, heaven forbid, it would be disbanded and sent back to Palestine, or even sent to fight in the Far East, where the war had not yet ended. There, according to rumor, Orde Wingate, the British pro-Zionist officer nicknamed "the Friend" by the Yishuv, was requesting that the Brigade be sent to join him in Burma. The dispute persisted for as long as the Brigade served in Europe. "Among the Jewish Brigade, nothing brought more controversy than the topic of vengeance against the Germans [. . .]. There was no end to the arguments—organized ones and spontaneous ones."[20]

THE AVENGERS AMONG THE JEWISH BRIGADE,
AND THEIR ACTIVITY FROM TARVISIO

In the end, decisions in principle and discussions of ethics were one thing, but the reality of confronting the Germans was another. The Jewish Brigade continued northward, and on May 19, 1945, its advance guard reached

Tarvisio on the Austrian-Italian-Yugoslav border. Toward the end of the month, the rest of the units arrived. The soldiers remained there for two months or so, as part of the Seventy-eighth British Division. Having been contested land for centuries, the area boasted complex ethnicities and politics that reflected and emphasized the welter of problems facing the Jewish Brigade. In and around Tarvisio, against the background of a beautiful Alpine vista, the soldiers met a population—Italians and Yugoslavs, Germans, and especially Austrians—who had collaborated with the German occupiers during the war.

Tarvisio was located in an Alpine pass on the escape route south of Germany. Former SS men retreated into the area, and with help from the local population, they helped Nazis flee through Austria to Rome and, from there, to the ports of Italy and Spain on the way to refuge in Latin America. When the Allies arrived, the collaborators hid or suddenly became adherents of democracy and socialism. Some managed to obtain jobs in the military government. Thus, all at once, the question of vengeance became immediate and tempestuous: there were war criminals hiding in the vicinity or passing through on their way to ports of escape. The Jewish Brigade tracked down some of them, and even found documentation on the deportation of Jews from northern Italy and of the robbery of their property. In addition, because of the city's temperate climate and strategic location—hidden in a valley—the Germans had set up a number of military hospitals in town. After the war, the Jewish Brigade was assigned to guard the ailing Germans who remained in local hospitals, essentially imprisoning them. Immediately, suspicions arose that German physicians still working in the hospitals were hiding SS men there.

Another pool of Germans was the healthy captive soldiers working in roads in the Austrian and Italian areas. The Jewish Brigade was assigned to guard them too, and neither the captives nor the captors concealed their hostility. Thus, for example, Brigade soldiers sent German prisoners to clean synagogues that had been desecrated and to clear a large area with landmines that the Jewish Brigade was responsible for making safe. In a number of cases, prisoners were hit if they saluted one another out of habit in stiff-armed Nazi style or if they walked on the pavement. The Brigade deemed the pavement forbidden to the prisoners, in retribution for the Nazi regulations that had humiliated Jews in the ghettos. If the German prisoners strode around confidently and defiantly, they were slapped and their insignia were torn.[21]

When the Jewish Brigade soldiers came to Tarvisio and began, as noted, to find Germans, Austrians, and others, there was fear that discipline would break down as the soldiers continued their outbursts against the prisoners and in the hospitals. Worse yet was the concern that the British would conclude that the Brigade was a nuisance rather than an asset and not allow it to serve as an occupation army in Germany. So at the initiative of some of the soldiers, a squad was set up and tasked with methodically interrogating prisoners, the wounded, and local civilians in order to locate war criminals. The information that this squad gathered would be used later by the Avengers who were organized from within the Jewish Brigade. In the meantime, spontaneous operations were forbidden, officers held long talks with soldiers, and gradually the flare-ups mostly subsided.[22] The squad included Israel Carmi, Shaike (Yeshayahu) Weinberg, and Robert Grossman (Dov Gur)—all foot soldiers and young officers seconded to the intelligence corps of the Jewish Brigade and tasked with collecting the information. They received lists from German and Austrian informers, and they showed the lists to the officers of the Jewish Brigade who were also members of the Haganah, particularly Meir Zorea and Haim Laskov. Both would later serve for many years in the Israel Defense Forces and become well known as a general and a chief of staff, respectively.[23]

Zorea and Laskov approved the campaign, and the information was passed in full to the British Army's Special Investigation Branch (SIB). The SIB rewarded them with information from its own sources and agreed that any hidden sums of money discovered would be channeled toward the treatment of survivors. The campaign itself was, of course, carried out on a need-to-know basis, with those outside the squad unaware, by soldiers "among the best people in the Jewish Brigade and among the truest of the true, who consented to embrace the purpose of revisiting the blood of the Jews upon the heads of the Nazi murderers [. . .] by decision of the pioneering Hebrew community." The group that was set up was called *Gmul* ("Recompense") or *Nakam* ("Vengeance"), with a cadre of roughly ten soldiers supported by dozens more. Johanan Peltz, for example, was one of them "because my mother was incinerated at Treblinka and my father was hanged at Auschwitz, and that was enough for me [. . .]. When we caught someone who had acted directly against the Jewish people, to me he represented my mother's murderers."

The members of the group worked in highly compartmentalized teams of two or three, a mere few dozen who had been sworn to secrecy, primarily to avoid reflecting on the Jewish Brigade and its top commanders should the operations become known. Thus, each participant knew only a piece of the overall picture, and because of this careful compartmentalization, it is difficult today to determine how many Germans and Austrians they killed.[24] They would set out at night, disguised as British military police and driving a suitable military vehicle, to an address they had pinpointed in advance on the basis of interrogations. Then, after verifying that the person they found was the one they were seeking, they would bring that individual to a pre-selected spot—generally a line of fortifications in the mountains that included reinforced out-of-the-way caves or to the shore of a cold, deep lake. There they would detail the accusations, in German, and announce the sentence. Most of the condemned lost their composure when they heard they had fallen into the hands of Jews; they begged for their lives and for pity upon their wives and children, who would be left without them—a plea that sounded absurdly ironic to the soldiers. The sentence was carried out on the spot, by strangulation or gunfire.

"Those weren't glorious deeds," Laskov said in a rare remark on the matter. "Acts of vengeance are the province of the weak, and nothing to be proud of. We were weak, we'd lost the war, we'd lost six million Jews, we had no country—and we took vengeance."[25] It bears emphasis that these acts of vengeance by members of the Jewish Brigade were a first objective, undertaken when the soldiers believed that the Jews of Europe were extinct and that they were inflicting vengeance at the final behest of the victims. At this stage, immediately before and after the war's end, there was still no contradiction between vengeance efforts and the attempts to care for the survivors of the Holocaust, since only a few survivors had begun trekking southward to Italy and the Jewish Brigade.

Brigadier Benjamin, the high commander on behalf of the British, was of course not told of the squad, so he was unaware of its existence. The Haganah commanders in the Brigade—Shlomo Shamir and subsequently Ben-Gal—were of two minds. On the one hand, said Ben-Gal, even to a man like himself, who was accustomed to operating according to military directives, it was clear that no particular instructions were necessary for "exterminating those who were active in exterminating Jews; it is a positive, desirable undertaking, and my duty is to contribute to it. Every Nazi who was active and who personally carries responsibility for actually exterminating Jews is deserving of death for that reason."[26] However, he took exception to the squad's methods, and he addressed his complaints to the Haganah command that operated within the Jewish Brigade unbeknownst to the British military authorities. He considered the activity of the Jewish Brigade regrettably "partisanlike." Weinberg, who was one of the Avengers, agreed: "In general, the Jewish character is partisanlike to a great extent." In their circle, the word "partisanlike" meant disorderly, ad hoc, offhanded, and unprofessional, by way of reference to the way partisans operated. Ben-Gal contended that just a few squad members were trained to work in intelligence and that they received approval from him (or, earlier, from Shamir) only when they could demonstrate that there was well-founded intelligence. Kalman Kitt, one of the Jewish Brigade's prominent officers, whose opinions tended to be heeded, emphasized the dilemma: "The proposed plan of executing them one by one wasn't accepted but wasn't forbidden either."[27] But according to Ben-Gal, there were more than a few incidents in which Laskov, Zorea, and Carmi decided to approve their own operations without offering sufficient evidence against those they executed and cases in which their excursions left suspicious traces, and even bodies, in the field.

Carmi admitted that the squad was small, acted "without obeying authority," and refused to accept instructions from the Land of Israel or even the Jewish Brigade's internal committee, which was aware of the revenge campaign. In Carmi's opinion, it was "orderly vengeance" because it was based on lists. Ben-Gal, in his testimony, recalled that Carmi had not asked anyone for permission and had not considered himself obliged to do so. Moreover, in Ben-Gal's opinion, justice must be witnessed to be considered done; he wondered what international importance there could be to executing a low-level Gestapo officer here and there—executions that merely raised suspicion among the British—and whether such secret killings would be a stain on both Zionism and Jewry.[28] The operations were not backed by consultations with the appropriate figures from the Land of Israel, nor by the institutions of the Yishuv. "On most matters, they relied [...] on the people"—that is, the Yishuv leadership relied on the soldiers and delegates to make the right choices on the spot—but when the operations came to light, messengers arrived on behalf of Meir Grabovsky (later Argov), a top political figure and confidant of David Ben-Gurion. The messengers asked the Avengers of the Jewish Brigade to set up a court martial and not execute Germans without trial—neither then nor later, as an occupation army in Germany, where its duty would be to bring suspects to court for a fair trial. The Avengers refused, claiming that the existence of a court martial could become known to the British, and maintained that those punished were truly guilty. The disagreements were over matters of principle: at the command level, the highest priority was keeping the Jewish Brigade's reputation unsullied, since the Yishuv was interested above all in preventing friction with the British and Americans. In contrast, the highest priority of the Avengers who served in the Brigade was inflicting vengeance on the guilty.[29]

Moshe Shertok, whose son Yaakov (Kobi) was serving in the Jewish Brigade, was aware of the plan's focused attacks on the guilty, specifically on SS officers "who voluntarily participated in the slaughter." In addition, he received reports from the field: Argov notified him when the Jewish Brigade soldiers had collected names and addresses in their "card file" and told him that they had already attained important results. "We have the right to avenge the copious blood that was spilled," Argov wrote to Shertok—not to request permission or plead the justice of the operations but in a matter-of-fact tone, indicating that the matter had already been settled between them.[30] In identifying the guilty and exacting vengeance, the Jewish Brigade had help from the so-called German Unit, which Shimon Avidan had established in the Land of Israel in May 1942 under the Palmach. (The Palmach was the elite strike force of the Haganah.) The German Unit was intended to help the British Army from behind German lines, and it consisted of roughly fifty well-trained, well-consolidated German-born fighters who were deeply familiar with the local language and customs. It was incorporated into the British Army in November 1944 as the Palmach's contribution to the Jewish Brigade, and it set out for the Italian front in April 1945. At war's end, the soldiers of the German Unit of course had the ability, because of their qualifications, to identify and win the trust of German and Austrian murderers in hiding. For that reason, the British attached the unit to the Jewish Brigade as reinforcements for its Third Regiment, under the command of Yehuda Brieger (later Ben-Horin) and Mondek Pasternak (later Moshe Bar-Tikva). Brieger, a former communist, was a member of the leftist Kibbutz Hazorea. The soldiers of the unit, according to Weinberg, became the main operational arm of the Jewish Brigade's vengeance activity: "We employed them in the arrest and vengeance operations," Carmi confirmed.[31]

The soldiers of the German Unit established close ties with the followers of partisan commander Josip Broz Tito, later the prime minister and president of Socialist Yugoslavia. An alliance seemed natural, since there were many leftists among the Jewish Brigade's soldiers, and it yielded a great deal of information about SS officers in Austria. When access to those officers was easy, they too were arrested in their homes at night and hanged, "with no speeches or ceremony," in the nearest forest.[32] Soldiers in the Jewish Brigade's other units also executed Germans, according to the testimony of a sergeant who belonged to an ordnance unit stationed elsewhere a few months prior: they sought out SS officers who were in hiding, and when they discovered the telltale tattoo near the armpit, or the attempted obscuring of one, the man was shot on the spot. Those actions were carried out independently of the Jewish Brigade's avenging group because "it was simply an inner urge driving us to vengeance. Everything was organized internally, within our unit. We took revenge instead of sending them to a prison camp."[33]

In summation, said Laskov, "We didn't liquidate many, to my regret"; Zorea contended, "We came too late and did too little." Motke Hadash concluded, "There wasn't anything organized with a big *mashtab* [Russian for "scope"]. The operations actually carried out weren't large in number." Mordechai Gichon, the intelligence officer for the Avengers of the Jewish Brigade and later a war historian, estimated that the number of Nazis executed might be in the dozens. Ben-Horin recounted: "There were just a number of operations."[34] Naturally, no notes or documentation were preserved. Laskov and Zorea, who were the top leadership, were completely silent on the matter for years, and when they did finally speak, it was sparingly. Carmi said that later, when German-Israeli relations began to develop, the directive was to avoid the topic.[35] Carmi's testimonies changed over the years, and his estimates of killed Germans increased with the passage of time. It seems that his most reliable accounts are the earliest, included in his memoir published in 1960, before the first German ambassador came to Israel. The tone and the figures are much more modest: "We managed to get our hands on quite a few criminals," he says in the book, eschewing any mention of killing.[36] Apparently—and even this is a high estimate—150 or 200 men is the maximum. This number takes into account that the group had forty-five or fifty nights to operate after their arrival and that they needed time to organize, obtain information and create lists, and travel to Austria and southern Germany. Even if as many as three or four squads set out on a single night and each squad found one man, there were necessarily nights when an operation could not be mounted and the figure would drop to 150 to 200 executions at most.[37]

CARING FOR THE SURVIVORS AND
THE ENCOUNTER WITH THE PARTISANS AND AVENGERS

As the soldiers of the Jewish Brigade began to encounter more survivors, they felt a desire to help them as much as they could. In the words of Ben-Horin, the commander of the German Unit, "We turned our energies to saving the survivors [. . .]. We were seized with a real obsession [. . .] to give them all the comfort we could and to take revenge to the extent of our power." Ben-Gal said frankly, "We stole from the British Army; we set up border-crossing points." Shaike Weinberg testified, "Our patrols [in search of clusters of refugees] were the lever that opened a dam"; he also said that he and Carmi organized a detachment to seek out Jews who were being freed from the camps.[38]

After they visited Mauthausen, which was considered the worst of the concentration camps, and saw weeping survivors—mere skin and bones, speaking only with their eyes but repeatedly kissing the Star of David on the soldiers' arms as evidence of a dream come true—the urge for vengeance burned again. Once more, a visit to the site of recent torture and murder kindled emotions: "For anyone who hasn't seen those sites of concentration camps and crematoria, it's impossible to understand what they [the Germans] did to us," said Laskov. Ben-Gal and Shamir visited Mauthausen together: "The moment an everyday person visits an extermination camp like that one, the yardstick by which they measure their life changes," Shamir wrote later. When soldiers entered the liberated concentration camps, the sight of the gallows, the torture equipment, the piles of bodies strewn like dung over the fields, stunned them. The survivors generally asked two things of the soldiers, wrote Carmi: to exact vengeance on the Germans, and to bring them quickly to the Land of Israel. The soldiers thus faced a dilemma: which of the projects took precedence, or could both be pursued simultaneously?[39]

The more refugees streamed southward, the clearer the scale of priorities became: Any rescue took precedence over vengeance, and certainly over vengeance that might endanger the rescue activity. The argument over vengeance versus rescue "ended very quickly. [. . .] If we pursued vengeance, we would make [the survivors'] lives more risky and more difficult because the avengers could well be taken to be associated with them rather than with us [. . .]. Of course, a living Jew was immeasurably more important to us than a Nazi we could kill."[40] And indeed, the members of the German Unit invested all their efforts into caring for the survivors. Thus, for example, they returned as promptly as possible to Mauthausen and smuggled the survivors to the Jewish Brigade in trucks that they had confiscated from Austrians. As the Soviets expanded their influence into Eastern European territory, there was fear that the four Allies would redraw the map of Europe; because it would be impossible to operate behind the Iron Curtain, time was of the essence. This sense of urgency was compounded by the awareness that the Jewish Brigade would not be in Tarvisio much longer.[41]

At the start of July 1945, after Jewish Brigade soldiers searching for survivors met scouts from Kovner's group who had been sent from Romania to search for the soldiers, word spread among the Brigade that a group of partisans led by Kovner was approaching and that they were being followed by hundreds of refugees dauntlessly crossing borders in order to reach their waiting brothers. "We awaited them with curiosity and with warm interest," Ben-Gal recalled.[42] "We were excited and amazed," wrote Yehuda Tubin, a member of Kibbutz Beit Zera, to his wife, Shlomit. She would pass along his detailed letters, as was the practice in those days, to Hashomer Hatzair leaders Ya'akov Hazan and Meir Ya'ari. This correspondence was the only means of communication, and delivery often took weeks or months. A few weeks earlier, the Jewish Brigade soldiers had been wondering about their postwar assignments, and now they had their answer. On July 15, near the evening, Abba Kovner and Vitka Kempner arrived at the camp in Tarvisio along with Pasha and Dorka Reichman, Haya and Haim Lazar, Yulek Harmatz, Shlomo Kless, and Bezalel Kek. Some of their group, who had arrived previously as agents for the Bricha, rushed to embrace the newcomers. Without a second thought, those agents adopted the cause of vengeance as a continuation of the struggle in the ghetto and in the forest. As Shlomo Kenet recalled, "Every surviving comrade joined the Avengers."[43]

They received a heartfelt welcome from everyone there. "The Jewish Brigade gave us a wonderful reception [. . .]. We [. . .] who were tough, cynical [. . .] we were as emotional as children who fall into the arms of their families," Vitka said later. Cesia recalled "tanned faces, boundlessly emotional, smiling warmly [. . .] as if the motherland had sent messengers to receive us as we, the homeward bound, approached its gates."[44]

The partisans themselves made an enormous impression. "Meeting them was among the most moving moments my life was blessed with [. . .]. Not miserable survivors and scraps of humanity, but people like us, and maybe even nobler than us, who fought under the most inhuman conditions for human dignity and for their national pride." And more: "They were a thousand times stronger and smarter than all the soldiers and emissaries [. . .]. Some of the most excellent people in existence!"[45]

The next evening, July 16, a mass meeting was held out in the open, among the spectacular scenery, for hundreds of Jewish Brigade soldiers and Holocaust survivors. "A tremendous experience," the participants said of the event. Kovner was invited up to an improvised podium. He in turn invited up the fighters who had survived the ghettos and the forests; thus, he emphasized the solidarity of the Hativa, the band of survivors from Eastern Europe, and the standing of the fighters in their forefront. One of those present describes the tears that gleamed in the eyes of the listening soldiers and Kovner, "trembling with emotion, closing his eyes, raising his hands [. . .] as if he wished to embrace everyone, and begging them to believe his words, but it was hard, hard to believe the scenes of horror that he described to us."[46] Kovner expressed amazement at the miracles that had spared the survivors and happiness at the wondrous meeting of those from the Land of Israel with those from the lands of the Holocaust. For two hours or so, he continued a narration of events from the days of the Holocaust in Vilna. Then he arrived at the message he intended to convey: The survivors know that despite the long narration, and the narrations that will yet follow, the listeners may not understand what happened. But it is imperative that they recognize their duty to take up arms immediately against "the ax that is swinging close. The ax that is ready in every corner of Europe." Kovner tried to impress on his listeners a profound fear of the next war, which he believed would occur soon. He prophesied that when war broke out again, Jewish children would go to the pyre—the Yishuv too, with its children, just as the Jews of Europe had. Millions would again join in the killing, scions of dozens of nations, because they saw in the fields of Majdanek, Ponar, and Treblinka how it was done, "with what ease, what simplicity, what tranquility," how permissible the killing of Jews was, how profitable. "We are approaching a cruel new attempt that may come upon us in a burst of brimstone and blood," he said, and asked, "Are we not approaching our fate with a passivity resembling—if not exceeding—that of the victims before us?" The tragedy must be transformed into strength for reaching the land of Israel and for disrupting its everyday routine, he said. He ended by vowing to stand up to the significant trials ahead.

Regarding the duty that the murdered imposed on the living to take vengeance on their behalf, Kovner did no more than hint. After addressing—and no doubt shocking—the soldiers sitting before him with the fearsome assertion that they and their children would go to the pyre, he continued with a question that was no less fearsome: would they show even more passivity than their predecessors had? Then he finished: "I have something else in mind. Something more." But he provided no details and no explanation. He did not contend that vengeance at that point, immediately at the war's end, might obviate the next pyre no less effectively than an army by proving that killing Jews had stopped being permissible and profitable. He presented the relocation to the Land of Israel and the spreading of the message of solidarity there as challenges that must be met.

Thus, there remained an open question. He titled his speech "The Mission of the Last Ones." What mission did he mean? Who were the last ones? And specifically, what was their mission for the immediate term? Are the last ones only the survivors from Europe, or are they the entire remaining

Jewish people with its entire Brigade? Regardless of its uncertainties, however, Kovner's speech would be remembered for years to come as emblematic of the meeting between Holocaust survivors and Palestinian Jews, an occasion when its listeners sat for two hours "with bated breath [. . .]. A new, theretofore unknown world was revealed before their eyes."[47] According to Meirke Davidson, who was among the founders of Kibbutz Eilon and prominent in the Palmach, "Abba Kovner was the Jews' strongest expression of themselves" when he appeared in Tarvisio. Motke Hadash called the unforgettable evening "the Night of Vilna"; after that, the atmosphere in the Brigade and in the regiments was different. Having considered Kovner's words, as well as a report brought by Aharon Hoter-Ishay—an officer of the Brigade who headed the search for survivors on behalf of the Brigade and its internal command and who looked for liberated concentration camps and death camps—the Jewish Brigade was inspired to devote all possible resources to organizing a voyage to Land of Israel for Europe's survivors, in parallel with the campaign of vengeance already underway.[48]

When Kovner and his companions arrived in Tarvisio, the question of vengeance—whether personal or collective/national, spontaneous or organized—was already at the center of the Jewish Brigade's discussions and activities. Both before and after his speech, vengeance was adumbrated at a series of meetings about various other subjects as well. For example, Hadash wrote about a meeting with the partisans in which Kovner uttered the principal points and matters and Hadash ended his description with the expression "the annihilation's conscience"[49]: this was an abbreviated way of conveying the stirrings and whispers that surrounded the partisans and their objective, and it expressed the inherent contradiction of vengeance: the conscience demands vengeance because vengeance is inflicted at the behest of the murdered; however, vengeance in the form of annihilation offends the conscience. "We told only a few people about our intentions," said Yulek. Yitzhak Ratner, one of the members of the Vilna underground, went walking with Hadash on one of the first nights of their acquaintance and revealed to him that inside the Hativa they had a vengeance organization. When Hadash met Kovner, he told Kovner about the Jewish Brigade's approach to vengeance. Kovner was excited but undemonstrative, not having known "that there are thoughts along those lines." Later, Hadash introduced him

to the heads of the German Unit, who were dealing in vengeance.[50] Carmi
too sat with Kovner and informed him of what the Jewish Brigade had accomplished so far. But despite Kovner's subdued excitement about the idea
of vengeance that had already taken hold in the Jewish Brigade, it was clear
to Kovner and his companions that their own intentions were something
else entirely, not secret nighttime executions by conventional means, without worldwide ramifications.[51]

Another meeting engendered a harsh argument between Kovner and
Mordechai Surkis, who, like Argov, was a central figure in Mapai, the largest party in the Yishuv, headed by David Ben-Gurion. Surkis had befriended
and greatly assisted the members of the group. But Kovner was decidedly
anti-Soviet, and according to Surkis, till his dying day Kovner never forgot that Russian partisans had killed Jews in the forest. Indeed, how could
Kovner forget that his beloved younger brother Michael had been killed in
the forest with thirty-four of his fellows when the Russians directed them
into a German ambush? How could he forget that the great majority of his
fellow underground activists, whom he trained in the Vilna Ghetto with
love and effort, had been humiliated and scorned in a manner he could not
forgive? Surkis begged Kovner not to speak against the Soviets publicly in
Austria and Italy, and certainly not in Russian—many Jews had deserted
the Red Army, including an entire artillery unit that had discarded its uniforms. That unit had been taken in by the soldiers of the Jewish Brigade
nearby, and the NKVD, the secret Soviet police, had come searching for it.
But Surkis could not sway Kovner.[52] In subsequent meetings, Kovner continued to speak "harshly and bitterly" against the Russians for encumbering,
harassing, and killing Jews. However, the image of the Soviet Union was entirely different in the Yishuv, and naturally also among the soldiers of the
Jewish Brigade as fighters in the war. The Yishuv felt outright admiration for
the Soviet Union's wartime dauntlessness—and for such cities as Leningrad
and Stalingrad, which became symbols of determination and steadfastness.
Kovner contended that the Jews had no future in the Soviet Union, and he
even spoke of rebellion against the Russians. Later, he was taken aside and
told, "Restrain yourself. Your leeway is limited."[53]

And of course there were meetings with the members of his own
movement—Tubin, Moshe (Miyetek) Zilbertal (later Zertal), and Shaike

Weinberg, who made up the secretariat of Hashomer Hatzair in the Jewish Brigade. After his speech, there was no need to speak further to them about the Holocaust, and at that point he revealed to them the secret of the Nokmim, whose oath constrained them from revealing it themselves. He spoke of the duty to exact vengeance and to do so before proceeding to the Land of Israel, because any people who were considering a resumption of the Holocaust should be made to know that their lives were the price and it would spell their end.[54] According to Weinberg, Kovner did not detail any specific plan but tried to convey the overall idea to them. He spoke of the East European Survivors' Brigade (the Hativa), a concept that was hard for the members of Hashomer Hatzair to swallow. They had waited for years to reunite with fellow members who had survived, and now they were being asked to unite with others. It was difficult for them, as part of the Yishuv, to understand a project like the Hativa, which was ostensibly apolitical but planned to unify all the forces of the Yishuv and the Jewish people. Kovner made clear to them that if he, along with the other Hashomer Hatzair members among the arrivals and further members yet to join them, returned to the confines of the movement, they would not be responding to the needs of Kovner's other followers, who had come from different movements, ranging from the Beitar to the communists. Such a move on his part would push some of them "into complete despair, or into terrorism or something worse." To their credit, said Kovner, Tubin and the other members understood, despite the discomfort they felt as Hashomer Hatzair members, that the Hativa was a "project not subject to ordinary classification."[55]

Long letters were sent to the Land of Israel in the wake of the meetings with Kovner and his associates, first of all to Hazan and Ya'ari, the leaders of the movement, in order to explain to them who Kovner was, and especially what the Hativa was, and to ask the leadership in the Land of Israel to treat them with warmth and friendliness rather than merely weighing whether the Hativa constituted a threat to Hashomer Hatzair. Kovner himself told them, in his remarks about the Hativa—perhaps partly because he realized that the idea of unification would be foreign and raise suspicions in the political climate in the Land of Israel—that the whole purpose of the Hativa was merely to camouflage the project of vengeance. The three of them were supporters of vengeance in principle even before Kovner arrived, and Weinberg was already a participant in any case. Thus it was agreed that Weinberg would serve as the Hashomer Hatzair liaison to Kovner; and at that juncture, a deep friendship began to form between them that would continue for decades in Israel.[56]

There were also meetings with members of Mapai who were enthusiastic about the idea of the Hativa, were charmed by Kovner and his mission, and used terms such as "holy," "miraculous," "messianic," and other expressions of admiration. While the topic of vengeance did come up for discussion with the Mapai representatives, it was not in the same frank and direct manner as in the discussions with the Hashomer Hatzair members. Still, it should be emphasized that even among the Mapai members of the Jewish Brigade, including the oldest and most levelheaded of them, the sentiment was widespread. Ben-Zion Israeli, of Kvutzat Kinneret, was one of the eldest soldiers and a revered veteran. He wrote: "There is only one just response—vengeance against that nation, on its own land! As I continue encountering some of our few brothers who escaped from the concentration camps [. . .] my blood boils inside me and restraint is difficult."[57] The discourse brought about a different result: according to Eliyahu Ben Hur (previously Cohen), a senior figure in the Haganah and an officer in the Jewish Brigade, Kovner succeeded in bringing together, for the first time in the company's history, all the commissioned officers, sergeants, and activists of Transport Company 462 for the speech. Kovner "told about the Holocaust visited on the Jews of Europe, using all his talent as an orator and writer. Military men sat aghast as he described the horrible calamity." That time, Kovner "gave an eight-hour account of his story, of the exile and of the forests." At the end of his address, everyone was called to a special parade and received detailed orders on how to allocate time and forces to the care of the survivors: "And that is an order!" The meeting complemented and deepened the impression that Kovner had made with his arrival speech, and it spurred the soldiers to examine the flow of refugees, the "migration of peoples" taking place in Europe, as well as the sense of having a mission set before them.[58]

However, after these emotional meetings, Kovner sat separately with Davidson, Carmi, and Ben Hur to present them with the problem of pursuing both vengeance against the Nazis and close, warm relations with the Land of Israel. "It must be said, to his credit," writes Davidson, "that he wanted to see the Haganah predominating, if it would agree to his intent. We informed him that we would give every assistance to the Nokmim and I would serve as liaison." Apparently Davidson meant to be liaison on behalf of the inner command of the Haganah, and thus he pinpointed the core of the problem, a problem that would resurface as events unfolded. Kovner and his associates wanted recognition from the Haganah and the opportunity to work under its authority, but in keeping with conditions and plans of their own devising. Therefore the meeting was not uncomplicated, and participants walked away with mixed impressions of it. The Kovner faction regarded the delegates from the Land of Israel with great suspicion, considering themselves superior in their understanding and evaluation of the Holocaust, Davidson writes, adding, "They saw us as small fries who hadn't suffered from the war [. . .]. What they wanted first was weapons, so then we confiscated small arms, like pistols, from the unit, and we willingly gave them to the Nokmim and provided them with money, but they looked on us with scorn." They had courageous men and women among them, Davidson continued in his testimony, and ways of their own to obtain money. A creative and adaptable woman by the name of Irena (i.e., Irena Gelblum, a fighter in the Warsaw Ghetto uprising who had joined the group in Bucharest) passed money from Italy to Romania speedily and at a great profit. They numbered about thirty people, Davidson estimated, and already they had a presence in Germany. "Regarding vengeance," he said bluntly, "we couldn't consider ourselves qualified judges, and since we had already found a group [that wished to handle it], we relied on them" unofficially.[59]

Ben-Horin was appointed liaison officer to the partisans. He was the third liaison mentioned in the testimonies: Weinberg had been appointed to represent Hashomer Hatzair, Davidson to represent the internal command of the Haganah in the Jewish Brigade, and Ben-Horin was the appointee from the Land of Israel—from the "high command," as he emphasized in his testimony, apparently meaning the Haganah command at the national level in the Land of Israel. He said that he had argued intensely with the partisans because vengeance had become their life's ambition and they increasingly pressed for a large-scale operation with no holds barred. "[They] came to us with a wild plan to poison entire cities through the water supply. We were placed in a difficult position, since that perception was incompatible with our perception." Their argument was ultimately backed by much justice, said Ben-Horin, but the focus on vengeance could have endangered other, more vital activities. The Nokmim disagreed. The Haganah command in the Land of Israel considered the matter important and central, as attested first and foremost by the fact that Ben-Horin, the commander of the German Unit, was appointed the liaison between the Nokmim and the Jewish Brigade and assumed responsibility for ensuring that acts of vengeance would be "supervised and compartmentalized." Not only that, but when tension over the issue reached its peak, Ben-Horin was sent to Palestine at his own request to confer about the form and character that the operation of vengeance should assume.[60] The next chapter will go into more detail regarding the consultations in Palestine and Ben-Horin's meeting with Kovner there.

THE JEWISH BRIGADE DEPARTS NORTHWARD

At one of the meetings held in the wake of the partisans' arrival, a professional discussion was held in Russian with the top command of the Jewish Brigade. Ben-Gal defined it as "speaking fighter to fighter." Yet just a few days later, the commanders of the Jewish Brigade were told that they would be proceeding not to Germany ("And it's good we weren't sent into Germany") but, in three days, to Belgium and Holland instead.

According to Ben-Gal's testimony, Kovner came to him as soon as the partisans heard about the change of destination and told Ben-Gal "that they were assigned, having volunteered and agreed, to pursue the interests of vengeance." Kovner asked to bring his group onward along with the Jewish Brigade because from Holland and Belgium they could more easily infiltrate Germany. However, Ben-Gal was skeptical. On the one hand, he was satisfied that the task had been assigned to the partisans, who were especially eager and prepared—and all the more so, now that they were otherwise idle and unorganized, without a ship to take them to the Land of Israel. He was also glad to have the task of vengeance fall to the partisans rather than to his own soldiers, uniformed members of the Jewish Brigade (it may be inferred that to his mind, surreptitious killing was unbefitting of men in uniform). On the other hand, said Ben-Gal, "It grated on my ear when he came to tell me he had orders that hadn't reached me through the chain of command. I'd received nothing." Ben-Gal didn't ask for a note to this effect signed by

Ben-Gurion or Shertok; however, although he had five thousand soldiers to transport in three days and "the usual commotion had started" in response to the move-out order, he took the trouble to check with the Diaspora Center in Milan. He apparently contacted Surkis, who had been appointed by the center to head the Bricha and was on warm, fatherly terms with the Nokmim. The Diaspora Center activists were in regular contact with the leadership in the Land of Israel, and even though the matter was a secret, they let Ben-Gal know that such a plan did exist. So Ben-Gal agreed to move the Nokmim northward, in uniform, as a platoon of the British Army.[61]

However, Mordechai Maklef (later Israel's third chief of staff) had been assigned to organize the platoon and dress it in uniform, and he returned to Ben-Gal, saying that Kovner insisted on having women travel with them as well as a one-armed man—Haim Lazar, who had lost an arm during his time in the forest. Ben-Gal informed Maklef that there were no one-armed men circulating in any unit of the British Army and that female soldiers did not travel sitting on male soldiers' knees, he said. Female soldiers traveled separately, in their own units, the way it should be. It was useless for Kovner to explain that they had all arrived together from "back there," which is to say that they were inseparable, having endured the Holocaust together. Ben-Gal and Kovner were speaking different languages, just as when, in Romania, Kovner spoke with emissaries from the Land of Israel about what was and was not possible. One man lived in a world of regulations: Ben-Gal considered himself disciplined and "regimental," operating within the framework of the regiment. The other man followed no regulations, accepted no authority, and considered nothing impossible after what he and his friends had experienced. "When we left the forest, we were savages," said Yulek. "For almost a year we hadn't seen a fork," said Senka Nissanilevich.[62] But Ben-Gal believed that the Nokmim should stay behind if they did not comply with the regimental regulations.

In his own way, Kovner presented matters to Ben-Gal as if the Yishuv had proposed the mission of vengeance to the Nokmim and they had volunteered to perform it. His approach indicates that he already understood, shortly after reaching the Jewish Brigade, the type of person he was addressing and the structure of authority that prevailed in the Jewish Brigade. There was a command structure known to the British, there was an internal command structure that was responsible to the Haganah and represented the

Yishuv, and the soldiers of the Jewish Brigade saw the internal command as overriding the British-backed command. The Yishuv leadership, which was the first and final decider, was held in high regard by the soldiers, and Kovner quickly understood that he had to bring Ben-Gal a directive from the Yishuv, a task that the Yishuv assigned, and a demonstration of volunteerism, which was a central value. Most of the Nokmim had been members of Zionist youth movements before the war, and their connection to the Land of Israel, to its leaders and its landscapes, was the very fabric of their lives. When they met the soldiers of the Jewish Brigade, that feeling of belonging to the Land of Israel began returning to them, along with the view of the land as a supremely desired destination whose priorities must be obeyed. Vitka testified that for them the Jewish Brigade came to be considered a foretaste of the Land of Israel.[63]

However, the way Kovner presented matters to Ben-Gal was not accurate. The task had not been assigned to him and his group by anyone in Italy from the Yishuv's leadership, nor by any representative of the Jewish Brigade's leadership. He and his associates had conceived of the idea and were burning with the ambition to carry it out. That ambition was their lodestar.

For his part, Kovner had complaints against Ben-Gal's behavior toward him and his group, and when he reached the Land of Israel, he sent instructions telling Pasha and Vitka to avoid contact with "James," that is to say Ben-Gal, because of the man's unfriendly stance. After Kovner left, Pasha too—according to his testimony—encountered palpable disrespect from Ben-Gal and Shamir, and they "gave him the runaround," promising meetings that were never held. Shamir's memoirs reveal that Kovner and Pasha saw the situation accurately; he writes that although Kovner did speak with him, ask him questions, and request his advice, Kovner kept his plans to himself and jealously guarded the independence of his group at the Tarvisio camp. Then Shamir openly adds that "if we had felt that the plan could be carried out according to the gist of Kovner's suggestions, we wouldn't have needed him. In other words, had there been someone with a serious proposal by which a million Germans could be liquidated, quite possibly we would have implemented it, even at the cost of disbanding the Jewish Brigade." But looking back from the perspective of advanced age as he wrote his memoirs, he was not at all sure that the elimination of a million Germans had been worth risking the Jewish Brigade's dissolution and, consequently, the abandonment of the survivors.[64] Do his words mean that the commanders of the Brigade were not actually opposed to vengeance as such, only to Kovner and his associates as the wreakers of vengeance? That if not for the fear that the Jewish Brigade would be dismissed and the survivors not offered help, the commanding officers would have led the Jewish Brigade in that campaign? And that in his old age, he was still of two minds?

In deciding that the Jewish Brigade would depart through Germany to Belgium and Holland, the British command was acting on the suspicion that the Brigade's soldiers, if part of the Allied occupation army in Germany, could not be stopped from inflicting terrible revenge upon the Germans. There was also fear among the soldiers that at the sight of Germans continuing everyday life as if nothing had happened, they might lose their composure.[65] But there was another, possibly more significant reason for the decision that derived from British policy: the British knew that from the moment it emerged that Jews, perhaps many Jews, had survived, the Brigade soldiers had begun diverting much of their hours, days, and resources to the discovery, systematic assembly, and handling of the survivors. For that purpose, the soldiers were setting aside part of their food rations and pocket money (Laskov testified that 20 percent of their food was passed to the survivors; Yehuda Tubin claimed it was a quarter). They were diverting a great deal of time and effort that should have been devoted to their military duties, at the expense of the army and its own resources: vehicles, petrol, uniforms to replace the striped prison clothing, meals, tents, blankets, beds. The refugee camp that sprang up near Tarvisio, for example—at Pontebba—was fed, supported, and financed as if it were part of a British unit. It accepted fifteen thousand people to be cared for by the soldiers, and the Jewish Brigade's transport unit was operating above capacity because the entire project served the purposes of the Yishuv in its attempts to bring in refugees. From where they were massed, the refugees were brought south and west to ports of departure for the Land of Israel. They were consigned to agents representing the Mossad for Aliyah B "because the word had gone out everywhere in Europe that in order to reach the shores of safety, you need only make your way to the Jewish Brigade [. . .]. The Jewish Brigade's soldiers tirelessly took

care of everyone with devotion and efficiency [. . .]. They showed endless understanding and patience [. . .]. They considered it a divine labor."[66]

A description from Pasha depicts the rescue of exhausted survivors,
loaded onto trucks and brought to the camp, in the period after the Nokmim joined the soldiers of the Jewish Brigade in helping to care for the refugees. Soldiers of the Jewish Brigade arrived at the Yugoslav-Austrian border at night to meet the trucks full of refugees. The soldiers lifted the back
tarp of the truck, one of them aimed a flashlight inside, and another helped
the refugees out; they would then kiss each of the refugees, weeping at their
condition: "Those bruisers, our soldier boys, they cried just like babies." And
the refugees too, seeing Jewish soldiers with the Star of David on their shoulders—salvation, after year upon year—embraced them, kissed them, and
wept; together, they cursed the Germans, the Austrians, and the progeny of
Germans and Austrians.[67] Had the soldiers of the Jewish Brigade been transferred to Germany, they could have continued bringing southward survivors
of the concentration camps, death marches, and forced labor, as well as the
others who came later to the displaced persons camps. But from Belgium
and Holland, according to the British assessment, the soldiers would certainly have had difficulty doing so. The British prohibited the entry of Jewish soldiers into Germany, even those visiting or looking for relatives; soldiers were obliged to find ways around the prohibition.[68]

A few days before leaving Italy, while still unaware of the British decision
and hopeful that the Jewish Brigade would be part of the occupation army in
Germany, the Brigade's commissioned officers and sergeants were called together by Brigadier Benjamin, and he forcefully demanded that they refrain
from harming German prisoners and civilians and that they uphold their
reputation as soldiers and as human beings with morals.[69] In addition, at a
formal assembly of all the soldiers before their departure, there was a recita-
tion of thirteen rules of behavior for Jewish soldiers on German soil, a sort of
Thirteen Commandments, which the assembly was sworn to obey.

> As a soldier of the JBG [Jewish Brigade Group], remember and preserve
> the following:
>
> 1. Remember your six million slaughtered brothers and sisters!
> 2. Through the generations, preserve hatred for those who slaughtered
>   your nation!

3. Remember that in this battle, you represent the nation!

4. Remember that the Jewish Brigade in Germany is a Jewish occupation army!

5. Remember that the presence of the Jewish Brigade, with its flag and its insignia, before the eyes and in the country of the German people, is vengeance!

6. Remember that blood vengeance is the vengeance of the collective. Any irresponsible action will hamper the collective!

7. Present yourself like a Jew who takes pride in his people and his nation!

8. Do not be associated with Germans, and do not attend their gatherings!

9. Give Germans no regard, and do not enter their homes!

10. Disallowed are they, their women, their children, their property, and everything they have! Banned through the generations!

11. Remember your mission: Rescuing Jews, immigrating to the Land of Israel, and freeing the homeland!

12. You have a duty of dedication, fidelity, and love toward the survivors of the sword and of the camps!

13. Your aspect must be worthy of the military and of the Jews. A proper appearance, discipline wherever you go!

And finally, in a loud and emotional voice "which shook through the entire assembly," and later in bold type for the printed version, came the declaration "**Cursed be he who fails to remember what they did to us!**" Above the Thirteen Commandments, there stood the words of Ezekiel 25:15—"Vengeance with a despiteful heart to destroy, for the old hatred." That verse is followed by a divine promise to deal the Philistines "great vengeance with furious rebukes; and they shall know that I am the Lord, when I shall lay my vengeance upon them."[70]

The matter of vengeance has a central place in the Thirteen Commandments, but it is a symbolic vengeance consisting mainly of the presence of the Jewish Brigade, with its flag, as a representative of the Jewish people face to face with the defeated German nation. Poets and writers, particularly those who enlisted in the British Army and in the Jewish Brigade, repeatedly mentioned vengeance as a national wish that rested emphatically on the Brigade's shoulders. The upcoming entry into Germany gave special meaning to the poems and songs written for the soldiers. There, the soldiers were viewed as having saved the honor of the Jewish people by the very act of fighting and by "the ability to avenge millions of our brothers and soothe the boiling blood of theirs that shouts from all the soil of Europe."[71] Verses called upon zealous, hardy Jews in arms to be a sharp avenging arrow, a sword of revenge, a bearer of the banner of vengeance, and so on. There were marching songs, popular songs, and songs intended for community singing. A "song of vengeance" by poet Ya'akov Orland, which he wrote as a soldier in the British Army, became the anthem of the Hativa, and a poem by Amir Gilboa—who served for four years—ends with the words that were figuratively tattooed on his hands as a vow: "My martyrs' behest: the dew of revenge!"[72] There is a certain contradiction between the poems, which the soldiers embraced, and the Thirteen Commandments, insofar as the poems call on each soldier to take revenge both for the nation and as an individual, whereas the commandments address the military volunteers as a community with a shared responsibility. The sixth commandment contains a warning against individual acts of vengeance that are not endorsed by the collective, lest such acts spread uncontrollably within Germany.

On July 27, 1945, two months after the Jewish Brigade reached Tarvisio and twelve days after the partisans arrived, roughly a thousand trucks left Italy and crossed into Austria, carrying the soldiers and their equipment. The next day, at ten in the morning, the first of them entered Germany. The trucks displayed the familiar banners, but with the addition of *Die Jüden kommen!* ("The Jews are coming!"). With bated breath, a long convoy of soldiers passed along with their flags and insignia: a blue-and-white tag, with a gold Star of David on each sleeve. Thus, five thousand soldiers from the Land of Israel came to Germany, a clear majority of them either having left their families behind or being survivors of the Holocaust themselves. They had been definitively informed, while crossing Italy's border into Austria, that they would merely pass through Germany, not stay as an occupation force alongside the Allied troops. Great anger and disappointment set in as they traveled through the untroubled and contented "evil land" of Austria, and there was a strong urge to leap from the truck, strike a match, and send it all up in "flames of vengeance"—particularly when they passed through the area of Leinz, which they mistakenly took for Linz, where Hitler was raised.

The trip all the way through southern Germany took four days, "and we had the pleasure of seeing with our own eyes the destruction and ruin of

the land, and seeing its people, who had been so arrogant in victory, humiliated and servile in defeat. It would have been humanly impossible not to rejoice in their suffering." The soldiers deemed each city laid waste a "beautiful city"; even the British officers, who accompanied the convoy and whose
attitude toward the Germans was usually restrained and formal, saw in the
ruination of Germany revenge for the bombing of London, Coventry, and
Plymouth. They mentioned their own bombing of Dresden as revenge for
Coventry, and Hamburg as revenge for Plymouth. In Hamburg, forty-two
thousand people had been killed in one week of bombing.

The motorcycles that kept the sections of the long convoy in touch with
one another deliberately stopped traffic as much as possible, so that locals
would be forced to see the flags and the messages written on the trucks. But
along with the glee, there also arose the question—every day and every hour,
in all its weightiness—of how to exact vengeance, how to do so without sinking to the level of the debased Germans, who were now visibly strolling the
cities and villages as if everything were back to normal. Enjoying life as if
they hadn't wreaked terrible destruction and brought death to tens of millions all over Europe and the entire world.

How to stay human but still take revenge? The soldiers solved that dilemma in their own way, as individuals. Although the journey can be said
to have been peaceful overall, there were a number of severe encounters with
members of the German population.[73]

In the evenings, individuals and small groups from among those whose
families had been murdered drove away from the bivouacs, distanced themselves from the long lines of vehicles, and raided nearby towns and villages.
They visited their wrath upon the residents, using their cars to knock bicy-
clists and pedestrians into roadside ditches, "caught up in a divinely mandated war against everything German—to burn it, shatter it, destroy it,
and obliterate it," especially when they knew that the Germans in particular locations had abused the survivors. The apex of their campaign was a
conflagration in a village near their bivouac at Kaiserslautern. Testimony is
not unambiguous, but it appears that only a few of the soldiers volunteered
to help with the firefighting, and they came under suspicion of arson. After the incident, a special assembly was gathered at which the rabbi spoke,
with rebukes, warnings, and calls for responsible behavior. Kalman Kitt also
spoke—not about the injury to the Germans; despite the rabbi's words, this

was considered legitimate by all—but about the danger that such operations posed to diplomacy and worldwide sympathy. The operations ceased.[74]

However, the soldiers protested strongly against those who cautioned them not to take revenge during their time on German soil. They remembered well that before they had entered the fighting on the Italian front, they were given speeches about mass vengeance and were even read to from the booklet *A Year in Treblinka* in order to boost their motivation. And now, the soldiers complained, the call was for restraint! The same policy prevailing in the Yishuv, the exact same restraint vis-à-vis the British and the Arabs, had arrived here with an additional rationale. If they didn't curb their actions, the survivors would suffer—no one would care for them if the soldiers were punished by dismissal. This was an argument no one could refute.

At a camp in Landsberg, near Munich, one of the largest of the displaced persons camps still fenced in, a large sign was prepared in advance, in Hebrew, saying, "Welcome! Long live the fighting Jewish Brigade!" The DPs stood on the side of the road, waving and weeping, while the soldiers handed them the contents of their rucksacks. According to one of the survivors who met the soldiers, the survivors wanted

> those men to see the death camps, to learn what the Nazis did to us—and to avenge our blood, avenge the murdered fathers and mothers. To avenge; and beyond that, to let the murderers see the proud Star of David on blue and white, on the shoulders of the military uniforms, as revenge for the yellow patch we were forced to wear.[75]

On August 1, at the end of a journey totaling close to nine hundred miles, they reached Belgium. Ben-Gal having agreed that some of the Nokmim would travel with the Jewish Brigade, Carmi took a number of them with him when the convoy of trucks departed from Tarvisio; he left behind Yehezkel Rabinovitch (later Baharav) as liaison, with a military vehicle, money, and "everything necessary." At the same time, Shaike Weinberg left uniforms and British military IDs for the Nokmim who stayed behind. In subsequent months, Carmi would send provisions and equipment to Germany from time to time, when the Avengers infiltrated into it.[76] According to Yashek Ben-Zur and Poldek Maimon, they left with the Jewish Brigade, in Brigade uniforms, through Germany to Belgium and Holland; Yehuda

(Idek) Friedman related that the Brigade provided them with clean clothing and uniforms and drove them to their specific assigned destinations. Shlomo Kenet confirmed that they were given British uniforms, with the help of Haganah members, and that they received counterfeit papers and were sent to Munich via train.[77]

KOVNER LEAVES FOR PALESTINE,
AND THE NOKMIM LEAVE FOR GERMANY

After arriving in Italy, why did Kovner so quickly set off for the Land of Israel? Was it his own choice, or was it imposed on him by a decision that he wasn't even aware of? According to one testimony, "They dressed him pretty quickly [. . .] in a Jewish Brigade uniform and transferred him to the Land of Israel." That direct phrasing hints that Kovner's departure for Palestine was rooted not in his own planning and desire to request support from the Yishuv but rather in his reluctance, as a leader, to tread the conventional path. He led the Hativa, which was considered suspect in its agenda, he spoke against the Soviets, and he demanded vengeance. Mordechai Surkis, that same central figure of Mapai who had begged Kovner not to disparage the Soviets, especially not in public, entreated him to come to the Land of Israel and make a "pilgrimage to Mecca"—that is, to visit Meir Ya'ari in his kibbutz, Merhavia, and fall into line. This idea appealed to Kovner not at all. Accordingly, "We notified Ben-Gurion of the matter, he demanded immediately that he [Kovner] be brought to Palestine, and it was done," Surkis testified.[78] In other words, it was decided then to dress up Kovner and dispatch him in uniform. On the very same day Kovner reported to the Jewish Brigade, July 15, Yehuda Tubin wrote in a detailed letter addressed to the Land of Israel that "the question of his immediate travel came up," though he does not mention who brought it up. Kovner promised an answer within a day or two, and Tubin promised to handle the matter.[79] From these testimonies, it appears that the members of both Mapai and Hashomer Hatzair wanted Kovner to make that journey.

There are other testimonies, however, such as one from Davidson. He said that after the meeting at which it was agreed that the Nokmim would receive every assistance, "the first thing was to send Abba to the Land of

Israel"—it will be recalled that Kovner had said that he favored primacy for the Haganah. "It was decided that Abba must come to the Land of Israel, present to the institutions of the Yishuv the situation in the Diaspora, and return to Europe with a plan for continuing the efforts," testified Jacquo Yaron of Kibbutz Hatzor, a Hashomer Hatzair member and a soldier of the Jewish Brigade. Ben-Zur testified that Eliyahu Ben Hur, who had heard, along with his officers, Kovner describe the Holocaust in detail, insisted that he come to the Land of Israel, just as Ruzka Korczak had been sent there previously from Romania. People must know in the Land of Israel: they must know what happened in the Holocaust and know that thousands are now on the roads with the Land of Israel as their destination.[80]

Kovner, we realize, already understood the standing that the leaders of the Yishuv enjoyed in the eyes of the soldiers, the trust that the soldiers placed in them, and the questions that the leadership faced at that time—weighty questions that a stroke of vengeance could complicate or render unsolvable. Michael Elkins, whose book Kovner recommended as a reliable source for the sentiment of the times (if not its factual accuracy), writes that for the soldiers, the Haganah was the sole supreme Jewish authority. Vitka recalled, "They didn't bring Abba there. Abba wanted to go," and Kovner himself, in a letter summarizing the matter of vengeance, wrote: "From the very unenthusiastic reaction of Shlomo Shamir and of Ben-Gal, I learned—as advised by Shaike Weinberg, Meir Davidson, and Yehuda Tubin—that the most appropriate course for me is to come quickly for a personal meeting with the leadership in the Land of Israel."[81]

It may not have been the ties Kovner formed with the commanders of the Jewish Brigade but rather the warm relations with the lower ranks that led him and his associates to question whether they had the right to initiate vengeance on their own initiative and without the approval of the leaders in the Land of Israel. Acts of vengeance could have amounted to an abuse of trust from the many who had welcomed and assisted them; those people, some of whom had become genuine friends of the Nokmim, "couldn't move beyond gestures of friendship unless there is approval from higher up." It would be impossible for the Nokmim to wreak the kind of vengeance that they wished and then, if they survived, suddenly show up in Palestine. Kovner hoped that the leaders of the Yishuv, and the leaders of the Haganah above all, would understand the sentiment underlying the quest for vengeance and would lend approval, money, documents, and cooperation. In retrospect, Kovner saw the attempt to secure the understanding and approval of the Yishuv's central figures and institutions as a continuation of the attempt in the ghetto to find intellectuals who would approve of the underground's methods. "We aren't crazy, we aren't defectors, we wanted to do this in the name of the Jewish people," Poldek said more than once. After the fact, Kovner asked himself: Had it been a "correct but miserable idea" to sail to Palestine? He answered, in a letter written to Vitka en route, that an analysis of the situation showed that he must go in order to determine whether there was anyone to rely on; however, "at the same time, I realize that in fact I will not succeed, and the deeper I look into the problem, delving into the nature and psychology [of the Yishuv leaders], the more strongly despair takes hold of me and I feel that this trip will be the end of me."[82]

At the same time, a ship was being arranged for soldiers who were due for leave. There was the opportunity to take Kovner to Palestine. "We saw Kovner's trip as a project for serious handling. He was a major figure," Davidson testified later. Kovner was given the address of Yitzhak Sadeh, the commander of the Palmach, because it was important that Kovner acknowledge his authority. Shmuel Ossia, serving in Transport Company 462 under Ben Hur, received an order to prepare Kovner to accompany the soldiers who were sailing to Palestine on leave, and Shalhevet Freier (son of Recha Freier, the founder of the Youth Aliyah organization) saw to procuring documents and a uniform for him. The documents identified Kovner as Sam Lehmann, a soldier from Moshav Kidron. On the way south, Kovner's escorts stopped in Milan and had Kovner's cloud of hair trimmed to a soldierly length. Vitka, who accompanied him for part of the journey, could hardly recognize him. At Via Unione in Milan, Kovner told the members of the Diaspora Center about how Vilna was caught up in the Holocaust, and about the ghetto, the underground, and the forest. Once more, his account filled listeners with energy and determination: if the partisans could struggle like that, and under impossible conditions, then the soldiers certainly could "struggle and sacrifice for [. . .] the Holocaust refugees."[83]

In the meantime, the Hativa—the East European Survivors' Brigade— had disbanded on July 23, 1945, roughly three months after its founding, largely because of the desire for vengeance. Among the non-Nokmim Hativa members, some worried that the engine of the Hativa would find itself pulling the wagon of the Avengers. There were certainly other causes that contributed to the disbandment of the Hativa, such as the lack of specificity of its ideas, the emotional attachment to former political movements, and encounters with Israeli emissaries and soldiers who had an ideology incompatible with the Hativa's message of unity. Kovner was well aware that the Hativa had little chance of surviving in the Land of Israel, and its members were apprehensive about what to expect from the members of their former movements when they got to Palestine. But the disbandment was caused primarily by the disappearance of the core group, led by Kovner, which had charted its course. From the three avenues of action that had been conceived in Lublin as a result of the fear engendered by the return of murderous antisemitism, the only one remaining was the one most important to the group's members: vengeance.

The final action of the Hativa as an organization was to send a manifesto to the participants of the Potsdam Conference, which began in July 1945: Prime Minister Winston Churchill of Great Britain, Soviet ruler Joseph Stalin, and US president Harry Truman. It announced, in the name of the concentration camp survivors, that they were unwilling to spend one more minute on German soil in the same camps, alongside the murderers whom the Allies had arrested, and they wished to be housed in special camps for Jews until the granting of their wish to immigrate to the Land of Israel. Otherwise, they could sink into absolute desperation.[84] Was this a veiled threat that they might commit acts of desperation, such as revenge attacks?

In his dedication to the idea of vengeance, Kovner committed political suicide: The Hativa, which had been an original and symbolic concept, was dissolved. The Bricha, in contrast, had accomplished striking success by any standard. By the time Kovner left for Palestine, some ten thousand survivors had reached Italy, primarily from Romania, Hungary, and Poland. Afterward, the Bricha continued, and survivors arrived by the same methods and along the same routes pioneered at the end of 1944 by the first to head south from Vilna. Bricha activists received assistance from other facilitators, such as Jan Masaryk, who allowed Czechoslovakia to serve as the main way station; the Joint Distribution Committee, headed by Joe Schwartz, which provided support and food; and the Jewish soldiers and officers of the Red Army and the US Army, who offered a helping hand and rescue from danger.[85]

If not for the vision of vengeance, Kovner would have continued organizing the Bricha with his associates and with the Jewish Brigade —which, as described, adopted them enthusiastically. They felt trust and affection, they longed for a leader who would be there to bring the nation's survivors from the valley of tears, and they treasured the echo of his impressive speech. If he had come to the Land of Israel sometime later, being a "representative of the survivors' definite majority opinion" (as he was to understand years afterward); being the author of the first manifesto that called for organized resistance to the utter annihilation, with the iconic headline "Jews! Let us not go like sheep to the slaughter!"; being one of the founders of the ghetto underground; being a commander of the Jewish regiments in the forest; and being the initiator of the Bricha that had brought Jews southward from Lithuania—if he had left the matter of vengeance to be an ethical/symbolic issue to be solved on the broad national level, then Kovner would likely have been welcomed in the Land of Israel as a leader of great stature, a prophet of Jewish unity bringing to the Land of Israel the lessons from the experience of the Holocaust. However, the vengeance project distanced him from the members of the Hativa who had trusted him and followed him for its sake; he consigned the Bricha to the faithful hands of the Jewish Brigade soldiers and the emissaries from the Land of Israel. He and his group disappeared from public view, Kovner frankly acknowledged,[86] and they found themselves the focus of a dispute waged behind closed doors, as if they bore a grim and undeciphered secret. The explanation for this series of events may be the same as for Kovner's statement to Ben-Gal claiming support from the Yishuv: he and his associates were possessed by the quest for vengeance, and it had become the substance of their lives to the point where it was their frame of reference for everything. The fiery urge to avenge derived from the loss of their entire previous world. It filled the emptiness that followed the end of the war, and it took the place of hopelessness in a world they had despaired of.

Within two weeks of Kovner and his associates' arrival in Italy, they distanced themselves from their friends among the Jewish Brigade, the Bricha, and the Hativa and outlined a practical plan for vengeance. It had been conceived in Lublin, and the basics sketched out in Romania. The force would be organized, its number and composition suitable for the purpose—which is to say roughly fifty men and woman ready to spend an unspecified amount of time among the Germans, friendless and unknown, and to operate under assumed identities without cracking. They would enter Germany as promptly as possible, locate the necessary chemicals, insert agents into the workforce of the municipal waterworks of three or four large cities, and poison the water in them all at once, on the same day. They would have to forswear individual acts of terror, and they would need to raise sufficient money.

At this point, Kovner revealed to Weinberg in detail, for the first time, the Nokmim's waterworks scheme. Weinberg objected absolutely, since masses of innocent people would die, and by his own account he immediately urged Kovner to pursue "Plan B," which would focus on killing or seriously harming tens of thousands of imprisoned SS officers, like the ones he had seen in camps run by the Allies. Weinberg gave Kovner the names and locations of the camps.[87]

Meanwhile, the "financial department" of the Nokmim continued its trade in currencies, which it had begun back in Budapest. It converted Italian money into Austrian schillings, schillings into German marks, and so on in a cycle. Dan Arad recalled: "One day I was walking around with a bag of eighty thousand marks, which was a lot of money. I slept on top of it." The department's agents traveled by train through hills and snow. There were extortionists and police to be wary of, "but an order is an order [. . .] and even when our shoes were worn out, not even a little of the money came our way. It was all sacred to the purpose." Friedman attested: "Bolek [Ben-Yaʿakov] was in charge of me, and I received an order to pass along a rucksack full of money." They would transfer piles of phony pounds sterling that they had bought for a song (the counterfeit currency necessitated rucksacks and suitcases; these are often mentioned in the testimonies). They were arrested in Strasbourg, where luckily they found themselves in the hands of a military chaplain who was an American Jew. He released them without examining their rucksack. Here it should be added, with emphasis, that the picture Kovner paints in his testimony—of the Nokmim as detaching themselves from everyone they knew in the Jewish Brigade and Bricha and immersing themselves solely in the project of vengeance—is not entirely accurate. Kovner went to Palestine, unaware that in practice the rest of the members maintained close ties with the organizers of the Bricha and with the soldiers of the Jewish Brigade while still participating in the overall activity. Thus, for example, the funds that were obtained served the needs both of the Nokmim and of the Bricha. Even while they were on the move, they swapped news, agents, and necessary equipment.[88]

To conclude this chapter, one could say that from the testimonies regarding meetings between the partisans and the soldiers, it emerges that the concept of vengeance in the form of "Plan A," in its "horror and magnitude," was at first only whispered and then voiced more clearly by some of the soldiers, and thus, when Kovner left for the Land of Israel, there were already those in the Jewish Brigade who knew of Plan A, as testified by Weinberg and Ben-Horin, and exemplified by Motke Hadash's reference to the "annihilation's conscience." Thus the leaders were also aware, at least at the top level of the Haganah in Palestine, even before Kovner disembarked. There was no chance of secrecy for such a plan in a small, close-knit community such as the leadership of the Yishuv; as little as a single Sabbath dinner in the dining halls of a few kibbutzim, which hosted Jewish soldiers on leave, would suffice to spread the rumor. The issue of vengeance, along with news of the founding of the Hativa and its disbandment on Italian soil, as well as the anger of the partisans against the Soviets, who were admired in the Land of Israel, came to the notice of the Yishuv in advance of Kovner's arrival and certainly figured as context for the attitude toward him that formed even before he reached the shores of Palestine.

At the start of August 1945, the Jewish Brigade was already on the march. The Hativa had dissolved, and Kovner was on his way to Palestine. Behind him, he left a force that was scattered and feeling orphaned. Vitka was alone, and Pasha carried a difficult task on his shoulders. He assumed command of the group in Kovner's place, but since he had disapproved of Kovner's leaving for Palestine at such an early stage of the group's formation, they had agreed, before Kovner left, that the group would operate even if Kovner could not obtain support for their operations from the institutions of the Yishuv. Kovner's trip sparked a stormy disagreement among the group, a dispute that lingered as long as the Avengers lived. Menashe Gewissar said that it was unnecessary to travel to Palestine in order to bring back poison. At that time in Europe, everything could be had for money or the equivalent.

Pasha claimed, in contradiction, that under the conditions then prevailing in Europe, setting up a laboratory would have been nearly impossible.[89] Kazhik (Simcha Rotem) protested, until his very last day, more than seventy years later: Why did he go? Who authorized him to go? What makes a commander leave his troops behind? Was that a way to behave, without asking anyone? I wasn't asked! Manek testified more mildly, saying that although he wasn't angry at Kovner, Kovner shouldn't have gone to Palestine. Lena Satz-Hammel added that Yitzhak Hammel, her husband, charged again and again that "Abba went off to Palestine without asking us; he abandoned us. It made us very sad. We felt he would be a long time away from us and he would be sorely missed [. . .] and who could deny that in the Land of Israel they might possibly prevail upon him not to come back?" But Hammel himself, who had accused Kovner of abandonment, also claimed more than once that Kovner had a comprehensive sense of history and felt responsibility for the Yishuv and the forthcoming state. Rachel Galperin was indignant that Kovner hadn't asked them whether they agreed for him to be replaced by Pasha. Leibke Distel, for his part, said that it was impossible to operate without support, that the Jewish Brigade showed understanding, that it cared for and looked after them, and that the Nokmim saw the Brigade as representatives of the Land of Israel operating under instructions from the leadership at the home base, whom the Nokmim didn't know. For that reason, Kovner went there—realizing that without support from the Land of Israel for their idea, the Nokmim would lose their Jewish Brigade connection. Poldek testified that the Nokmim took for granted that the commanders of the Haganah in the Land of Israel would accept their plan, agree that it was the proper course, and enable the group to carry it out, as the Nokmim were the best of the Jewish pioneering youth and had voluntarily undertaken a sacred and vital task. Bezalel Kek-Michaeli disagreed, saying that it had been a mistake and that action should have been taken as independently as possible, with minimal Haganah involvement and approval. But in retrospect, Pasha continued, throughout the war there had been no leadership to confer with; in Tarvisio, Kovner finally met some leaders and understood that in the Land of Israel there was high-level leadership that could be consulted before he took such action. He wanted his operations to be responsible deeds from a national viewpoint, not deeds that would result in damage.[90]

Considering the protest from Kazhik, as well as the stern opinion of some of his comrades, the question immediately arises whether Kovner's departure from the shores of Italy engendered a sort of fissure in the triad of Kovner, the Nokmim, and the Palestinian Jewish leadership. Arriving in Israel, Kovner met a leadership that wanted to examine and assess him and to influence the path that he and his comrades would take. Perhaps the group scattered around Europe had little knowledge of that; they may not have fully understood the nature of Kovner's relationship with the leadership or, later, that between Pasha and the Haganah. The group's members had no direct contact with that leadership, and it is true that they were not consulted. It must be remembered, too, that following the war, communications were sparse between the Land of Israel, which was under the British Mandate, and the conquered German land, which was under the control of four occupying powers, thus adding to the sense of disconnection.

On August 7, three weeks after coming to Italy, Kovner set out from the port of Sorrento in the south, and he wrote to Vitka about the heaviness of his feelings and the fear for his comrades (whom he called "our family"), particularly Pasha. He asked Vitka to watch over the project and see to it that Kek-Michaeli departed with the members at all costs and as quickly as possible—meaning, of course, from Italy to Germany. A few days later, the soldiers' ship anchored in Alexandria, and they took a train by way of El Arish into Palestine. Kovner was registered on arrival as Uri Kovnai; "Uri" had been his nom de guerre in the ghetto of Kovno.[91]

From That Fire

HAIM GOURI

From that fire which marked your charred and tortured body
We carried a torch which lights our souls
We lit with it the flame of freedom
We carried it to battles for our land
We took the pain, the unimaginable pain,
And we poured it into stonecutters' tools and sharpened plows.
We turned your humiliation into guns.
Your eyes became a beacon directing ships at night.

We took a sooty and broken stone
From the calamity of your destroyed town.
It became a cornerstone and a foundation
For an impenetrable wall.
Your words, smothered in flames,
Are sung by our frontline units.
Honor and courage accompany it.
Also the ancient hope, which will not disappear.

We have avenged your bitter and lonely death
Our fists are heavy and strong.
Here we built a memorial to the burnt-out ghetto.
It is a living eternal memorial.

Published in *The Book of the Ghettos' Wars*, p. 696, Ghetto Fighters' House and Hakibbutz Hameuchad, translator unknown. Courtesy of Gouri's widow, Aliza Gouri.

FIGURE 1. A group of partisans after the liberation of the Vilna area by the Red Army in July 1944. The second row includes Vitka Kempner (first from right), Abba Kovner (center), and Ruzka Korczak (third from right). The photo was taken by a photographers unit led by Jewish-Soviet author and journalist Ilya Ehrenburg.

FIGURE 2. A plaque drawn by Otto Walish in May 1945 calling upon the Yishuv youth to join the Jewish Brigade in order to take revenge on the Germans: "To me Belongeth Vengeance and Recompense."

FIGURE 3. Poldek (Yehuda Maimon), second from right, pictured with others in Jewish Brigade uniforms, on the road to gather Holocaust survivors, July 1945.

FIGURE 4. German prisoners guarded by the Avengers and Jewish Brigade soldiers, July 1945.

FIGURE 5. Abba Kovner (top right) on board the *Champollion* on his way back to Europe with the poison, December 1945.

FIGURE 6. A US military investigation of the bakery close to the Nuremberg prisoners camp after the poisoning of the bread, April 16, 1945.

FIGURE 7. The Avengers in Tradate, Italy, in June 1946, a month before leaving for the Land of Israel. Back row, left to right: Eliezer Lidovski, Yitzhak Ratner, David Bowilski, Manek L., Yashek Ben-Zur, Poldek Wasserman, Yulek Harmatz, Ruvke Schneider, Willek Shenar, and Grushka Agasi. Front row, left to right: Itka, Dushia, Genia, Machush (Michael) Derez, Shimek Lustgarten, Leibke Distel, and Max Wacksler.

FIGURE 8. Landing in Haifa, July 1946.

FIGURE 9. Lena Satz-Hammel's diary.

FIGURE 10.
Dora (Dorka)
Goldreich-Reichmann
(Avidov).

FIGURE 11.
Yitzhak
(Pasha)
Reichman-Avidov.

FIGURE 12.
Pinchas
(Yashek)
Bencelowicz–Ben-Zur.

FIGURE 13.
Dov (Bolek) Ben-Yaʿakov
(Gewirtzman).

FIGURE 14.
Irena
Gelblum.

FIGURE 15.
Rachel
Galperin-Gliksman.

FIGURE 16.
Zygmunt (Zygi)
Gliksman.

FIGURE 17.
Arie Leib (Leibke)
Distel.

FIGURE 18.
Helena (Lena, Lenka)
Satz-Hammel.

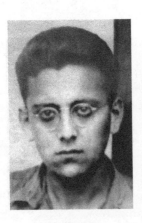

FIGURE 19.
Yitzhak
Hammel.

FIGURE 20.
Mira (Mirka)
Verbin-Shabetzky.

FIGURE 21.
Hasya (Hashka)
Taubes-Warchavchik.

FIGURE 22.
Jechiel (Chilik)
Warchavchik.

FIGURE 23.
Yosef (Yulek)
Harmatz.

FIGURE 24.
Shimon (Shimek)
Lustgarten.

FIGURE 25.
Eliezer
Lidovski.

FIGURE 26.
Levi Yitzhak
(Ludwig) Mairanz.

FIGURE 27.
Yehuda (Poldek)
Maimon (Wasserman).

FIGURE 28.
Moshe
(Manek) L.

FIGURE 29.
Zelda Treger-
Nissanilevich.

FIGURE 30.
Netanel (Senka)
Nissanilevich.

FIGURE 31.
Theodore (Dzhunek)
Dan Hershderfer-Arad.

FIGURE 32.
Yehuda (Idek)
Friedman.

FIGURE 33.
Abba
Kovner.

FIGURE 34.
Reisl (Ruzka)
Korczak-Marla.

FIGURE 35.
Vitka
Kempner-Kovner.

FIGURE 36.
Shlomo
Kantorowicz-Kenet.

FIGURE 37.
Yehiel (Ka-tzetnik)
Feiner–De-Nur.

FIGURE 38.
Bezalel
Kek-Michaeli.

FIGURE 39.
Ze'ev (Velveleh)
Rabinovich.

FIGURE 40.
Zila (Cesia) Rosenberg-Amit.

FIGURE 41.
Simcha (Kazhik) Rathajzer-Rotem.

FIGURE 42.
Yitzhak Ratner.

FIGURE 43.
Ze'ev (Willek) Shutzreich-Shenar.

ATTEMPTED VENGEANCE

4

Palestine and Europe, August 1945–March 1946
Kovner and the Yishuv

THIS CHAPTER WILL DEAL WITH the months of Kovner's stay in Palestine, his meetings there, and the consolidation, during that time, of a stance among the Yishuv leadership with respect to the idea of vengeance. The chapter will also follow Kovner's departure back to Europe aboard a British ship, his arrest as the ship neared the shores of France, his confinement in British prisons in Cairo and Jerusalem, and his release.

What was the nature of the Yishuv when Kovner arrived there to advocate vengeance? At the end of 1945, there were 592,400 Jews in Palestine, and they amounted to 32 percent of the population, the other 68 percent being Arabs, who were both governed by the British Mandate. During the 1930s, roughly 90 percent of the Jewish immigrants to Palestine had arrived from Europe, primarily Poland. The average age was low, because of the immigration of trainee pioneers and young people. The Yishuv was organized with institutions for self-administration that rested on the public's trust in its leadership and on its willingness to volunteer in the face of existing challenges. That significant aspect was already known to Kovner and his associates from their meetings with the Jewish Brigade. A large majority of the Yishuv, roughly 95 percent, was under the umbrella of its largest domestic

Jewish organization, *Knesset Yisrael*, and internal affairs were managed by the Assembly of Representatives and the Jewish National Council. The Jewish Agency was in charge of building the national home, under authority of the Mandate and as a representative of the World Zionist Organization, and it was considered "the government of the state-in-formation." The dominant political party in the Yishuv was Mapai, and the Histadrut—the General Federation of Laborers in the Land of Israel—was the most important force in the economy. The Haganah, the military arm of the national institutions, was linked in an ostensibly unofficial manner to the Jewish civil/political echelons but was fully under their authority. Thus in 1945–46, any decision on behalf of the Yishuv regarding the *Nokmim* was in the hands of David Ben-Gurion, chairman of the Jewish Agency; Dr. Chaim Weizmann, president of the World Zionist Organization; the leaders of the Haganah, Yisrael Galili and Moshe Sneh; the Palmach, led by Yitzhak Sadeh; and the heads of Aliyah B, led by Shaul Avigur.[1]

During the period covered by this chapter, more than ten new settlements were established, and, despite the prohibitions against immigration and the blockading by the British of settlements that had been taking in immigrants, the clandestine immigration to Israel continued unabated. The two breakaway undergrounds, Lehi and the IZL, attacked police buildings, telephone lines, and bridges, and confiscated money and weapons. Constant, bitter tension prevailed between the organized Yishuv's policy of restraint and these two breakaway movements. (Galili, in his correspondence, called them the *sitra achra*, which is the unholy "other side" in the Kabbala.[2])

Some months before Kovner arrived in Palestine, the tension peaked. That time, from December 1944 to February 1945, was called the *saison* (the hunting season), and it was characterized by the struggle between the Haganah and the IZL. This struggle resulted from harsh measures taken by the British, who had warned the leaders of the Yishuv that if the IZL were not reined in, the activities of the Jewish Brigade would be jeopardized and the British Army in Palestine would be forced to enact strict measures against the entire Yishuv. The leaders of the Haganah instructed its troops to turn against the breakaway movements, and the troops kidnapped, detained, and interrogated many of the members of those movements. The Haganah passed information to the British about hundreds of the members, who were then imprisoned and sent to detention camps in Eritrea. When the British felt that the Haganah was assuming too much independence in the campaign, they put an end to it. In addition, there had been strong opposition among the Jewish public to the steps taken during the saison. Throughout the Yishuv, a bitter taste remained from this period, and its aftereffects influenced the attitude toward Kovner, as some soldiers of the Jewish Brigade had come to associate the Nokmim with activism of the breakaway type. Moreover, most of the officers and leaders responsible for the policies enacted during the saison were the very ones whom Kovner had met when he came to Palestine, the ones whom he asked for assistance and understanding.

In response to British policy, especially as directed against clandestine immigration, in October 1945 the Jewish Resistance Movement (or United Resistance Movement), known as the *Meri*, meaning "revolt" in Hebrew, was founded. It included the Haganah, the IZL, and Lehi, despite the severe tensions between them. Within the Meri, the Palmach constituted the strike force of the Haganah. During this time, it participated in field operations, particularly against installations that tracked immigrant ships. The UK foreign secretary, Ernest Bevin, condemned the violence, announced that he would not increase the limit of 1,500 immigration permits per month, and threatened that "if the Jews, with all their sufferings, want to get too much at the head of the queue, you have the danger of another antisemitic reaction" on a broad scale.[3] His words—an offensive parody, given that severe antisemitism on a broad scale was already rampant in Europe following the war—brought about a general strike, with protest rallies and a public fast. A fast day was also declared by the Jewish Brigade in Europe.

After an extensive diplomatic effort by the Yishuv and its leadership, along with pressure from the US, an Anglo-American Committee was established that recommended bringing one hundred thousand displaced persons from Europe to Palestine. The Yishuv was called upon to house the expected immigrants; to raise money "for saving the remnant," a first relief team set out for the displaced persons camps in Germany, under the auspices of the United Nations Relief and Rehabilitation Administration (UNRRA); and extensive procurement and training got underway in anticipation of a Jewish struggle against the Arabs. Among the Jews of Palestine, in the meantime, civic life was highly variegated in terms of political parties and ideologies.

The Yishuv lived modestly, but culture was lively. A building for Habimah, the national theater, was erected; a public scandal erupted over the awarding of a prize for a masterful translation of Goethe's *Faust* from its original German, a language with blood on its hands; and Chanukah celebrations, which hadn't happened since the start of the war, were revived with the carrying of a torch from the graves of the Maccabees.[4]

It was into this ferment that Kovner tumbled in August 1945, when the full tragic picture of the Holocaust was beginning to come into focus. Most of the Yishuv had arrived in the Land of Israel from Central and Eastern Europe before the war and left relatives behind. Some three hundred thousand members of the Yishuv lost their families. Calls for a terrible revenge were expressed in newspapers, on the radio, and at every public meeting. The general opinion, firmly voiced, was that the impure German nation as a whole was responsible and deserved total revenge and a complete ban. But how, and by what means, is there a contradiction between revenge and justice? Would every German person be punished? Kovner was facing a pivotal question: was there a discrepancy between the deep feelings of pain and grief; the desire for revenge on behalf of the individual, the family, and the nation; and the view in the Land of Israel regarding the plan of vengeance that he had brought with him? Had the Holocaust been experienced in the Land of Israel in a way that would enable those there to understand the feelings of the survivors? The answer was not long in coming.

There was a two-sided impetus behind Kovner's trip to Palestine: On the one hand, the leadership of the Yishuv wanted to become acquainted with him, to hear his reasoning, and to ultimately persuade him to accept the "national authority." On the other hand, Kovner himself hoped to receive recognition and support for his plan, to relate the survivors' stories, and to spur preparations for their expected arrival. Thus, when the train from El Arish pulled into Rehovot, members of the Mossad for Aliyah B were waiting for him. They took him to Shaul Avigur's parents' home, where for three days he and Avigur talked; the latter questioned Kovner, paying characteristic warm and friendly close attention to his responses. Yisrael Galili too, one of the Haganah leaders, came to visit, and he must have given an account to Moshe Sneh, who was then the national chief of staff for the Haganah and worked shoulder to shoulder with him. Kovner was cautious. He did not explicitly mention Plan A, and he refrained from using concrete examples, instead speaking in general terms. This first meeting with the Land of Israel and its leadership left Kovner with a bitter taste in his mouth. However, it is clear—and he must have understood this—that the time and attention devoted to him were evidence of the importance that those in the Land of Israel attached to him, to the Hativa, to the idea of vengeance, and to the desire to investigate matters. Avigur may have told Kovner that the issues at play were "too serious to allow him [Kovner] to play politics for himself."[5]

After being released from that marathon meeting, which even the heads of his movement knew nothing about, Kovner began four months of feverish activity in the Land of Israel, from August to December. He knew that his comrades in Europe were anxiously waiting for him to return. Each passing day brought Germany more Allied soldiers, more refugees either passing through or staying a while before continuing on their way, and more Jews arriving at displaced persons camps, so the chances of successfully focusing on one specific population or another were dwindling. Kovner had to establish relationships of trust, enlist support for the plans of vengeance, and obtain the means of carrying them out. His feeling of urgency was out of step with the tenor in the Land of Israel, which swept up newcomers into a whirl of activities, but he never for a moment forgot why he had come. In late August, he sent a letter to Vitka peppering her with questions about how she was doing; about the Nokmim, whom he had left behind, Pasha and Bezalel Kek-Michaeli in particular; and, above all, about the likelihood of finding "our doctor" in Europe—that is, a chemist who could prepare the poison. In a subsequent letter sent only a few weeks after his arrival, Kovner asked again about the latter, this time referring to "the engineer," adding, "I am very pessimistic about the concrete results of my efforts, although the matter is making a strong impression and arousing deep, serious thinking." He concluded the correspondence with the following surprising sentence, exclamation point and all: "Tell Pasha that I require them absolutely [*umbadingt*] to work in full seriousness [*mit der ganze Ernstkeit*] on the second plan!" Is the upshot that Kovner immediately felt Plan A would not be met with understanding? That he may have suspected he would not find the tools he needed to carry it out, or that doubts had begun to eat at him regarding the justification of the plan? In any case, the Land of Israel, the cynosure of the Jewish diaspora, was still strange and unfamiliar to him, and he was being treated as a stranger as well.[6]

Kovner met with a lengthy succession of leaders and organizations, and he spoke to various assemblies. One of the most prominent was a meeting of his movement's secretariat, where shortly after his arrival he gave a very long speech, delivered in installments, that lasted more than a day. The severe matters that he presented were similar, even in their phrasing, to those he presented to the Jewish Brigade in his Tarvisio speech, yet he added an emphasis on recompense, which he saw as a must, a nation's judgment upon a crime against the nation.

Then he continued with a comprehensive survey of the conditions of the surviving Jews in each country of Europe, and he suggested a plan of action that focused mainly on inculcating the same inner disquiet into the Yishuv, uniting all its forces, and immediately bringing the survivors to the Land of Israel—the thousands, the tens of thousands, who were trying to make their way to the homeland. But he did not explain what he meant by "not thinking specifically of armed self-defense," he did not use the word "vengeance," he did not detail the recompense for the crime, and he did not specify the judgment to be pronounced by the nation.[7] If those assembled had any reaction to his words, no record of it exists. However, it isn't hard to imagine the feelings of the leaders sitting opposite Kovner at Kibbutz Merhavia, where the fields were blossoming and the song of building and of future times was in the air, being warned about the immediate threat of knives at their necks, about their children being led to the pyre, and about merging their political forces. Beyond a doubt, Kovner was right that the Land of Israel was alien to him, and vice versa. Certainly he was received there as a foreigner, as a raven of ill omen.

He eagerly read the Hebrew literature that had been written since he and his comrades had been confined in the ghettos. He met with Yitzhak Sadeh, the commander of the Palmach, requested his support for the Nokmim, and won much understanding. Sadeh was "one of the few who realized that there is an essential truth in this madness," Kovner said.[8] Sadeh took Kovner to Nathan Alterman, then the poet laureate, and thenceforward their conversations revolved around the Holocaust and the reaction of the Jewish public and leadership during that time, rather than the subject of vengeance.

Before their meeting, Kovner had become acquainted with Alterman's *Joy of the Poor*. The collection of poems had been written before the war and was published in 1941, after the Yishuv had been seized by a fear for its future, in the wake of the bombing of Tel Aviv and Haifa by the Italian air force in the summer of 1940, which killed more than two hundred people. Italy, as was well known in the Yishuv, was Nazi Germany's ally. Alterman wrote of a Tel Aviv that had been hypothetically conquered by the Germans. His words, although penned three years before the Warsaw Ghetto uprising, and about Tel Aviv, are eerily prophetic. He describes the founding of an underground in one of the ghettos, the comradeship that formed among its members, the revolt that was both transcendent and suicidal: "To Gladness and Joy let our prayer go up—we perish!" This is a quest for meaning in death during rebellion, the likes of which had perhaps not been undertaken in all of Jewish history: "This once in a thousand years, for our death there is morning's light!" In *Joy of the Poor*, Kovner must have read the poem "Prayer for Revenge," which conveys the feeling of humiliation, the back scarred by the whip, and the appeal to God the merciful Father that the spilt blood of his servants be avenged: "Arise, Father! Arise and devour! Be thus the Father that you are! / For the degradation of your servants by their enemies must end!" And when the vengeance succeeds, the poet insists that his God not halt it.[9] But despite that, despite the deep understanding that Kovner found in such poetry for the feelings of the ghetto fighters and the Nokmim, there is no evidence that the two men discussed the subject. Even so, as soon as they were published, the poems of *Joy of the Poor*, including "Prayer for Revenge," became compulsory reading for the contemporary generation.

RUZKA IN THE LAND OF ISRAEL

When Kovner arrived in the Land of Israel, Ruzka Korczak was already there; and the relationships she had formed since her arrival aided his acceptance. Ruzka, it will be recalled, acceded to Kovner's request that she leave Lithuania once it was liberated and contrive a route to Romania. Having succeeded in that, she met emissaries from the Land of Israel in late November 1944 in Bucharest; once they, shocked to tears, heard her description of the Vilna Ghetto, the underground, and the partisans' forest, they decided on the spot to send her to meet the Yishuv. She adamantly resisted: in her opinion, her duty was to return to her comrades, to whom she was linked by every fiber of her spirit, and inform them that the route was open. In counterargument, Moshe Agami, the most senior of the emissaries, pointed out three objectives that required her to travel immediately. First, Avigur, "whom everything depends on," must hear firsthand about the conditions and intentions of the survivors and must prepare for the arrival of waves of refugees into southern Europe. Second, she was told that "in the Yishuv they don't know the situation" and still do not understand the scope of the killing and destruction. (These contentions from Agami strengthened the feeling, which Ruzka had carried since the ghetto, that the Yishuv was unaware of what had happened and that therefore everyone remaining alive was duty-bound to describe and retell it, leaving no stone unturned, in order to inform them.) Third, as a determined partisan, fighter, and member of the underground, and as a young woman with a radiant personality and a winning manner, Ruzka was the right person to keep morale from flagging in the Land of Israel and spread the word that there nonetheless was a future. There were those who had fought and remained alive, and who were set on arriving there.[10]

When Ruzka arrived, she did indeed invest all her energy in describing the Lithuanian Holocaust to various institutions of the Yishuv. She went from place to place, quietly telling the story in Yiddish and singing the songs of the partisans. And she wrote *Flames in Ashes*, a book about the Vilna Ghetto and its underground—an account clearly influenced by Alterman's *Joy of the Poor*. In her talks with many leaders of the Yishuv, she told them about her experiences and discussed questions relating to her comrades in Europe. Amidst all of that, and amidst the difficulties of adjusting to an unfamiliar country and a new home, in Kibbutz Eilon, she eagerly volunteered to help her comrades scattered across Europe after she heard of their plan for vengeance. Ruzka had not undergone the harrowing experience that her friends had of visiting the Majdanek camp near Lublin, where the apparatus of extermination remained intact and terrifying. She had already left by that point. That may be why, in her testimony upon arriving, she repeatedly described the urge to avenge as "the only thought" that impelled her comrades to action. She reached as far back as the days of fighting in the forest, when

German trains were derailed: "All that time, the passion for revenge was the ruling emotion in our lives [. . .] an emotion that never let up and never faded."[11] She spoke in particular of the possibility of vengeance after the Holocaust, in the form of building and creating in the homeland, "thinking of vengeance by means of the handheld plow [. . .] and of our revenge embodied in the value of constructiveness." Even beyond that, she knew that the urge for vengeance was "so foreign to you," as she repeatedly told her listeners.[12]

Roughly eight months after Ruzka arrived, she met Kovner, who told her in detail about the plan for vengeance; she wrote to her comrades in Europe—including, most importantly, her close friend Vitka—that the plan was "something new by way of practical action" but not unexpected. "By the feeling, the conception of the thing, the idea, I wasn't surprised. I see it as a direct continuation of the path, of *our path*. I see it as necessary and as repayment of a debt." From this point on, summer 1945, Ruzka was committed to Kovner's course "heart and soul," especially to convincing the leaders of the movement and of the Yishuv, who already trusted and respected her, that the principles and practice of the concept were just. She saw herself as the voice of those comrades who had stayed behind in Europe, and she may have hoped that the relations she had established and the regard she had earned would net a certain measure of moral support for the idea. Sadeh was one of those whom she had deeply impressed: he took her to meetings attended by Palmach members, and he referred to her as a "Palmach woman from the Diaspora" and himself as a fellow partisan. It may well be that his meetings with Ruzka influenced his attitude toward Kovner and toward his plans. Kovner reviewed the manuscript of *Flames in Ashes*—he even helped her choose the title—and it is not implausible that the work on the manuscript, which chronicled the tragedy of the Vilna Ghetto and the Jewish regiments in the forests, strengthened in both of them the sentiment that the world would not be righted until the question of vengeance found its solution.[13]

Ruzka tried to tip the scale in favor of Kovner and the plan of vengeance, but this attempt was complicated by news that arrived from emissaries who returned from Romania. They were the first who had met the partisans—initially Ruzka in December 1944, and then Kovner and his associates in March 1945. Afterward came reports from Italy, starting in mid-July 1945, when the Nokmim met the Jewish Brigade. For the elite of the Yishuv in general and the leadership of Hashomer Hatzair, all these dispatches, those about the Hativa in particular, were cause for great concern. Evidence of this concern can be seen in an invitation Kovner received as early as the end of August 1945, barely three weeks after his arrival, to a meeting at the Mapai central offices "to discuss matters concerning the Hativa." The meeting apparently took place at the start of September, with the participation of the most central figures in the party's top echelon.[14] Later came vague reports from the Jewish Brigade, through letters and word of mouth from soldiers on leave, about a group organized to wreak terrible vengeance on the Germans, though it was unclear exactly what vengeance and at whose instigation. These worries mingled with broader questions that had been facing the Yishuv since the war but even more so since its end: Who are the survivors? How many are there? How can they be defined? How have they been marked by the Holocaust? (At that point the details of the Holocaust were not yet fully known to the Yishuv.) And thus other questions emerged: how to prepare for the encounter with the survivors and for their absorption into the Land of Israel, and what their place should be in the political plans of the Yishuv.[15]

As the survivors' arrival neared, chief among the concerns of the Yishuv leadership was the question of how to receive the partisans, who had positioned themselves at the head of the survivor community and been accepted, with love and willingness, as their leaders. The partisans were considered a segment of the Soviet fighting force, and in some central blocs of the Yishuv—and certainly in the top echelons of its leftist movements—there was a feeling of solidarity with and sometimes even ardent admiration of the Soviet Union. In the local culture, Russian citizens in general, and perhaps the product of Soviet education in particular, were depicted as warm, openhearted, generous, down-to-earth, and worthy of emulation. On the leftist side of the Yishuv political map, youth and Palmach soldiers sang Russian songs, wore embroidered Russian-style shirts, read *Panpilow's Men* and other Russian wartime classics translated by the finest Hebrew writers in Palestine almost in real time, and were disinclined to heed the words of the Jewish partisans, who had fought under the aegis of the vaunted Red Army: the complaints and sharp criticism the partisans directed against the

Soviet Union were viewed in the Land of Israel as proof that the Holocaust had distorted their discernment and understanding. Second, rumors of the Hativa's existence were interpreted among the left as a distancing from itself, or at least not a continuation of the loyalty to Hashomer Hatzair that had prevailed before the war. Third, because the Jewish Brigade soldiers associated the Nokmim with the breakaway militias of the Land of Israel, a sort of equation was being written in which Nokmim = breakaways = activists with no respect for the national-level command; and in contrast, restraint = the Haganah = responsibility on the public and national level.

MEIR YA'ARI AND THE QUESTION OF VENGEANCE

The concerns and the doubts discussed here were felt by Meir Ya'ari in particular even before he met Kovner in Palestine. They were intensified by letters he received from members of the senior leadership of Hashomer Hatzair in Romania and Hungary and from members of the movement who were soldiers in the Jewish Brigade. The top leaders of Hashomer Hatzair in the Land of Israel were unsettled and fearful that a "horrifying calamity" would beset the movement because of the founding of the Hativa and because of the description of the partisans as outlined in the letters that reached Palestine.[16] Near the end of July 1945, when he was about to set out for London for the first postwar Zionist Congress—and while the Jewish Brigade was preparing to leave Italy and go north and Kovner was expected to make his way to Palestine by sea—Ya'ari sent a dour letter to Yehuda Tubin in Italy. Ya'ari, who had been a soldier in World War I, was fearful of those who did not know how to doff their uniforms and "relearn the colorless heroism of the everyday," those who scorned the home front and in whose hands the *Nagant* (a Russian firearm) might go off by itself. Similar sentiments were expressed by others returning from or living in Europe, such as Antek Zuckerman, in Krakow, who as early as June had sent the members of his movement, Dror-HeHalutz, in Bucharest a harsh letter that later reached the Land of Israel. When Kovner learned of the correspondence later, he considered it a knife in his back. Antek wrote that the partisans radiated a bullying, hooliganist spirit and that if they were not firmly restrained, they would be the first to join the *Terroristen-Bande* or, heaven forbid, turn into criminals. They love the Jews, wrote Antek, "and they would face death for them, but that doesn't prevent them from stopping a carful of Jews and ransacking them from head to toe." Of course, he qualified, they weren't all like that, and he closed by saying that he loved them. The letter strengthened the fears and misgivings about the temperament of the partisans, hostile to authority and quick on the trigger, and the way that might translate into politics. Further accounts were heard at other institutions—at a meeting of the Histadrut Executive Committee, for example—from responsible personalities, such as paratrooper Yoel Nussbacher (later Palgi), who infiltrated Hungary with fellow paratrooper Hannah Szenes, about partisans who weren't ethically compatible with the workers' movement of the Land of Israel and who, if given the requisite resources, would bring an additional element of terrorism that would overshadow the deeds of Lehi.[17]

In addition to all the above, a leader had already been found for them, "a magnetic personality, with a splendid record among the partisans, a man with powers of persuasion who can put a stop to conversation with his own laconic words and ends them with 'ponyato' [Russian for 'understood']. Fate has amused itself with us and hatched a Revisionist demon in Hashomer Hatzair guise," wrote Ya'ari to Tubin. That startling sentence was based on what Ya'ari heard from Ruzka. "She knows," he went on, "that despite their pure hearts and intentions [. . .] they have adopted concepts that are almost fascist." It is certain that Ruzka herself never thought of her comrades in such terms—it would have been terribly insulting to their struggle against fascism in all its forms and to their political stances, which were mainly Socialist and far removed from those of the Revisionist Party. But Ruzka was deeply respected by Ya'ari and his fellow leaders and by Kovner and his comrades, so she took it upon herself to try to bridge the gap. She called upon Ya'ari to amiably listen to the partisans when they arrived, and he assented—on the condition that *they* present themselves amiably. But if they "distance themselves to begin with and try to set up their own organization and their own kibbutz, then of course," Ya'ari threatened, "we will have no choice but to suppress them."[18]

These remarks provide context for the way Ya'ari viewed Kovner before they met, before he heard directly from Kovner about the plan for vengeance. First, he was anxious about the Hativa that Kovner had founded, the idea of which ran contrary to Hashomer Hatzair's self-image of a "singular avant garde." Here was an organization founded by a young leader who had emerged from the ranks of the movement in Europe but had not even consulted the sage of Merhavia before taking action. Second, he was stunned by the fierce anti-Sovietism of Kovner and of the "Asians" who saw him as their leader and obeyed him while assuming the role of central activists in the Bricha. And the Bricha, after all, was a proclamation that the Jews remaining in Eastern Europe believed that there was no future for them under a Communist regime and that they must quickly flee—a conviction that the Hashomer Hatzair leadership considered heresy. The Bricha was also a proclamation that there was no rebuilding of the movement in Soviet-dominated Eastern Europe, especially not in Poland, the cradle of the movement. Ya'ari took this revelation badly. He was still unaware that most of the Hashomer Hatzair members had been killed in the rebellions and in the forests and that there was no core of members to accomplish the rebuilding.

Thus, it could be said that those trepidations on the part of Ya'ari, before his meeting with Kovner, were already generating in him deep suspicions of the man, ones that perhaps influenced his attitude toward vengeance. He may also have feared Kovner's charisma. When the letters arrived from the Jewish Brigade, Shaike Weinberg testified, Ya'ari "was maddened upon hearing of the union [the Hativa] and ran straight to Ruzka to hear from her who Kovner was"—and it appears that the rumors initially engendered exaggeration of the size and power of the Hativa.[19] Only a year or so later was Ya'ari able to voice a definition of the actual role of Hashomer Hatzair in Europe, with a short and telling motto: "To be a compass for those who leave and an anchor for those who stay." In that aphorism there was a certain compromise between himself and Kovner.[20]

On September 17, 1945, which was Yom Kippur, the Day of Atonement, a few weeks after Kovner arrived in Palestine, the two men met in Merhavia for an uninterrupted eleven-hour conversation, with Ruzka in attendance. It was the first session of a dialogue that continued until their deaths in 1987. From the outset, each was uncompromisingly grappling with someone whom he deeply respected despite, or perhaps because of, trenchantly arguing every question of principle for more than forty years. After the meeting, Kovner wrote to Pinchas Gruner, who was one of the Hashomer Hatzair members in the Jewish Brigade: "One thing is clear to me, we'll be joining forces." And he expressed the hope that Ya'ari, whom he recognized as a great Jewish leader, would adjust the movement's direction to the new postwar reality that faced the Jewish people. However, Ruzka had more reserved hopes regarding the movement's future direction.[21] This aspect of their relationship, based on mutual esteem, would come to the fore when Kovner, imprisoned in Egypt by the British, clung from afar to the figure of Ya'ari with all his might.

Apparently Kovner did not mention vengeance in that first conversation with Ya'ari, even though Ruzka was present—or perhaps, on the contrary, because she was. She ardently supported vengeance, but after a few months in Israel she was able to discern the point of view held by the Yishuv and its leaders and "the tension and the readiness to sacrifice," and she sensed that "the struggle . . . concerns itself with life and not with death, and in this struggle everyone is willing to stand or fall."[22] Kovner looked forward to an additional meeting, since for his purposes the opinion of Ya'ari, the head of the movement, was of utmost importance. His plan had become the purpose of his existence, and so he needed to carefully consider every step he took.

Kovner didn't know that half a year earlier, when he was still in Lublin, Ya'ari had already taken a position on vengeance, while speaking to Yehuda Ben-Horin and soldiers of the German Unit who were about to join the Jewish Brigade. In February 1945, before the German Unit was due to set out for Egypt, and thence to Italy, Ben-Horin met Ya'ari in Palestine for a long talk. It was apparently the first time Ya'ari had discussed vengeance. After their conversation, there was a farewell meeting in which Ya'ari commended the soldiers of the unit, who, within weeks, would be at the front. He told his listeners that in their long conversation, Ben-Horin had called for the establishment of "an Order of Avengers that would redeem the blood of the millions. This talk was one of my most profound experiences during the years of that war. And Y. [Ben-Horin] made good, as the members of our movement characteristically make good. He and his comrades were entrusted to serve as the core troop of avengers in the Hativa [meaning the Jewish Brigade]." That was how Ya'ari recounted the enlistment of the German Unit in the Brigade's actions of vengeance, which he had certainly learned of from Ben-Horin. He added: "We don't distinguish between the masses of the German

nation and a few rabble-rousing leaders. There is no tight pinnacle of Nazism, there is an enormous swath," and there was no telling when the poison would dissipate from it. On that occasion, he didn't call for indiscriminate vengeance against the German people, but he said explicitly, "We have
not strayed after the temptations of forgiveness," and he sent the soldiers off
on their mission "with love, faith, and confidence." Those words were published in the movement's journal *Mishmar* shortly afterward, and some years
later in *The Book of Hashomer Hatzair*, where they were titled "Be the Core
Troop of Avengers!" Yet they faded from memory.[23] Ya'ari, they show, did
not oppose the Jewish Brigade's approach to vengeance and did not propose
forgiveness for the German nation in general.

Ben-Horin set out with the soldiers of the German Unit, and in July
1945 they met the partisans who had, as described in the previous chapter,
come to the Jewish Brigade. After that introduction, "we were under growing pressure from [. . .] the partisans to mount large-scale missions of vengeance inside Germany," wrote Ben-Horin, adding that the officers of the
Jewish Brigade found such activity repellent. He personally felt great apprehension that the partisans, in their hopelessness, would commit such acts on
their own, so his preference was that "we should take charge of this"—"we"
apparently referred to both the Jewish Brigade and the German Unit. After Kovner left for Palestine in August and the Jewish Brigade moved north
to Holland and Belgium, Ben-Horin occasionally met with Pasha, who was
taking Kovner's place. According to Ben-Horin, Pasha continued with the
same demands that Kovner had, and tension developed between the partisans and the Jewish Brigade's command. Although there was mutual understanding between Pasha and Ben-Horin because of their shared Communist background, when the tension peaked, Ben-Horin traveled to Palestine,
on special home leave at his own request and with his commanders' approval, in order to consult with the leaders of the Haganah and of Hashomer Hatzair regarding the missions of vengeance.[24] Obviously this indicates
a state of alert, unbroken since Kovner's "house arrest" at Shaul Avigur's parents' home: the leadership of the Jewish Brigade and of the Haganah both
devoted full attention to the Nokmim and refused to let matters take an
uncontrolled course. Thus, the commander of an important unit traveled
to Palestine for consultations, although the Jewish Brigade still had many

duties to fulfill (duties it continued to fulfill for almost an entire year afterward) and the means of communication and transport were still convoluted and time-consuming.

When Ben-Horin arrived in Palestine—he didn't specify the date, but it was apparently in September 1945, a month or so after Kovner came—he told the Yishuv's leaders about the moral and practical uncertainties of vengeance that troubled the soldiers of the Jewish Brigade and the German Unit, as well as about the operations that had been carried out thus far, actions that, as mentioned, had been directed individually at Nazis whose guilt was beyond doubt. By all indications, it was Ben-Horin who conveyed to the Haganah leaders, and to Ya'ari and Ya'akov Hazan, the leaders of the movement, as much as he knew about Plan A. To his gratification, he found them all, from Galili and Sneh to Hazan and Ya'ari, agreeable to the approach that had emerged in the Jewish Brigade and in the German Unit, an approach that he also supported: to execute as much vengeance as possible upon the Nazis, but on them alone—that is, against those individuals found guilty, and without harming the activities of rescue and of immigration to the Land of Israel.[25]

Meanwhile, Kovner met again with Ya'ari, who was also firmly committed to that approach. Although, according to Kovner, Ya'ari was shocked by the plans of the Nokmim, Ya'ari calmed himself and gave Kovner his approval at the level of Plan B.[26] To Kovner's surprise, vengeance did not stand out as a point of argument in that conversation: "He said, 'I don't want to hear details. If Yehuda Ben-Horin is on board with it, I approve.'" Mordechai Roseman claimed, in retrospect, that Ya'ari was not really comfortable with vengeance; however, at that time it was seen as despicable for someone who had not experienced the Holocaust to display open opposition. "I'm sure that Ya'ari mutely disagreed in his heart, but no one had the nerve to say to Kovner, 'Forget it.'"[27] A kind of lip service was paid to the principle. A Hashomer Hatzair newsletter stated, after the Jewish Brigade had returned to Palestine, that "the creation of the Brigade served to change our course [as a movement]. The call for vengeance and the encounter with the Diaspora [...] became a reality, to the joy of us all."[28] In any case, Ya'ari provided not "any hint at all" of his position on vengeance to the Hashomer Hatzair members of the Jewish Brigade, such as Tubin, Moshe Zilbertal, and Weinberg, even though they had been waiting for months for him to express it. They were even hoping that Ruzka would come to Europe from Palestine with Ben-Horin, but they received no answer in that regard either.[29]

KOVNER'S MEETINGS WITH BEN-HORIN,
BEN-GURION, GALILI, SNEH, AND SHIMON AVIDAN

Ben-Horin agreed to be the Haganah appointee in charge of vengeance operations and in charge of official relations with Kovner's group of Nokmim, who had stayed in Europe. He was preparing to return to the Jewish Brigade with clear instructions after guidelines for action had been, by his account, formulated by the Yishuv leaders. Kovner, it will be recalled, had arrived in Palestine at the start of August. He met with Ben-Horin, and doubtless Ben-Horin made his appointment known to Kovner. Thus, Kovner was aware that the Yishuv's institutions meant to curtail the freedom and independence of the Nokmim by giving the responsibility of inspecting vengeance operations to a man acceptable to those institutions and to the Haganah. However, it is not clear whether Kovner passed along this information to Pasha, with whom Ben-Horin had already met more than once, and to the rest of the Nokmim. In any case, Kovner's letters to Vitka and to the leaders of the Nokmim in Europe make no mention of Ben-Horin. What Kovner himself thought of the inspection officially imposed upon him and his comrades is certainly a question. Ben-Horin understood the difficulty: it was not assumed that the Haganah commanders, located in Palestine, were in a position to give orders to all the Jews of the Diaspora, he said. And so Kovner was invited to meet Ben-Gurion, and then Kovner met the leaders of his own movement, beginning with Ya'ari and continuing with Hazan, with whom he established a friendly relationship; together, they induced Kovner to accept the ruling, at least ostensibly. "Our attitude, mutually, was 'Respect him but suspect him,'" Ben-Horin recounted, "and I was never sure how thoroughly he accepted the orders." Ben-Horin returned to Europe and found that the Brigade's officers gladly left this troublesome sphere of responsibility to him.[30]

Kovner described his meeting with Ben-Gurion as dealing with other topics. He wrote later that it was a very lengthy conversation, that he opened it with a description of the Holocaust, and Ben-Gurion spoke of Soviet antisemitism in the forests and of the possibility that in the Land of Israel Kovner might take on the role of a youth leader with the membership of Mapai. Kovner responded that he was still a member of Hashomer Hatzair, that he was a leader only for the duration of the emergency, and that he was dedicating himself to one purpose only—though, as Kovner's testimony states, the issue of vengeance did not explicitly come up in their conversation. According to the schedules of Ben-Gurion and Kovner that summer, the conversation could have occurred only in the two weeks between November 21, 1945, and Kovner's departure for Europe at the start of December. Ben-Gurion had left Palestine on June 10, 1945, and stayed alternately in Europe and the US in the intervening months before returning to Palestine on November 21, after his well-known visit to the DP camps. Despite energetic searching, no record of the conversation could be found in Ben-Gurion's diaries or in his rich archives, nor is there any record of his stance regarding vengeance. We remain facing the contradiction between the topics of their conversation according to Kovner and according to the testimony of Ben-Horin, which claims that Kovner was brought to meet Ben-Gurion so that Ben-Gurion could bring him to heel and explain the limits of vengeance to him. How could it happen that Ben-Gurion never asked him about the purpose that Kovner was dedicating his life to? After all, Avigur was his right-hand man, and the members of Mapai in the Jewish Brigade, such as Mordechai Surkis and Meir Argov, kept him constantly updated; they had sent Kovner to Palestine to meet Ben-Gurion. Even without an archival document attesting to this, it may be assumed that if Ben-Gurion had considered vengeance a correct action to be undertaken immediately, he would have given appropriate instructions and put the mechanisms of the Yishuv into action, with consequences that would echo into the present. In any case, this meeting too left Kovner with a bitter taste in his mouth, and he felt it added an element of delay and distrust to the handling of his requests.[31]

Meanwhile, Kovner continued having meetings about vengeance. He spoke with Galili and with Sneh, who both expressed solidarity and understanding with respect to the matter, though no more than that, and without revealing that they were already aware of Plan A. In his meetings with them, Kovner asked about procuring particularly effective poison—an odorless, tasteless substance that would dissolve in water and leave no trace—believing that it would be difficult to obtain it in Europe, as well as assistance in the form of reinforcements: a vehicle for the group's transportation needs in Europe, and an order from the Haganah that the avenging mission in Europe was not to be disrupted. Kovner vowed that for their part, the Nokmim would operate without involving any elements of official Jewry, whether in the Land of Israel or in the Diaspora, and that if they were arrested and tried, they would assume full responsibility. Galili promised Kovner that he would make Haganah liaison officers available in Europe and would see to arrangements for Kovner's return there, provided that Kovner accept the authority of the Haganah and that the Nokmim carry out only Plan B, which targeted camps where SS veterans were concentrated. As for the poison, Kovner would have to seek it elsewhere. Kovner realized that "for the idea of poisoning the wells of cities, approval can be found among perhaps three people only," but even those people were trying to persuade him to bring the Nokmim home to the Land of Israel. They had done their duty, they were tired, and "we will take care of it." Again the scenario arose, as it had from the mouths of Shlomo Shamir and Ben-Horin, that "we," the Haganah, which had authority over the Jewish Brigade, "will take care of it" instead of the Nokmim.[32]

Kovner accepted the conditions, but Ben-Horin could sense that the acceptance was a sham. "I admit and confess that with Galili, with Sneh, and with Shaul I was two-faced. I agreed dishonestly. I sent a coded message telling my comrades in Europe not to talk with anyone about Plan A until I arrived." Kovner wrote those words three or so months before he died, in a document that he asked to have deposited in the archives in Israel. It contained his summation of the chief events of the affair. The document clearly indicates that he intended to continue with Plan A, in contradiction of the assurances he had given and with the knowledge that the plan had not been approved. "I lied with a clear conscience," he said, years later, to his comrades in Israel. "Not for a moment, even until now, have I had any doubt that Plan A was correct and was a necessity." After meeting with the leaders mentioned above, Kovner met with Shimon Avidan, who understood him and supported him in his solitude among the Yishuv, and they became fast friends. Afterward, Kovner said that he might have behaved differently had he met Avidan to begin with, before meeting the others.[33]

In mentioning a coded instruction he sent to his comrades in Europe, Kovner was referring to ongoing correspondence that started at the port where he departed from Italy. The correspondence continued throughout his stay in Palestine, primarily by means of soldiers serving in the British army and the Jewish Brigade, as well as emissaries from the Land of Israel. The letters were addressed to Vitka, and she read them aloud to Pasha and Kek-Michaeli. Such procedures were common at the time because the war had disrupted the mail service, but the system must have negatively impacted Pasha's standing as Kovner's replacement during his absence. The letters included a growing number of terms that constituted code readily understood by the recipients: the revenge operation was called the "educational program"; the camps housing the SS veterans were called "children's houses," as on a kibbutz; the prison was called the "hospital"; the poison "medicine"; and the chemist or engineer who would prepare it the "doctor." Pasha was called Izya, Kek-Michaeli was Danny, Vitka was Yehudith, and Kovner himself Yehuda or Uri. Vengeance, as a concept, was named Hadassah, the name of Kovner's first girlfriend, and similarly, Kovner was sometimes referred to as Hadas. In the Bible, Hadassah was the Hebrew name of Queen Esther, while the name "Esther" itself resembles the Hebrew word for concealment (hester)—and she indeed concealed her ethnicity in order to save her people. In the Yishuv at the time, code names were common for members of the undergrounds and leaders of the Yishuv, for their operations, and for the locations where they stayed; the use of nicknames and antiphrasis was a regular practice, particularly in correspondence, to avoid detection by the British.[34]

On September 8, with the Rosh Hashanah (New Year) holiday beginning the Hebrew year 5706 and having been in the country for roughly a month, Kovner referred to "the most important thing for our purpose" in another clear order, in which he once more wrote of prioritizing Plan B. He mentioned that he "categorically" wanted Pasha to make the best use of his time for preparing Plan B. "This does not mean abandoning the first one (no!)," but the search for the means to implement Plan A had not yet ended, and it would involve great effort and long, difficult preparations. Still, he expressed a New Year's wish for a "grand achievement." In this letter and subsequent ones, Kovner continued instructing his comrades to take action without the assistance of others, to independently assemble the tools for the job, and to form no additional ties. Once more, his desire to work without the members of the Haganah, and to not submit to their authority, is evident. The reason for this may be that at his meetings it had already been made clear to him that the independence of the Nokmim was considered undesirable by the leadership of the Yishuv. Kovner did instruct his comrades once more, at all costs, to find the "engineer," or the "doctor"—meaning Yitzhak Ratner, a veteran of the Vilna Ghetto underground, and a chemist by training, who could help them prepare or procure the necessary poison.[35] Chapter 6 will deal with the Nokmim in Germany, this instruction, and the way Pasha and the other Nokmim responded to it.

Chaim Weizmann, Ephraim Katzir, and the Poison

In addition, Kovner continued to search for financial backing and for a suitable poison once he realized that Sneh and Galili would not fulfill his request. His letters show him exerting himself, hurrying about, and even imposing a tactical hiatus on himself; for a month or so, he did nothing about the mission because he didn't want to trigger an irreversible refusal.[36] In later descriptions of the meetings where he discussed vengeance with leaders and public figures, he gives exceptional attention to a dialogue with Dr. Chaim Weizmann, then president of the World Zionist Organization, at a meeting he says was arranged by Mordechai Shenhavi of Kibbutz Mishmar HaEmek. Shenhavi had already set up a meeting with Weizmann for Ruzka in February 1945, a few months after she arrived in the Land of Israel, and that meeting had been long and friendly. She gave him an account of the Holocaust, and he listened attentively, allowing no interruptions.[37] According to Kovner, Shenhavi—of whom Ruzka spoke highly—was the one who had suggested, in September 1945, that he meet Weizmann. Kovner describes Weizmann as listening silently, as if closed off, and then finally saying that if he were younger and in the position of Kovner and the Nokmim, he would have acted similarly. Kovner wrote that Weizmann referred him to Professor Ernst David Bergmann, a pioneer of nuclear research. Bergmann in turn tasked the brothers Aharon and Ephraim Katchalsky (later Katzir) with preparing the requested substance. They accomplished the task in two months, knowing of no more than Plan B, like Bergmann. In addition, Weizmann permitted Kovner to use his name in approaching industrialist Hans Moller, owner of the ATA textile works, and Moller gave him a sum of money that Kovner converted into gold coins. This much appears in Kovner's testimonies regarding the meeting.[38]

However, there is no mention in Weizmann's diary—or in his memoirs or archive—of his meeting Kovner in summer 1945. Any such evidence would be surprising because Weizmann was not in Palestine during those months. In fact, during the war years he was absent from Palestine most of the time. In March 1945 he left for London, and from there he proceeded to the US for November and December, finally returning to Palestine from London at the end of February 1946. Kovner had already embarked for Europe at the start of December 1945. Bergmann's biographers refer briefly to the poison issue and describe it as "accusations and rumors" that any scientist serving the security needs of a nation could fall prey to. Shenhavi's biography doesn't mention the meeting; Kovner appears in it only briefly, in other contexts.[39] And Ruzka, who had visited Weizmann at Shenhavi's suggestion and later went with Kovner to an important visit to Ya'ari, writes nothing about visiting Weizmann with Kovner. One would have expected her to accompany him, as she did in the case of Ya'ari, and at least mention it in her testimony.

Historian Yehuda Bauer, who took a long testimony from Kovner in 1964 regarding the Bricha and the Nokmim, deposited the lines of testimony describing the meeting into Weitzmann's archive on the condition, stipulated by Kovner, that they be archived as confidential material and exposed to no one without his consent. In a letter accompanying that section of testimony, Bauer wrote, with justifiable caution, that the meeting between Weizmann and Kovner had taken place "in Rehovot in 1945 (apparently)." Indeed, today the only existing indication of the Kovner-Weizmann meeting, other than Kovner's own testimony, is a peculiar-looking card in the Weizmann Archives. It also came by way of Bauer, in 1965, with the lines of testimony and the letter; it is dated March 1, 1946, and on it, written in English, are Kovner's name and the words "Talk with Dr. W." The number 6,000,000 appears in parentheses, in order to indicate that the six million were the topic of their conversation.[40] It may be assumed, then, that Kovner and Weizmann did meet at Weizmann's home in Rehovot. Be it not said that Kovner's imagination invented that meeting. Yet it happened not in summer

1945 but rather after March 10, 1946, that is, after Weizmann returned from the US by way of London at the end of February and after Kovner was released from the British prison in Jerusalem—an episode that will come up shortly. According to the testimony of Jewish prisoners who were incarcerated with him at the central prison in the Russian Compound, Kovner was released during the second week of March. Kovner himself, in a testimony given later to Sarid, specified that March 15 was the approximate date of the meeting or of his release. So there is a discrepancy between the date on the card and Kovner's release date: clearly on March 1 he was still in prison.[41]

The date of the meeting in which the two men spoke of the six million has decisive importance in the scenario of the poison's procurement and in the question of whether Weizmann was involved. Professor Katzir, later the fourth president of the State of Israel, testified to me in 1998, confirmed by his signature, and later wrote in his autobiography that in summer 1945 he and his brother Aharon were research assistants in the Department of Organic and Micromolecular Chemistry at the Hebrew University of Jerusalem. One day that summer, a student of Aharon's, Yehiam Weitz, a member of Hashomer Hatzair, introduced Ruzka and Kovner as fighters and Holocaust survivors, and in Ephraim's words, "they began an abbreviated account of [. . .] the ghettos and the extermination camps, as well as the desperate efforts by small groups to rise up against the Nazis." It was the first time the brothers had been told about the Holocaust in such a shocking, firsthand way: "We had heard something previously, but it seems that only then [. . .] were we exposed to the true story." Kovner told them about the plan for vengeance against SS veterans who were imprisoned by the Allies, and he emphasized that such an operation had sheerly symbolic value.

> We had no disagreements with him. We were old hands in the Haganah, and we'd been educated that Jews must actively defend themselves. It was immediately plain to us that we would be helping Abba Kovner as much as we could. Aharon and I approached the man in charge of the university's chemical warehouse [. . .] who was also in the Haganah, and he agreed without hesitation too. Together with him, we made a list of effective poisons that he could obtain. He assembled them and relayed them through us to Abba Kovner.

One milligram of these substances was downright fatal, said Katzir, and Kovner said the quantity was enough for Plan A twice over.[42]

In that same 1998 interview of mine with Katzir—a conversation that was recorded and transcribed, then signed by Katzir himself in the presence of another witness—Katzir was surprised to hear that the furnishing of poison for Kovner's use was ascribed to Weizmann: "That attribution is baseless, not only because the poisons reached Abba Kovner in the way already described but also because that entire approach was in complete opposition to Weizmann's worldview. He was unenthusiastic, to say the least, about that kind of operation, and certainly about the involvement of scientists in such operations." At this point, Katzir provided some examples touching especially on Weizmann's opposition to attempts at preparing unconventional chemical and biological weapons before the War of Independence: "In any case, Aharon and I never discussed this business with him. In summer 1945 we didn't even know him personally." The brothers arrived at the institute in Rehovot, which at the time was named for Daniel Sieff, in 1948. All these details indicate that Aharon and Ephraim Katzir weren't under orders from anyone—certainly not from Weizmann, as he was out of the country and couldn't have given orders to Bergmann anyway. The brothers weren't connected with the institute in Rehovot, they were unaware of Plan A, and as young men active in defense matters, it wouldn't have occurred to them that a full-fledged assault on SS veterans required any authorization at all. Two or three days after their meeting, Kovner dropped by in person to appropriate the poison, and for years the brothers knew nothing about what became of it.[43]

In fact, Kovner told Vitka in a letter at the start of October that he had already found a "specialist doctor" with a "hospital" (that is, a laboratory) who was wholeheartedly willing to help and that Kovner would be traveling to Jerusalem (not Rehovot) early the following morning to meet him. In another testimony, Kovner mentioned Mount Scopus, the location of the Hebrew University at the time. Regarding the financing that he wished to obtain and bring back to Europe, he wrote that he had finally found "a hand extended by one of our good acquaintances—a paragon in Zion!" He hoped this acquaintance would help him approach a philanthropist who, in turn, might provide continuing support, even in cash. Kovner mentioned that the philanthropist didn't want to be identified, so Kovner identified neither him nor the good and helpful acquaintance. On only one occasion did Kovner tell his comrades that the poison had taken some two months to prepare, not merely a day or two. Two members of the Haganah had called him to a cache where the poison had been stored, packed in powdered and condensed milk cans, and they asked him whether the packing was satisfactory. Afterward, when he had received the gold coins from Moller, the Haganah paymaster slipped them into a tube of toothpaste or shaving cream. As Kovner mentioned in his testimony, the Haganah knew exactly what he had received and from whom, as well as what he had taken with him.[44]

Did Kovner meet Weizmann in spring 1946—in the middle of March, upon his release from prison, after three months of being isolated from his comrades with no news of their activities? Perhaps, then, he might have related Plan A to Weizmann on the level of possibility or theory, since he didn't ask Weizmann for anything and didn't even know, for his own part, where matters stood. There is no clear answer or testimony in that regard; Weizmann didn't mention such a meeting in his diary or in his many letters, and Kovner was aware that he must be careful to speak to the leaders of the Yishuv about Plan B only. The American journalist Michael Elkins, a good friend of Kovner's, quoted Kovner as saying he had indeed spoken with Weizmann about Plan A out of a desire to give the German people a taste of "the same agony," and Kovner recommended Elkins's book as a reliable source on the question of vengeance.[45] Perhaps at that long and noncommittal meeting in which Kovner, recently released from prison, didn't ask for anything, Weizmann replied hypothetically that if he were a young survivor he might think similarly. However, Kovner said repeatedly and in testimony that he met Weizmann in summer 1945 and that he was presented with the poison upon Weizmann's instructions.[46]

Is it possible that Kovner approached Weizmann and requested such and such a poison that would kill millions? And if he asked for poison that would kill only some tens of thousands, is it reasonable that Weizmann would respond favorably right away, with an instruction to Bergmann and others, without consulting anyone else in the Yishuv leadership about such a fateful proposal? Without explaining that he had to consult and think before he could respond to the request? To that improbability, it must also be added that Weizmann followed a pro-British policy all his life and such a revenge operation, under the nose of the British Army in the British-occupied zone of Germany, would have dealt a palpable blow to relations with them. Aharon and Ephraim Katzir were young Haganah members, and they met Kovner the young partisan but not Weizmann the president of the World Zionist Organization, whose office carried authority and obligations. And Kovner spoke with the brothers about an assault on SS veterans only. It should also be borne in mind that Bergmann was close to Ben-Gurion and advised him on scientific matters, which were Bergmann's expertise; therefore, if he had received such an instruction from Weizmann, it may be assumed that he would have revealed it to Ben-Gurion, who opposed vengeance.

A meeting with Weizmann, and his approval for vengeance, would have legitimized the Nokmim and incorporated them into the Yishuv. If Weizmann had been in agreement with them, his word would have dictated the attitude toward the Nokmim in the Land of Israel then and for generations to come. In that case, the Nokmim would have felt among the Yishuv not like a foreign minority but like a group embraced by the admired president of the World Zionist Organization. Elkins, having spoken with Kovner, wrote: "A man honored as none other by the Jewish people had given moral backing to help answer the question that had unnerved them [. . .]—'Who set you as leaders among us?'" However, Elkins does not specify the date or place of the meeting.[47] Elkins's book, with the paragraph about Weizmann, came to the notice of Zalman Shazar, who was president of Israel from 1963 to 1973, and he was shocked at the story. Fearing it would besmirch the presidency of the country, he wrote to Yulek Harmatz, insisting that the veterans of the Nokmim thoroughly deny that it was Katzir who had given them the poison, which they did not.[48]

Hanoch Bartov, who visited Kovner in the 1960s at a resort on the Carmel mountain, heard the story of Kovner's being referred to Bergmann and of Weizmann remarking, "If I were your age, I'd do the same thing." Bartov recounted, in retrospect, that the partisans were loyal, upstanding comrades one and all—including Ruzka, with her "purity and wisdom"—and that because they had lived so intensely with one another in wartime, if Kovner had told them anything untrue, they would have rejected his leadership. They were all convinced, and to this day remain convinced, that Kovner's account was correct. Bartov is certainly right that complete trust is necessary between leader and followers, and all the more so regarding someone of Kovner's stature as a human being and as a leader—with the exception of the vengeance scenario. Vengeance was aflame in Kovner's very body, an overriding imperative for righting the moral order. His behavior toward James Ben-Gal demonstrated that; so did his own written admission that he was not honest with Avigur, Sneh, and Galili; and so do the details that he reported regarding his meeting with Weizmann and the peculiar card that was deposited in the archive. They all indicate that apparently the issue of vengeance must be seen as constituting an episode different from, and atypical of, the rest of Kovner's life and behavior. He could not bear the thought that the world would return to routine after the appalling crime of the Holocaust without justice being visited on the foremost criminals, the German nation. Kovner was a person of exceptional stature, as everyone who knew him agrees. Yulek, at the age of ninety, said, "I never met such another man in my life." Pasha also said so, until his dying day.[49]

The Consolidation of the Yishuv Leadership's Stance

The meetings of Kovner and Ben-Horin with the leaders of the Yishuv provided clear evidence that the top officials of the Yishuv and the Haganah were aware of Plan A. The secret may have leaked into the Land of Israel by way of the Jewish Brigade's soldiers, and it may be that Kovner spoke to them about "the transcendental aspect of it," as he said he did to a certain few, whom he refrained from naming. It may be inferred that he meant Avigur, Galili, and Sneh (from whom he requested the poison); Ya'ari (who was shocked by the idea); Sadeh and Avidan; and perhaps Weizmann too, whom he did meet later. In a nutshell, a number of the Yishuv's top leaders stepped forward to help Kovner, but only with Plan B.[50]

It is also clear that among the leaders of the Yishuv, none agreed in any way with Plan A, at any stage. On the contrary, they all stipulated the condition clearly: "Plan B only." Kovner's personality impressed Sadeh, Baruch Rabinow—another Haganah central figure—and Avidan more than it impressed the others, and according to Kovner, they "profoundly understood the intent of vengeance and embraced it." But they—even Avidan, who later undertook a revenge operation of his own—expressed solidarity and understanding without discussing or advancing Plan A. "The approach of Kovner and his band, who favored indiscriminate revenge, was unacceptable to me," Avidan said.[51] Ben-Gurion had obvious priorities that were shared by his fellow leaders, by most of the soldiers in the Jewish Brigade and in the British Army, and by the emissaries sent to Europe: the refugees must be rehabilitated and brought to the Land of Israel for the sake of their welfare and of the state's creation—which are inseparable.

Sneh headed the national command of the Haganah from 1941 to 1946. In a 1967 interview, he spoke in retrospect of the attempt by the Yishuv's leadership to formulate a policy on vengeance. He too believed, like the rest of the leadership, that the matter was embroiled at the time with the other matter of preparing for the influx of refugees. He said frankly that he believed the underground groups that had begun to form in Europe at the end of the war, including partisans and anti-Nazi underground fighters, were aiming to wreak revenge on the Germans but had another objective as well: to preserve the interpersonal and social structures that had been established in wartime.[52] Sneh's tone implies that the goal of preserving those structures was counterproductive, and such an attitude indicates an unfortunate failure of understanding on the part of the Yishuv's leadership, including Sneh himself, regarding the position of the survivors. His tone even clashes with other statements that he made in the same interview to the effect that the leadership was aware of the terrible trauma experienced by those people. Did this leadership ask itself why, having lost their families, their homes, their communities, and the other collectives of which they were members, and being left only with the few friendships, forged literally in blood and fire, that now served as family, the survivors would want to give them up? Why should they not continue to follow the leaders who had proven themselves in the most difficult of times, even if forces beyond those leaders' control had led to occasional failures? Sometimes, when they came to the Land of Israel, partisans set conditions for joining the War of Independence—only together, in the same platoon or company—because their friends were all they had left. Anyone associated with the survivors, and certainly with the groups of partisans and Avengers, knows that to this day, even as grandparents in the plenitude of their years, they consider the friendship among them to be the air they breathe.[53]

"Many of those fighters simply didn't know what to do with them-selves," Sneh continued. "Idiosyncratic groups sprang up, like the Nokmim led by Abba Kovner, whose agenda did not seem useful or constructive to us." The expression "sprang up," implying an appearance ex nihilo at the war's end, shows again that Sneh did not understand the groups as a contin-uation from the days of the ghetto, the forest, the camps, and the roads that were wandered between them. He didn't understand that the Nokmim, and above all else the very urge to vengeance, were rooted in the events of the Holocaust. Sneh makes no reference to the source of the fiery passion for revenge, or even to that passion itself. He contends that those people had no direction, because they completely rejected political party allegiance and that what they all had in common was a "unitary national, unitary Jewish outlook." His statement is astonishing, all the more so for being voiced not immediately after the war but more than twenty years later. Is it really a ter-rible sin to adopt a unitary national, unitary Jewish outlook? And does it, moreover, demonstrate a lack of direction? Even if we take into account that at the time of the interview Sneh was already leading MAKI (the Israeli Communist Party) and communism rejects nationalism, there was an im-perviousness here to the feelings of the survivors, and his words lacked hu-man empathy.

Thus the Jewish national vision that underlay the founding of the Ha-tiva, the East European Survivors' Brigade, was understood not as a neces-sary lesson to be learned from the Holocaust but as the dismantling of a framework by people unable to regain their footing in life after a great di-saster. As Muki Tzur, the historian of the Kibbutzim movement, put it as-tutely, in the Land of Israel there was a failure to realize that their identity as Holocaust survivors was deeper than their political identity, which, al-though dating farther back, had lost its significance to them.[54] The leader-ship, Sneh testified, feared that survivors might descend to extreme actions, and so it considered that the solution to their plight must be found within its own eyeshot. The decision was to try to funnel "the enormous accumula-tion of national/Jewish/fighting energy into constructive channels" by send-ing delegates and resources from the Land of Israel to establish a European self-defense organization for the Bricha campaign that would train young people in weaponry and combat but first and foremost protect the Jews who were living in the shadow of immediate lethal danger from murderous gangs and individuals.[55]

A few years later, one of the volumes of *The History of the Haganah* published remarks similar in content to those in the abovementioned Sneh interview but more sharply worded. It should be remembered that Sneh headed the national command of the Haganah for years, and the book's editors, who included Shaul Avigur, still embraced the narrative that during World War II, Jewish underground groups rose up and operated within the overall framework of the partisan movement—the writers, like Sneh, do not mention the ghetto fighters among them—and that after the war, their members found themselves idle in refugee camps and having constant friction with the despised German population. In the Yishuv, there was concern that irresponsible elements would exploit the rage, despair, and thirst for revenge among the survivors, beginning with the partisans, in order to mount impetuous attacks. Not only do the ghetto fighters go unmentioned, along with various undergrounds organized by great effort and at great cost in order to preserve the honor of the Jewish people, but the book's authors go on to write that among the refugees there was no lack of "belligerent and aggressive" elements "replete with the spirit of rebellion and of the protection of their honor, sometimes to an excessive degree arising from deep feelings of inferiority [. . .] aspiring to unbridled acts of vengeance [. . .] primed for a fierce reaction to the slightest act of provocation,"[56] a description that is by no means consistent with the human qualities of the fighters among the survivors, or of the survivors as a whole. Once or twice, the book states that those "irresponsible elements" were the breakaway organizations in the Land of Israel, which is to say the IZL and Lehi, whose representatives in Europe might harness the "spirit of rebellion" in order to enlist desperate refugees for their purposes, to win the support of the Jewish masses, and to harm the central interests of the organized Yishuv, which were immigration and statehood. Again and again the expression "harnessing" appears, and "steering and directing the feelings of rage and vengefulness into positive channels," which is to say orderly and organized training of young people in self-defense—first against antisemitic attacks that were continuing after the war, and afterward for the needs of the future state.

The book's authors depict a clear bipolar situation, which is also what the soldiers of the Jewish Brigade perceived in some cases: At one pole were the breakaway organizations and the partisans, representing the wild, irresponsible course, and at the other pole stood the Haganah, which, in battling the organizations that broke away from it, was fighting for the souls of the refugees in order to calm them and help them self-rehabilitate and contribute to the community and its future.[57] The message is clear, it is severe, and it may well not reflect the opinion of the entire leadership since, as noted above, there were those who sympathized and who understood the attitude of Kovner and his followers, and who respected Kovner for his leadership during the Holocaust and for his unique personality, even if they did not support his plan. "Here he was not halted," Ruzka wrote to Vitka, saying that he had received support and assent and letters of recommendation.[58] It bears emphasizing again that the agreement covered Plan B only, and only under Haganah auspices, and that sympathy and support for the person do not necessarily imply support for the policy or the methods. Nonetheless, it is difficult to accept the remarks of Sneh and the narrative from *The History of the Haganah*.

KOVNER'S DEPARTURE AND ARREST

Kovner stayed roughly four months in Palestine, from early August to early December 1945—a very long while, from the viewpoint of the comrades who were waiting for him in Europe, scattered in small cells, all intent on their duty. He lingered not in anticipation of arranging the poison—his letter to Vitka said that in early October he had already been to the "specialist"—but because he wanted to return to Europe with an order, sent to him or handed directly to him, from the top echelon of the Haganah, especially from Sneh and Galili, addressed to the European command of the Haganah and ordering them to ensure that the Nokmim received assistance for taking with as much freedom, and as little supervision, as possible.

However, the top echelon of the Haganah did not meet to discuss the question comprehensively—or at least there is no evidence that they did. Kovner was aware that they were consumed by "heavy, daily, fateful worries for the Yishuv and for the Zionist cause."[59] In addition, he was dependent on the members of the Haganah to arrange for his papers and his escort, and he was obliged to wait for a clear answer regarding how and when he would return to Europe. It is not evident whether the high command delayed his departure intentionally on the assumption that time was working against the plans of vengeance, whether its resources of time and attention were insufficient for the matter among the continual day-to-day happenings in Palestine, or whether the departure of other people for Europe—such as the agents of clandestine immigration—was considered more urgent. It must be remembered that arranging passage abroad for someone who had arrived illegally using forged military documents, and who would be returning the same way, was by no means a simple task.

The Nokmim who had remained in Europe were unable, all that time, to understand what was delaying Kovner, and suspicions arose. The rumor mill began to churn, possibly because Ya'ari had written to Europe that Kovner had "reformed," meaning he'd returned to the mainstream of the movement and would not be continuing with the vision of the Hativa; in fact, Ya'ari wrote, Kovner had founded the Hativa in order to draw the politically uncommitted toward Hashomer Hatzair. If so, then it could be that he had abandoned the idea of vengeance too. The rumors reached the ears of the Nokmim in Europe, and Kovner was shocked. Vitka, who felt that with each passing day the fissure between him and his comrades grew, sent him a harsh letter. In it, she scolded Kovner for not writing to the rest of the group, and she reported an atmosphere of isolation and a complete focus on the original objective. She was witness to the angry disputes that broke out in the wake of Kovner's instruction to concentrate first on Plan B. That instruction could have been another source of suspicion about a change in Kovner's stance. In her letter, she told him that work had started around the prisoners' camps despite the bitter arguments. The correspondence also reflects disagreements about relations with the Jewish Brigade. Vitka maintained friendly ties with the Hashomer Hatzair soldiers there, whereas Kovner opposed the ties between Pasha and Ben-Gal. He urged Pasha to reduce them to the necessary minimum in order not to cause palpable damage.[60]

Ruzka tried to defend Kovner against the anger of his comrades, explaining in letters to Europe that his return had been arranged and cancelled

several times; in contrast to her normally restrained nature, she became upset with those who had begun to doubt his loyalty to the vision of revenge.
Despite knowing him for years and having "believed in him as in God," they
now looked on him as, heaven forbid, a traitor. Throughout Ruzka's letters
during those months, sent from Kibbutz Eilon to Vitka in Paris, it is obvious that she misses her close friend. Her messages are full of affection for
Vitka on the one hand, and, on the other, appreciation for the healthy mo-
mentum of building in the Land of Israel and for the positive attitude of the
movement toward its members everywhere. The letters repeatedly aver that
Kovner is busying himself with the issue of vengeance every hour of every
day and that she is giving him all the help she can. She upbraids Vitka for giving up on the prospect of his return and expresses encouragement: in a little while, Vitka and Kovner will be reunited. However, the frank correspondence between the two close friends indicates doubts in connection with
the virtuousness of vengeance: "Vitka, the main motivation for our existence
and our work mustn't be strictly negative. [. . .] It's wrong to live at death's
side. [. . .] On such a concept, you can't build a life and the outcome will be
disappointment." After Kovner was arrested, she wrote to her friend: "At all
costs, the work [of the Nokmim] must continue. Your last letter shocked
me," meaning that Vitka had sent Ruzka a letter containing serious doubts,
and Ruzka felt there was no other way out except to hang fast and continue
"the work."[61]

Kovner's sailing to France, his arrest by the British, his imprisonment,
and his release constitute a story that has been, and still is, a source of theories, assumptions, and even questionable conclusions, some of which have
retained their hold to this day. One persistent narrative has Kovner setting
off while still looking like a partisan, with long hair and boots. It was in fact
very difficult to persuade him to get his hair cut and leave his boots,[62] but
in the end he did comply. That myth must be debunked because in a photo
of him and his four traveling companions, snapped on the ship as it headed
from Palestine to Europe, he looks like any soldier; the appearance of those
other four, who were arrested with him, drew no comments. Another persistent assumption is that Kovner was arrested because of a tip-off connected
with the vengeance plan, and furthermore that the tip-off came from circles in the organized Yishuv—that is to say, from the Haganah and from the

Jewish Agency. That assumption is contradicted by various sources at that time and by the contemporaneous situation and events, as well as a couple of simple reasons. First, such a tip-off would have incriminated the Haganah itself, which supplied Kovner's papers and uniform, packed the poison and gold that were among his effects, and arranged for his voyage. Second, if the British had arrested him because they knew he was on his way to murder millions of men and women, or even if they had found the means for murder among his possessions without knowing in advance, they would doubtless have first let him lead them to his comrades in Europe before capturing and arresting them all. Together, the Nokmim would while away the rest of their days in pitiless confinement.

Here is the arc of the story as the facts bespeak it: Kovner left for Egypt early in December 1945 with an ID that belonged to Benjamin Beit-Halachmi, a discharged soldier whose physical appearance was very similar to Kovner's. On December 14, at the port of Alexandria, he boarded a ship named the *Champollion*, which was packed with some 4,500 or 5,000 British soldiers on leave. The soldiers included some from the Jewish Brigade and some other Jewish soldiers, making up a contingent of 27 who were on their way back to their units in Europe at the end of leave. They were under the command of Moshe Eisen (later Barzilai), a native New Yorker and sergeant-major in the Jewish Brigade who had been on special family leave at his kibbutz, Ein Hashofet. The Haganah assigned him five more men, including Kovner, who weren't soldiers but had been furnished with phony documents. The four others were on assignments for managing clandestine immigration and for the Palyam, which was the marine unit of the Palmach. The five were assigned an escort of two, one of them being Ya'akov "Jacquo" Yaron of Kibbutz Hatzor. Kovner carried a duffel bag with him, which Eisen called a "sack" and Yaron described as a "white bag." It held the poison he had obtained from the Katzir brothers, packed in twelve cans of powdered milk or (according to Eisen) condensed milk, and gold coins concealed inside toothpaste tubes.[63] The voyage was uncomplicated, although Kovner felt ill and spent most of the time reading in his hammock with the sack in his hand. He never set it aside for a moment. He never afforded the ghost of a clue about the sack's contents to the four men accompanying him, nor to the two soldiers accompanying them all, according to his testimony and theirs.

Eisen, who had responsibility for all the Jewish military travelers, was the only one who knew what was inside the sack.[64]

Shortly before the ship reached the port of Toulon, a loudspeaker called out the assumed names of Kovner and the three others whose documents were false. The poison quickly found its way to the bottom of the sea. A military police launch that had come from shore took charge of the four men, and they were brought for detainment to the military installation near Toulon, a huge camp suitable for the shipload of soldiers in transit. Moshe Rabinovitch (later Carmeli), the seaman in the group of detainees, escaped one rainy night, but the remaining three were returned to Egypt aboard the *Tour de France* at the end of December. Kovner sat for about two months in an isolated cell there, not knowing exactly where he was being held. He and his two comrades were interrogated as if they were Lehi agents intent on assassinating British figures. Nothing came of it, and Kovner was relieved that there was no questioning about vengeance or poison. The three detainees stuck to their cover story: they had secured military IDs and uniforms in order to search for any surviving relatives in Europe. At the end of February, the three were transferred to a prison in Jerusalem, the so-called *Kishleh* near the Tower of David, and a few days later to the central prison in the Russian Compound. In the second week of March 1946, they were freed in a release that was routine and customary between the British and the Haganah, according to testimony from additional prisoners and the diary of a Jewish prisoner who shared their cell. That prisoner, Michael Ashbel—a well-known member of the IZL and a native of Vilna—testified that he had conversed at length in prison with Kovner, who presented himself as "Michael Kaminetzky." Michael was the name of Kovner's younger brother, who had been killed in the forests of the partisans, and Kaminetzky was the surname of his first girlfriend, Hadassah; however, to date there is no evidence that Kovner carried any additional document with any name other than Benjamin Beit-Halachmi, the name on the document with which he left Palestine.[65] Although the process of his release was routine and customary, apparently Golda Meir was involved in it. On the day that Abba Kovner received the Israel Prize in 1970, she related that she had seen to the transfer of Kovner and his fellow prisoners from Cairo to Jerusalem and that she had sent the attorney—one with experience in previous cases involving both the Haganah and the British—to free them from the Russian Compound, in her capacity as liaison between the Histadrut and the British Mandate.[66]

How and Why Did the Poison Reach the Bottom of the Sea?

According to Kovner, when the four men's names were called out over the ship's loudspeaker, he hastily asked Yaron—one of the escorting soldiers who knew nothing about what the sack contained—to take the sack to an address in Paris, in other words to Vitka and Pasha, if anything happened to Kovner. If such delivery was impossible, he urged Yaron to destroy the sack in any way feasible. Kovner opened the bag, took out half of the contents, and dumped it out of the bathroom window into the sea, according to his testimony: "I had that bad a feeling."

For his part, Yaron claimed in his testimony to have run to Kovner's hammock as soon as Kovner was arrested, where he found—just as he had expected—the mysterious white sack that had aroused his curiosity throughout the voyage. He ran frantically to the deck and threw it into the sea unopened. Furthermore, when he met Kovner again in the detention camp, Kovner repeatedly asked him about it, disguising the question by inserting it into a sort of song: "What about the poison?" Only when Yaron managed to decipher the message in the singing did he realize what had been in the mysterious bag. He answered immediately that the sack had been jettisoned. "Abba almost collapsed. He clasped his head in anguish [. . .]. His face looked pale as a mask. 'Why? Why did you do it?' he asked in a hoarse, choked voice."

Eisen, as noted, was in charge of the group and was the only one who knew what Kovner was carrying. Apparently he had been informed of this by members of the Haganah. ("They told me. They had to tell me.") He testified that Kovner had given him a burlap bag, easily carried, containing cans that were labeled as condensed milk. Suspecting that the military police would interrogate him as well, Eisen went immediately to the bathroom window and tossed out the contents of the bag, "can by can." Afterward, he was haunted by the fear that the cans would be found, since some of them had floated, and this at a time when food was scarce and food for children even more so.

According to Rabinovitch, it was only when the four were under detention at the transit camp that Kovner told them about the mission of vengeance and about his fear that the mission would fail because of his imprisonment; then he gave Rabinovitch a letter, addressed to Vitka in Paris, and some gold coins.[67]

Can the testimonies be reconciled? If so, how? Might Kovner have discarded half the cans and left the rest in the hands of Eisen? Did he entrust the entire sack to Yaron? Did he really leave the white sack in the hammock, hoping that the summons to report would prove to be for a simple matter capable of solution and not for arrest and imprisonment? It is difficult to decide among the testimonies. Being arrested compels quick decision-making under pressure, and according to Yaron's testimony, a rumor rapidly spread aboard ship that a squad of Jewish terrorists had been caught on their way to England to assassinate the royal family. And the twenty-seven Jewish Brigade members, with five more Palestinian Jews, were in the midst of a force of thousands of soldiers, some of whom demonstrated hostility against them after the arrest. One way or another, the poison was thrown from the ship into the sea near the shores of France.[68]

Could it be that Kovner had actually changed his mind about Plan A even before he left the Land of Israel and therefore hadn't prepared a plan for the eventuality of being caught? Because he was carrying false papers, he must have known that arrest was possible; nonetheless, he didn't maximize the chances of saving at least some of the poison by consigning a portion to one of the others who carried false papers, nor even to an actual soldier, nor—when he was summoned to report—to several reliable soldiers by prearrangement.

If he had told at least one of the two escorting soldiers something that would have helped keep the poison safe, something more than the hasty request that he flung at Yaron a moment before he went to the police launch, then there would be some evidence of his commitment to the plan. "If I'd known, maybe I would have taken a risk," Yaron said regretfully.[69] Maybe the reason Kovner kept the poison in his sole possession and told no one about it was that he had no desire to implicate anyone else. Indeed, he had promised Galili that in the case of imprisonment, all guilt would be assumed by him and the Nokmim who were in Europe. Or had the grisly Plan A perhaps palled on Kovner during his stay in the Land of Israel, what with its firm rejection by all the Yishuv leaders he met, the promise he had made them not to carry out the plan, the atmosphere of constructive impetus and liveliness that had washed over him during those four months, and the change of conditions in Germany that would have caused non-German victims as well? A possible answer to those questions is that Kovner took the poison with him, intending to endanger no one along the way but himself, before persuading his group to carry out Plan B only.

Why Were Kovner and Three Companions Arrested?

According to Kovner, he was told years later that the informers were Haganah circles that were less than happy with the plan for vengeance and that wanted to sabotage it, so they gave him up. Shimon Avidan, ever trustworthy, testified heatedly later that he knew for a fact that "apparently in the Jewish Agency,"[70] which was from the start among the opponents of the entire plan of vengeance, a source had passed the information to the British.

Kovner rejected Avidan's version of events despite Avidan's reputation for reliability, and it is indeed difficult to believe that when gold and poison were on Kovner's person, a Jew of the Haganah or of the Jewish Agency would betray him to the British. Kovner was a role model: a hero of the Holocaust, a commander of an underground, a partisan, and a survivor with no family left. The Haganah had more than enough ways to prevent the Nokmim from implementing their plan without resorting to such an underhanded maneuver, which recalled the ugliness of the saison and could put Kovner in danger of lengthy imprisonment. Moreover, the Haganah gave Kovner the ID with which he was traveling, and Haganah members who arranged his voyage—and could just as easily have prevented it—packed the poison and the gold for him. Information passed to the British by the Haganah could have backfired by revealing its ties to Kovner. And certainly the Haganah had no interest in helping the British capture the Palyam agents it had sent to Europe to assist in illegal immigration.

In fact, Ben-Horin's memoirs include clear testimony on the matter:

> I was warned by Haganah headquarters not to take with us any unauthorized soldiers who were trying to infiltrate the ships in order to search for relatives in Europe, because secret travel with the Jewish Brigade soldiers was our only way of sending emissaries. I knew that likely the Haganah

would soon be sending Abba Kovner and other Haganah and Bricha emissaries to Europe and *the channel must not be endangered*. (Emphasis added.)

It will be recalled that Ben-Horin had been appointed liaison with Kovner's group in Europe; he certainly was thoroughly aware of how the institutions regarded the voyage, and his testimony clearly indicates a desire to help Kovner, not to endanger him and the method of operation. Returning to Europe himself aboard a different British ship, Ben-Horin experienced tension with the ship's British officers and a nervous restlessness on their part that expressed itself in multiple recounts at assembly and in developing and finding systems for positioning the desired number of soldiers on each deck. When he heard that Abba Kovner and his traveling companions had been arrested, he understood that the British had learned of the Haganah's method for sending emissaries.[71]

Ze'ev Grudjinski, of the Mossad for Aliyah B, also testified regarding "the sending of people overseas on various assignments, such as procurement (Munya [Mardor]) and vengeance (Abba Kovner)," meaning that Kovner was on assignment on behalf of the Yishuv.[72] Eisen writes in his memoirs that upon being summoned over the ship's loudspeaker, Kovner ran to his cabin and brought Eisen the sack, telling him, "This must be smuggled to the Haganah agent in Marseilles."

Yaron backed up Eisen's testimony with respect to the involvement of the Haganah command in Kovner's voyage. He testified that on the night of his departure to Egypt with the five other men, he was hastily instructed by the person in charge of the journey (whose identity he didn't know and whose face he didn't see) just before boarding the train in Rehovot: "You must stay with these soldiers all the way to Marseilles in France. Protect them, and teach them to obey orders in English." Then the man thrust a small note into his hand, said, "Read this, memorize it, and destroy it!" and then disappeared into the darkness. The note told Yaron to go to a certain address in Toulon and deal there with someone called Willy, who would take charge of all five soldiers. If something went wrong, Yaron was to immediately send the message "The pomegranate has rotted!" for the attention of "Y.H. – M.E." in the Land of Israel. Only afterward did Yaron realize that the initials referred to Ya'akov Hazan at his kibbutz Mishmar HaEmek. Years later,

Hazan confirmed to Yaron that he had been the addressee for the message. He also whispered the name of the top commander for the mission but reminded Yaron that "silence is still strength."[73]

Not only that, but the Mossad's emissaries in Paris received notification, even before the ship's scheduled departure, that the five men were expected to arrive and must be helped on their way after the voyage. Therefore, the arrest triggered an extensive correspondence between the Mossad for Aliyah B, the European branch of the Palmach, and the Yishuv. The Palmach in Europe wrote that it had received orders from the top to put itself at the service of the three arrestees and to cooperate among themselves, and it requested further information for the purpose. Yaron, who had been one of those thousands of soldiers taken from the ship and confined to the transit camp, slipped out of the camp and sped through the pouring rain to Toulon for all he was worth. Once he arrived at the address, he knocked at the door and uttered the password (*Feinkuchen*, which is "omelet" in Yiddish), with the rotted-pomegranate message on the tip of his tongue. Willy berated him for considering Kovner's arrest the principal news because "to us, everyone is equally precious," and sent him to report at the Bristol Hotel on Rue Jean Jaurès, where the Haganah maintained its center.

At the Bristol, a number of representatives gathered to consider whether to break into the camp and free the four despite the ceaselessly pouring rain, the barbed wire surrounding the camp, and the armed sentries at the gates. They sent a messenger to the camp to communicate with Kovner from the outside and ask him first, but he ruled categorically against any such venture because if it managed to free fewer than all four, there was no telling what fate would befall whoever was left behind. His stand was either everyone or no one. Kovner refused to make his escape even when conditions permitted it. Eisen, the commander, came to the camp office, demanding that the British provide written confirmation that they had taken four soldiers away from him and that they tell him the suspicions against those four soldiers. He even threatened not to move from the spot until they did, but to no avail. According to the camp commander, the order had come from the Middle East and he didn't know the reason. However, Eisen was permitted to communicate with the four and was asked to tell them, in translation, the orders of the British. He came from New York, whereas they didn't know a word of

English. Eisen brought good cigarettes for their guards, and one day when Kovner and another soldier were carrying pots of food under the eye of a distracted guard, they came close to the gate—the camp had turned into a pool of mud—and Eisen suggested they escape. Kovner had an idea of his own, to drug the guards with sedative-laced cigarettes or candy, but then it emerged that Rabinovitch had escaped on a rainy night, on the spur of the moment—barefoot, because the guards had taken his shoes, but carrying gold coins and a letter that Kovner had entrusted him with when they were detained at the transit camp. It soon became clear that there was no point breaking into the camp to free the three men: after Rabinovitch's escape, the camp commander informed Eisen that he had been instructed to deposit the three remaining detainees on the *Tour de France*, which was about to sail back to Egypt. Eisen telegraphed the news immediately to the Land of Israel.[74]

All those details form a picture completely incompatible with the theory that someone from the institutions of the Yishuv was an informer. It is a picture of involvement in Kovner's travels by a number of institutions, and by one figure after another from the Yishuv concerning themselves with the success of his mission and maintaining constant communications between all the offices responsible for it, including the highest echelons. Someone was appointed to prepare the five for their journey, another for the departure, another to escort them to Marseilles, and yet another to await them there. Consideration was given to freeing them by force from their detention, Kovner in particular; and as mentioned, there was Eisen presenting demands to the camp commander.

Because Kovner was never interrogated regarding the project of vengenace, because he was arrested as Benjamin Beit-Halachmi rather than under his real name, and because the three other man arrested with him were truly innocent of any connection with the affair, it may be concluded that neither the informer (if there was one) nor the arrest was connected with the project of vengeance. And in that case, it must be asked: If there was an informer, who was it, and who was informed on? But if there was no informer, why the arrest? Indeed, the reason for arresting Kovner and his companions was apparently quite unrelated to him, and his fellow detainees, as an individual. As it happened, on November 6, 1944, roughly a year before they left Palestine, Lord Moyne, the British minister resident in the Middle East, was assassinated by Eliyahu Hakim and Eliyahu Bet-Zuri, two members of Lehi. Moyne, an ardent opponent of Zionism and of Jewish immigration to the Land of Israel, was suspected of direct involvement in the sinking of the *Struma* on March 1942 near the Turkish shore, which resulted in the drowning of hundreds of Jewish refugees. The tragedy shook the Yishuv and was painfully remembered. It must be recalled that Kovner embarked at the very time when Moyne's two assassins were being tried in Cairo. In mid-January 1946 they were sentenced to death. The British were at the end of their patience following the assassination, and they were increasingly intensive and suspicious in their search for Lehi members in particular.

Moreover, in December 1945 the British found out about a postwar method of illegal immigration happening right under their noses, as Ben-Horin worried they would. Known as Aliyah D, it had been developed to smuggle activists in illegal immigration, such as seamen and radio operators, out of Palestine and illegally bring survivors in. Only a few people were smuggled that way because it was necessary to supply appropriate documents to those exiting and entering and teach them the routine of a military unit and enough English so that they would not attract suspicion during travel. The practice was to assign a soldier to assist each emissary or illegal immigrant, or each few of them. There were failures anyway, especially when the British punctiliously compared rosters or when the documents and the voyage had not been well prepared, and such failures had occurred in the weeks prior to the arrest of Kovner and his companions.

Kovner's voyage had had every reason to go wrong: it had been hastily arranged in December, just as protocols were tightening. He and his companions knew neither English nor of the rules of a British Army unit, and theirs was a larger-than-usual contingent of impostors. There might generally be one, maybe two, per ship. The men did get smoothly through the paperwork in Palestine, and they set out as if they were among a total of thirty-two soldiers. However, since they were dispatched in haste, they were never brought to the camp in Rehovot for the usual few days of instruction, instead proceeding directly to the train station there, according to testimony from Shalom Singer (later Ron), who was responsible for that camp. And indeed, in Egypt they were already arousing suspicion because of their relatively advanced ages, their hesitancy in following orders, and their nonmilitary deportment. Suspicion of the four men only increased after they did not immediately respond to the loudspeaker summons, being unaccustomed to their false names, and did not answer in English. When they asked Eisen for an explanation before being turned over to the military police, he told them they were being arrested "on suspicion of not being soldiers."[75]

Were they arrested because the British themselves, during their customary head count in advance of reaching shore, discovered that the list of thirty-two soldiers was forged and five of the so-called soldiers were impostors? Or were the British alerted by someone—by an informer? The existence of an informer is suspected because the order for arrest was relayed from Alexandria to the shore at Toulon and from there to the ship.[76] Avigur, for his part, told Kovner later that the informer was an IZL member settling scores against the Haganah rather than specifically operating against Kovner and his companions, and that the man had been killed in 1948, meaning that it was all water under the bridge. Kovner accepted Avigur's account as true. And Eisen indeed testified that before they sailed, members of the Haganah—who, it will be recalled, put him in charge—told him that members of the IZL (or Lehi; he didn't remember precisely) had asked to join them as well, but the Haganah had refused because the assassination of Lord Moyne and the assassins' trial in Cairo had further strained relations between the Haganah and the breakaway movements. The Haganah members had warned Eisen to take into account that those movements were angry and making general threats.[77]

The Committee of Inquiry

A committee of inquiry set up to examine the matter—with Lyova Eliav, a man of undisputed integrity, as chair—invested lengthy thought, examined various possibilities, interviewed all available parties (including, as Rabinovich had fled the camp, the other two detainees, who had been released in the meantime), and concluded that there could not have been an informer in the Land of Israel "who knew the entire plan from beginning to end." In other words, there could not have been an informer from among the institutions of the Yishuv who had knowledge both of the plan for vengeance and of the activists in illegal immigration, because in that case the men would have been arrested before boarding the ship. The informer was more likely someone who had the opportunity to leaf through the documents and suspected that some of those aboard were illegal but was ignorant of the reason for their voyage.

At this point, the committee of inquiry inserts criticism of the departure procedures, of the substandard preparation given the five passengers, and of the carelessness whereby "many people knew of A.K.'s departure." The committee's conclusion was that the informer either was in Rehovot or, more likely, was a "canary" employed by the British at Port Said who told them that the ship was carrying extra passengers.

Another possibility, raised by Eisen himself, is that he may have made an honest mistake when he handed his list to the British upon boarding the ship. He had two envelopes, one with a list of twenty seven and the other with thirty two—the former authentic, and the latter forged to add five—and he may have erred by handing over the wrong list.[78]

Besides all the above, including the conclusions of Eliav's committee, there is a form that Kovner filled out many years later, "Request for Recognition of the Right to Be Decorated as a Former Prisoner of the Mandatory Government." In it, he unambiguously told why he was arrested. Under "Details of the Accusation," he wrote: "Purported suspicion of terrorist intent to assassinate Bevin," and under "Sentence," he wrote: "Not brought to trial." Kovner was kept in isolation and interrogated—according to the answer he provided for "Type of Imprisonment"—but the interrogation did not lead to a trial because there was no proof of the intent to assassinate Bevin. In a long interview that he granted to Levi Arieh Sarid, Kovner repeated, "They interrogated me in Cairo on being a Sternist [a member of Lehi, led by Yair Stern] and I didn't understand why they were interrogating me on being a Sternist on my way to kill Bevin [. . .] it didn't cross their minds that I was an avenger." In that connection, he repeatedly and unequivocally accused Antek Zuckerman of writing the letter that arrived in the Land of Israel branding Kovner a Sternist and essentially bringing about Kovner's arrest.[79] Kovner filled out the form and was interviewed by Sarid in 1984, only a few years before his death. It is a sort of retrospective summation: "How that entered Antek's head, so that he smeared me and my friends, God knows," Kovner wrote before his death in a letter that he archived recapitulating the affair, "but his words fell on feverish ears. From every side, I began to sense an ambivalent attitude: positivity and solidarity alongside mounting suspicion."[80]

In light of the Eliav committee's conclusion, the Haganah decided that although it would continue to send emissaries to Europe under Aliyah D, it would insist and ensure that the emissaries be much better prepared. Munya Mardor, for example—who was sent to replace Yehuda Arazi as the head of clandestine immigration—testified that he underwent exacting preparations: in response to the arrest of Kovner and his companions, Mardor's identity was hidden in a different way, and the preparations for his departure were several times as careful.[81]

Kovner Under Detention and in Prison

Before he was led from the ship to detention in the transit camp, Kovner managed to pass a small note to Pinchas Gruner, a member of Kibbutz Mesilot and a soldier in the Jewish Brigade who was nearby at the time of Kovner's shipboard arrest. In the note, Kovner instructed him to immediately contact Ruzka and Hazan and tell them "Pasha's story"—in other words, that Kovner had been arrested onboard before reaching his comrades, headed by Pasha. Hazan, it will be recalled, was the address in the Land of Israel, and Ruzka was to serve from this point on as a contact person. As mentioned, she was dedicating all her energies to the vengeance project: "I live only for the Hadassah affair. It is the substance of my life." Gruner was asked to tell her to prioritize the European passage of Shimon Avidan, whom Kovner wished to have replace him as the head of the operation. Vitka testified later that Kovner's and Ruzka's letters to her expressed doubt as to whether Pasha could manage the whole project, and that it was obvious Kovner wanted someone to be sent from the Land of Israel to take command.[82]

From detention in Toulon, Kovner passed a letter to Pasha and Vitka, along with some gold coins, in the care of Rabinovich. When Rabinovitch reached Paris—carrying the bitter news, the letter, and the coins—Pasha was thunderstruck: "I'm not embarrassed to say I started crying. First time any man saw me cry."[83] Kovner's letter provided final instructions because their paths were diverging, possibly for years. All might not be lost, though. They must consult Ruzka, who could provide all Kovner's contacts in the Land of

Israel for assistance and medicine (meaning poison). He asked Vitka and Pasha to send her their Parisian address immediately and, when they wrote, to
use their prearranged code names because Ruzka had those names listed.[84]

On the assumption that their separation would last for years, Kovner
sent a strict demand to Vitka that she do some soul-searching and understand that she and her comrades belonged to the Hashomer Hatzair movement. That demand was engendered by Vitka's anger at how often he mentioned the movement in his letters, as if the mission of vengeance depended
on the movement. She wrote, "And I certainly don't agree with that"—
whereas Kovner was concerned first and foremost with the future of the
group's members. Because of his stay in the Land of Israel and because of
the close ties he formed with the movement's leaders, Kovner was no longer
aware that Vitka and the other Nokmim were still loyal to the credo of the
Hativa of East European Survivors. According to that credo, even if the Hativa itself were disbanded, there would remain the commitment not to affil-
iate with any other movement but rather to hold fast to the idea of unity under the Hativa alone as a message to the Yishuv. Self-identifying as members
of the movement did not stand in opposition to vengeance, Kovner wrote,
because the movement had given him the warmest and most fair-minded
support he'd received for vengeance, with the blessing of its leaders Hazan
and Ya'ari.[85]

Ruzka went to work on the task. She contacted the headquarters in Paris
through Binyamin Cohen, then a soldier in the Jewish Brigade (and afterward a historian); she searched for someone to substitute for Kovner (with
the knowledge of Ya'ari, who specifically recommended Ben-Horin); she
raised funds; but primarily she focused on finding poison to replace what
now lay on the seafloor. She stayed in the Land of Israel to carry out these
vital assignments and did not sail for Europe, despite longing to join her
friends there.

She wrote explicitly to Vitka that Kovner had managed to also tell Gruner
that "instead of Uri, someone from here will carry on alongside Pasha, and he
said that it is a person who knew everything from the first moment, someone
talented, knowledgeable, experienced in this work, and properly focused. I
know that he cannot entirely replace Uri, but he can help greatly and keep
the project running." She was presumably referring to Avidan.[86]

From the ship that was bringing him back to Egypt, Kovner managed to send another note. In it, he repeated the instruction to arrange for Avidan's arrival and to tell Hazan and Ruzka of his arrest. Jacquo Yaron testified, as mentioned, that the initial instruction, before Kovner left Palestine, was to inform Y.H. at M.E. (Ya'akov Hazan at Mishmar HaEmek) in the event of a failure and arrest; as Kovner's detention lengthened, Ya'ari sent worried letters to the Jewish Brigade.[87] The fact is that few people knew then, and few know even today, about Kovner's appreciation of Hazan's and Ya'ari's favorable attitude toward vengeance and about their involvement in the matter. Ya'ari's words of farewell to the German Unit before they departed for Europe were, as mentioned, "Be the core troop of avengers!" In urging Vitka and his comrades to remain loyal to the Hashomer Hatzair movement, perhaps Kovner—fearing that if his confinement continued for too long, his zealously committed comrades would be left rambling in Europe with no anchor point and no support force—was hoping to assure them of comfort in the warm bosom of the movement, which would provide help on a personal basis even to those who were not among its most ardent members.

From the stern prison in the western desert, Kovner did not succeed in sending a single message. Only after he was transferred, at the end of February, to the Kishleh—an enormous and chilling structure in Jerusalem that served as a prison and police station during the Mandate—could he promptly write an emotional, poetical letter to his comrades saying he laid hands on their heads and blessed them, hoping wholeheartedly to learn what had occurred during his confinement. Upon his release from the Kishleh in mid-March, he wrote again. It was a long letter, in marvelous Yiddish, even more poetical and emotional than the one before, but in its dozen-odd pages he expressed suicidal thoughts. "He nearly went mad," Elkins wrote in a characteristically frank description of Kovner's troubled mental state after imprisonment.[88] In the letter, Kovner describes the Holocaust, the crises that he endured at that time, his family and its history, and the loss of his first love, Hadassah, who was murdered while walking with her mother to the death pit near the Vilna ghetto. Considering Plan A lost cause, he consoles his friends on their inability to exact vengeance, and he once more writes about Ya'ari: "A believer, one of the great believers. One of the few. A sort of pure though distant reincarnation of a great ancestor," a grandparent extending a hand to Kovner in his distress and showing him the way to the sunlight, where the movement is the home at the end of the pathway.[89]

Yonat Rotbein-Marla, Ruzka's daughter, now believes that Kovner changed his mind as he sat in prison. Evidence is that the poem that he wrote there about the partisans' forest, "Until No Light," focuses on life. Until then, he had aspired with all his heart, like the rest of the Nokmim, to carry out Plan A, which amounted to "let me die with the Philistines"—in other words, choosing death. His term in prison, perhaps as added to his months in the Land of Israel, brought him to the conclusion that now was the time to choose life. Choosing life meant choosing to continue, to meet the future, to immigrate to the Land of Israel, and to build the state, so choosing life also meant abandoning Plan A. But he couldn't say so to his friends the Nokmim, and there wasn't one of them whom he could command to live. It was a personal decision that had to come from inside, and external coaxing would be of no use.

The letter he wrote to his friends before his release from prison in Jerusalem includes a passage that supports Yonat's opinion. Kovner wrote: When I set out on my way to you, I had a bag of medicines to strengthen your abilities. But I was carrying something else with me as well, *dem Otem von dem Leben* ["the breath of life"—emphasis Kovner's] that I breathed here in the Land of Israel, and I hope that we all can breathe it [. . .]. In the margin of the page alongside the words "the breath of life," he added a note later: "The first hint of a return to reality!"[90] Michael Eshbal, who spoke at length with Kovner when they were both confined in Jerusalem's central prison, also reports that Kovner relented: Kovner told him about the Vilna Ghetto, the underground, and the partisans. "There, in prison, in the months of isolation that were imposed on us, Kovner decided to give up on his aspiration for vengeance. There he wrote [. . .] 'Until No Light,' about the fighting of the partisans," noted Eshbal.[91]

And he may have had that change of heart even earlier, before the voyage, knowing that time was working against him because occupied Germany was filling up with Jewish refugees and Allied soldiers. How could an attack on the mass of Germans not harm the others? In addition, his stay in the Land of Israel also drove home the pressing need to solve burning political issues, foremost among them the matter of bringing the survivors home—which was a top priority for Kovner as well; he was, after all, the founder of the Bricha movement. To all that, add Kovner's clear knowledge that no one he met agreed with Plan A, a knowledge demonstrated when he wrote to his comrades, after less than two weeks in the country, about freezing Plan A. But there is, nonetheless, no definitive proof of a change of heart. He set out equipped with the poison that the Katzir brothers had furnished him and intent on joining his comrades who were aflame with the urge to avenge as a means of redemption for the world and for their own lives, even if his course was subsequently obstructed.

Be that as it may, in the months of his stay in the Land of Israel, the top leaders of the Yishuv and the Haganah, wary of breakaway militias and fearing that the attack would become ungovernable, established a clear policy limiting the Nokmim to Plan B and stipulating that the Haganah supervise it. What steps did the Haganah take in order to safeguard that stipulation? How were its relations with the Nokmim who had remained in Europe? What occurred while Kovner was under confinement? The following chapters will investigate these questions.

Prayer for Revenge

NATHAN ALTERMAN

For what does your servant want, Father High?
Across their smooth necks with his fingers to pry.
And what does he seek to find in their haunts?
Just the lights of their eyes is all that he wants.
O bitter's his heart, his sorrow heavy lay,
He's been beaten by foes on this earth of clay.
With their spittle, wet—
There's revenge, he said.
Silenced, he seemed—
The reckoning he schemed.
So when as Sabbath and New Moon Your revenge You'll keep.
May he with one eye, at Your Holiness peep.
And when greater than telling, joy beams from his face,
Tell him not: Have pity! Say not: Show grace!

Forget not, forget not them nor their name,
Forget not the one whom hundreds overcame.
Accept Thou the wrath of the few even now—
O Lord of the Dead, Blessed art Thou.

From *Joy of the Poor: Poems*, Mahbarot Lesifrut, Tel Aviv, 1959, pp. 65–67. Translated by Dov Vardi, in Dov Vardi, *New Poetry*, WIZO, Tel Aviv, 1947, p. 105. Courtesy of Nathan Slor, Alterman's grandson.

5

Paris, February–June 1946
The Haganah and the Avengers

IN FEBRUARY 1946, after Kovner was imprisoned by the British in Egypt but before he was transferred to Jerusalem—also after the Jewish Brigade had gone to Holland and Belgium and while the Avengers, the Nokmim, were located variously around Germany—Nahum Shadmi set out for Europe. He had been Haganah commander of the Jerusalem district but was now part of the national command. As a matter of fact, in October or November 1945, when David Ben-Gurion was in Paris, he had already appointed Shadmi to head the Haganah in Europe.[1] One of the major reasons for setting up a Haganah headquarters in Europe was the realization that the Bricha was going to be a lengthy project. Until the refugees could all be brought to Palestine, their safety had to be assured because they were "strangers, uprooted from their homes and surrounded by haters on all sides," constantly scrapping with the locals and openly contemptuous of Germany's postwar regulations and arrangements. Roughly a quarter million people were gathered in the displaced persons camps, with 185,000 inside Germany, in the British-occupied zone and especially in the American-occupied zone; 45,000 in Austria; and 20,000 in Italy, mostly near the Jewish Brigade. Because old people and children had been the first to be targeted for death, few of them survived, so most of the survivors were young adults. As viewed by the Haganah, the young survivors were sitting idle in the DP camps and could well invest their time in training for life in Israel, primarily for self-defense. The DPs, and especially certain groups among them—the nature of which was not yet known in the Land of Israel—were rife with "the natural urge for vengeance."[2]

Shadmi's responsibilities were defined only in general terms. They rested on the framework of the May 1942 "Biltmore Program," with its aspiration for the founding of a Jewish national entity, and on Ben-Gurion's plans, within that framework, to help the European Jews fight to live and to leave:

> Quick work across a broad arena. We need to bring tens of thousands of survivors to the Land of Israel. We need to set up new kibbutzim in the Negev and at the borders. [...] The Holocaust survivors will be glad to join us, and we must train them in the use of weaponry before they immigrate. [...] We will also bring weapons to Palestine, in order to defend ourselves when the hour of reckoning unavoidably arrives.[3]

It was Shadmi's responsibility to handle the Jewish Brigade's internal affairs, and he received full authority over the Haganah soldiers in the British army and other armies as well, so that he could deploy them for various purposes. Later, his son Yiska (Issachar) said: "When he arrived, he was told not to create too much order because wherever representatives of the Yishuv were operating in Europe, they lived on disorder!"[4] Shadmi was also responsible for obtaining weapons and shipping them to the Land of Israel; for setting up an organization among the survivors "to educate the Jews in self-defense" against any outbreak of unbridled antisemitism; for training survivors, especially the young ones, to defend themselves in an orderly and systematic way; and for "sorting out the problem of vengeance against the Nazis," which was considered one of the most urgent issues that Shadmi faced upon arriving in Europe.[5]

The very phrasing "the problem of vengeance against the Nazis" may not be a direct quote from Ben-Gurion, but it still indicates the atmosphere and the attitude that had come to surround the issue—an issue that the Haganah saw as an immediate problem. In his memoirs, Shadmi focused on the topic and wrote that one of the most difficult, most sensitive tasks assigned to him was to discover what the organization of Avengers was, "whether it was necessary," and how the Haganah could activate it if authorized by the Yishuv to do so. Yehuda Ben-David, who was a member of the Haganah delegation responsible to Shadmi and was close to him, stated in retrospect that the Nokmim were an organization "that sprang up then under the leadership of Abba Kovner" and were "a much more dangerous organization" than the vengeance group that operated within the Jewish Brigade.[6]

The leaders of the Haganah in Palestine understood that the urge for vengeance was burning in many hearts, and that because the Jews had suffered from a crime of such magnitude (a magnitude that was becoming ever clearer after the war's end), that fiery urge was more than could be satisfied in the near term. For the very reason that there was clearly no appropriate punishment available, the urge for vengeance robbed many good people of their tranquility—particularly those who had undergone humiliation and physical torture and who had witnessed cruelty against others. The editors of *The History of the Haganah*, which reflects the atmosphere among members of the organization at that time, wrote that vengefulness against the Nazis filled the entire being of many survivors; that the passage of time had not diminished their ambition to unleash it and had robbed them of their calm; and that with senses sharpened by the vicissitudes they had endured, they understood that the world at large was preparing to resume business as usual and reconcile with the murderers. At this point, the editors included three stanzas from Shaul Tchernichowski's poem "Baruch of Mainz," which had been republished in 1943—the worst year of the genocide. The stanzas all begin with the word *Ve'nakamnu*, meaning "and we will take avenge": avenge the days of bloodshed, the defilement of women, the corpses of the aged, the dishonor of our martyrs, and the eternal hatred that debased our name.[7] The quotations from the poem and the tone of the description indicate that the aspiration to vengeance on the part of the survivors in general, not only of certain groups among them, won understanding and even solidarity. It bears repeating that most of the people in the Yishuv had lost their families in the Holocaust. Accordingly, there is reason to investigate the difference between the understanding and solidarity regarding the feelings of the survivors after the war on the one hand and the attitude of the Haganah toward actual vengeance operations and toward the groups that decided to carry them out, on the other. The Haganah considered those groups, Abba Kovner and his Nokmim first and foremost, an urgent problem: unrestrained adventurism could cause great damage to the rescue of the refugees. Thus a fine line had to be drawn between the need to prevent that damage and the need for "an outlet of some kind for the vengeful impulse that they had cultivated year upon year."[8]

As mentioned, that "outlet of some kind" became Shadmi's job to find. First of all, upon coming to Europe he needed to assess the existing "movement of avengers" and the urgency for any such movement at all. Ironically, in February 1946 the Nokmim, who supposedly needed someone in charge, were already deployed around Europe, especially in Germany, ready for action, and headquartered in Paris, the very city Shadmi was headed for. It was not merely ironic but a reliable recipe for friction between the sides: On one side, the Nokmim were young, determined, and independent, having coped with impossible dangers and predicaments; they were secretive; they were ready for any sacrifice; and they were loyal to one another, to their leader, and especially to the memory of their dead and to the vision that united them. On the other side, a commander had been sent from the Land of Israel not only to impose restraint on them but also to govern them from outside and to fulfill the assignment that Moshe Sneh had defined as "taking over the avengers' group." Shadmi testified that he received authority to command "the Nokmim and their operations," with Yehuda Ben-Horin—who had moved on to other activities, such as purchasing arms and the training of young Jewish volunteers—transferring to Shadmi the assignment that had been given to Ben-Horin during his visit to the Land of Israel: liaison between the Nokmim and the Haganah's German Unit.[9]

THE NOKMIM'S HEADQUARTERS IN PARIS

Pasha Reichman and Vitka Kempner had arrived in Paris before Shadmi. For a short while after the Jewish Brigade left Italy, they had remained in Tarvisio, receiving assistance from Israel Carmi, Shaike Weinberg, Yehuda Tubin, and others in the form of money, documents, food, and equipment, and had tried to discuss revenge matters with those soldiers who, having stayed behind, became in essence delegates of the Yishuv. Then Pasha sent

Vitka to Belgium in order to maintain communications with the Jewish Brigade, particularly the central figures from the Land of Israel, such as Meir Argov, Mordechai Surkis, and Motke Hadash. Vitka recalls: "They were all very good friends, and when Abba went away they took it upon themselves to look after me. We'd meet every day, we'd talk, and they knew very well who we were"; from time to time they also saved some of the Nokmim from arrest and imprisonment. Vitka went to Belgium with three men, with counterfeit money, and with written information about the camps where German prisoners were being held. It had been necessary to ferret out their locations.[10]

Vitka, who would be joined by Pasha later, reached Antwerp and Ghent too, where the Jewish Brigade's three regiments were stationed. Yet in hopes of entering Germany and coordinating the group's activity there, they decided to relocate to Paris. Not only did they expect entering Germany to be easier from Paris through the American-occupied and French-occupied areas (because in the British-occupied area, order was more strictly kept), but there was another reason, which had proved decisive for them: the headquarters for the Haganah and the Bricha were being established in Paris. Weinberg, who served as a transport sergeant for the first regiment of the Jewish Brigade, managed to persuade drivers from his regiment that the two must be transferred, and so, in late October, Pasha and Vitka were driven to Paris. In addition, Pasha and Vitka managed to set up communications between Weinberg and a Hashomer Hatzair member in Vilna, apparently Yitzhak Zohar, who was appointed to lead the mobile squad of Nokmim and who in turn established a link between the Nokmim's financial department and the Jewish Brigade. He would travel to Bratislava, purchase gold with dollars, and repeat the cycle: gold from east to west, dollars from west to east. Some of the gold he brought was converted to cash for Pasha to distribute among the teams of Nokmim and to activists in Paris as required. Thus, as he passed money to figures such as Weinberg, Zohar was serving the soldiers in the Jewish Brigade who were handling the needs of the Bricha and the rehabilitation of the refugees.[11]

Every few weeks, Shaike and Tubin would pass through Paris; by meeting with them, Pasha and Vitka maintained a connection with the Jewish Brigade. In their testimonies, Tubin and Weinberg recalled that at those meetings, Vitka and her comrades continued telling them about the Holocaust, over time granting them a better understanding of what the survivors had endured, what burned within them, and how much more respect they deserved. According to Weinberg, he obtained for the Nokmim, at their request, the first poison at their disposal: a small quantity of strychnine from a Communist woman, a chemist who had been liberated from Auschwitz and was working in a laboratory. He was helped by Henry Bulawko, a well-known Yiddish-speaking journalist from Lithuania, one of the leaders of the Jewish underground in France and a former Hashomer Hatzair member who had been imprisoned for two years in Auschwitz—just the man for the job. They tested the strychnine on dogs, but it didn't work efficiently.[12]

Disappointed in the strychnine and not knowing when—or even if—Kovner would return with poison, the Nokmim decided to see about manufacturing their own poison. In his letters from Palestine, Kovner had told them repeatedly that they should urgently locate the "doctor," meaning Yitzhak Ratner. Ratner was a chemist from Vilna who had joined the group in Lublin, at Kovner's suggestion, and worked closely with it, motivated by hearing, as he roamed Poland by train, antisemitic invectives that led him to understand that Europe was no place to continue living. When Kovner called for him to be sought out, he was in Milan functioning as the treasurer for Aliyah B. Poldek Maimon and Bolek Ben-Ya'akov had, as noted, stayed in Italy when the Jewish Brigade and the rest of the members moved north, and they hurried him to Paris, furnishing him with a passport, a uniform, and details about where to cross the border. The activists of Aliyah B were dumbfounded. Where had such a responsible man, no longer young, disappeared to? They suspected the Nokmim and wouldn't forgive them. They also suspected that Ratner, as treasurer, might have vanished because of some impropriety, but that suspicion dropped away because not a penny was missing.[13]

Ratner sat himself down in the library at the Sorbonne to refamiliarize himself with the relevant chemistry, having had his mind elsewhere during the war years, and he quickly realized that without help, he couldn't manufacture what Pasha was requesting: one type of poison that was soluble in water, and another that could be smeared on the bottom of a loaf of bread. He concluded that atropine would be suitable for mixing with water and arsenic for use on bread. The challenge was notably complex: a laboratory was necessary, arsenic was available only from disreputable black marketeers who were capable of double-crossing and turning informer, and the whole project would cost a fortune. According to Vitka, "Pasha did incredible work on that, with all sorts of people." She didn't provide details, because, even though she was Kovner's representative, the closest secrets were unknown to her. No one but Pasha knew the complete picture, not even Bezalel Kek-Michaeli, who was responsible for all the teams located in Germany.[14]

In Paris, the Résistance had been active underground, fighting the Germans and their collaborators, and Pasha tried to establish ties with their members—particularly the Jews among them. For their part, they tried to connect him with the Maquis, who had been the guerrilla fighters of the Résistance, and particularly with the communists. The communists had their own agenda of vengeance and were looking for partners in pursuing it. Poldek had ties of his own with a group of French Jewish communists who had been imprisoned with him at Auschwitz. Thus Ratner, through acquaintances from Vilna, made contact with the owner of a tannery who was in the French underground. Once he had been let in on the secret and had overcome his astonishment at the request, the man gave Ratner forty-five pounds of the arsenic used for tanning, in packages of four and a half pounds each.

The packages of arsenic were hidden at the home of another member of the French underground, a divorcée of the well-known Yiddish actor Avrom (Silva) Morewski, who was close to the group both ideologically and personally. Ratner received the atropine from a Jewish acquaintance, a senior employee of the Red Cross, whom he had known in prewar Vilna and who agreed—after long conversations in which Ratner described the horrors of the ghetto and Ponar—to divert a substantial quantity before it was signed out and pass it to Ratner. The next chapter will continue the story of that poison, which was refined and prepared not in a laboratory but at the sleeping quarters of Pasha and his wife, Dorka, and with her help. Suffice it to say that later, in Palestine, Ratner told Kovner that the arsenic was of good death-dealing quality.[15]

During that first period, in late 1945, Pasha was in command at headquarters, Kek-Michaeli was his deputy, Dorka and Vitka were communications officers, and Poldek was plying the roads. Others came, stayed a while, and went on their way as decided. Afterward, Kek-Michaeli went off to Munich to take responsibility for the Nokmim in Germany.

The Paris headquarters was split up among various shabby hotels and the homes of acquaintances. Vitka testified:

Pasha was very deep underground. I didn't even know where he lived. We met from time to time in cafés to swap information, and I connected him up with the Brigade. I was living at Saint-Michel, in a low-class hotel, and the hotel owner complained that men in uniform were visiting me all the time [. . .]. I was in Paris half a year [from the end of October 1945 to mid-April 1946] and I didn't see a single play. I dressed in the same clothes that I'd come from the partisans with—a skirt and sweater. Nothing interested me. Normal life was outside our sphere of interest.[16]

The commanders would also convene in the Nineteenth Arrondissement, at the home of Leah Rabinovich (Czeczja), whose nephew Velveleh Rabinovich was one of the Nokmim. Comrades came and went, carrying falsified Polish passports. "She received us like a mother, and we were actually forsaken people, and very young," said Poldek. Leah's daughter Paulette would marry Ludwig Mairanz in Israel in the 1950s. He was a pleasant, charming man and, most notably, a master of his craft. For nights on end, he would stay up forging documents for the Nokmim. He had begun the work during the war, forging documents for his family. He could easily falsify checks, adding zeros to them, and deposit or cash them. In order to not endanger Leah, he operated in the hotel rooms of the headquarters—sometimes in one, sometimes in another. She knew his secret, and she protected it. His tools of forgery arrived in Israel along with him, and today they remain in Paulette's attic in the town of Shoham.[17]

Heniek Wodzisławski, one of the contingent of Nokmim from Częstochowa, also came from Italy to Paris, and he too had an aunt there. Pasha equipped him with a Jewish Brigade uniform and appointed him as liaison between the Nokmim headquarters and prominent figures of the surviving Western European Jewish community, particularly the wealthy ones. Heniek, who was fluent in several languages, candidly told those people that he was collecting money for vengeance. He explained to them about the Nokmim, the Jewish Brigade, and their common purpose, and for the most part his appeals were received favorably. He passed the money to Pasha or directly to the members that Pasha would specify. Thus, for example, one day he met with Zygi Gliksman on the German-Alsatian border and handed him a bag of gold coins.[18]

The headquarters operated under conditions that were by no means simple. It will be recalled that Kovner would write to Vitka from Palestine and she would read the letters to the others, starting with Pasha. There was tension between them, said Vitka in her last interview—which dwelt more on feelings than on items of fact—because she was "Abba's representative, his voice to the group" generally and to headquarters specifically. According to her, Pasha did not share with her or the rest of the Nokmim in Paris all the information that he possessed.[19] These remarks indicate why the testimonies and memoirs of the Nokmim who operated in Germany make no mention whatsoever of Shadmi or other top figures of the Haganah or emissaries in Paris from the Yishuv with whom Pasha was in touch, and primarily mention figures from the Jewish Brigade who provided the Nokmim with support. Pasha and Vitka were in fact the two central, permanent presences at headquarters in Paris—he as commander, and she as liaison between Kovner and Pasha, between Pasha and the teams of Nokmim, and between Pasha and their staunch friends in the Jewish Brigade.

It was a trying period in Paris for the two, with their separate burdens. It lasted half a year, with heavy responsibility on Pasha's shoulders: although he had been a prominent and central figure since as far back as the group's formation in Lublin—where, because he had been in charge of the operational side of the vengeance project, he considered himself a natural choice to replace Kovner—he was surprised that Kovner, as soon as he was imprisoned, asked that Shimon Avidan or Yehuda Ben-Horin take his place. Pasha's past as a communist would not have endeared him to Shaul Avigur and Shadmi, communism being an ardent foe of Zionism, and certainly not to Ben-Gurion. Avidan, who had been a member of the Communist Party in Germany, was not a beloved friend of theirs either. But Ben-Horin too had been a communist in the past, and Yulek Harmatz was not only in the Komsomol but filled a position on behalf of the Soviets in the forests, and no one held it against them. All four men had later embraced Zionism heart and soul.

Pasha faced very difficult conditions as he started his job. To begin with, he had to support some fifty or sixty members of the Nokmim, since they had all emerged from the Holocaust with, quite literally, only the shirts on their backs. Secondly, being dispersed to several different places, the Nokmim were difficult to keep in touch with. Third, he had the Haganah, the Jewish Brigade, and the Yishuv to consider. Above all else, though, he was of course obliged to pursue the mission. As Kovner's substitute, Pasha found the admired leader's shoes hard to fill. By any account, it would have been a thorny challenge for whoever tried to take Kovner's place. Pasha had admired Kovner ever since their first meeting, and although he understood immediately that Kovner intended to appoint not him but Avidan or Ben-Horin, his overall view of Kovner as a leader remained untarnished, as did his grasp of the needs of the moment. Thus Pasha showed a greatness of spirit in transcending personal issues.

Vitka too had a hard time in Paris. Although her job as liaison was a pivotal one, it was insufficient to fill her days, and she was a young, naturally active woman. Being separated from Kovner bothered her, and the passage of time was not beneficial for her frame of mind. As noted, Kovner set out for Palestine at the start of August, and he was sent to prison in mid-December. For quite a while, no one at headquarters knew about his arrest. Their only means of communication was letters carried in hand, and conditions meant that the correspondence could be neither continuous nor speedy. The Nokmim in Germany began to ask themselves what had become of Kovner and whether he was still loyal to the vision of vengeance and the responsibility he had undertaken by traveling to Palestine to enlist support for that vision. Thus Vitka was torn between now-suspicious comrades and her loyalty to Kovner. In fact, in a frank interview she said that at times she herself doubted Kovner's constancy—a sentiment that, as will be recalled, she voiced to Ruzka.

A number of Vitka's close friends from the movement, from the ghetto, and from the forest were scattered throughout Germany at that time, including Cesia Rosenberg-Amit, Mira Verbin-Shabetzky, and Lena Satz-Hammel, but she seldom saw them. What with the bleak, spartan conditions under which the teams in Germany lived, and with Pasha and the others around her in Paris devoted single-mindedly to the attainment of vengeance, Vitka was detached from the city's life, which had begun to revive after the war, and from local Jewish social and political life. In effect, Vitka and her friends inhabited a capsule of their own making, completely insulated from their environment. Anyone daring to speak of living normally in the Land of Israel was considered a renegade. The terrible vision that swirled within them gave them no rest.[20] Kovner wrote Vitka letters telling her how much he missed her, asking continually how she was doing and how she was feeling; she answered that she missed him too, using endearments and wishing for their reunion: "I'm alone, so alone!" she exclaimed to him across the miles. "My life has been so hard these past months," she admitted in another letter, a long and aching one. "I have no clear standing, I have no path ahead." Ruzka wrote to her, as a friend to her soul and as one who missed her; the way she wrote contradicts the gossip that had trickled Franceward from the Land of Israel regarding an affair between her and Kovner during his months there. The gossip must have been painful to Vitka, but Ruzka, putting her thoughts and heart straight onto paper, was apparently unaware of the rumors.[21]

Pasha was present at a gathering of Jewish fighters from all the armies, held November 1945 in Paris, with Ben-Gurion as the paramount figure, and Pasha spoke with Avigur, Ben-Horin, Ehud Avriel,[22] and lastly Ben-Gurion. In testimony later, Pasha said that he hadn't personally wanted to meet Ben-Gurion because he assumed Ben-Gurion would oppose vengeance, but friends of the Nokmim in the Jewish Brigade had urged him to meet him. Argov, who supported the Nokmim from start to finish, arranged the meeting as soon as the gathering of fighters had concluded. After waiting a long time, Pasha was received by Ben-Gurion, who was standing impatiently outside his hotel, with a car waiting and with his wife, Paula, urging him onward to another, more important meeting. Ben-Gurion reassured her and stepped into the hotel lobby with Pasha. They sat down for a moment, and Ben-Gurion listened as Pasha explained the group's intent in general terms. "He was ready for it"—meaning that Ben-Gurion had been briefed in advance—and he said, "I'm not promising what we'll do if you don't cancel it," giving the impression of a threat. Ben-Gurion also told him that a state was already under formation, implying that this was no time to be concentrating on less important projects. In conclusion, he told Pasha, in friendly Yiddish, that "in history, vengeance is a very important thing" but went on to ask rhetorically whether it was possible that "killing six million Germans will bring my six million Jews back" (he called them "my Jews"). Unless that were possible, he said, he wasn't interested. However, Pasha testified that he perceived in Ben-Gurion's eyes, and in his attitude, a great regret about being unable to openly agree on taking such-and-such actions.[23]

Two weeks after that gathering of fighters, Pasha met with Avigur again for a longer talk, this time at Avigur's hotel—the Metropol, in Paris—and they established good relations. As they spoke, they were joined by Avriel, who was staying at the same hotel, and he was congenial. "Those are very good guys," Avriel told Avigur later. Avigur asked to hear first of all not about vengeance but about the Holocaust. Pasha recapitulated it for five or six hours, and Avigur listened attentively as always. Avigur also questioned him about the Avengers, asking for details about who constituted the group, what they lived on, and how many they numbered. Millions, said Pasha, and Avigur responded: "If millions are busied with vengeance, we won't have a state." Munitions must be amassed, millions of Jews must be brought to the Land of Israel, and vengeance was not part of the picture. "We're about to establish a state, and events elsewhere will also have significance for that future state."[24] A few weeks later, after Kovner had been imprisoned and the Nokmim had begun to reorganize their headquarters, Avigur told Pasha what had happened to Kovner, promised assistance, and asked what was needed. Pasha answered that the poison for the SS veterans had already been prepared in Paris (by Ratner), and for transferring it to Munich he requested some men in uniform with authentic military identification—there were always inspections on the roads and at the borders, and if the poison were noticed, the smuggling would be punished as black marketeering of the worst kind, incurring long imprisonment.[25] Avigur promised to help, and when the time came, he was as good as his word.

WHO REPRESENTS THE JEWISH PEOPLE?

Nahum Shadmi's first job was to gain the trust of the Nokmim in order to bring them under his authority, so he began establishing ties with them. After the meeting between Pasha and Avigur, Avigur transferred the handling of the matter to Shadmi as of February 1945, and two days later Shadmi sent for Pasha. Shadmi testified a number of times about what occurred, but his testimonies are inconsistent both in tone and content, and they certainly do not coincide with what Pasha recounted in his own testimonies.

The History of the Haganah presents a mild version, based on Shadmi's memoirs, which described the first contacts with Nokmim headquarters in Paris as having begun with "a thorough sorting out of principles," as Shadmi put it. Shadmi called upon the Nokmim to accept the authority of the Jewish people expressed by the organization authorized to represent it in this matter, namely the high command of the Haganah—represented, in turn, by Shadmi. He stressed that he was not minimizing anyone's pain or the upheaval that caused it, but he insisted on agreement to the basic principle that no group of individuals must arrogate to itself the right to carry out acts of vengeance on behalf of the entire Jewish people.[26]

According to other testimonies from Shadmi, which were not published and therefore, while less official, are more revealing of himself—especially because they were spoken to Ben-David, who was close to him—Shadmi told the Nokmim more sternly that following the Holocaust, the Jewish people were focusing on their sole priority, which was the founding of a state in the Land of Israel. It was the single overriding objective at that moment. Someone had to take responsibility, he said, and decide which activities were permitted and which forbidden. "You aren't in charge. It's my call first. Then you can appeal. I'll tell you, when the time comes, who you can appeal to. Maybe it'll turn out I was wrong, and in that case they'll correct me." He also said, "The Jewish people are in charge, and they're represented by the Jewish Agency," which was in charge of the Haganah.[27]

Thus, the only option for the two sides was a collision course. Not only was one side trying to exert authority over another side that had stopped obeying authority years before, but the central challenge in their discussion was the weighty question of who actually represented the Jewish people and spoke in their name after the Holocaust: The survivors, whom the Nokmim represented by expressing the urge for vengeance that burned within each and every one? Or the representative of the Haganah, which in turn represented the Yishuv and its aspiration to build a state and welcome into it those who had escaped the sword?

Moreover, there was the obstacle of an underlying contradiction that neither side had noticed: the Nokmim carried with them the dying wish of millions of victims and the wish of many survivors, to avenge. The Haganah, on the other hand, feared that exacting vengeance would bring harm to those same survivors because it would interfere with the work of assembling and caring for them. Another factor was the gap between young people who had experienced the evil of the Holocaust, most in their early twenties, and Shadmi himself, a fifty-year-old from the farmland of Menahemia, south of Lake Kinneret, who came to Israel in 1921, served in the Haganah and various campaigns, and apparently knew little about the Holocaust when he was sent to Europe.

There is a third source, though, in which Shadmi is even more revealing of himself: a number of surprising documents that he wrote in Paris during the days when those very meetings with the Nokmim were occurring. They are detailed reports that he regularly sent to Palestine for Yisrael Galili, which the latter then passed to Sneh. In those reports—written at that time rather than as memoirs or retrospective testimony—Shadmi revealed his true feelings. Toward the end of February, which is to say a few weeks after arriving in Paris, "Dov" (Shadmi's code name) sent an overall report of the situation to "Ram" (one of Galili's code names) discussing the issue of vengeance, titled *Nechama* ("consolation" in Hebrew, which stands for Nekama, vengeance; in other words, vengeance for Shadmi is consolation). He started by describing the friends of "Nechama": they are incensed, consumed by doubts, "full of bitterness and disappointment from their contact with us" (which is to say, from meeting representatives of the Yishuv), focused on their sole friend Nechama, and already engaged in a practical process of serious, ramified, and concrete preparations. "She [Nechama] has put me to a lot of thinking, balancing of judgment, and soul-searching," he wrote, and he presented the following conclusions:

a. *The fact is, I love Nechama and I wish her to succeed. My conversations with you at home have led me to believe that you regard her in the same way.* [Emphasis added.]

b. Responsibility for her must by no means be held by only a few individuals. With all due respect to those people, with all the smallness I feel as I stand among them, and in the shadow of the suffering of European Jewry, I say nonetheless *that something as majestic and sacred as our sister Nechama must not be consigned to the responsibility of the abovementioned people* and certainly not become political capital for our dear colleague Rivka [a code name for Hashomer Hatzair];

Responsibility must rest with the entire community, and in this case I see myself as the sole authorized representative of the entire community." [Emphasis added.]

c. In the plan for attending to Nechama, the following priorities must be respected: (1) "Maximum effectiveness" in order to stand up to complaints arising afterward; "and maximum effectiveness starts at ten thousand and up," which is to say it starts with at least ten thousand Germans killed. (2) "Nechama must be attended to within the limits of conscience—to the point where even maximum effectiveness remains confined to those who deserve Nechama," without harming the members of their households, their relatives, or Allied personnel. (3) "Nechama must be attended to in a coordinated fashion along with the fulfillment of a fundamental promise" to the survivors, in order that they not, heaven forbid, suffer harm [from Germans or Allied authorities believing them to be the ones taking revenge]. (4) "The organization of Nechama's friends must be disbanded and dismantled as promptly as possible. They will each benefit personally, and we as a community will benefit as well."[28]

Those remarks from Shadmi, who sent them to his commanders, once more show emphatically that the leadership of the Yishuv opposed Plan A—the indiscriminate killing of millions—but supported Plan B, the attack on SS veterans, as uncontroversial. The remarks bring other points into focus as well:

First, there was a deeply emotional attitude toward the question of that friend Nechama. Shadmi writes explicitly that in conversations with his commanders at home, which is to say in Palestine before he left, he could tell that they too were in favor of her and that she was not merely a friend but even a sister who was considered majestic and sacred. His remarks are consistent with those of Shlomo Shamir, who, as noted, wrote that if a serious proposal had reached the Jewish Brigade for the liquidation of a million Germans, they might very well have put it into action. They are also consistent with the words of Kovner, who wrote to Vitka that Ben-Horin had actually let him know in Palestine that "we will take care of it," as well as those of Yehuda Arazi's brother Tuvia, who turned to Moshe Shertok and Ben-Gurion

at the end of 1945, when his brother took ill, with a suggestion for a reshuf-
fle: he would replace his brother in Italy in order to continue the work of
clandestine immigration, and Yehuda would be sent to Paris, where he could
work on planning the vengeance operations in Germany, which would likely
assist indirectly in the Zionist struggle against the British as well, "since they
will demonstrate that it is dangerous not to remove the Jewish survivors of
the Holocaust from Europe."[29]

Second, Shadmi's remarks indicate that the question was not whether
to carry out Plan B but rather who would carry it out if the order to do so
was given. Shadmi focused on the point, which he had already forcefully
presented to the Nokmim, that he represented the Jewish people after the
Holocaust and the war, and he stated unambiguously that regarding vengeance, responsibility must rest with the entire community rather than with
a small group. Should a decision be issued in favor of executing the plan,
then it must be executed only under the conditions Shadmi set forth: the
group of Nechama's friends must be disbanded and dismantled as promptly
as possible, he wrote. Those harsh words raise further questions: Did that attitude toward the Nokmim derive from the attitude of the Yishuv's leadership toward the survivors in general? Was the refusal to leave the matter in
the hands of the survivors, even under close supervision (as had been agreed
between Galili and Kovner before the latter set off on the way back to Europe), the product of a growing suspicion that the survivors, having undergone terrible experiences potentially beyond human endurance, might have
emerged from the inferno in imperfect mental condition? Ben-Gurion, on
his return from visiting the DP camps, said at a meeting of the Mapai Central Committee: "I found, to my astonishment [. . .], that the people were
nonetheless healthy, first of all in body, but also in spirit. Most are precious
Jews, precious Zionists with deep Zionist instincts." Although the Nokmim
were made up primarily of partisans and ghetto fighters who, having stood
up to the challenge, were viewed differently (and the emotional reception
they received when they came to the Jewish Brigade's camp is confirmation),
they too were to be approached with care, for fear of extremism and impul-
sive responses, and therefore the Nokmim must be disbanded and dismantled as an organization, for their own good and for the good of all.[30]

SHADMI'S MEETINGS WITH THE NOKMIM HEADQUARTERS

Now a chain of meetings began between Shadmi and representatives of the Nokmim. The first three meetings took place in as many successive days. It was out of the question, Shadmi said, that a group of individuals, even excellent ones, could take action in the name of the Jewish people. "This asset"—a term that, applied to revenge, further reveals his attitude toward Nechama—must be at the entire community's disposal, and what justification exists for their being "separate, closed off, and differentiated"? Why don't they integrate with the Jewish community at large and accept its authority? According to Shadmi, the Nokmim gladly accepted the community's authority, in full awareness and with a sense of responsibility, but were categorically unwilling to disband before implementing one of their plans; lengthy and difficult preparations over a period of months had left the Nokmim "in a very bad state, psychologically and personally." After the meetings, Shadmi informed them that all the assistance to Nechama would be subject to his authority and that he was assuming responsibility for immediate implementation once the practical plans solidified. After one encounter with Nechama (in other words, one stroke of vengeance), the group would disband, and Shadmi would designate some for immigration to Palestine and others to stay and help him with other impending work. Shadmi issued assignments to those loyal to him: to Shmuel (Uli) Hacker (later Givon), who commanded the German Unit, in place of Ben-Horin and apparently also to an officer from the Jewish Brigade. He gave them a month to investigate the details, and in the meantime two more meetings were to be held before the time came for the operation and for the group's disbandment.[31]

But developments were not as clear-cut and decisive as Shadmi described them in the report he sent, and it is worth examining how the other side saw them. Progress in negotiating with the Nokmim headquarters was sluggish, Shadmi himself admitted in unpublished testimony. He repeatedly mentioned three figures he met at three meetings, but the only one whose name he remembered was Pasha. Two men who accompanied Pasha, presumably the ones unnamed by Shadmi, were Bezalel Kek-Michaeli and Ben Meiri. Pasha testified that as a pair by themselves, he and Shadmi met little. Yehuda Ben-David, who set down the testimony, added for his own part that even though most of the Nokmim had participated in pioneer movements and truly saw their goal, once vengeance had been achieved, as immigration to the Land of Israel and integration into life there on a kibbutz and in the Haganah, the Nokmim did not at first accept the authority of the Haganah in full. On the contrary, Pasha testified, "we spoke like people [who were] an integral part of the organized Yishuv," not outsiders or opponents of it.[32]

Indeed, the leaders of the Nokmim were uneasy about external interference. Shadmi tried to convince them that as a matter of principle, neither he nor those who sent him had any intention of preventing acts of vengeance. Far from it, he said in later testimony. The Haganah supported in principle the execution of vengeance operations, but on three conditions, which he returned to and emphasized in additional meetings: first, that the operations have a "sufficiently realistic foundation;" second, that the operations not harm the most essential concerns of "the masses of Jews in the camps;" and third, that the operations "comply with our moral standards." The last point is easily understood: by "*our* moral standards," in first person plural, Shadmi meant the standards of the Yishuv and the Haganah, not the standards of those sitting across from him. If he meant the standards of the Jewish people as a whole, he didn't explicitly say so.[33]

"I tried to imagine myself in the position of those bitter people," Shadmi wrote after his first meetings led him to the conclusion that "it" amounted to an insane venture past the limits of human retaliation. (And by "it" he apparently referred to Plan A, which was discussed immediately before he wrote the remark.) "A phenomenon outside the bounds of any human thinking whatsoever. It's a kind of disease." It was clear to him, by his account, that he had to act quickly to defuse this ticking bomb before vengeance awakened fresh waves of antisemitism—before survivors who had managed to weather the cataclysm met their deaths because of deranged acts of vengeance.[34]

Moreover, while the teams in Germany were preparing for their mission, a written report reached Chaim Yahil (previously Hoffmann)—who was leading the relief teams that had come from the Land of Israel and were working under the auspices of the United Nations Relief and Rehabilitation Administration—that a Nazi underground was awaiting the opportunity for an open fight between Jews and Germans. That underground, he said, had done everything in its power to make the occupying forces also hate the

Jews: "The Jews are on edge," the document said, and dangerously vulnerable to provocation.[35] Shadmi also feared greatly that acts of vengeance would make the nations of the world lose their sympathy for the survivors and stop supporting the Jewish people's just demand for a state. After all, the Jews were the aggrieved party; they were not supposed to be the offending party.

The Nokmim put forward a different view: they had heard from Jewish officers in the US Army who had met Germans that the German masses were expecting the remainder of the Jewish people to exact a terrible vengeance. The Germans knew very well that it would be the appropriate punishment for the unforgivable crimes they had committed. Most of the Nokmim believed that the fears felt by the Yishuv leadership, and reflected in Shadmi's words, were baseless and that indeed the opposite was true: the Germans would not respond to deeds of vengeance, and all the populations that the Germans had conquered and tormented would merely rejoice and appreciate the deeds of the Nokmim. Years later, Shadmi told his son Yiska that of course the Germans deserved no mercy, and whatever could have been done should have been done. To Yiska he again enumerated the conditions that the operation had to meet: orderly coordination among all the parties, no telltale evidence (although it must also be made known that the vengeance was a stroke of "Jewish Work"), and no disquiet in their relations with the British.[36]

According to Shadmi, Pasha claimed to be speaking, in concert with his comrades, on behalf of thousands of members within his organization, but by Shadmi's estimation the number couldn't be more than 150, with only 5 to 7 truly active members and another 15 or 20 looking after the financial aspect. In the course of Shadmi's efforts to assess the numbers and the nature of the Nokmim, but perhaps at the initiative of the Nokmim leaders themselves, a young woman in uniform who had come from Romania to Paris met with him. Shadmi testified that he learned a great deal from her about the Nokmim. That woman—who carried false papers and whose name he did not remember, although Vitka is mentioned on his schedule of work and meetings—led him to understand that if he offered the group a concrete plan of some kind, it would be welcomed enthusiastically by most of the members she knew, roughly 90 percent of the total membership. In the wake of that meeting, as well as in a close succession of further long meetings, the leaders of the Nokmim agreed, according to Shadmi, to have him appoint two more officers to their top command and to set up a sort of inner quadrumvirate, two from each side, that would require his approval for any action.

In addition, Shadmi notified them that he had authorization from the Land of Israel to give them assistance—presumably the assistance that Pasha had requested from Avigur—and that in Palestine they had already spoken with Kovner, who at the time was imprisoned in Jerusalem. Indeed, Shadmi assigned to them Yehezkel Baharav of Kfar Monash and Dov Schenkel of Kibbutz Neot Mordechai and the German Unit. The help that the two men provided to the operation will be detailed later. Shadmi's two men on the quadrumvirate had clear instructions to oppose any plan that did not differentiate SS veterans, who were guilty ipso facto, from the civilian population.

At this point, the interviewer remarked to Shadmi that such an agreement recalled the agreements from the time of the conflict with the breakaway movements. His remark indicates that although the testimony was delivered fully forty years after the war, the supposed equivalence between the Nokmim and the breakaway movements was still being invoked and perpetuated.[37] It must be added immediately that the Nokmim, most notably Pasha, deny the existence of any such agreement in either of its two aspects (outsiders joining their top command, and the conditioning of all operations on Shadmi's approval) and that there is indeed no confirmation of the agreement in the testimonies of the Nokmim, nor in materials relating to their activities in Europe.[38]

In his own testimony and in his book of memoirs, Shadmi goes on to describe a series of terrible large-scale plans that his men told him were part of what the Nokmim intended, most of which he vetoed. It must be clearly emphasized that the plans mentioned by Shadmi are also unsupported by any other testimonies or in materials remaining from the Nokmim. Among them are committing simultaneous arson in Germany's large cities, with a projected death toll of hundreds of thousands of Germans; blowing up German bridges and tunnels; and carrying out attacks not only in Germany but also in other countries, especially in and around Paris—a plan that had no connection to revenge against the Germans. Could it be that Shadmi and his faction were overly fearful of what the Nokmim might have in mind?[39]

Shadmi apparently had a misunderstanding regarding Paris. The group's members, young, active readers who knew the literary scene, must have read

Bruno Jasieński's novel *I Burn Paris*, which had enjoyed broad commercial success in Europe in the 1920s and 1930s. The book was penned as a Communist response to the novel *I Burn Moscow*, which was written by a right-winger. *I Burn Paris* was published originally in installments, in the newspaper *L'humanité*, which spoke for the French Communist Party. After appearing as a book, it was translated into ten languages, including Yiddish and Polish, and it went through many printings, six in the Soviet Union alone. Jasieński was deported from France on charges of disturbing the public order because his protagonist plotted to take revenge against the world for his woeful life, destroying it to build a different one instead. The protagonist goes to prison, where fellow inmates arrange work for him at a water purification plant and find him a fatally poisonous powder, which he places in the city's drinking water in order to exterminate the entire population. The urban government collapses, the city is divided into domains controlled by warring ethnic groups (the Jews rule the Jewish Quarter, Le Marais), and ultimately everyone is killed except the prisoners, who build a model Socialist society on the ruins of the old order. A call for solidarity with the Soviet Union, at the end of the book, won the author a hero's welcome there after his deportation from France, but this did not avail him in the end: he was executed during one of Stalin's purges in the late 1930s. Still, the book lived on in Europe at large—and in the East European bloc in particular, after Nikita Khrushchev rehabilitated the author's name.[40] Among the testimonies of the Nokmim, Lena Satz-Hammel's and Ben Meir's mention the book without elaboration, apparently because it was so well known that the idea of burning the French capital, and especially of poisoning its water as unmitigated collective punishment, had been in the air since the first printing, even if readers considered the story an allegory rather than a procedural guide. It could be that the expression heard today, "Is Paris burning?," comes from that era, even if it became more famous after Hitler used it.[41]

The title *I Burn Paris* came up in Shadmi's conversations with the Nokmim, but they had no intention of harming the Parisians in theory or practice, and no such thought is mentioned in their testimonies. On the contrary, Pasha wrote that the headquarters was moved to Paris not only in order to obtain the poison there but also to benefit from the assistance of former members of the Résistance and Maquis in doing so, because as leftists and fighters who had also been oppressed by the Germans, they would understand the Nokmim. The Nokmim intended to attack Germans only. In a letter that Kovner wrote in the 1960s, after reading Shadmi's book, he wondered at the intentions attributed to the Nokmim. "To attack not only in Germany but in other countries all over Europe—and in Paris [. . .] when were there ever any plans like that?"[42]

It could be that because the talks between the Nokmim and Shadmi had aroused mistrust, the Nokmim preferred to have an additional, parallel channel for communicating with the Yishuv and created one through the close friends they had made in the Jewish Brigade. Thus, for example, Zygi Gliksman testified that he was sent by Pasha with another of the Nokmim, dressed in Jewish Brigade uniforms and furnished with appropriate papers, to the Brigade's camp in Belgium, where they were meant "to establish appropriate communications with the Land of Israel in order to inform the group which of the three plans we had been promised support for" (Plan A, Plan B, or Plan C—the latter of which targeted individual Germans). Gliksman was told to wait for an answer and bring it to Pasha when it arrived. He put the appropriate communications in place. For three weeks, he slept at the camp, while the man he'd traveled with returned to Paris and made some financial transactions along the way. One day Gliksman was summoned by someone (he doesn't say who) and informed that Plan A had been canceled and only Plans B and C approved. Immediately he set out to inform Pasha.[43] This account is one more indication that the top officers of the Haganah and Bricha—Shadmi, Avigur, Ehud Avriel—had a particular opinion of the Nokmim. However, lower in the hierarchy of the Jewish Brigade, among those who personally knew and assisted the Nokmim, the opinion differed; there was more understanding and solidarity regarding the purpose of the Nokmim, and their needs were given greater consideration.

From another direction came further proof of the opinion the Yishuv's top leaders had formed of the Nokmim. Shortly after Shadmi arrived in Paris, Ben-Gurion (who, as noted, spent time there on his way back to Palestine) appointed a team to coordinate all the Jewish resistance forces in Europe in order to prepare a force there for the expected conflict with the British. The combined force was named the Jewish Resistance Movement in Europe, essentially terming it the European arm of the *Meri* ("revolt" in Hebrew), the Jewish Resistance Movement that had been formed in Palestine.[44]

To the coordinating team, Ben-Gurion appointed Ruth Kliger (Eliav), a central activist from the Mossad for Aliyah B, to represent the Jewish Agency; Avriel; and Shadmi to head the team in his capacity as overall commander of the Haganah in Europe.

At a meeting of these three, Avriel was appointed to serve both as liaison between the high command of European Meri and the Nokmim and as liaison between the high command and Ben-Gurion. Upon his arrival, Avriel realized the approach of the Nokmim, he later testified. Although they presented their plan of action to members of the Haganah and to "figures of national authority," at the same time they declared that they would be taking action in any case, even without support from the institutions, as they had previously declared to Meirke Davidson and Ben-Horin. Avriel, according to his testimony to Yehuda Bauer, was shocked to discover certain ideas of the Nokmim that at least some people, upon hearing them, "considered absolutely mad and harmful and unethical and altogether inhuman." In response, the Meri leadership's attitude hardened along lines that were approved by Ben-Gurion and others who were "highly against it" and that were reflected in the stance that Shadmi had taken: to tell the Nokmim that their objective was sacred and just; to acquire their trust and attempt to influence their course of action because otherwise "they will simply disdain us and do all kinds of terrible things that we will have to answer for later"; and to help them by providing logistical assistance coordinated with the Haganah and headquarters. To that, Avriel's testimony included the following remarks about Kovner, which are consistent with what Ben-Horin said:

> [Kovner] had a foot in each camp. He was one of our people, but he was also in one of those gangs. We didn't completely trust him. We didn't believe them, because they said, "We're fibbing to you. We're not telling you everything [. . .]." We were more willing to help them than they were to be helped by us, because they considered us an obstacle to their operation, even though they understood that we were providing them with professional help and with levelheaded people.[45]

Despite all that, even though the three top officers had formulated a clear policy that was coordinated with Ben-Gurion, they did not continue their headquarters' activities in the realm of vengeance. For practical purposes, the authority remained in Shadmi's hands, although Avriel helped him by means of his good relations with Avigur and "exposed them all"—probably meaning that he revealed their names. From Shadmi's, Avriel's, and Ben-Horin's testimonies, it emerges unambiguously that they had clear knowledge of Plan A, that they informed Ben-Gurion of it, and that all the leaders were dead set against it. Ben-Meiri testified: "We kept in close touch with Ehud Avriel and with Avigur," who were opposed to vengeance operations and took action to prevent them. He added a key point, "They simply pitied us," a remark that sheds light on the relations that continued in force and the assistance that was given to the group despite opposition to its program, as well as emphasizing the question of the relations between the Yishuv and the survivors. Yulek saw the relations with Shadmi differently: Shadmi was instructed to keep an eye on his group because they thought "that we had come unhinged"; Shadmi was critical of us, "but he had respect for us too, because he saw our seriousness and he understood that we had lost everything."[46]

When the Nokmim understood that a large-scale plan would not be approved, and Kovner in Palestine issued them the instruction, they turned their energies to an operation against tens of thousands of ex-SS and Gestapo personnel, former officers, and enlisted men who were being held in prison camps. The primary reason for targeting them was the suspicion that the Allies would free them without trial—an inkling that proved correct.[47] Once more, according to Shadmi, the idea of poison came up—this time, poisoning the drinking water in the prison camps. The poisoning of prisoners in Stalag 13, which was near Nuremberg, by adding arsenic to the flour at the bottom of bread loaves, was one plan he approved; Shadmi also enumerated other operations that he had approved for three camps, including poisoning the water.[48]

Shadmi was wary of the consequences of such operations; therefore, he did what was necessary to protect the camps of the Jewish DPs in case, after it became known that the operations were the work of Jewish survivors, the local population responded with violence against them. No force, he wrote, must set out on its mission before steps have been taken, and tested, to protect the survivors. Another precaution he took was to prepare arrangements on the roads and at the borders for the participants in approved vengeance operations so that immediately after the deed they could retreat to assembly points on the shore in anticipation of leaving for the Land of Israel rather than being hunted down by the British and Americans. The arrangements included a number of spots at the border that were prepared beforehand. Because of the great trepidation associated with the operations, the operatives' immediate departure was coordinated in advance with the Mossad for Aliyah B and even prioritized above other departures.[49] Shadmi and Yehuda Ben-David said unequivocally that this arrangement "was the way to dissolve the group"—a consideration that, of course, was not revealed to its members—and that it had been agreed that each of the Nokmim could participate in one operation, thereupon being sent off to the Land of Israel as promptly as possible. However, Ben-David emphasized that those same Nokmim were "likable men" who worked shoulder to shoulder with the Haganah on everything necessary for the Bricha, clandestine immigration, and procurement. Shadmi even stressed that they integrated into the Yishuv as soon as they arrived, as laboring settlers and in the Haganah, as if to say: Those I sent to the Land of Israel were no goldbrickers, and I did well to send them.[50]

APPROACHING ANTEK ZUCKERMAN
TO LEAD THE VENGEANCE OPERATION

At the end of 1945, as mentioned, Menashe Gewissar, an emissary from the Nokmim, was sent to meet Chaika Grossman in Poland and convince her to join their activities, but she immediately and categorically refused. At the start of 1946, Gewissar, then treasurer for the Bricha, approached Antek Zuckerman in Poland as well and asked him to lead the groups following Kovner's arrest.

Gewissar testified that he knew the Nokmim from back in Romania and that they "came to me in Paris and bewailed their distress to me." Poldek Maimon told him then for the first time about Plan A and about Kovner's journey to Palestine and arrest, and revealed to him that the teams in Germany were still unaware of that arrest. He said there was despair in the Paris headquarters; the news had hit them like lightning from a clear sky, and they felt helpless. According to Gewissar's testimony, Poldek requested that he persuade Antek to come to Paris and meet the headquarters staff.

Gewissar was well suited to the task: first, he knew Antek from as far back as Vilna; they had trained together as members of HeHalutz before the war, Antek serving as one of the leaders. Second, he was close to Poldek and to the group's activities. Accordingly, Gewissar traveled to Warsaw, where he spoke with Antek and Zivia. She was quite familiar with the Nokmim from her time in Bucharest—and she immediately objected. But she nonetheless suggested that Antek go to Paris and decide there, at the place itself. Gewissar returned to Paris and told the Nokmim that Antek was on his way.[51]

According to Antek's testimony, a meeting of the HeHalutz movement's leadership convened in Lodz, with emissaries from the Land of Israel participating, to discuss the future of the movement; it considered the request as well, and the participants decided in favor, on the condition that before Antek give explicit approval he meet with the authorities responsible for issues of defense and security in Paris—in other words, with Nahum Shadmi. Antek said he traveled to Germany and met with the groups there, but no such meeting is mentioned in the testimony of anyone from the German-based teams, nor in their memoirs. It must be added that they were continually moving from place to place in search of prisoner camps, so a meeting with them would have been difficult to accomplish.

Gewissar testified that when he returned to Paris, Shadmi took the initiative to contact him and when they met, Shadmi told him about himself. As a veteran Haganah member, he asked about Gewissar's experiences during the Holocaust and told him explicitly that there was a decision from the top institutions of the Yishuv—he may have mentioned Moshe Shertok's name as proof—to bring the Nokmim who were scattered around Germany to the Land of Israel and have "all the activities that were theirs to carry out" handled by the German Unit of the Palmach and its soldiers. The phrasing is Gewissar's, but it does once more imply that the Haganah believed vengeance should be taken, although not by the Nokmim.

Shadmi asked Gewissar to persuade the headquarters of the Nokmim to give up the idea, but Gewissar refused. It was not the Yishuv that set up the group, he said, and so it is not for the Yishuv to disband it. The Yishuv did not experience the Holocaust and did not understand those who did. These people had come together for a purpose, and they wouldn't abandon it. They couldn't be asked to agree to anything contrary to their conscience and to the thoughts that had occupied them for years, and for the past year they had been investing their entire selves in the project. Gewissar agreed only to pass Shadmi's information about the Yishuv's decision along to the Nokmim. Then Gewissar left for Germany, where he met Antek and told him the same, leaving the decision in Antek's hands.[52]

After the war, both Gewissar and Antek were members of the Ghetto Fighters' Kibbutz, living as close neighbors for eighteen years. They never again raised the subject and never sorted it out between each other. Grossman was a member of nearby Kibbutz Evron, and apparently the subject didn't come up in meetings with her either. Each of them remembered the events differently. Antek testified that from Germany he traveled to Paris, where he had a very long talk with Shadmi and with other Haganah members; he told Shadmi about the proposal and about the decision in favor that was taken at Lodz, and he expressed his uncertainties and hesitancies regarding courses of action. In response, he was asked by Shadmi (referred to in Antek's testimony by his original name, Kremer) whether in principle he, Antek, accepted the decisions of the national institutions. When the answer was affirmative, Shadmi said: "If one single person remains from those teams in Germany, that one person will be overmuch."

Antek was quoting Shadmi's answer from memory, but he did repeat it at least twice, word for word, after a number of years.[53] Antek was surprised at Shadmi's attitude, which was much more critical and severe than he had expected. Thus, after receiving that "definitive, decisive" answer from the responsible representative of the Haganah, Antek gave the teams in Germany a negative reply and returned to Poland. His interviewer asked the obvious question: did Antek accept Shadmi's words as a warning to be heeded, or was Antek himself convinced that the operations should not be mounted? Antek answered clearly: he was convinced that the operations should indeed be mounted, but, he explained again, when the members of HeHalutz in Lodz said yes, and he said yes, the understanding was that if he headed the vengeance operations, they would be an integral part of the overall operations of the pioneer movements. "I don't need to explain here that we'd been vengeance-minded for years. I think it's no exaggeration if [I say] that there wasn't a Jew who participated in forming an armed organization, a Jewish fighting force, and wasn't imbued with the idea of revenge against the

Germans and wasn't in search of a plan. [...] The fact is that I was about to replace Kovner as commander of the Nokmim," he testified, "and if I were leading them, I would have brought about vengeance but differently."[54]

Now we have reached the limits of the discipline, and we remain with one testimony weighing against another. In Shadmi's testimonies and books, there is no mention of the meeting at all. The Nokmim insisted that they never met Antek—not in Paris or on German soil. Pasha claimed unequivocally that there was never any request on behalf of headquarters. Indeed, why would Pasha ask to be replaced in a position that he was fully dedicated to? Poldek and Vitka answered, separately, that it never happened. They never heard of any visit by Antek to the German teams, and they never met him in Paris. Poldek testified: "I had a totally private conversation with Gewissar, and various ideas came out of the despair that hit us after Kovner's arrest and the loss of the material, the money, and the support that we'd been waiting for. True, I did raise the idea in that conversation, but I had no authority to offer Gewissar a commitment. He was a loyal friend of the Nokmim as well as the life-force of the Bricha movement, highly valued and close to Antek." However, Poldek and Vitka said they were very happy to hear that the institutions of HeHalutz in Poland approved the appointing of Antek to lead the Nokmim.[55] Be that as it may, this affair reflects the centrality of the issue then and later.

In Paris, additional consultations were held; James Ben-Gal made a practice of meeting with Shertok during Shertok's occasional visits to the city, in order to receive instructions from "the higher-ups," as he called them. Ben-Gal asked Shertok what the instructions regarding vengeance actually were, because the Jewish Brigade had never received a straightforward and comprehensive directive from the Yishuv leadership. Ben-Gal testified that Shertok's answer surprised him in its clarity: If vengeance was to be taken on behalf of the Jewish people, then it must be vengeance worthy of the name, and the target must be plain to all. The vengeance must be wreaked on a scale that will leave an impression on the entire world, so that the world will realize that Jewish blood is not forfeit and that vengeance is serious, rather than a corpse here and a corpse there. (Those words may express his displeasure at the clandestine assassinations of Germans who were not fully identified.) If some thousands of SS veterans, or all the detainees at a camp where the

Allies were holding war prisoners, could die at once, and if later it was leaked that this had been Jewish vengeance, then according to him the vengeance would have the proportions "of the things that Shertok told me should be done." In other words, a very senior figure in the Yishuv leadership, the man who founded the Jewish Brigade, not only approved of but encouraged far-reaching vengeance against the imprisoned SS veterans. Ben-Gal's response was also clear: "It was obvious that we would assist in vengeance operations." Later, Ben-Gal expressed regret that the Nokmim hadn't succeeded.

Shertok's words to Ben-Gal are congruent with his stand on the matter, a clearer stance than that of other Yishuv leaders. They are consistent with the report that Argov sent him regarding the avenging deeds of the Jewish Brigade, of which Shertok was aware as they were happening. They also complement Shadmi's words regarding the instructions received from the leadership of the Yishuv, according to which the German Unit of the Palmach would be doing what was necessary. Although the Jewish Brigade was disbanded on July 10, 1946, even afterward, a band of some 120 soldiers stayed in Europe, integrated with the emissaries, and operated in all spheres—38 of them, mostly from the German Unit, were recruited for "operations of the Haganah in Europe: vengeance, military training in the DP camps, and handling of armaments"—in that order of importance, as it turned out.[56]

In other words, vengeance was not dropped from the soldiers' agenda. The next chapter will deal with the fortunes of the project from August 1945, when the Yishuv contacted the teams of Nokmim and their headquarters and the Jewish Brigade set off northward, to July 1946, when the Nokmim joined the Yishuv in Palestine. The chapter will focus on those operations spoken of with Shadmi that were executed in part, as well as how and when they were executed, and with what results.

Baruch of Mainz

SHAUL TCHERNICHOVSKY

Accursed be thou forever, cruel race!
Accursed forever be thy veil name!
The wrath of God shall dwell with thee forever.
The blood that thou hast sacrificed, the tears,
The Moaning of thy victims, shall arise
In one wild flood against thee, and the sound
Shall be a horror in the stormy night.
[...]
Ha! How fearful is the night!
Here in the dark I feel
The cold that cuts into my heart
Like driven steel.
But through the town are crimson flames
As from a furnace blown.
And the hand that lit the furnace there
Was mine alone.
Look! The dull-glowing clouds of smoke
Roll further, higher.
The monastery burns and wraps
The town in fire.
When I had lit the funeral pile
I lingered there
And joy was in my heart to watch
Their fierce despair!

From *Poems, 1910–1920*, Schocken Books, Tel Aviv (republished
in 1943 in Hebrew), p. 197. Translated by Maurice Samuel, in
A Golden Treasury of Jewish Literature, selected and edited by
Leo W. Schwartz, Rinehart & Company, Inc., New York, 1937,
p. 623. Courtesy of Schocken Books.

6

Germany, August 1945–June 1946
Life Apart from Life

AN AFTERNOON IN SPRING, at a modest but well-kept apartment in Tel Aviv. The year is 2010, and Yehuda (Idek) Friedman is seated on the sofa. To his left is his wife Ruth, I am on his right, and Hava Zexer is standing to the side with a camera. Opposite us are shelves loaded with books and knick-knacks. Idek repeats that he has little new to tell us researchers. Surely we've already heard everything from the group's other members. His wife cautions us that his health isn't what it once was; he is in his nineties. We promise to be brief, merely to clear up a few points that have remained uncertain, and that's all. Something to eat? No, thank you. Please don't bother. But a cup of tea would suit us fine.

The interview begins, and it flows smoothly: What were your experiences in the war, where were you, how did you join the group of Avengers? "After what I went through, I couldn't think of anything else but revenge, even for a minute. I knew that we couldn't return; we couldn't get out of it [alive]. We were burnt out, and we knew that we were going to die [when caught, but] it was obvious that there should be vengeance." We ask further: Who was with you on the team in Germany, what was life like for you, and how did you plan together for the operation in Hamburg and at Dachau?

Idek is a very modest person, mild-mannered and a man for productive work rather than a *tongiber*, as he defines someone purporting to set the tone as guidance for others. The interview starts to draw to a close. The central topic had been the operation at Dachau, which was not carried out.

Then, suddenly and without warning, Idek disregards the present time. He sits tensely forward, his eyes fixed on a point above the shelves, and from his throat comes a howl:

> Why?! Why?! Why was the operation stopped?! Father and Mother will never forgive me for not doing anything! Mama, Papa, I did nothing! They stripped them and shot them [at the Płaszów concentration camp]. I went home, and the place was empty. We were seven children. My uncle had ten. We should have tried again and again!

His howling seems endless, a terrible burst of fury. Hava is frozen at her camera. I don't dare jot anything down. His wife fidgets on the sofa and asks in a whisper if, on second thought, we wouldn't have something to eat. Idek continues:

> It hurts horribly, it hurts, it hurts! What a waste, what a waste! We were all in favor of the operation, we were unified, these were fighting men and fighting women, each chosen individually for the group, and we hung around there for a whole year! Why? Why did we agree to call it off? Last Holocaust Day [a few days before the interview], I was pacing around like a madman![1]

Ruth extends a hesitant hand and places it on his arm. He slowly composes himself, returns to the present, and resumes the fluent conversation, continuing to lay before us his complaints and bitter disappointment. When we take our leave, we are apologetic and regretful about what we have elicited. As we stand in the doorway, he is already regaining his pleasant disposition. On the way home, Hava and I speak about the conflict between the duty to collect testimony while there is still time and the distress that the interviewer triggers in returning survivors to the past to relive it, wearing down and penetrating the protective walls that they have constructed over the years. By what right? Dogged by a sense of guilt, we phone the next day to ask after him.

DIFFICULTIES OF LIFE IN GERMANY

The Germany where the Nokmim arrived, a few months after its surrender, was a ravaged land. Bombing by the Allies had left enormous destruction, particularly in the cities, and tens of millions were homeless. In Berlin alone, 75 percent of the buildings were unfit to be lived in. Some fourteen to sixteen million Germans had been expelled from Czechoslovakia and Poland, crowding the country further. Infrastructures and industries had been damaged. Electricity had been cut, and it took months to return. Hardest of all was the severe shortage of food. Rations were distributed by the Allies against printed coupons. The black market flourished, and inflation ballooned. Some seven and a half million Germans had been killed, four million of them soldiers; a million and a half or so had been captured by the Soviets, and they included many youngsters who had been drafted in Germany's last-gasp war effort. One German in four had lost a family member, and women were a majority of the population. There were at least 50,000 orphaned children in Berlin, and another 150,000 to 200,000 "Russian babies" born in the Soviet-occupied zone after the incidents of mass rape. The four victorious Allies—Britain, the Soviet Union, France, and the United States—divided the country among themselves and tried to replace the old institutions of government that had collapsed. Germany essentially had no societal institutes and no leadership in any sphere. It was everyone for themselves.

The Allies had hoped to punish the Germans and take revenge, and the Morgenthau Plan—originating with US Secretary of the Treasury Henry Morgenthau—instructed the American occupying forces not to take any action for Germany's economic rehabilitation. The plan even gave thought to requiring heavy war reparations from Germany to the victimized countries. But with time, it became clear that a ruined Germany would be a burden on Americans. Thus, after as little as a year, a change of policy began emerging, and by summer 1947 the Marshall Plan had superseded its predecessor. George Marshall, chief of staff in the US Army, initiated a program of healing for Europe, on the theory that only significant investments in infrastructure would bring economic recovery and thus strengthen the democracies and hold the line between them and communism. Thus rehabilitation began for sixteen countries, foremost among them Germany. In a short

time, Germany turned into an economic miracle; and it was into that trans-
forming country that the Nokmim stepped. They followed the happenings
in Germany at close range, gratified by the defeat and the difficulties suffered
by the Germans that they met and resentful about the signs of rehabilitation and of a return of the German lifestyle before the country faced justice.[2]

The teams of Nokmim who came to Germany in summer 1945 were
small, and they were isolated from one another. Sometimes it was each man
on his own, each woman on her mission, alone and under false identities,
with assumed names and forged papers. As a precaution, each of them had
several IDs; sometimes the requirements of a cover story meant denying a
previous identity, abandoning a language, lying and dissembling, fabricat-
ing new details and dispelling old ones. They lived among the hated Germans in conditions of scarcity, because the money collected was earmarked
for the operation and not for personal needs. They were immersed in preparing the groundwork, the connections, and the workplaces—while awaiting the poison. Among the members, there was compartmentalization; not
everyone knew the locations of the others at any given moment or their assignments and activities. Each of the teams had its own assignment, because
their overall number—roughly fifty members—was relatively scant for the
task they had undertaken. According to the testimonies, the Nokmim were
constantly shifting their locations, both for the purpose of the Bricha, which
they were still assisting, and for the purpose of vengeance. They traveled
from country to country by truck and by train, often together with Soviet
troops but always with daring and resourcefulness, among men who had not
been home for years. Their vengeance project had them meandering from
place to place in Germany, despite not having recovered or taken healing
time for themselves after the torments of the Holocaust. "I was the very figure of a nomad," said Mordechai Roseman. There were arrests from time to
time; a month's imprisonment was the invariable sentence from the Soviets
for black marketeering, followed by release, rearrest, and escape. It was difficult to follow the testimonies and create a clear picture from them: "We were
here today, there tomorrow. Day or night, who noticed?" said Hasya Taubes-
Warchavchik. "No identification card for a real identity, no surnames, we
were switching documents all the time, we lived from hand to mouth. Nothing mattered to us," testified Mira (Mirka) Verbin-Shabetzky.[3]

Over time, the members of the group formed a deep friendship that continues to this day. Thus for example, Yehuda (Idek) Friedman related that
when Hilik (Yehiel Warchavchik, later Hasya's husband) took ill, they immediately raised money for medicine. A spirit of dedication and frugal living prevailed among the Nokmim. In Paris, Yitzhak Vilozni looked after
Zygi Gliksman, who had developed jaundice, and saw to his needs. "What
trust we all had in each other. No one was asked to do anything out of line
or anything they couldn't accomplish," Manek L. says today. Yashek Ben-
Zur added: "I agree to be interviewed only on condition that the members
who have already passed away after decades of close friendship all are mentioned." There were, of course, couples as well. They got together, they broke
up—they were young people whose world was lost, and they were looking
to one another for warmth and closeness. When Lena Satz fell in love with
Yitzhak Hammel, she wrote in her diary: "Could it really be wrong for me to
be happy? [. . .] Is it against the mission? I have the mission in mind, but also
love, also my own life."[4] The devotion to their purpose was complete. They
were restless; they were ready to burn the world down and be burned with
it. They didn't for a moment expect to exit Germany alive; in Hasya's words:
"We were fully taken up by the idea of [killing] six million. No one was left
from our families, life promised me nothing, I wasn't a living person. We
were all ready to die, and death was constantly before us."[5]

There was also a sense of loneliness because they had postponed the
dream of immigrating to the Land of Israel. Most of the refugees shared in
that dream, and the emissaries from the Land of Israel, including soldiers of
the Jewish Brigade, were working to make it happen. The Nokmim may have
been wary of encountering the Land of Israel and the unfamiliar form that
the dream might assume in reality, but in any case they were obliged first to
settle accounts with the Germans and only then to reapproach the dream.
They were apart from their environment and the rest of the refugees. They
often had to confront difficulties single-handed as they fulfilled their tasks;
both teamwork and solo work were necessary. Pasha sent Vitka from Paris to
visit the members of the various teams in Germany. She didn't reach them all
because they were dispersed and mobile, but she returned with certain conclusions: "People in their great isolation are so despairing," Vitka wrote to
Abba Kovner, "so invested solely in one single idea that leads directly to the

depths of death. They [...] are hardly occupying this world [...]. We are completely cut off from all the social and political life of the Jews here in the Diaspora, and all the more so from life in the Land of Israel."[6] There were more than a few moments of crisis: "Something is pressing on my heart; pressing and stifling [...]. I wish that for once it would just follow through to the end," wrote Lena in her diary. Alongside the fear arising from personal danger, there was never a moment without fear of what would befall the Jewish people unless change came soon. After some of the Nokmim heard Yitzhak Lamdan's poem "Masada," which was read aloud among the Jewish Brigade and which won great popularity in the Zionist youth movements of Europe for promising that Masada, the mountain on which that last rebels against the Romans took their lives, would never fall again—Lena was beside herself: "How it [the poem] underscores our calamity, the fact that we truly are perishing [...]. If nothing happens to awaken the world, and our own pitiful people especially, then our fate will be to perish [...]. Must we in fact perish now?"[7]

As individuals and as family members, they paid a heavy price. Almost all paid it on the understanding that they had no choice, since the secrets must be kept from the few surviving relatives that they had and even from spouses who were not Nokmim. When Kazhik left Bucharest for Poland in order to guide Jews across the Polish border southward, he left his parents back in Poland. When he learned that the vengeance operation would be a lengthy project that would delay his immigration to the Land of Israel, he asked that his parents be allowed to join a troop of immigrants bound for Italy. And so, after managing to locate them in the ruins of Warsaw, he didn't see them again for almost three years.[8]

Yulek Harmatz's memoirs repeatedly mention his mother. He in fact parted twice from her—upon leaving the ghetto, and then after an emotional reunion in Lublin—and neither his longing for her nor his pangs of conscience subsided until after the vengeance operation, when he could feel that her sacrifice, and her isolation, had not been in vain.

Lena's diary says: "My mother has sailed for the land of Israel, and I did not go with her." Manek was one of the very few who had two sisters and a brother still alive; and Yulek, his commander, was unaware of this until he found out later that Manek had cut himself off from the group and disappeared for a few days in order to see his siblings and search together for their parents. After returning, Manek felt guilty that he had left his position for a number of days in order to see family, particularly when an operation was about to be mounted.

Idek had received two weeks' leave while they were still in Italy, in order to meet with a sister who had survived, and when the group was in Germany afterward, he felt it wouldn't be appropriate to ask for another leave. After all, if everyone went off to look for relatives, the group would fall apart. Shimek (Shimon) Lustgarten almost lost Shifra, the love of his life. The two of them were liberated from Auschwitz after a year and a half there, but at that point, despite the "very heavy cost," he insisted on going his own way. He wrote to her that he had in his very hands a certificate for immigration into the Land of Israel but he couldn't use it yet. He couldn't immigrate while there were still accounts to settle. He couldn't allow their future children to experience another Auschwitz. Therefore, for the time being, immigration was out of the question.[9]

Rachel Galperin-Gliksman, assigned to serve as an emissary in Budapest, tried to return to Romania to say goodbye to her sister and mother, both survivors, before they set off for the Land of Israel; however, she didn't get there in time. The ship left, and she remained deprived of a face-to-face farewell. It would be another year before they saw each other again. Poldek Maimon traveled many hours from Paris to an Italian port in order to say goodbye to Aviva Liebermann, whom he was head-over-heels in love with, and to tell her he did not have the right to suggest a solid contact.[10]

By means of letters, and principally in notes sent to Lena in Weimar by Yitzhak, who was in charge of the Berlin district, he would tell her that he was tired after days of running from pillar to post, that his head hurt, that it was a lonely job when you had to stay isolated for a certain term, and that he missed her. The idea of personal relationships as a factor in who is assigned to live together or serve on the same team was completely foreign to their thinking, especially since the relationships were not always permanent or long-term. Each of the Nokmim received an assignment and handled it together with whoever else was assigned. "I had no right to a life," Yitzhak wrote Lena, fearful of how the long isolation might influence his sanity. "I'm going mad, but not completely."[11]

Yulek wrote again and again in his diary about terrible migraines, which he attributed to the burden of responsibility—everyone considered him a champion at getting things done—and he was also troubled by continual problems with his teeth because of malnourishment in the ghettos and forests and a lack of medical care even after the war. Even as tens of thousands of Jews around them were resuming their lives and building a future, the Nokmim cared for one another when they were ill and refrained from contacting physicians because they were, in essence, living for months on end as an underground once more. Each of the Nokmim experienced internal tension that demanded resolute faith and resilience, and they say that only their friendship compensated for the lonely isolation.[12]

The Nokmim emerged from the Holocaust with no possessions, and most of them had no education and no trade either. Most were in their early twenties, and the war had robbed them of six years. They lived from hand to mouth, in conditions of scarcity, and they counted every zloty and mark. They received an allowance that Pasha sent from Paris, and they managed on it. The sentence "There was nothing to eat" appears in most of the testimonies, along with recollection of the amazing occasions when some kind of food did appear.

Hasya found a sheaf of money on one of the trains that they wended their way on. She didn't tap into it but asked permission to use part of it to have her worn-out shoes repaired—not to, heaven forbid, buy new ones. Sometimes she traded her monthly bread ration for salt herring. Mira Verbin-Shabetzky related that they each had one dress and a pair of shoes that was long worn out. It seems so harsh, looking back, said Shlomit, who had been a member of the French underground and was married to Heniek, who, as mentioned, handled a great deal of money from the Jewish communities. However, there was a special atmosphere then—no one pilfered. Poldek, who slept on a mattress stuffed with worthless money, discovered that his brother too had survived; while excitedly planning to go meet him, Poldek asked Pasha's permission to take a few dollars and purchase a proper gift for him.[13] Aharon Kagan was the head of the so-called financial department and managed it high-handedly together with his younger brother Yashka. Aharon and his wife, Dinka, were accused of pocketing money, and Pasha sentenced them to death. Lena testifies that mentally, the group still hadn't left the underground and the Soviet forests behind, and therefore everything immediately drew a death sentence. Many of the Nokmim considered the sentence extreme, and it was, of course, not carried out—another reason being that in the days of the ghetto and the forest, a strict rule forbade killing a Jew before killing a German. But the couple left the Nokmim and relocated to Los Angeles.[14]

For the Nokmim's lodgings, the headquarters required each to individually rent a room in a separate place so that the group's members would not be seen together. When they chose a room, they had to avoid risks: never reside at the end of a hallway, preferably have a separate entrance and an outward-facing window, preferably rent from elderly landlords who were not involved in the war and would not ask unnecessary questions. It must be borne in mind that in Germany's difficult times directly after the war, the landlords were gladdened by any gift of food they might receive from tenants and were often willing to look the other way and avoid asking certain questions. Those landlords were waiting for sons and fathers to return from the war, and they had yet to internalize Germany's fall from lofty hegemony to defeat. For example, in Fürth, near Nuremberg, there was an office with a list of houses that would rent rooms on the condition that the tenants prove that they were transient foreigners waiting for a visa in order to travel farther, generally to the US or Canada.

Yulek rented a room with Manek in Fürth, at number 32 on the Heiligenstrasse, the "Street of Saints." They presented themselves as Poles who, having been sent to Germany for forced labor, were unwilling to return to now-Communist Poland and who were waiting for a visa. They presented documents that they had received from Pasha—handwritten, without photos, and of course with false names.

Mira also rented a room in Fürth, from a German widow whose husband and son, as photographed in German military uniforms, held a position of honor in the apartment. It was very difficult to look at the photos with seeming nonchalance, to listen to excuses such as "we had absolutely no idea," to hear and speak the hated language. Mira was undercover as a Volksdeutsche, an expatriate German, who was now searching for her family and, because of (supposedly) contracting tuberculosis amid her wanderings, had been permitted to live in Nuremberg. She was by herself, and a Nuremberg team commanded by Yulek would come to her lodging on weekends, when she returned from her travels ("I combed the whole of Germany"). "Mirka took care of us and looked after us [...] a kind of combination of mother, sister, and sergeant major," liaising among all the apartments and rooms. The doorkeeper said, "She looks like a decent girl, so what are ten boys turning up for?" Mira testified, "I was immersed in it, I worked deep inside it, and those were my finest months in Europe."

Yulek, who led the Nokmim in Nuremberg, said proudly that relations among them were admirable and there was a distinct attempt to keep life orderly and maintain a feeling of home. The sense of a goal and mission illuminated everything.[15] Vitka, serving as liaison among the teams in Germany and between them and Paris, was angered by the obsequiousness of the average German citizen, whom she perceived as willing to debase himself—or, even more so, herself—for the sake of sugar or a pair of stockings. When she found a photo album in the house where she rented a room and saw it contained an image of the family's son shooting Jews, she immediately left. For some weeks she lived in a former concentration camp that had been converted to accommodate refugees. Visiting the teams of Nokmim scattered across Germany was one of her more difficult duties; she felt depressed and humiliated. "I admired my fellow members for having the strength to live there, in Germany. They were a wonderful circle of comrades."[16]

Despite the hardships and the heavy personal cost, only one member asked to leave the group: Gabi Sedlis, the master forger (whose role was decisive at a time when a good fake document could save a life). In Lublin he had been uncertain whether to join the Nokmim. When he eventually met with Pasha in Germany, Gabi flatly requested to be relieved of his membership in the group. Pasha responded: Kovner recruited you, and only Kovner can dismiss you.[17] Be that as it may, Gabi's voice and presence stop appearing in the testimonies.

Mordechai Roseman remarked that although everyone shared a willingness to sacrifice, Pasha himself—the ex-communist—was wholeheartedly swept up in vengeance, more prepared for sacrifice than any of the others. Manek added: "Pasha was a wonderful man, more emotional than the rest of us. He was a friend you could talk to and argue with, not like Kovner, who was more of a leader than a friend." Pasha kept closely in touch with all the

Nokmim, meeting with and taking an interest in every member. Every minute of every hour, he lived the responsibilities that his job dictated—a job that risked ending in great tragedy. By Eliezer Lidovski's account, Pasha fulfilled his assigned duties with fidelity and energy, and his life partner Dorka showed initiative and foresight in helping him. Pasha's son Avi testified: The look with which Pasha's father saw him away to the forest is something Pasha carried constantly with him and never forgot to the end of his days. Kovner, for his part, left his mother behind; and Hasya Taubes-Warchavchik said, as they were sitting around a campfire in the forest, "Leaving a mother and father behind is going morally bankrupt."[18]

What did they talk about amongst themselves when they met between one task and another? Shlomo Kenet and Dan (Dzhunek) Arad testified: "We didn't talk about the moral implications of what we were going to do. We were, as Mira says, immersed in the work." And Lena claimed: "I didn't have a thought or a notion [. . .]. I didn't picture to myself what would happen. [. . .] I don't remember that even among our circle within the group we discussed or argued about it." And Leibke Distel, in response to the question of whether they thought about what would happen after Plan A was accomplished, said, "No, we weren't thinking about anything." The interviewer asked Kazhik Rotem: You were forming ties with people whom you intended to poison. Did you give any thought to that? He answered: I was completely disconnected. The interviewer turned to Poldek: Did you have any picture of how the city would look after the whole population was poisoned? Poldek answered:

No. If I'd pictured that, I wouldn't have been able to do it. I might have run away from it. I might not have wanted to see it at all in that way. If I'd looked at it from the other side, I wouldn't have been able, because however much they did to you—you're still a human being in the end, every one of us. Hitler and all his gang didn't manage to crush our humanity out of us.[19]

DIVISION INTO TEAMS AND THE SEARCH FOR TARGET SITES

Between August 1945 and February 1946, the Nokmim searched for suitable places in Germany for carrying out Plan A and Plan B. It will be recalled that Abba Kovner wrote twice from Palestine to Pasha and Vitka in Paris (at the end of August and on September 8, 1945) telling them to temporarily set Plan A aside—only for the time being, because the plan was not actually canceled—and to concentrate on Plan B. Thus, from the time they entered Germany until early 1946, when they learned of Kovner's arrest in January and Nahum Shadmi entered the picture in late February, the Nokmim were occupied for roughly half a year with seeking out and deciding on appropriate places to implement the two plans and with advance preparations. It was concluded that they would concentrate on five cities for starting work and for obtaining access to the water systems: Nuremberg, Hamburg, Frankfurt, Munich, and Berlin.

Berlin was quickly dropped from consideration. There was no point remaining in a city so thoroughly destroyed, despite the symbolic value that would redound from an operation there. Mira explored Berlin for a day and said there wasn't a single house left intact. It was the happiest day of her life so far—Berlin was in ruins! At the same time, others of the Nokmim were dispersed in other areas of Germany in order to find camps that contained large numbers of prisoners of war, preferably from the SS.

Munich was chosen as the logistical headquarters for operations in Germany. The activity centered in a sort of villa that had formerly served the Nazis, in the Grunewald neighborhood. It had been built by architect Walter Gropius, and after the war it housed refugees. Bezalel Kek-Michaeli was responsible for the center in Munich. There, meals were prepared, subject to constraints of budget, and soldiers from the Jewish Brigade such as Tubin and Shaike Weinberg would come to eat with the Nokmim. Although the building was local headquarters, group members came and went—receiving an assignment, leaving to handle it, and coming back for the next one. Besides Kek-Michaeli, who was in charge, Shimek Lustgarten from the Krakow group was posted there, as was Kenet. Their job was to transfer money to the teams, to handle communications, to receive information from and pass information to the teams, and to thoroughly familiarize themselves with the city. One day, Kenet was appointed the driver of an old but reliable Mercedes that the Nokmim received, apparently from a Jewish officer at the United Nations Relief and Rehabilitation Administration. Avraham Perchik was there, the oldest of the Nokmim, who had excelled back in the Lublin days at arranging a meeting spot at *Peretz Hois* (Peretz House) that conjured up warm meals out of nothing. Lena Satz-Hammel was there as well sometimes, as a liaison officer.[20]

After the Brigade moved northward, the Nokmim received supplies and equipment only occasionally from Israel Carmi and had to support themselves financially. Perchik served as treasurer, receiving funds from the financial department. Some of the funds were counterfeit money that had been produced by prisoners of the Germans that flowed into the marketplace after Germany's defeat. The Nokmim bought counterfeit pounds sterling on the German black market for a song and sold them as genuine, at a good rate, in Italy. There, the financial activity was handled by Bolek Ben-Ya'akov and Poldek. Senka Nissanilevich was the liaison, and Kenet passed the money to the teams with his car. In Munich there was also a quartermaster unit, which established a coffer for purchasing food supplies. Contact was established with a German local who served as supplier, purchasing food from farmers; thus, nourishment at the center was better than at the outlying posts. The Joint Distribution Committee set up a station at the Salzburg border crossing, and many refugees passed through it on their way. Dalia (Daicha) Kaufmann, who was from Vilna, worked there, and she also provided the Nokmim with food. Additional food, principally canned, came from Jewish soldiers of the American Army stationed in bases in Nuremberg. Vitka summed up by saying that there were little teams in Austria, Belgium, and Italy, each with its purpose. The headquarters and its annexes were in Paris, and the rest mostly in Germany, where at each of the posts the team numbered roughly five or six.[21]

It was difficult to find the POW camps because most were positioned away from the cities and the highways, and even more difficult to map them because the military authorities, primarily the British and Soviets but also the Americans, took a dim view of loitering near the camps. A few examples from that period of searching will illustrate the changing assignments and their problems.

According to Lena's diary, Yitzhak Hammel and Dan Arad reconnoitered in the vicinity of a POW camp in Mauthausen, the site of the terrible concentration camp that previously, as will be recalled, made a severe impression on the Jewish Brigade soldiers who visited it upon its liberation. The camp was very well guarded, and they couldn't find access to it. Yitzhak was responsible for the Berlin district until the decision to give up on that district and on the Hamburg and Weimar districts as well. He also led the search for camps of imprisoned Germans in Sachsenhausen-Oranienburg, in Buchenwald near Weimar, and in Ebensee, and for specific Nazis according to names on notes that they received from their colleagues in Munich or in Paris.

When Pasha arrived from Paris, he sat down with Yitzhak for a discussion that ended with orders being distributed. But orders began changing right and left as fluid circumstances continually altered the situation. One team of six, headed by Lustgarten, left for Frankfurt (by October 1945 they were already there), but soon only three of them remained; the other three continued onward because Frankfurt too was largely in ruins, so there was little point in staying.[22] Similarly, Pasha sent Manek with Hasya and Yulek to look for camps of SS veterans. Mira and Idek Friedman briefly joined Kazhik and Irena Gelblum in Dachau.[23] In February 1946, Hasya was ordered by Pasha to take up a position in Neuengamme, near Hamburg, where a POW camp was located, and to observe the camp's entrance together with her future husband, Yehiel (Hilik) Warchavchik, to see who entered and exited, how water and bread arrived, and if it might be possible to establish contact with the camp's authorities and receive jobs at workplaces that were connected with the camp and employed outsiders. They rented a room together in the village, an "icebox," as Hasya described it. Ice covered the walls, and they fueled the little stove with newspapers.[24]

Cesia Rosenberg-Amit came to eastern Germany from Italy in autumn 1945 and lived almost a month in eastern Berlin with the intent of joining a team that would be penetrating nearby Sachsenhausen. But the plan changed, and she was ordered to join a team that would be penetrating Buchenwald instead, in the Weimar area. There, five or six kilometers from town, some twenty thousand German POWs were being held, all former SS or Gestapo, crowded into wooden shacks behind fences of electrified barbed wire with guard towers stationed in the corners. Not far from there was an enormous camp belonging to the Soviet Army. They kept watch over the Germans. Lena worked in the kitchen of the Soviet camp, masquerading as a German woman—she had learned German, as well as French and piano, as a "well-brought-up girl" in Vilna. She had received a permit to reside in

Weimar in return for a pack of cigarettes—the first and last time in her life that she offered a bribe. She rented a room at the home of a German woman whose husband was missing, and every day she walked more than six miles to Buchenwald and back.[25]

Manek headed the Buchenwald team, and Arie Gutkind liased between the team and the Munich center. The proximity between the two camps, the Russian and the German, and the Russians' direct contact with the prisoners from Buchenwald increased the chances of the team amassing useful information. They befriended a Russian officer who was knowledgeable about the camp and its procedures, and throughout the winter of 1946 they "tirelessly, with endless dedication," collected every scrap of information. However, the Russians guarding the Buchenwald camp were determined and very suspicious; therefore, the Nokmim were not able to move further inward. They were tossed between hope and despair, between sky-high joy over each small achievement and the gloom of helplessness.[26]

Plan A and Its Cancellation

Despite the great effort invested in locating POW camps, mapping access routes to them, and attempting to secure employment at them, it was decided to gradually close most of the posts and concentrate on three cities from the original list—Hamburg, Nuremberg, and Munich—with three teams trying to reach their sources of water. Hamburg was discarded from consideration after a short time, according to Pasha's testimony, because the Nokmim found no method available to direct the water to target only Germans. So efforts were concentrated on Munich and Nuremberg.[27] Among the Munich team were Kazhik, Irena, and Idek. In Nuremberg there were two teams. One team of four was employed at the camp of POWs from SS units, which was run by the American occupation forces; that team went undercover as Polish refugees from Upper Silesia, speaking Polish and German. They were obliged to attend drinking sessions with the local German workers, who bandied about profanities. The American officers called them "fucking Polacks." The other Nuremberg team numbered six or seven. Yulek was the commander, and communications were centralized through Mira. Within a few months, the members of the Munich and Nuremberg teams obtained jobs that would give them the opportunity, when the time came, to open and close water mains so as to introduce poison and direct it as they wished. Only the poison was lacking, so they waited for it. As 1946 began, they were ready.[28]

As early as the start of August 1945, Yulek had been appointed to head the operation in Nuremberg. He was thoroughly excited and awed: Nuremberg symbolized Nazi Germany and its laws and had been host to the great conventions of the Nazi Party. There Plan A would come to fruition. Yulek was appointed while Kovner was still in Italy, and "I was grateful to be chosen for this task." He asked the Parisian headquarters to assign to his unit someone who knew how to solve technical problems, specifically in piping, and the headquarters sent him Willek Shenar from the Krakow contingent. Willek's family had all perished in the Bełżec extermination camp, and he, the only survivor, had kept with him a photo of his parents through thick and thin. Yulek had "relied on the people at headquarters" to make the best choice, as he wrote in his eulogy for Willek, and Willek exhibited the right qualities: talent, adaptability, diligence, and good cheer.[29]

Promptly enough, Willek was accepted for work at a very strategic place—the water purification plant for Nuremberg and the vicinity—and thus his role in the operation was pivotal. He was an excellent worker: he invested his all, he was undeterred by the rats and insects and by the difficulties of working with a system located entirely underground. He made surprising progress: he not only obtained the plans of the Nuremberg water system, but shortly after beginning work at the plant, he could control the main valve itself. As Poldek put it, "In his own hand, he held the key to the source of the water supply." Day in and day out, Willek and the other members of the unit examined the maps and conferred with one another. Finally he succeeded in formulating a detailed plan for directing the poisoned water toward Germans only and sparing the areas where the American soldiers' families resided. Over time, however, it emerged that the population of Germany was becoming more heterogeneous; thousands of Allied soldiers were interspersing with the Germans, while in addition, Jews continued to arrive, especially to the displaced persons camps. It was constantly necessary to update the plans for routing the poisoned water.

The original decision, to install water-steering valves in the large cities, was successful at Nuremberg. An estimate was sent from there to the

Parisian headquarters, via the Munich headquarters, of the volume of water passing through the valves, for the sake of calculating the necessary quantity of poison.[30] No one at the plant suspected Willek; he did his work in a quiet, unassuming, professional way. For its own part, the German family in whose house he lived was convinced that his atypical accent derived from the far-off environs that he supposedly came from. The family was pleased with him for taking care of his appearance, bringing them such foods as were permissible then, and helping with the house's maintenance.

But Plan A, although punctiliously prepared, was canceled, and there were two contributing factors. The first was Kovner. His September letter postponed Plan A until his return to Europe, and the plan was completely canceled after Kovner was imprisoned and the poison was jettisoned into the sea. When Pasha was informed of Kovner's arrest and of the poison sinking to the seafloor, he thought, "I couldn't go to people and tell them that we wouldn't be working on Plan A. They couldn't have handled that. [. . .] None of us wanted to give up on the idea."[31] He had to speak to the other members of the Parisian headquarters and break the news to Yulek. Yulek, in turn, had to tell his comrades, despite their expectation that the plan would be coming to fruition any day. For Willek, the "man at the mains" who had come so close to the objective, the news from Yulek was like the sky was falling. He collapsed and didn't recover for some time. His widow, Leah (Lucia), gives a pained account of what she heard from him again and again after they met in Israel: how his world was destroyed before his eyes and how he was driven to his sickbed. He remained loyal to the idea until his dying day, and he never put the murder of his family—particularly his parents—behind him. At Michmoret, where Lucia and Willek lived in Israel, the chairman of the council once asked him: How could it be that a man as warm and loving as you, so smiling and generous, wanted to kill millions of people? And Willek answered: You simply don't understand.[32] Willek personified the dissonance between that group of people, with their individual qualities and values, and the terrible deed that they hoped to execute.

Willek was out of sorts for a long time. Mira recalled that he wouldn't stop talking about the plan's cancellation, and his morale was dreadful. However, he tried not to darken the atmosphere among the group. Poldek recounted that in the end, Willek took the cancellation like a disciplined soldier, quietly and with neither anger nor protest, and was always ready to understand another's point of view.[33] The cancellation was a harsh blow not only for him, near as he had approached to the point of action, but for them all. Distel tried to console his comrades: There are still two plans on the agenda, and there's no conflict between them. Years later, he wrote understandingly about the halting of Plan A, given that innocent people might have been harmed. Vitka testified: The Nokmim felt that the cancellation of Plan A was not only a setback but also a true betrayal by Kovner—a sentiment they felt as early as September, when they received his letter from Palestine instructing them to concentrate on Plan B until he arrived. "Abba understood very quickly that Plan A was not going to happen," she said, and that very few people would have considered it a tolerable deed. According to her, no one doubted that the planned retribution against the Germans was moral, but they would consider the act immoral if it harmed anyone else. When Pasha sent her again to visit the teams in Germany to assess their attitude toward the transition to Plan B, Vitka was appalled at what she saw: demoralization, despair, cynicism, and even a lack of trust spreading among the Nokmim. And certainly no operation could be mounted without trust in the person who issues instructions and orders. Even when it became obvious to Kovner and Pasha that Plan A could not be carried out, the Nokmim in Germany did not see it as obvious at all. "Their point of view was very clear-cut, a matter of either/or. There was no middle way [. . .]. They felt that they were being deserted: [. . .] they'd prepared, they'd been sitting at all the locations, and now . . . where were their orders?"[34]

The second factor in the cancellation was Shadmi. In reports that he sent to Yisrael Galili, he wrote explicitly that he had thoroughly examined the two plans, had found that the preparations for carrying out Plan A were indeed serious, and had forbidden the plan outright for the very reason of its immediacy. Moreover, as he wrote to Galili, Shadmi had not been convinced that it was possible to avoid poisonings in the American and British military camps, and "I was not in favor of massive child casualties among the Germans. My reasons were not sentimental, since our own children had been wiped out no less cruelly; but I was apprehensive primarily of the external impression," which is to say how global public opinion would view the operation and its consequences. His decision encountered "enormous resistance" from the Nokmim, who had been working lengthily, and successfully, on their preparations. But Shadmi did not back down.[35]

And how did Pasha react, as commander? In his testimony, he emphasized again and again that his contacts with Shadmi were minimal and that the group operated on its own authority and with its own resources. There is no mention in his testimonies, or in those of the Nokmim, that Pasha relayed Shadmi's directive to them. He told them about what happened to Kovner and the consequences, and that was essentially what mattered to the group. The teams in Germany had no direct communications with Shadmi, and it is doubtful whether they were even aware of his decisive role in their lives. Pasha said in summary that after Kovner traveled to Palestine, "We waited for letters from him, because communication wasn't regular, and we were left in Europe by ourselves for a long time, fairly helpless." Despite the efforts of Bezalel Kek-Michaeli, who was responsible for activities in Germany, it was difficult for headquarters to communicate from Paris by way of Munich with some fifty men and women who were scattered without organized logistics or permanent vehicles. "We stopped the preparations for Plan A," Pasha explained, because for the time being the Americans were stationed around the camps and the Jews were in DP camps of their own; meanwhile, the suitable time to strike slipped past. He added that people were embittered, felt abandoned, and rebelled (he doesn't go into who rebelled or how). There were some members at headquarters who didn't give up on Plan A: "We were eliminating most of our posts anyway, and we left only Nuremberg and Dachau. At those two places, we started hurrying up with basic preparations [for Plan B]." The activities planned for Nuremberg and Dachau also had the objective of improving morale: for months they had waited for, worked for, devoted themselves to, and lived with Plan A, and now it was gone.[36]

At this stage, in February and March 1946, Pasha was facing intense pressure and was forced to make decisions. According to his first testimony in 1966, he realized in those months that given the scope of the work and his physical condition (he was emaciated after the war), he would be unable to continue without significant assistance. He looked for someone who could help him, "and I was alone then, simply alone." Kovner was in prison, Eliezer Lidovski was in Italy for the sake of the Bricha, and Kek-Michaeli was in

Munich. Vitka was in Paris too, but at a separate location, and he couldn't impose another burden on her. So he asked Shaike Weinberg and Yehuda Tubin, his closest friends from the Jewish Brigade, to send him someone, preferably from the Hashomer Hatzair movement, whose members he considered "good material." They sent Ben Meiri to help him in Paris. He was one of the "Asians" and had been a central activist in the Bricha, and Pasha was very happy with him. Meiri, for his part, renewed acquaintances with the members of the group and was deeply impressed "by their spiritual readiness for the bodily self-sacrifice of blowing themselves up in the operation" and by their scrupulous ethics. "Every penny was counted out sparingly. They were people who [. . .] contributed from everything they possessed."[37]

"Plan B": Poisoning the Bread at Nuremberg

At Langwasser, formerly a camping site for participants in Nazi Party marches and conventions held for a number of days, an American camp for POWs had been set up. During the war, the place had held a German-run camp, Straflager 13, for Soviet prisoners and forced laborers, but now the tables had turned: it was the Germans behind bars. The nearby city of Nuremberg itself was in constant tumult: "Lithuanians, Latvians, Estonians, and Ukrainians are roaming everywhere; how numerous our murderers apparently are," Yulek wrote in his diary. "The Poles are looting the homes of the Germans. The American soldiers are going around with German women. Many Jews are arriving. None of them is busy with anything but speculating."[38] And then one day Yulek contacted Pasha to declare he was ready. Pasha came to Munich to assess the preparations, and when he heard the scenario and realized that the Nokmim really were ready, he asked for a pan of cold water in order to soak his hands and relax. Yulek recalls: "Between me and Pasha, there was absolute trust, and one reason was that both of us were communists who had turned Zionist." And Pasha says: "Yulek was the right person in the right place."

They waited another two or three weeks, until Kazhik, who headed the team in Dachau, sent word that he too was ready. It was decided to strike in both places at once, on the night between Saturday and Sunday, April 13 and 14. Shadmi said: "I approved the operation, down to the details, and I chose the date" after ensuring protection for the concentrations of survivors in the vicinity. He'd also stipulated, when he met in Paris with the headquarters of the Nokmim, that after the first vengeance operation they leave the posts they occupied and immediately set off for the Land of Israel. Shadmi had been expected to have the operation authorized by "Ben-Kedem" as well, meaning Moshe Shertok, and "Amram," apparently Moshe Sneh, reminded him of the expected authorization in a telegram sent three days before the operation. When "Yonatan" (Shaul Avigur) asked how he came to approve the operation before receiving those authorizations from Shertok, Shadmi was obliged to explain, in a report that he sent only after the operation, that he hadn't had time to because Shertok was still on his way and arrived in Paris after it was over. In any case, Shadmi testified that as long as the operation hadn't been executed in Nuremberg, he wouldn't allow himself to go off to Palestine even on urgent matters.[39] Thus, officials at the highest levels of the Haganah and the Yishuv were involved in the decision to carry out Plan B, and the plan was, as noted, dependent on their approval; however, the Nokmim had no idea of the involvement of those officials in their plan, or of the importance that those officials attached to "Nechama" as a whole, and today the Nokmim are quite surprised to hear about it.

But to return to the scene: Once the date was set, the poison had to be brought from Paris. Avigur kept his promise to Pasha to allocate two soldiers in uniform with authentic papers to carry the poison that Yitzhak Ratner had refined in Pasha and Dorka's apartment, and Shadmi indeed chose two soldiers from the German Unit. Vitka confirmed that the poison was brought by two Jewish Brigade soldiers and that the Brigade also helped obtain money and establish connections all the way. The soldiers from the German Unit were Dov Schenkel, a member of Kibbutz Neot Mordechai, and Yehezkel Baharav of Kfar Monash.

Pasha testified that he traveled from Paris to Munich with Shlomo Kenet, the liaison officer, as well as the two soldiers; along the way, one of the soldiers, a sworn atheist, was driving and suddenly released the wheel, looked up at the sky, and said, *"Ribono shel oylam, soll mir matzliach sein!"* ("Lord of the Universe, may we meet with success!")

The poison safely reached the group waiting for it in Germany. Yashek Ben-Zur took the trolley to meet and accompany Schenkel, who brought the poison to him and Leibke Distel. Schenkel had tied rubber hot-water bottles to his body, with the poison inside them. He didn't have suspenders to secure them—no one had thought of that—and as the trolley made its way along, he stood in a corner and kept adjusting his uniform for fear that the bottles would fall out. Because arsenic tends to sink, the poison, which was in liquid form, had to be continually shaken. Schenkel was a tall and sturdy man, but he almost collapsed when he finally reached Mira's apartment and sat down. Baharav, on the other hand, received another portion of poison from a "chemical lab" in Paris, as he recalled years later, and went to a hotel in Paris where a special belt was waiting for him. Even years later, because of compartmentalization, he couldn't say who had given him the poison and the belt. With the poison in the belt on his body, Baharav arrived in Munich and turned it over to the headquarters there—not directly to Kazhik, who was in Dachau.[40]

Mira related in her testimony: "When the poison reached Dov Schenkel, we raised a toast. We sat with him all night, and we felt wonderful, even though we knew in advance that we would need to run away immediately." According to Mira, he asked for a large flashlight because, having arrived, he wanted then and there to dilute the poison that Ratner had prepared. He explained that he couldn't have carried the poison from Paris by himself after dilution; it would have been much heavier. Pasha was present when the liquid was mixed in Munich, but for reasons of caution he wasn't the one who brought it to Kazhik in Dachau or to Yulek in Fürth. Poldek and Yashek recalled: "After fifty or sixty years, shortly before Dov Schenkel died in Neot Mordechai, we heard from him that he had received an order to dilute the poison." Yulek testified: "Schenkel also hinted to two German journalists, who had come to Neot Mordechai to interview him for a book on the subject, that he mixed the poison with water." Those recollections raise a decisive question: Did the Haganah's representative, Shadmi, tell him to dilute the poison in order to lessen the severity and damage of the group's operation, yet cause enough damage so that they would still be obliged to flee? Shadmi made clear statements pertinent to the question. He blamed "amateurism in managing the preparations, especially in areas that require the scientific accuracy of a certified laboratory," implying that the poison prepared by Ratner did not, in his opinion, meet the required standards. But it must be remembered that Ratner told Kovner explicitly that the poison he'd prepared was high quality, and the American military authorities who tested the poison residue after the operation agreed with Ratner's assessment rather than with Shadmi's. This chapter will explore this topic in more depth later.[41]

Before the poison arrived, Distel received an important assignment. He had been a member of the United Partisan Organization in Vilna. Captured, tortured in a number of camps, dwindling to ninety-three pounds, and then fleeing the death march, he managed to reach Pontebba, and there he fell into the embrace of comrades from Vilna. Vitka immediately invited him to join the Nokmim.[42] Distel came to Fürth, met the Nuremberg team, and heard from Yulek about the immediate plans. At the end of September 1945, after Kovner's letter arrived, Distel was tasked with securing a job at Nuremberg's largest bakery, which provided bread for the German prisoners. It was a four-story building, ringed by red and brown bricks, and only those with permits were allowed to enter its gates. Distel openly presented himself as a Jewish survivor of the camps. He said that an uncle of his had a huge bakery in Canada and that he wanted to learn the trade in order to carry on the family tradition when he immigrated there. He received a job, rented a room at number 12 on the Urftstrasse, and began a wearying study of baking. Distel was obliged to work among Germans, who claimed that they hadn't known what the Nazis were doing to the Jews and asked him to tell them. Some of them doubted that Germans had committed the acts attributed to them, "and there were always arguments," while Distel was constantly occupied with thoughts of who among them, during the war, had done what. He initially thought of throwing poison into the sacks of flour in the warehouse, then he thought of pouring it into the dough mixers, but finally, after consulting others of the Nokmim, he concluded that the poison should be smeared on the underside of bread loaves. Meanwhile, he was promoted to a job in the bread storeroom. After two months of training, he knew the work procedures completely and learned how to arrange bread "by the German system of shelving bread loaves" when it was ready for shipping. He was able to distinguish between the dark bread that the German prisoners received and the more expensive white bread, which was delivered to the American staff and its assistants. However, most of the workers and supervisors were hostile toward him, and he was considering telling his commander,

Yulek, that he would rather drop the whole project. In the meantime, weeks passed, because according to the plan, the Nokmim were intending to coordinate simultaneous poisoning in two places, Nuremberg and Dachau.[43]

In April 1946, the squad was finally ordered to be at the ready. The Nokmim had chosen—by themselves, as far as they knew—to strike during the night between Saturday and Sunday, April 13 and 14. There were a number of reasons for the timing: a full moon was expected; on Saturdays there was generally only one shift working, and the number of guards outside was minimal; and on Sundays there was no baking, so a double supply was baked in advance, meaning that the bread would have enough time to absorb the poison. Distel received the rubber bottles of liquid poison from Schenkel to be smuggled into the bakery, and according to his testimony, at the ghetto he had gained smuggling experience that came in handy. He bound the bottles tightly to his body, he put on a roomy raincoat, and when he entered the bakery he stashed the bottles inside three water barrels that were positioned there as a precaution against fire. Later, he moved the bottles to a spot beneath the wooden floor until the right moment.

The exploit was assigned to a lean incursion force including Yashek, Manek, and Distel, under Yulek's command. Yulek brought Willek in as well, as his assistant, in order to compensate for the cancellation of Plan A. The force was intended to consist of six members, but unexpectedly the bakery workers mounted a strike, interfering with the scheme. Since the Nokmim couldn't routinely report for their shifts during the strike, fewer of them could participate, and they couldn't take in all the bottles. Some bottles remained at Mira's place. On Saturday, April 13, three men entered the bakery and hid inside large bread bins, taller than a man, until all the other workers left. There were unexpected complications, and hiding places were changed, but near midnight, with the light of the full moon flooding the place, they retrieved the bottles from under the floorboards, transferred the contents into two large buckets, and worked as one to brush the loaves with poison before returning them to their exact places. Two did the actual brushing, and Distel replaced the loaves according to the official German shelving system he had learned. They needed to stir the thick mixture again and again in order to keep the poison from sinking to the bottom. Arsenic does not dissolve completely in liquid, and in addition, the stirring was intended to keep the color of the mixture identical to the color of the loaf bottom, where the poison was to be absorbed. Caution was vital, because the odorless, tasteless poison could easily be confused with some other substance, and they must not touch it themselves.

They managed by moonlight to brush roughly a thousand loaves of bread—"When we finished the first thousand, we kissed each other," Leibke said—before the watchmen visited and the Avengers retreated to concealment with all their paraphernalia. The watchmen, seeing nothing out of the ordinary, moved on. The work of poison-brushing continued for another two thousand loaves or so. When the watchmen returned, this time to the vicinity of the building's doorway, a strong and noisy gust of wind broke panes of glass and unhinged a door. Yashek and Manek fled through the windows. The watchmen pursued them but failed to capture them. Leibke hid the brushes and the remaining mixture and stayed in his hiding place. The German police had been summoned, and he heard them conclude that two intruders had tried unsuccessfully to steal white bread. As mentioned, white bread was expensive and scarce, and so the scenario sounded plausible to Leibke, and he felt relieved. When quiet returned and first light arrived, Leibke left his hiding place and joined Yulek and the others, who were waiting in a vehicle arranged in advance by the Jewish Brigade to pick them up after they completed, or had to abandon, the operation.[44]

Results of the Nuremberg Operation

To determine the results of the Nuremberg operation, Yulek sent Rachel Galperin-Gliksman to the camp area for as close a look as possible. She was chosen because she was a woman who, having not previously roamed around Nuremberg because she had been mostly assigned to the routes of the Bricha, would not arouse suspicion or be easily remembered. In addition, she spoke Polish and German.

She reached the bakery but couldn't enter because there was no bread for sale. Something had happened, she was told, and the bread was "no good." She gathered information from around the camp and from the prisoners' wives who lived nearby, and the word was that many had fallen ill from an attempt at poisoning. From Jewish officers she learned that the Americans wanted to cover up the episode in order to prevent an international incident.

They enlisted all their modern technology, and with every ambulance and car at their disposal, they took the victims to the hospital for stomach pumping. According to the information that Rachel received, more than a thousand men and women were affected, but they did not all die.[45]

A day or two passed, and the Americans had yet to announce anything. In the meantime, conjectures were spreading, particularly in the German newspapers, and everywhere the number of victims differed. Generally there were no well-grounded sources, and articles merely quoting one another. Yulek, who kept the press clippings over the years, summed up from the Associated Press that 2,000 people or so had suffered stomach poisoning and, as of a few days after the incident, some were in very serious condition but none had died. The *Herald Tribune* wrote that 1,800 people had been affected but that it was unclear how many had died. In the Czech press, a small notice some days later reported that hundreds died despite American efforts to save them and hundreds more were sickened. Pasha relied on an article in the German newspaper *Süddeutsche Zeitung*, which wrote that German prisoners had suffered poisoning from a bakery, with 3,700 people affected, and hot-water bottles had been found containing residue from the mixture. But he believed that 8,000 had been affected—while admitting that the number was not verified—and that 860 individuals had died in agony. The German newspaper gave the poisoners credit, saying that the poison had been applied to the bottoms of the loaves with great skill. The *New York Times* ran two short items saying that 2,283 people had been affected, 207 of them had become very sick and were hospitalized, but none had died. Those numbers also appeared in The *London Times*, with the added statement that the hospital records too showed no confirmation that anyone had died. None of the articles mention that the poisoners were Jews or that they fled the site, and in fact no conjectures at all were raised regarding the identity of the poisoners.[46]

The upshot, as stated by Yulek, was that it was a "botched" mixture: thousands suffered stomach poisoning but without any deaths. The Nokmim attributed the effect's insufficiency to the sinking of the poison in the mixture, the concentration of poison, or the ratio of poison to glue. Despite the insufficient results, the Nuremberg team came away in good spirits because no other group had accomplished anything similar and because they had, in the end, managed to score an achievement. By their calculations, three thousand loaves of bread were distributed to twelve thousand prisoners from among fifteen thousand total at the camp, a quarter loaf to each POW, so that a significant effect could have been hoped for. Consequently, Pasha spoke of eight thousand prisoners poisoned. Pasha explained that he'd received part of his information from an American Jewish officer who constantly provided them with information and that the low number of victims reported was attributable to American efforts to quell the commotion and quickly evacuate the victims to hospitals. The Americans—fearing that, in their responsibility for the welfare of not merely those prisoners but all over their occupation zone in Germany, they would be blamed for negligence or worse—may have hastened to obfuscate the entire incident in order not to draw unnecessary attention to it. In Vitka's opinion, it was not important how many died or suffered, only the fact that the deed had been done.[47]

By way of evaluating the involvement of the Jewish Brigade in the operation, Vitka on the one hand kept enumerating some very good friends from the Brigade who worked hand in hand with them. However, "On the other hand, the ones on top made lots of trouble." Distel too said: "The understanding we received from the Jewish Brigade soldiers amounted to many times what we received from the higher echelons."[48] And indeed, some soldiers from the Brigade, and particularly from the German Unit, felt themselves to be part of the operation. From their ranks, after all, the men were chosen to carry the poison from Paris to Munich; and it was they who picked up the Avengers after the operation and helped them along to the border (as will be described later), and they who looked after the Avengers at the stopping points along the way. Yehuda Ben-Horin wrote: "From time to time I would meet with Pasha, and I was aware of the feelings among them. We set about planning a large-scale operation"—"we," as if he, an officer of the Jewish Brigade, were among the planners of the operation. And he continued: As the first target, a large camp near Nuremberg was chosen where the Americans were guarding fifteen thousand imprisoned SS veterans. "We executed the operation," Ben-Horin wrote, "without leaving clues." When his book was published in 1975, he remained of the opinion that the topic was best left in obscurity, and he remarked only that in the American press at the time, it generated a great hubbub that was quickly overshadowed by more important events. The operation, he said in conclusion, was mounted instead of other operations that he could not in good conscience have supported, meaning of course Plan A. It may be inferred that from his point of view, the Jewish Brigade and the Haganah brought about Plan B through his assistance in order that Plan A remain unachieved.[49]

Shadmi summarized the operation in two of the reports that he sent to the Land of Israel. In the first, written a month or so after the operation, he expressed disappointment in the dubious success, insofar as despite the efforts invested "and despite the momentousness of Jewish vengeance as a principle, these results are negligible." However, he suggested considering the big picture, in which there was something gained. First of all, like Ben-Horin, Shadmi revealed the opinion that the execution of Plan B prevented the execution of Plan A, which would have, heaven forbid, descended on millions "regardless of race and religion." Second, the entire group was already on its way to the Land of Israel, and his only fear was that during the long wait before they boarded ship, "the comrades might regain strength and start anew"; he was that wary of them and their tireless energy. Third, "Two thousand Amalekites are sleeping the sleep of the just." He believed that two thousand Germans, modern Amalekites, had died in the operation. He was unaware of what we know today: that the results were relatively mild. "Although I had hoped for a greater gain, still what was granted us is no embarrassment." And fourth, this small-scale incident made a great impression, although he regretted that the Germans believed it was not the work of Jews and "even are deliberately promulgating that assessment, in order to deny us even the gratification." The Americans, after attempts at denial and obfuscation, presented the incident as a clash between Poles and the SS veterans. What happened, or didn't happen, was no fault of the comrades, Shadmi wrote. They performed perfectly well, and the execution was exemplary. In a report afterward he wrote that he would stop dealing with the matter of vengeance—in view not of its unimportance but of its importance. He ended the report with an unambiguous declaration: "*In my opinion, we will be sinning greatly against our history if we do not engage ourselves seriously in the business of Nechama.*"[50] One may conclude that because the Jewish Brigade and Haganah both wanted Plan B to succeed and saw themselves as participants in it, they were very disappointed in the results, but they valued the behavior of the Nokmim. And Shadmi, at least, believed that the leadership of the Haganah and of the Yishuv should have engaged itself much more seriously in the business of proper vengeance.

Regarding the number of Germans poisoned, the quality of the poison, and its dilution before the Nuremberg operation, an answer may be found in the materials from the American interrogation, which were released in 2016, after seventy years had passed. For all those years they were classified material; even in 2016 they became accessible only after repeated written requests pointed out how old they had become. The investigation started on the day of the operation and continued into late February 1947, focusing in two directions. The first was the poisoners—and here the American authorities thoroughly failed. They neither identified nor located any of the poisoners, and they discovered nothing about the group or its members despite the residue and the objects that the escaping Nokmim left behind in the bakery. Extensive correspondence shows that they did search for four Jews, including a former Auschwitz inmate named Lipa Welner, who was designated the central suspect, and a man named Julien Broklyn, who lived in the building where Distel rented an apartment: number 12 on the Urftstrasse in Fürth. But the authorities found no clue connecting either to the deed. This ends the investigators' first summary, which was written on April 23, 1946, a week and a half after the operation. The second summary was written in February 1947, some ten months after the deed. Its writers—disgruntled that the items found in the bakery and Welner's interrogation are no longer available, and that they don't have any idea of where the suspects are being held—recommend closing the file for want of any discernible connection between the suspects and the deed.[51]

The second direction had to do with the details of the operation. The writers of the two reports, the one after ten days and the other after ten months, recapitulate the course of events as understood by the Americans, who were in charge of the investigation. The reports describe the encounter with the watchmen and the escape of two of the poisoners, exactly matching the testimony from Manek, Yashek, and Distel. Five days after the operation, according to the first American report, a loaf of bread was brought for analysis because symptoms of poisoning had appeared in some two thousand prisoners. The bread was ordinary in its dimensions and appearance, except that the bottom was white and powdery, glue was discovered beneath that white layer, and beneath the glue was sawdust. In chemical analysis of those layers, there was a reaction characteristic of arsenic. Examination of even a small quantity yielded an immediate and very strong reaction. Arsenic was present in a fatal concentration: 0.2 grams in 100 grams of bread. However, it must be emphasized that the quantity of poison per loaf was inconsistent, and that reading of 0.2 grams happened to be the maximum. On April 20, a week after the operation, the bakery was searched. A bucket was found that was partly filled with a white paste, along with some personal objects, three empty hot-water bottles, and a bag containing four more still-full hot-water bottles. Upon analysis, the liquid in those bottles proved to be almost 100 percent arsenic oxide mixed with glue and water, and if the seven bottles were identically filled, they would have held twenty-two pounds of poison in all, nearly pure, for accomplishing the deed. Such an extraordinary quantity could have poisoned thirty to one hundred thousand people. The second report put the number at no less than sixty thousand. Here, the American report sheds light on the question of the poison's dilution for use at the bakery: "It is impossible to dissolve a large quantity of arsenic oxide in water. Therefore it was impossible to prepare a usable solution at the necessary concentration, and the arsenic had to be mixed with water only to the point of forming a paste." A present-day chemical company provides clarification: arsenic oxide dissolves slowly and not uniformly in cold water; however, it can be dissolved in boiling water, which is why Ratner sent it in bottles intended for hot water. The paste arrived at the bakery in those same bottles, and they were emptied into a bucket together with material intended to dull the shiny white color of the paste. In other words, it was a quantity and concentration of poison capable of killing the inmates of four camps the size of the one near Nuremberg.[52]

Certain conclusions arise from the investigators' files and the two detailed reports: First, Ratner apparently did very professional work as a chemist, and the diluted poison, combined with the paste, sawdust, and color-dulling material, would adhere well to the bottoms of bread loaves and cause massive fatalities, as Ratner told Kovner when they met in Palestine and as the American investigators found to their astonishment. Second, Schenkel did receive an instruction to dilute the poison but not in order to diminish the results. On the contrary, dilution with a little water was the only way to achieve a paste that could be applied at the desired concentration. Third, no one was ever in fact put on trial for the poisoning; no one was found guilty of it; and no one, not even the Americans, mentioned Jews in connection with it. Fourth, no one died from eating the poisoned bread. From the physicians who were summoned, the investigators heard of diarrhea, vomiting, and skin rashes, but no further symptoms or consequences. Even if we recall that the Americans were eager to put the incident behind them as quickly as possible and understate the effects, still this is classified internal reporting that was left to collect dust on the shelves of an archive for seventy years. The conclusion is thus that the American press, which relied on the colonel responsible for guarding the German POWs, Samuel T. Williams, and emphasized that no one died from eating the bread, was relaying factual information. Speaking a few days after the incident, the colonel gave a general account and mentioned no suspects. No official American announcement was ever published to mark the conclusion of the inquiry, and public interest subsided within a short time.

A question presents itself: if the poison was of high quality and the quantity was sufficient to kill tens of thousands of people, how is it that no one died and only two thousand had medical treatment for any symptoms? It seems that the remarks from Yulek, the group's commander, bear remembering: there were two thousand people poisoned, but no one died, and the mixture failed because the poison sank and was not in the right ratio to the glue. And in fact the American report found that the substance spread on the bottoms of the loaves was not uniform. Manek, Leibke, and Yashek, the three men who applied the mixture, testified that one of them was in charge of ceaselessly stirring the thick mixture—a very difficult job—because the arsenic constantly needed to be kept from sinking to the bottom of the bucket.

After the operation, Pasha wrote an emotional letter to Yulek: "We have accomplished an important deed that will be remembered forever. But with it, our path has not ended; and although at this time we must retreat, we will return and continue."[53] Not only Pasha felt that the campaign might continue. In a press clipping contained in the American investigators' files, an anonymous writer says:

Who would want to kill 15,000 agents of a terror regime that was the dread of occupied Europe? Anti-Nazi Germans, or a Pole, Russian, Frenchman, or Czech [a Jew didn't cross the writer's mind]. And why? Because the former prisoners lost faith in the intention or ability of the Allies to punish the SS criminals and destroy their organization for all time. That loss of faith is well based, and if the Allies do not properly fulfill their duty of tearing out the war criminals by their roots, then we may anticipate more episodes like the smearing of arsenic on bread, to be committed by the victims of Nazi barbarity.[54]

And that was precisely the complaint of the Nokmim.

The Affair at Dachau

Even seventy years later, the affair at Dachau remains an open wound that may possibly never heal, a basis for bitter unresolved arguments among the Nokmim themselves and between they and those who converse with or interview them. At the heart of the affair is one principal question: why was the Dachau operation canceled, after being scheduled for execution simultaneously with the Nuremberg operation? And who caused it to be canceled after the great efforts invested in it? "It's hard to describe how much went into preparing for that operation, including the cost in work, in irritation, in health as people sometimes say figuratively—but in this case literally—and the cost in time. [. . .] Almost a year of preparations. [. . .] Long months of excellent planning," said a still-angry Kazhik Rotem, the head of the team, to author Yonat Sened.[55]

The preparations at Dachau proceeded simultaneously with the preparations at Nuremberg, and their original objective was to poison the water mains. A team of four Nokmim—Kazhik, Irena Gelblum, Idek Friedman, and Willek Shenar—came to Dachau as early as autumn 1945 in order to gain an understanding of the factors surrounding the sources of drinking water, and they established personal relations with Poles who handled various duties around the camps and with Germans holding civilian jobs in the town. When Lena told the team that Plan A was canceled, they were all dumbfounded and couldn't understand what had happened. However, as disciplined members of the group, they decided that Plan B would have to suffice for the time being. They began to prepare an operation similar to what was anticipated at Nuremberg. Kazhik agreed to head the preparations, assenting to a request from Pasha that had been passed along by an emissary from Paris. The Dachau team was much smaller than the Nuremberg team, but Pasha said that it included two very good members from among the Warsaw Ghetto fighters, Kazhik and Irena. The latter was one of the best of their women, he said.[56]

They were expected to learn the site well, especially the bakery. They did exceptional work, said Vitka. They positioned themselves inside the Dachau camp itself (that is, in the camp of the Polish unit that was guarding the POW camp, not among the POWs), they assumed false identities, and they visited all the places that were vital to carrying out the operation. Kazhik related: "I was already a soldier in the Polish unit, in uniform, and I was considered a Pole. I did sentry duty like anyone else, and in that way I learned the camp's procedures." The commander of the Polish unit was very fond of Pernod, the French drink, and from time to time the team in Munich sent a bottle of it from Paris. One day a delegation of high-level Polish officers arrived, and they were led on a tour of the POW camp itself where the German prisoners were. This was Kazhik's opportunity. He went with them to see the camp, both the large area for the general population of SS veterans and the boundary between them and the area for senior German officers. Each German general had an individual room with his name on the door. Kazhik was gratified to see them jump to attention at the approach of the Polish officers.[57] He introduced Idek as a machine technician (in the ghetto, he'd worked at a garage), and he befriended the Poles who ran the bakery, drinking with them and supplying a bottle of good liquor here and there, thus strengthening his ties with them. Irena and Kazhik presented themselves as a brother and sister in search of their father. Once they were on truly warm terms with the bakery's Polish manager, they got drunk with him, took his bakery keys, duplicated them, and returned the originals while he was still inebriated.[58]

With the approach of April 13, the day set for the operation, the team was still waiting for the poison to arrive for smearing on the bread loaves. They had no qualms at all about the task: they knew that the people in the Polish camp ate one kind of bread and the many prisoners ate another kind, so only the German prisoners would suffer. Shlomo Kenet, accompanied by

Yehezkel Baharav, was on his way to them with the substance. They were unaware that in the meantime the operation had been called off and they should be leaving immediately or that someone was carrying an order from Pasha to Kenet to stop the transfer of the poison and have it buried in the earth. Meanwhile, however, Kazhik, Idek, and Irena, still unaware, entered the bakery and waited there for the poison. At midday someone arrived— apparently Lena again—and Kazhik went out to hear what she had to say. The door creaked and scared them. They left, were picked up by a Jewish Brigade jeep that was waiting outside, and were driven to Limoges, in France.[59] It was left to Kenet and Shimek Lustgarten to destroy the poison, but Kenet refused. He wanted to bury it, for use when a new opportunity arose. In the end, with great regret, they poured out the poison in the forest, including what had remained with Mira. "That was the hardest moment for me. To take that material and personally throw it away."[60]

Why was the operation at Dachau canceled at a moment's notice, when the poison was on its way to three Nokmim who were already inside the bakery? Nahum Shadmi tried to provide an answer in a concluding report that he sent to the Land of Israel: "For unanticipated technical reasons, one camp in the American territory was excluded." But he didn't explain those technical reasons. There remains the question of what Shadmi told Pasha in ordering him to cancel and what Pasha told Lena when he sent her to notify the comrades at Dachau. No less important, and still echoing today, are the doubts, speculations, and assumptions of the Nokmim, and they will be enumerated here:

- Why were only two or three people on steady assignment at Dachau— Idek and Willek weren't there the whole time—when it was an enormous POW camp of twenty-eight thousand inmates with an additional special camp for a hundred generals of the Wehrmacht, while at Nuremberg there were at least seven of the Nokmim under Yulek? Lena raised the supposition that Yulek still hoped for the implementation of Plan A and therefore assembled and prepared a team for that eventuality.[61]

- Did Kazhik and his team misbehave? In drinking together with the Poles, did they take a step too far? Idek said that it didn't appear so to him.[62] Was Kazhik endangering the group by participating in unseemly activity? There was, in fact, a police file opened. Kazhik was arrested for being found with dollars that he intended to exchange, and the American military police kept him imprisoned in Munich for a month. Kazhik said, frankly, in a meeting of Nokmim decades afterward: "I believe that it was one of the mistakes that I should have avoided making." That is, he shouldn't have taken a sum of funds to be exchanged at a shady haunt of moneychangers and smugglers.[63]

▪ Some of the Nokmim raised yet another theory: Irena and Kazhik were somewhat self-important and had distanced themselves from the rest of the group because they had fought in the Warsaw Ghetto uprising and were considered close to Antek Zuckerman and Zivia Lubetkin, and they may not have entirely accepted discipline.

▪ In Mira's opinion, Kazhik had been done an injustice: If his behavior was not as expected from a member of the underground, and if some of the Nokmim believed he was failing to meet expectations, then the higher command should have straightened him out or replaced him rather than criticizing him after the fact. Irena was well liked by all; she was friendly, vivacious, helpful, beautiful, and impressive, and it bears adding that in a small group, a distinctly beautiful woman could have been a complication. Poldek Maimon said: It was the only stain on the group; let's not dwell on it.[64]

▪ Were there other reasons—not what Shadmi called technical reasons—for canceling the operation? Yehuda Ben-David claimed that suspicions had arisen in the camp (meaning among the Polish guard unit).[65] Vitka, Kenet, and Pasha cited a similar reason. Vitka, who shared some of the hard deliberations as a member of the headquarters, says that the cancellation had no connection at all to what Kazhik or Irena had done or left undone. According to her, on the day of the operation, a message came from the Jewish Brigade soldiers saying that the local authorities (apparently the American Army) had uncovered all the group's members, not just at Dachau, and were about to arrest them; thus, Pasha ordered the Munich team to stand down but, believing that the Nokmim must achieve something, ordered that the Nuremberg team proceed and then everyone leave Germany right away.[66]

- A time was set—the night between April 13 and 14—when the two operations could be carried out simultaneously, and the poison was ready for both places: "The material was at hand. For Dachau, it was just like for Nuremberg." But one or two nights before the scheduled date, Pasha received word from an American Jewish officer who knew not only that they were about to attempt something but also that the team at Dachau was not Polish but Jewish. "This Jew ran up to me, all in a panic, that I've got to get the guys out of there right away" because there were suspicions among the guards at the Polish camp. Now, according to Pasha, the Nokmim headquarters faced "a terrible dilemma." If the Americans were aware of Kazhik, then they might quickly follow the trail to Yulek as well. But if neither of the attacks were carried out as scheduled, another chance might not occur for such an operation, not even in a different place. At this point Pasha concluded that it was impossible, come what may, to tell the Nokmim that Plan B too was to remain unaccomplished. Pasha consulted with Vitka, with Yulek, and with Bezalel Kek-Michaeli, and they unanimously decided to cancel the operation at Dachau but proceed in Nuremberg.[67]

As long years passed, Idek remained unreconciled to the cancellation. In his testimony, he said: "We were a group with such solidarity. We were individually handpicked fighters, we worked so hard, we went hungry, we traveled the roads for a year, we were all in favor of the operation. So what if the door creaked? Why did we run away to France? We should have tried again and again! Did the guys who were completely *varbrennt* (burning with zeal), like Pasha and Bezalel, agree just like that to accept the say of the Yishuv? We could have got that business done even without the Yishuv, and if we got caught—so what?! Why did they agree to dump the poison away, after getting it was such an effort?!"[68]

Idek does point to a contradiction, which may be difficult to resolve, between their readiness for utter self-sacrifice and their willingness in practice, without exception, to participate—despite having their hearts set on continuing with the plan—in the retreat and escape that were arranged for them.

Kazhik, as the commander, was shattered and mortified by the cancellation; subsequently, he refused to speak to Irena or Idek in Limoges, where they stayed for two weeks at the home of a Jewish family, nor later along their way. He remained mortified for many years; and in his testimonies and at meetings with his comrades, he repeatedly raised angry questions and doubts. Only in his last testimony, in 2009, did Kazhik say that he might have judged others too harshly, might have made groundless accusations, and might still be seeing things from his own perspective rather than from the broader perspective that characterized the Haganah and the Yishuv with respect to the damage that vengeance might cause to the Jewish people and to the state-building. Those remarks might be the beginning of rapprochement between him and his fellows.[69]

THE NUREMBERG TRIALS

The Nuremberg trials, which the victorious Allies began conducting in October 1945, did not leave the Nokmim indifferent, particularly since the Nokmim had come to Germany only a few months before and were able to follow them from the very start in the local press. Moreover, the building where the trials were held was located on the road between Fürth, where they rented their rooms, and Nuremberg. It was the only building left whole in an area otherwise laid waste, and the seven Nokmim of the Nuremberg team passed by it almost daily. The idea that an international trial intended for punishing the top officials of the Nazi regime, a regime that had ruined their young lives and taken their entire families from them, would be conducted without any representation of the Jewish people—the principal victims—gave them no rest. And the thought that the attempt to exterminate the entire Jewish people was not in itself defined as a separate and special criminal act, but rather thrown in as part of the overall criminality, also gave them no rest. The Nokmim, like many others, feared in their hearts that justice would not be done; that not all those responsible would stand trial; that the sentences would not correspond to the severity of the crimes, the past would be forgotten, and a new order would step forward. Certainly every one of them was apprehensive about the eventual outcome of the trial, an event that would last for months, because of its unprecedented legal and ethical complexity.

The Germans' treatment of the Jewish people, and just the Jewish people, had violated every law known to the local and international legal systems. They saw Europe as an open arena for arbitrary murder and torture. That being the case, thought the Nokmim, why should they receive the courtesy, after everything that they'd done, of a trial by the book? The Nokmim believed it would be a good idea to commit an act that would incur arrest and trial, providing an opportunity to loudly and clearly tell the whole world the story of the Holocaust against the Jewish people, so that the Nuremberg trials could not continue to ignore the voice of the Jews.

Accordingly, the Nokmim decided not to wait for the results of the legal process. They intently discussed it, in all the details they could learn, and Eliezer Lidovski repeatedly warned his comrades that the international court was not to be trusted: no vengeance or real punishment would emerge from its proceedings; the judges were arguing over every clause and precedent in a legal system created for a long-gone era, and therefore it was up to the ex-partisans themselves to deliver an "act of vengeance" against the Nazi leaders.[70] So a number of them decided among themselves to take action but keep other members unaware in order not to endanger everyone. Lidovski set himself an objective: to assassinate Hermann Göring, Hitler's most important henchman among the defendants as well as the most repulsive and self-indulgent of them all, when Göring was entering or exiting the courtroom. The idea prodded ceaselessly at his mind, occupying him night and day. He determined to act without saying a word to even his closest comrades, with the exception of two, and without informing any officials of the Jewish people or of the Yishuv, who would certainly have thwarted him.

Lidovski kept his secret until the mid-1980s, when his memoirs were published and the Nokmim began to tell their stories. At the end of 1945 he was vice chairman of the Diaspora Center, in Italy—a key position with significant responsibilities. He managed to obtain a document from the Joint Distribution Committee attesting that he was traveling to Germany to meet with officials of Jewish institutions; and Bolek Ben-Ya'akov and Poldek came with him, dressed in uniform and equipped with false documents. Soldiers were allowed to cross the borders freely, and the two men in uniform passed inspection on the train; however, the British arrested Lidovski himself, whose ID was genuine, for carrying false documentation. He was handed over to the Americans, and it was no use explaining about the positions he held or about his past as a partisan. He was thrown into a holding cell together with a Ukrainian who had murdered Nazis in revenge. The Ukrainian had also been planning to assassinate one of the Nazi leaders, apparently from among those under arrest in Nuremberg, but he was ambushed and arrested amid the thorough security efforts of the British and Austrian police. Lidovski stood trial and was sentenced to a month in jail along with an assorted batch of arrestees. His comrades smuggled him fifty packs of hard-to-find Camel cigarettes to help improve his conditions.[71] Clearly many people, not all of them Jewish, were potential assassins of any vulnerable Nazi leaders; the British and American authorities therefore were strictly on guard against such eventualities, whether because as representatives of democracies they opposed execution without trial or because they didn't want the quiet in the areas they controlled to be disturbed by attacks on the defendants.

The groups in Germany knew nothing of the initiative by Ben-Yaʿakov, Poldek, and Lidovski, who were based in Italy, and therefore they assigned Manek L. and Leibke Distel to assassinate the culprits, Göring first and foremost. According to Poldek's testimony, Manek was the primary candidate for shooting Göring. The point was not necessarily to kill Göring. It was to arouse a commotion and be arrested, on the assumption that Manek would go to trial and there have the opportunity, as a former Auschwitz prisoner, to tell the world about the horrors perpetrated at the camps. Distel recounted: "The plan, as presented to us, had already been worked out in detail, apparently at the Parisian headquarters of the Nokmim, but the main problem in following it was obtaining permits to enter the courtroom. In order to receive a permit, it would be necessary to befriend some of the soldiers who were guarding the building and the courtroom—the Jews among them would be the natural prospects—and glean some information about the switching of sentries." The building was under very tight watch, with strictly followed procedures for the defendants' passage into and out of the courtroom. The location, as mentioned, was in an area of devastation; thus, there was nowhere to hide nearby, and sentries could easily see who was approaching.

At an apartment in Fürth rented by a survivor from Będzin, survivors from that town gathered from time to time, including Manek and a

Jewish American press liaison officer. The officer promised Manek, as a fellow Będziner, to admit him into the courtroom. Apparently he didn't know then the purpose of the visit, but after some conversations and intimations, he put two and two together and evaded following through on his promise.

Distel made a practice of traveling to Wiesbaden, where the Americans had their headquarters, in order to cultivate relations with a Jewish American soldier from Krakow and through whom Distel hoped to obtain a permit to attend the trial. In this case too, though, the promises went unfulfilled, and they ended in refusal.[72]

Göring had been the first target not only for the Nokmim. Because the Jewish people had no official representation, Ilya Ehrenburg saw to it that the Yiddish poet Abraham Sutzkever would take the stand and testify to what had happened in the Vilna Ghetto. Before his testimony, which was delivered in Russian on February 24, 1946, Sutzkever confided in Ehrenburg that he intended to smuggle a pistol into the courtroom and shoot Göring. Ehrenburg persuaded him to abandon the plan, on the grounds that it would result in Sutzkever's death and the Nazis weren't worth that kind of sacrifice.[73]

With no perceptible connection to the attempts by Lidovski and by Manek and Distel to gain access to the courtroom, word reached Shadmi at the Parisian Haganah headquarters that the Nokmim intended to execute all twenty-one defendants without waiting for the endlessly delayed verdict. Their plan, as he gathered, was to plant a time bomb in the courtroom or to burst in with guns and shoot every one of the defendants. Obviously none of the Nokmim themselves told him of the plan, and they had no idea how he became aware of it. The idea of coming into the courtroom and attacking some top Nazis, according to testimony from Manek and Distel, had been contained in an order from Pasha, but later his order was changed. Did Shadmi, hearing of the plan and opposing it, bring about the change? No proof exists.

Still, the longer the trial stretched out, and the more starkly it emerged that the central issue was not the systematic and indiscriminate murder of the Jewish people and their sufferings, the stronger the desire for vengeance. It became clear that in the eyes of the world, Jewish blood was forfeit. For Jews, there was no justice and no judge. The Nokmim's demand for vengeance fell into a void, "an immense and conscienceless vacuum," as Elkins called it,[74] with a circumference and depth that they were starting to understand. The absence of any real legal reckoning for the guilty multitude, the wholesale release of suspects from the camps that the Allies had built only to hurriedly dismantle, the escape of Nazis and their disappearance into countries across the sea, particularly in the Americas and with European and even Vatican assistance:[75] those all led to the bitter conclusion that no one had cared either during the Holocaust or afterward, that no justice would be done at this trial, and that it was therefore up to the Nokmim to wreak justice for themselves. They hadn't succeeded in penetrating the courtroom, but they consoled themselves that if they had mounted their attack against the top Nazis and been caught, they would have endangered the greater operation that they still hoped for. There was also a bit of consolation in the fact that a dozen defendants were sentenced to hang: ten indeed were hanged, and Göring killed himself in his cell on October 15, 1946, the eve of his scheduled execution—after the Nokmim reached Palestine.[76]

The press in the Land of Israel, particularly at the start and end of the trial, also expressed severe dissatisfaction that no one officially represented the Jewish people at the trials. It was feared that the trying of the top Nazis meant that all the other criminals were absolved and that the German nation bore no collective guilt; the manner in which the trials were conducted appeared to perpetuate the dismissive attitude of the Allies, during and after the Holocaust, toward the Jewish people. An item in the *Davar* newspaper opined that everyone deserved a single and immediate punishment because "predatory animals aren't judged, they're shot." The leadership of the Yishuv, on the other hand, was almost silent on the topic, and there was rage in the press over the Yishuv's indifference to the trial.[77]

LEAVING FOR THE LAND OF ISRAEL

After the operation that the Nokmim mounted had certainly put the military authorities on alert, the Americans in particular, the departure of some dozens of Nokmim from their scattered posts—fifty seven or so people, according to Pasha—and their transfer to safe locations and passage onward to ports of departure for the Land of Israel could by no means be described as easy. The process took two and a half months overall, including crossing borders, finding temporary lodgings, preparing suitable documents, boarding ships, and disembarking in Palestine. The chain of preparations and performance began with Shadmi, who had approved the revenge operation on the condition that the operatives leave immediately afterward. The next link in the chain was Pasha, who had planned the departure jointly with Ben Meiri. Shadmi wrote to Yisrael Galili: "The people did fine. [. . .] They were able to carry out the plan for returning home and despite serious difficulties, everyone arrived at the right place."[78]

The task of moving some of the group members into Czechoslovakia was assigned mainly to Zelda Treger and Poldek, who were in Italy at the time. Pasha instructed Zelda "to handle security, to assemble the people after the revenge operation, and to pass them across the border."[79] For that purpose, she was sent to Prague and joined Poldek there as early as March 1946, weeks in advance of the operation. Poldek had been summoned to Pasha in Paris, and Pasha assigned him responsibility for preparing lodging and documents both for the Nokmim involved in the operation and for those who would be evacuated in advance. Zelda and Poldek both stayed in Prague for some weeks on the assumption that after the operation, the Nokmim would arrive there in need of freshly forged papers and a route for immediately fleeing onward. Zelda, who had gained expertise with Vitka in the routes of the Bricha, in the obtaining of documents, and in the transit of groups of Jews across fluid borders, worked together with Poldek to find a route from Nuremberg and Fürth toward the German-Czech border and to prepare crossing stations or at least participate in the crossing stations that the Bricha guides had established.[80] Even reaching Prague, which was under Russian control, involved risks, first among them the risk of arrest for carrying false papers. The two of them tried to arrange lodging and authentic permits for residence in order not to endanger the comrades who would be arriving. They crisscrossed the city, seeking help at every possible address, but although they were equipped with a letter of recommendation from the Haganah, the problems were resolved only after Poldek, who had been connected with the Communist underground in Auschwitz, appealed to a Jewish communist whom he had befriended there and who had become deputy foreign minister in Soviet-dominated Czechoslovakia. Then authentic permits for residence were provided for the comrades. Obtaining equipment and food wasn't easy the first year after the war, but Zelda and Poldek very much wanted their comrades to have a comfortable stay after the great stress that could be expected.[81]

In the meantime, the day for starting out approached. On that day, April 13, 1946, the two of them traveled to the border and waited on the Czech side till nightfall for their comrades, at the crossing point that the Bricha movement had set up. The tension was heavy: Had the operation succeeded, and had the attackers made a good escape? The Nuremberg team had ridden away in a jeep that picked them up in order to sneak them across the border, but they ran into trouble and were placed under arrest. They made a scene, and the police, unable to find any responsible officer to provide instructions on a Sunday, let them go, and the crossing went safely that time. On the other side, Poldek and Zelda were waiting with Levy Argov (Kopelevich), who was a Jewish Brigade soldier from Kibbutz Ha'ogen who treated the Nokmim as if he were their brother, and with some sympathetic Czech police officers. After two days, they were all relieved to join the rest of the group in Prague.[82] There they could breathe freely and even celebrate an actual Passover Seder, even if not in a holiday atmosphere: Although they did not yet know the full details, they understood that the poisoning had not gone as expected. Yulek recounted that because Radio Prague had reported the poisoning, extra caution was exercised, and they were transferred for a brief stay in Bratislava. But within a few days they were among those celebrating the liberation on May 9. They watched the festive parade and enjoyed the Czech people's benevolent attitude toward foreigners. The people of Prague "went crazy with joy, and we were alone with our bitter tears."[83]

Aside from the escape routes that Zelda and Poldek prepared, Pasha had ordered further sites to be made ready. He sent Zygi Gliksman, Velveleh Rabinovich, and Heniek Wodzisławski to look for an additional route. They got to a town near the French border, and there they waited for comrades coming away in the wake of the operation, not necessarily from Nuremberg. At the time, there were Nokmim in various other places who had been told in advance to leave immediately and report to headquarters in Munich without delay. Their orders were issued before the date of the operation, and "with a sinking heart" the comrades assembled their few belongings; then, when they arrived, they were told to leave Germany right away because the discovery of the poison residue had kicked off a search for Yulek's team.

Each of them had traveled independently to Munich. Hasya Taubes-Warchavchik related that upon receiving the order, "we grabbed a bag and ran." Still in haste, one more team went off to Czechoslovakia, then to Austria, and later to Italy; another reached the border of France, proceeded to Paris, where they were concealed in a heartbreaking orphanage, and went from there to Marseilles; and a third and last team, which had gone from Munich directly to Paris and onward from there, included Pasha and Dorka and was escorted by Jewish Brigade soldiers. "The Brigade took us almost by force from Germany to Paris," Dan Arad recounted. The soldiers, whom they hadn't known previously, shadowed their every step, even to the lavatory, said Yitzhak Hammel. Glumly and regretfully, they left the places where they'd been living, laboring, and hoping for results, and headed for the borders.[84]

"Who gave Shadmi the right to dissolve us? And Pasha knew it was happening," Rabinovich complained years later. He had been among those who prepared the site for border-jumping into France. Still, it should be said that they fled after the operation not only because the institutions of the Yishuv didn't want them continuing but also because the operation turned them into lawbreakers wanted by American and British intelligence agencies. But the emissaries of the Bricha begged them to stay and not be forced away to the Land of Israel. "Alon"—Yehuda Arazi—knew full well the enormous contribution that the Nokmim made in the initial period of the Bricha movement. For their part, the Nokmim naturally felt that their place was still not in Palestine but rather in Europe, where their work was incomplete; however, Shadmi disagreed. It must be remembered that after relations deteriorated between Britain and the Yishuv, it was decided to conclude the functioning of the Jewish Brigade. The Brigade would be disbanded and sent to Palestine in June. In May, that step was already doubtless under preparation, and it was clear that from the Haganah's point of view, the Nokmim could by no means remain in Europe without the help of the Jewish Brigade and without close supervision. Poldek noted: "We even said that if the order to stay came from Kovner, we would stay." In their eyes, Kovner was still the commander and still an admired figure, despite a year's separation from him.[85]

Abba Kovner supported the transfer of the Nokmim to Palestine, not because he respected and obeyed the authority of the Yishuv institutions but because he hoped that the other Nokmim would decide, like him, to choose life—in other words, to abandon Plan A. In addition, he understood they could reach that decision only in the Land of Israel, in the place where he underwent a similar change himself. The decision must come from within themselves, not from external persuasion or instruction. However, since he knew that the Nokmim wished to continue, Kovner tried to persuade Shaul Avigur, in Palestine, to assist the group after the operation; that is, to let them remain in Europe and continue with more limited operations, transitioning from Plan B to Plan C, which meant operations against known Nazi war criminals, a scheme that the comrades had previously considered incompatible with their desire for comprehensive vengeance. Avigur's response to Kovner included, among other things: "If you personally don't succeed in persuading them to come to the Land of Israel, I will order all measures to be taken in order to ensure that they cannot take action and that they come one way or another."[86] In a letter that Kovner sent to Vitka in early May after his release from prison and after the Nuremberg operation, one of a stack of letters in which his longing and his plans for the future were expressed to her and, through her, to all his comrades as well, he wrote: "If they want to separate you, don't agree. Come only together" and beware those who would do anything to divide you—"*un zebrecklen eich* [and to crumble you]."[87]

In the meantime, the Nokmim continued their way out. At the end of May, an order came from Pasha, and those who remained in Austria took a train that passed through Vienna and took them to the border region between Austria and Italy. A truck from the Jewish Brigade brought them closer to the crossing, and they traversed the Brenner Pass on foot. The comrades stayed in Italy for another month. They were viewed with honor both by local Jews and by the Jewish immigrants who, like them, were waiting for a ship. Word had gone out that these comrades had "mounted an operation in Germany." In Milan a festive gathering was held in mid-June to mark two months since the operation.[88]

Another part of the group reached Lyons, in France, and later stayed at a little fishing village near Marseilles. There, they received instructions for setting up a fishing kibbutz. A Palmach trainer taught them defense techniques, and someone else taught them English. While they were at the fishing village, a letter suddenly arrived from Kovner. It was warm, emotional, and poetic. At the conclusion of its reading to the assembled members, voices were raised, and torrents of anger and bitterness spilled over. The letter contained a suggestion or veiled instruction to come to Palestine because a pause was necessary for reorganization and for creating a robust infrastructure in advance of continuing the activity and the struggle. Best that they all be together, at least for their first steps in the Land of Israel. The stormy reaction built upon itself, despite all the explanation. The comrades felt that although they had sacrificed, endangered themselves, and knocked about the roadways endlessly, the dream had not been achieved. They had gathered in France and Italy in the belief that there they would regroup and continue to operate; they hadn't realized that in fact they had been brought together for immediate transport to Palestine. They were human beings, said Ruzka's daughter Yonat, who had opted out of resuming life; they were convinced that they had no right to resume life, and to be sent to the Land of Israel, under a directive not involving their agreement, was to them tantamount to being ordered back to life. They hadn't reconciled themselves yet to being alive; they weren't ready for life, certainly not everyday life. Kazhik called it in English "unfinished business": who has the right to decide that I must live, when I prefer to die? I won't forgive it.

Kovner perceived their difficult psychic condition, Vitka said, and he believed that they needed to come to the Land of Israel for rehabilitation. She supported that idea: if they hadn't come then, they would have disintegrated from the inside out. Pasha added a practical rationale: the economic difficulty of supporting dozens of mouths. Rachel Galperin-Gliksman pointed to the ambivalence of mind and the clash between simultaneous feelings. On the one hand was frustration, arising from an operation that had not exactly been successful and could be pursued further. There was the resentful feeling that some higher-up was deciding their future, and there was rage against Kovner and his instruction to join him. On the other hand was an opposing thought: maybe it really was time to go. The letter arrived when they were already partway to the Land of Israel. Thus they arrived at a "unanimous tacit decision," Rachel wrote. "For a while, until the time comes to continue the project of vengeance, we are moving to the Land of Israel." Some of the

Nokmim had relatives there, the last survivors from their families other than the Nokmim themselves—mothers and loved ones and sisters whom they wanted to embrace. And having been on the road for an entire year since the end of the war, they longed to see the Land of Israel.[89]

They left on two separate ships; they were intended to meet on the high seas and transfer to a single ship, but this didn't work out. Those who had come from Czechoslovakia left from La Spezia, Italy, aboard the *Josiah Wedgwood*, a rust-bucket teetering with more than eight hundred crowded, seasick people. That ship reached Haifa on June 26, 1946. Another portion of the group departed Marseilles on the *Haganah*, which arrived in Palestine on July 2, 1946. The ship found itself in a difficult confrontation with the British. Two destroyers were waiting for her at Haifa. The ship's name was changed to the *Biria*, after a location near Safed that had become a symbol of the struggle against the British, and it was feared that if the ship were caught, the British might claim that partisans had seized it in an act of piracy.

All the testimonies describe the outburst of weeping and the excitement when the lights of Haifa came into view on Mount Carmel. As they disembarked, the hundreds of clandestine immigrants were received with oranges, juice, and cookies, with smiles and open arms. The British took the Nokmim to detention at Atlit, the camp near Haifa where all newcomers were first brought, but released them when the space was needed for those arrested in another operation. The *Biria* was the next-to-last ship—afterward, all further ships that the British stopped were taken to Cyprus.[90] Once released, the comrades began their new lives.

A Testament

ZIPPORA BIRMANN

Kibbutz Tel Hai, April 1943

All is lost. This is our fate: To expiate the sins of the prior generations.

We have mourned them all; we have ached with their loss. History's greatest possible horror descended on us. We saw, we heard, we suffered, and now it is our lot to disappear forever. Not even a Jewish grave is afforded to our bones. It is hard to bear. The only counsel is to fall honorably, together with all the thousands on their way to death, without weakening, without fear. This we know: The Jewish people will not expire. It will rise in rebirth, grow and thrive, and avenge the spilling of our blood.

Yes, I hereby turn to you, wherever you comrades may be: You are obliged to avenge. By day, by night, be not deaf to the command of vengeance, of redressing the spilling of blood, just as we are not silent while face to face with death.

Cursed be whoever reads this, sighs, and returns to his daily work.

Cursed be whoever sheds tears, eulogizes us, and says: Enough.

Our demand from you is not that! We did not eulogize our own parents; we looked silently at the discarded bodies of our dear ones who were shot like dogs.

We call upon you: Avenge. Avenge without mercy, without sentiment, with no "good" Germans. For the "good" German, an easy death; but death. He must be killed in the end. They promised too, to the Jews they deemed good: "You'll be the last one shot."

That is our demand, the demand of us all. That is the wish that burns in people who may fall tomorrow among the fallen, may fight with strength and fall with honor.

To vengeance we summon you, you who did not agonize in the hell of Hitler. That is our demand, and you must perform it even at the risk of your life.

Our shattered bones, which are strewn to all ends of Europe, will know no rest, and the ash of our bodies, which is sown in the wind, will know no silence until you deliver our revenge. Remember this and do so. Our entreaty is your duty.

Zippora Birmann, born in Rozhyshche in the Volyn Oblast (Poland), was a member of HeHalutz HaTzair (the Young Pioneer) and the Jewish Fighting Organization in the Bialystok Ghetto. She fell defending the ghetto in August 1943. After the war, her writings were found among the effects of Mordechai Tenenbaum-Tamaroff, commander of the uprising. These words of hers were published in *The Book of the Ghettos' Wars: Inside the Walls, Camps, and Forests*, p. 692. Courtesy of Ghetto Fighters' House and Hakibbutz Hameuchad. Translated by Mark L. Levinson.

Conclusion

"If Jesus had been through the Holocaust, he would have joined us."

PASHA AVIDOV, September 19, 1995

AFTER THEIR FIRST ENCOUNTER with the country and a turbulent attempt at integration at Ein HaHoresh, most of the Nokmim split away to various other communities: they hoped to return to Europe and resume revenge operation, but their repeated angry requests were denied. Still, revenge attempts continued in two lines. Shimon Avidan left for Europe in August 1946, with the full support of the Yishuv authorities, though the Avengers were out of the secretive circle. He operated in eastern Germany, helped by high-ranking Soviets and accompanied by German communist comrades, and enlisted a number of those soldiers of the German Unit still stationed in Europe. There is no knowing what he and his group actually accomplished, since he refused to his dying day to disclose details. According to rumors and hints I could not fully verify, they did execute a number of identified German war criminals before returning in August 1947. Also, a group of about twelve members who could by no means accept having their request denied left Ein Hahoresh and sneaked back into Europe in November 1947 on their own. Although they devised many detailed plans, they could not operate without backing, and they got into trouble time and time again due to dubious attempts to secure funds—they remained known as "the second group."

Kovner, Vitka his helpmeet, and Ruzka Korczak stayed in Ein HaHoresh. Avidan returned to his kibbutz, Ein Hashofet. The War of Independence ended, and gradually the second group of Nokmim returned from Europe as well. All the comrades continued living day to day in their communities, but despite their distance, the close friendship between them remained and even strengthened over the years. They met frequently at Ein HaHoresh at the Kovners' home and at Ruzka's. (She had started a family there with Avi Marla.) They continually phoned and visited one another. As time passed, they began bringing their children to the meetings, and thus the meetings grew in size. They continue to meet to this day, though the Nokmim are now in their nineties. Their children and grandchildren come to the gatherings and repeatedly ask to hear the story, trying to understand how their parents, quiet and loving people who go off about their business every day like everybody else, had it in them to champion the cause of vengeance. Then they listen and hear and once more respond with empathy and solidarity.

Even after they had undertaken job responsibilities and had started families, the Nokmim did not leave their past behind. The Mossad saw them as good candidates for recruitment: young people who kept secrets, who thought outside the box, who could work both alone and in teams, who could cross borders with forged papers and assume false identities. They were loyal Zionists, regardless of their prewar political backgrounds, and like many other survivors, they saw the establishment of the State of Israel as a miracle for the Jewish people in the wake of the Holocaust, a treasure that must be meticulously preserved. Most of them fought in the War of Independence, having enlisted in combat units, principally the prestigious Palmach.

Ludwig Mairanz returned to Israel in 1950 with an immigrant's certificate that he had prepared for himself with great adeptness. Despite the questionable activities of the second group, among which he numbered, he was sent again and again to Europe during the 1950s under assumed names, with double-bottomed suitcases. Apparently he went on arms procurement missions and operated mostly in Paris, where he felt at home, in close coordination with official Israeli contacts who were still positioned in France and with Yosef (Yulek) Harmatz. Yulek was active for many years as a central Mossad figure in Geneva. Later he served as the director general of the World ORT educational system.[1]

Pinchas (Yashek) Ben-Zur became an agent for the Shin Bet (the government's General Security Service) and the Mossad, and he carried out many secret missions. Shimon (Shimek) Lustgarten performed missions that he declined to speak about afterward. Yehuda (Poldek) Maimon worked for Nativ, a branch of the intelligence community set up in the early 1950s to maintain contact with the Jews locked in Eastern Europe. In 1963 he was sent to Poland as First Secretary of the Israeli embassy in Warsaw. Afterward, as a representative of Israel in Vienna, he helped bring the remnant of Polish Jewry to Israel and pave the way for the emigration of Soviet Jewry.

Yitzhak (Pasha) Avidov was sent by Shaul Avigur, then deputy minister of defense, to serve at the Israeli embassy in Warsaw. "It's an irony of history," Pasha said later, "considering the things Avigur said about us when he suspected we were seceders, that after a while we became friends and developed complete trust in one another."[2] When he returned from Poland, Pasha became a senior executive of an insurance company.

Hasya Taubes-Warchavchik helped design the Uzi, the first Israeli-made weapon, and then was a librarian for many years. Manek L. studied musical composition with composer Paul Ben-Haim and later became a successful businessman. Arie (Leibke) Distel and Mira (Mirka) Verbin-Shabetzky joined Kibbutz Yakum, Shlomo Kenet moved to Kibbutz Beit Zera, and Zila (Cesia) Rosenberg-Amit joined Kibbutz Givat Brener. Yehuda (Idek) Friedman opened a garage in Haifa and a plant for auto parts in Tel Aviv. Zygi (Zygmunt) Gliksman worked in sign painting. Yitzhak Hammel was a pioneer in developing computers as well as a senior executive at a major construction company. Zelda Treger and Netanel (Senka) Nissanilevich married and opened a delicatessen on Tel Aviv's famous Dizengoff Street. Simcha (Kazhik) Rotem managed a large supermarket chain. Ruzka became an educator and a central figure on Kibbutz Ein HaHoresh, and Vitka became a sought-after clinical psychologist. Ze'ev (Willek) Shenar was in charge of sanitation for Moshav Michmoret and the surrounding region.

In conversations with them and at their meetings, the Nokmim repeatedly stressed that they had essentially kept their silence for forty years and then, as a group, revealed their story only in the 1980s, a few years before Kovner died in 1987. Actually, their story had reached the public in the mid-1960s by way of a number of documentary films produced in Israel

and elsewhere and a handful of press accounts and brief chapters of research studies; but until the mid-1980s, only a few of the Nokmim, including Kovner himself, had agreed to be interviewed for those films and publications, generally withholding their names but without requesting the entire
group's permission. When the other Nokmim did find out, most of them
became angry with the interviewees. They considered that a vow of silence
had been broken, and they believed that most of the publications and films
were of insufficient quality and misrepresented the story. They decided, accordingly, not to respond regarding such publications, which included exag-
gerations and distortions, because it was "beneath their dignity," as Poldek
put it. Lena tried to explain the anger, which was directed at Kovner as well:
"Feelings were very strong with respect to revenge. For most of the members,
it was the summit of their lives, something sacred that wasn't to be touched.
Life was very special there; the passing days were different, the ideology was
total. Every thought was focused on it."[3]

In spring 1987, shortly before he died, Kovner wrote a summation of the
group's history and deposited it in the Moreshet archive. The title was "About
the *Nakam*: Filling Out the Earlier Testimonies." In it, Kovner explained
that the edict imposed by the Nokmim upon themselves—not to make public any comprehensive and detailed history of the group—was valid for forty
years. Thus he was explaining to his comrades that those who had been interviewed in the meantime, including himself, revealed little and did so anony-
mously because "there was self-censorship, in the national interest, regarding
that sensitive topic during a generation of terrorism and counterterrorism."
In other words, they feared that someone might be inspired to imitate their
project or that in response to their story, acts of terrorism might be directed
against Jews or against Israel.[4]

Their silence was also based on the belief that most of the Israeli public, which had not endured the Holocaust, had no understanding of the ve-
hement urge for vengeance that the Nokmim felt. During those years, the
Nokmim were unaware that there actually was a fervent desire in the Yishuv
for vengeance against the Germans. That desire has come to light today, as
described above, in documents that until now lay undisturbed in archives.
It was present even at the highest levels, which the Nokmim had perceived
as hostile to them and to their project. And they certainly did not know of

the reports that Nahum Shadmi sent back to the Land of Israel—that same Shadmi who in fact "loved Nechama." Moreover, some of the press accounts, and even *The History of the Haganah*, hinted that the Nokmim may have been less than sane in the wake of the Holocaust, and when the Nokmim saw such assessments, they regarded them as dismissive of the deep trauma that all the survivors bore. Shlomo Nakdimon, the first to write about the group, quoted three without naming them: "The emissaries from the Land of Israel called us crazy, and we answered: If such a Holocaust leaves 50 people crazy, then we're entitled to go crazy."[5]

Another reason for staying quiet was fear that their stories might disrupt the rehabilitation and protection of the survivors in Europe and, later, that it might interfere with the absorption of the survivors in the Land of Israel and the respect for them among society there. "We tripped over a kind of a seam between the Holocaust and the national rebirth. Our ideology embodied the past, since vengeance is a reaction to what has already happened [. . .] whereas the policy of the Zionist movement and of the Yishuv embodied a struggle over the future," Yulek said at one of the gatherings.[6]

And then, after Kovner was diagnosed with laryngeal cancer in the mid-1980s, the core members of the group met. Their stormy initial discourse lasted two days, and it was continued at a further meeting shortly afterward. At that meeting, the Nokmim chose Levi Arieh Sarid—a publicist and a researcher of the Zionist pioneering movements in Poland—to serve as the group's historian. The meeting was recorded and transcribed, and the recording, which Kovner called "the most reliable" of material, was given to Sarid. Kovner had sat with him for many hours before the meeting, and after the meeting Sarid interviewed the Nokmim thoroughly, one by one. The article he wrote was the first to set forth the entire story and was also the most comprehensive in terms of its scope and its use of testimonies. At that time, Kovner was still fearful that the publication of any book or booklet about the group's deeds would be "treated superficially both by the media in Israel and by the world. Who needs it?" he wrote to Pasha, and to the Nokmim he recommended waiting to see how Sarid's article was received. After some argument, particularly over the question of which magazine should run the article, it went to press in 1992, after Kovner's death. Despite going unseen by Kovner—and despite appearing in *Yalkut Moreshet*, a journal sponsored by Hashomer Hatzair and thus not representative of the entire group—the published article was greeted gladly by the Nokmim. They gathered at Kibbutz Yakum with their families in honor of the publication, and they expressed hope that the article would shield them from slurs and slander that had been cast them in a false light. From the 1990s onward, because the topic continued arousing curiosity, the Nokmim delivered testimonies of a freer nature, but still only after consulting one another. They even wrote memoirs, primarily for their families, and they printed their testimonies as individual booklets.[7] Some of them still wished sadly that Kovner had written their history himself and thus forestalled the scribblers and sensation-mongers, who, they felt, distorted and vulgarized it. Kazhik said: When you write, you burden yourself with a great responsibility; and Kovner wouldn't take that responsibility on himself. Lena noted: It's a great shame that he didn't write it himself instead of turning it over to Sarid to write, and it's a shame that he didn't call the Nokmim in and talk to them back in the fifties and sixties, before others started writing drivel. He would have explained to them, and we'd have made peace with one another. But Kovner decided not to write about the Holocaust in prose, only in poetry. He thought it was useless "to say to a stranger / Once there was a world here," because no stranger will understand.[8]

THE NOKMIM AND THE UNACHIEVED PLAN A

During their interviews, the Nokmim were asked for their opinions, in retrospect, on the shelving of Plan A. They answered as they were each moved to.

SIMCHA (KAZHIK) ROTEM (RATHAJZER)—In retrospect, he isn't sorry that the plan for poisoning the water supplies was not fulfilled; if it had come about, he supposes that he couldn't have gone on living in view of the consequences, by which he refers to the innocent people and especially to the children. It was an utterly lunatic idea. The Nokmim, it must be understood, had no desire to distinguish between one German and another—they wanted to target all the Germans. He does regret that the plan for Dachau wasn't carried out.[9]

ZILA (CESIA) ROSENBERG-AMIT—Today, she doesn't regret that the plan remained unachieved.[10]

RUZKA KORCZAK-MARLA—"This operation will be remembered as a national and human deed of power and scope, and a warning to further generations. The memory of the group, the pride of belonging to it, and the friendships that were forged then all nourish the comrades to this day."[11]

GAVRIEL (GABI) SEDLIS (SCHEDLITZ)—"To this day, there are two things I haven't gotten over: Leaving my mother when I went out to the forest [she was killed at Majdanek] and sharing the intent to murder millions."[12]

MANEK L.—"Obviously it's good that [the plan] wasn't achieved. But in 1945 you would have thought differently," he told me. Back then, they were obliged to sever ties and work alone in defiance of constant surveillance by the Haganah. They had the big plan to carry out, and he would have been glad then if it had been accomplished. It would have been justifiable very close to the end of the war, but not in 1946. A huge waste of time. Still, the Nokmim remained a wonderful group, he adds. They made life all the more worth living. People with integrity, with complete trust in one another, with independent judgment. Morally, they had set the bar, and they would not stoop any lower, come what may.[13]

HASYA TAUBES-WARCHAVCHIK—Today she is happy that they didn't poison the cities' water, but poisonings at the POW camps? Here they did too little, and with not enough victims.[14]

YOSEF (YULEK) HARMATZ—They knew and were deeply conscious that they belonged to one another. They sensed their public and national responsibility, and even though the basis of their ideology was the past, and the people they met [from the Land of Israel] were oriented toward the future, still they always found a common language with them. He is proud, happy, and gratified at belonging to this group. He is grateful both to his commanders and to his subordinates. The members of the group represented the noblest and the choicest Jewish youth from an Eastern Europe that was being burned alive. Nonetheless, today he thinks that Ben-Gurion was right to impede them. Everyone wanted to take charge of them, but they were stubborn and committed.[15]

SHLOMO KENET (KANTAROWICZ)—"It was an act of symbolism more than an act of vengeance. If I had pictured to myself what would be going on in those cities after the poisoning, I wouldn't have done it. But at the time, I found the operation morally acceptable. There was still an echoing scream that said we hadn't paid our debt, that we hadn't done enough to calm the screams away; but at that time, we were trapped in the dreadfulness of the Holocaust. Today it's impossible to understand our idea of vengeance. It's difficult to tell the story because it means handing a weapon to our enemies. [Today] I'm still carrying the feeling that the millions who were slaughtered, our parents and brothers and sisters whom the Germans murdered, imposed a sacred mission on us, and we left it undone." And in another interview: "I don't regret a single moment of my participation. On the contrary, I'm proud that I took part in this group, which did not care about its personal future."[16]

MIRA (MIRKA) VERBIN-SHABETZKY—It would have made no difference to her if a German, whether a child or a grown-up, was guilty or not. To her, there was no distinction. She was willing to see them erased completely from the face of the earth. She was an extremist then, and she doesn't feel she is less of an extremist now.[17]

ARIE (LEIBKE) DISTEL—"What we mounted was a symbolic operation, and it's good that we mounted it. Good that the Jewish people didn't casually leave the Holocaust behind without doing anything. A group of Jews did what they should, the way Jewish honor demanded. That's how I'd sum it up." And regarding Plan A: "You can assume that when they thought thoroughly about it, the planners decided not to poison the entire water system because that would be an attack on the innocent along with the guilty. Back then, granted, it was only reasonable and understandable that people would react after losing their families and after years of humiliation and oppression, but the reaction was held back by qualms that arose from emotion and from the mentality of members who nonetheless have to weigh their own actions by the standards of humaneness."[18]

YEHUDA (POLDEK) MAIMON—How much they accomplished doesn't matter. What matters is that the group arose and faithfully put into action the feelings of millions of Jews—every Jewish man, woman, and child. Does he still regret that Plan A was not executed? Certainly. He thinks that it was what they deserved. The German people, as a nation, cannot be forgiven.[19]

YITZHAK (PASHA) AVIDOV (REICHMAN)—If Jesus had been through the Holocaust, he would have helped to found the Nokmim. And if Kovner hadn't gone off to Palestine, they would have gone through with Plan A. No doubt about it. The comrades remained clean morally while doing foul, dirty work. They tried to do what God, if not imaginary, should have done.[20]

KA-TZETNIK – YEHIEL DE-NUR (FEINER)—At a meeting of the Bricha in Bucharest, Feiner spoke of the need to raise and advance the standing of the Jews in their own eyes and in those of other nations. Vengeance, to his understanding, carried a symbolic aspect that could convey a warning even without its practical dimension and could arouse respect toward the Jewish people. Years later, in his book *Nakam* ("Revenge"), he asked a question that has an obvious answer: Could the blood of a German child silence in our ears, for even a moment, the cry of a Jewish child? "Does blood have the power to wash away blood whose flesh exists no longer?"[21]

In Ein HaHoresh, at eighty-nine years of age, at her home among the grass and flowers that she nurtured, Vitka Kempner-Kovner spoke. Some years ago now, she moved back to other times and places, leaving the here and now. She speaks to herself, essentially, and summarizes for me and for Ruzka's daughter Yonat:

> It was a satanic concept, and commitment to it was total, unbending, and extreme to the bitter end. Nothing else existed. We lived, but we weren't living life. The campaign of vengeance was a powerful experience because it was very distant from everything human and normal; a destructive ideology. I felt fatigue after the ghetto and the forest and the rushing about from Lithuania all the way to Italy, and then back in the other direction to Belgium, Germany, Paris.

And at this point, maybe to clarify the past from the vantage point of a long, rich life filled with experiences that is nearing its end, she says—again, as if to herself—"Even if Abba had stayed in Europe instead of going to Palestine, the vengeance wouldn't have happened. Not because of the Land of Israel [that is, the objection of the Yishuv leadership and the Haganah] but because of *temporis mutantis*, the way the times change and we change within them. Time passed, and the vengeance we had in mind stopped being realistic." Some years before, she had said: "The most important thing about the campaign of vengeance was the very conceiving of such an idea. Like the Warsaw Ghetto uprising—it has to have a symbolic effect. [. . .] It was an insane idea, and it took over the lives of the people devoted to it. But at the time, I identified with it completely."[22] She repeated, on every occasion, that it was unimportant how many Germans were killed or harmed in the operations, just as it was unimportant how many Germans were killed in the ghetto uprisings, because even if the operation was on a tiny scale, the purpose was attained: They proved that genocide does not go unanswered.[23]

Some of the Nokmim still defend Plan A and are angry at themselves for its cancellation. They can allow themselves now to continue saying that they regret not having managed to kill more Germans, or at least more SS men from among the POWs in the camps that the Allies controlled. There is no doubt that some of them, if not all, still deeply wish a violent death to all Germans, but their wishes are no longer put to the test. They haven't betrayed their cause and haven't forsaken it. It was the circumstances, and in their opinion the Yishuv and its leadership as well, that stood in their way and prevented the operation; therefore, they can say that they continue to be loyal to it. But even so, perhaps they inwardly understand today a fact that some may have long understood: that it is good—very good!—to have left Plan A unaccomplished. After all, how could they stand before their progeny, their first- and second-generation descendants, while burdened with responsibility for that terrible deed? That is why they were ready for reconciliation with Kovner despite the great resentment that resounded when he remained for some four months in the Yishuv and failed to supply the poison within the expected time. They charged him then with treason against themselves and against the shared vision, the vision that he had initiated and that had lighted their way in his footsteps. They had kept the faith while he hadn't. Some of them refused to speak to him for several years after they reached the Land of Israel. Even now, when they recall those days, the anger is as still fresh, as if decades have not passed. But they understand that if waged on the enormous scale of their plan, vengeance would not have been tolerated in the Land of Israel—not then and certainly not now, not by the public and not by their own families, not by the enlightened world and not even by Germany. So for that reason too they spent years in silence.

ESTEEM FOR THE NOKMIM AND APPRAISAL OF THEIR PLANS

Esteem for the Nokmim as human beings did not interfere with opposition to their path, even from the people close to them. Chaika Grossman, for example, was invited to one of the first meetings of the Nokmim in the mid-1980s. Thinking back on it, she leveled sharp criticism against what she'd heard from them. She protested against the retrospective claim of the Nokmim that Plan A had been shelved because the times and conditions stopped favoring the plan. In her opinion, they should have based the plan's cancellation on compunctions, on rethinking from the humane perspective, on thinking ahead to the day when six million Germans have died and the deed brings consequences. The Nokmim depicted the operation as having promised, if carried out, to be a "bridge to a new day and to life" for the entire Jewish people. The mass vengeance was thought of as putting an end, once and for all, throughout the generations, to the antisemitic dream of crushing the Jews and their state. It could be, Chaika concluded, that the world might absorb such a lesson of deterrence, but the same lesson would lend legitimacy to similar acts and to methods tantamount to "Let me die with the Philistines." She tried to understand the attitude of Kovner, whom she respected and admired greatly: "The earth was burning under his feet. His profound experiences, his mind's reactions penetrating into his depths, always triggered extreme responses [. . .]. He lived the anguish of the past at another decibel level. His greatness was in his dissimilarity." But although she had come to recognize his extremism, she said after the meeting with her comrades of the roads and of the suffering: "It's hard for me to suppose that Abba meant literally what he said. [. . .] Plan A was just an abstraction."[24]

In 1988, Chaika took it upon herself to head Moreshet, the Mordechai Anielevich Memorial Holocaust Study and Research Center located at Givat Haviva. She would sit there at the abundant archive, turning the documents and manuscripts over and over, but she couldn't solve the riddle of the genocide. All the explanations from the mouths and pens of historians, psychologists, and others, failed to clarify it. The deeper the riddle plunged, the more sharply the question pierced: How could this appalling thing have happened? And she would return to the story of the Nokmim and say, "There is no explanation for the Holocaust. No explanation and not a speck of logic or elucidation to be found from any angle. So the Nokmim are all the more to be understood." She said this not with approval but with empathy, since if there is no reasonable causation and no logic and no explanation, it follows that an entire culture and millions of human souls were cut down arbitrarily, and therefore vengeance is not unthinkable.[25]

Similarly, Antek—Yitzhak Zuckerman—never stopped bringing up the topic in his later testimonies, reflecting a debate he continued to wage with himself:

> I had to disregard them, so that I could live my life in a way that I found justifiable. [. . .] They, the Germans, were reduced in my mind to something like nonexistence, because if they existed, I would have had to drop everything and devote myself to revenge. For that reason I didn't see them, I didn't visit their cities, I didn't see their country's splendor, I didn't see their museums. [. . .] To this day I don't reply if a German says hello. [. . .] I have no contact with them. And you may be sure: There will be no vengeance. It's all blather. But I wouldn't be willing to kill just any German, without differentiating.[26]

Antek speaks in present tense, as if the question of vengeance were still open, decades after the war's end. And in the statement that he must ignore the existence of Germans in order to live a life that he can justify to himself, he is essentially saying, albeit indirectly, that the Nokmim found their reason for living in not ignoring the Germans. Recall that Antek and Chaika were both asked to head the group after Kovner's arrest; it is thus no wonder that the matter continued to occupy their minds. Moreover, Antek and Chaika—he in Warsaw, she in Bialystok—were among the instigators of the armed revolts against the Germans, insurrections that had no equivalent in Kovner's Vilna, despite the organized underground set up and operating in the ghetto. It is perhaps for that reason the two of them did not strive for another deed of national and historical dimensions.

Mordechai Roseman, who was a close friend of the Nokmim, said that they were trustworthy and trusted one another, that a friendship had been forged, and that there was great admiration for Kovner. Obviously the Nokmim could not have operated, nor even have continued to exist, if not surrounded by supportive people.[27] And he said further: "The idea was historically righteous but politically insane." In contrast to Kovner, who contended that in order to fend off a new Holocaust, vengeance was a necessity for Jewish existence, Roseman contended that there was no such necessity. And consequently he perceived a severe moral problem: In principle, vengeance was called for, but how could killing be counteracted by killing? The proper method would be a constructive, intellectual, pioneering one, not a cruel partisan-style method. On the other hand, "It's good that there was such a thing, because only imbalanced people—and these people were in a daze—could produce anything like the necessary warning. What's important is that there was a group of Jews who were willing to sacrifice their lives if necessary."[28]

Even those who opposed indiscriminate vengeance called them "fine youngsters," as did Yehuda Ben-David. "True soldiers, each and every one," said Menashe Gewissar. Ben Meiri claimed: "In spite of everything lofty and noble about the idea of vengeance, it's of course a negative thing by nature, not constructive in any way and with no positive approach to life." And he would have waived the operation, although not the goal, which was righteous and correct. The main point, he said, is to emphasize that they showed devotion and willingness on a level "that I'd never seen in my life." Shadmi's book describes them as "among the best of Jewish youth. Pioneers whose ambition had been to reach the Land of Israel and integrate into the life there," until the war came.

> With their special sensitivity, they already realized that the world was about to resume its course and reconcile with the murderers. [. . .] They saw it as their duty to arouse the world and prevent the Holocaust from being forgotten. That objective became the central vector of their lives.[29]

Shlomo Nakdimon was, as mentioned, the first to write about the Nokmim. He was introduced to three of the Nokmim by Haim Lazar, the very man who had been bitter about being excluded from the Nokmim together with his fellow Beitar members. The Nokmim told Nakdimon their story, although retaining their anonymity. An article that Nakdimon published in 1966, in advance of the twentieth anniversary of the Nuremberg operation, is written with admiration and emphasizes that the Nokmim later integrated into the fight for Israeli independence and its state-building.

Michael Bar-Zohar followed Nakdimon as a pioneer of researching vengeance against Germany, and he published his book in 1969. Previously he had also had conversations with members of the Jewish Brigade and the German Unit who were active in vengeance. He reached the conclusion that all the Avengers were suffused with a feeling of historic and national mission and that from their fairmindedness, their high moral level, and the sense of justice engrained in their souls, nothing was lost in the thirst for vengeance that burned in their hearts, nor in the operations they mounted; they filled senior military and civilian positions in Israel afterward, and they won much recognition. Bar-Zohar also notes that revenge, in the minds of those who wreaked it, was not personal, not against those who had attacked their own dear ones, but rather a mission entrusted to the Avengers by all who were murdered and all who survived. The Nokmim tortured no one. And they took nothing for themselves from among the effects, the belongings, or the family property of those they targeted, at a time of scarcity, when such restraint was rare.[30]

Similar remarks came from Professor Israel Gutman, one of the pillars of Holocaust research, in answer to an interviewer's question about the idea, advanced in Germany in 2000, of putting Yulek and Distel on trial in the wake of a book published there by two German journalists, Jim G. Tobias and Peter Zinke,[31] that described the operation: "I know many of the Nokmim, who most actually have nothing violent or overbearing about them. They are completely pure in their humanity, and I am not exaggerating. That is how they really were." And in fact, as noted, there is a conspicuous gap between the personalities of the Nokmim and the mission that they adopted—vengeance without trial; and between themselves and the methods they were obliged to employ, such as black marketeering, falsifying documents, border-running, currency speculation, and bouts of drinking with questionable company for the sake of extracting information. Gutman emphasized that Jews had written on the walls, even the walls of the gas chamber—"Jews, Avenge!"—and thus, he said, the deed was by way of fulfilling that bequest. However, he ended his remarks with the Nokmim's contribution to the Bricha, to the Haganah, and to the resurgence of the People of Israel, and with the sweetest of all revenge: establishing a home in Israel under the flag of a state. "That is the bequest of those who walked to the gas chambers: from vengeance to resurgence." And he added: "What power did the Jews have to accomplish anything after the war? Everyone desired revenge, but the words and the ideas fell so far short of the possibility to fulfill them."[32]

Yehuda Tubin formed sturdy friendships with the Nokmim and earned their trust. Roughly a week before the Nuremberg operation, he wrote an emotional letter to his wife, Shlomit. Apparently he didn't know about the operation, so the timing of the letter was coincidental, but in it he prays for the welfare of those courageous and daring friends of his, ready as they are to follow wherever their chosen path leads them. Although they passed through hell, they weren't now taking the time to build their homes but instead remembering the dead:

> And may they be blessed for not reconciling themselves to *our blood falling forfeit* [. . .]. To consider their attitude a descent into terrorism, in my opinion, is to misunderstand the deep meaning of the Holocaust and the future dangers that Nazism introduced into the world; and given that the Nokmim did not succeed within the time frame of their activity, while we were in Europe, I dare contend that there is cause for regret.

But to those expressions of warm support, it must be added that despite Tubin's trust in the Nokmim, his strong bond with them, and his devoted care of them, it is unclear whether he was told of Plan A; according to his own account, he asked no questions and provided no suggestions. He always accepted, with understanding, whatever he was told.[33]

Shimon Avidan provided a summation too, looking back across the years: "I have to conclude, with regret, that we missed the only chance we were given to prove to the world that it can't make Jews into soap and chemical fertilizer without paying a price in blood." He was convinced that a proper campaign of vengeance could have given the survivors back a sense of safety and self-respect. Too little had been done, in his opinion, and what was done emerged from the independent initiative of individuals and small bands of survivors, partisans, and underground activists. The secret and anonymous operations occasionally deviated from their intended targets, he told his interviewers, and therefore some of them resulted in a bad impression and more than a little criticism. Today we know that matters had been directed clandestinely, naturally without documentation, and had left behind them a long swath of secrecy—of deeds best left untold, known to few in detail—so who can guess what truly happened over the course of it all? This explains why he said that since such activity can be waged only in secret, and since the weak cannot afford to join battle face to face, it is waged by "underhanded means," such as murder by ambush.[34] In these remarks, presumably Avidan included himself and the comrades who accompanied him through Europe to perform deeds best left untold. Who other than him knows what really happened in the course of them?

Haim Laskov and Meir Zorea agreed with him: "The side that deals in revenge is the weaker side. We were weak, with no state and no leverage; six million of us were lost. Too little was done, and that's regrettable." Zorea said: "In retrospect, those operations are fine with me, if only because they mean I can tell my son and my grandson that someone tried to give the criminals the retribution they deserved." And Avidan adds, "I'm content with my past. I don't consider that I sinned, when I stand before Bergen-Belsen and Dachau." And Mordechai Gichon remarks: "The Nazis we killed didn't deserve to live. It's a shame we didn't kill more of them."[35]

Generally, Avidan directed his criticism not against those individuals and small groups who did what the public at large should have done, but against the Yishuv institutions that decided to oppose vengeance operations—even those operations that would presumably have been mounted in a disciplined way. They decided wrongly, in his opinion. He believed that not only the SS officers but also the lower-ranking criminals, murderers with blood on their hands, tens of thousands of men and women, should have been targeted. Instead, they all went home, and the Germany he saw became populated by former Nazis who manned again most of the official positions. Continuing, Avidan claimed that since Europe was in chaos during the first year after the war, it would not have been difficult to target them, and leadership fell short by not hurrying to fulfill the mandate that the murdered millions had left behind: to avenge their blood. In essence, Avidan was ignoring the political considerations that guided the Yishuv's leadership: the need to maintain reasonable relations with the British and American occupation authorities in Germany for the sake of the hundreds of thousands of displaced persons under their authority as well as for the sake of the political future of the Yishuv and because the enlightened world, which had quickly forgotten or wanted to forget, "wouldn't understand our point of view." Avidan rejected that assessment of the enlightened world's reaction, and he suggested a different justification: World opinion had not been aroused at the time of the Holocaust, and the free world's leaders didn't lift a finger to prevent the slaughter of Jews; therefore, they couldn't be judgmental of Jews who decided to act against those who murdered their community.

That justification bears examining, since it never encountered the test of reality. It could be that had the plan been executed, the results might have been the opposite: Public opinion had become accustomed to seeing Jews as victims, and it had yet to realize how vast the genocide against the Jews was and how cruelly it was perpetrated. Thus, it might not have tolerated vengeance without trial, and certainly not in territories under the authority of the Allies, since at that time everyone was envisioning a new and orderly world. Public opinion could have seen the Yishuv and its behavior as irresponsible and not necessarily the proper foundation for an independent state. It might even have seen the Yishuv as a congenitally vengeful community, impelled by the affronts and tribulations of a long history, since as far back as the Bible the Jealous God repeatedly demands vengeance against the Amalekites throughout the generations. However, in a later interview Avidan said that he could well understand that the leadership had done its best to prevent a large-scale operation. He noted that the major priority in those days was the Bricha, "and who would defend the DPs if you smite the Germans?" It was the Yishuv's prerogative to identify the major priority, and they decided on bringing the DPs to Palestine, "although that doesn't rule out the idea that accounts must be settled." That was the last interview that Avidan gave, and the first that evinced any feeling of understanding for the stand that the Yishuv's institutions adopted.[36]

THE ATTITUDE OF THE YISHUV'S INSTITUTIONS

Compared with how Avidan and the Avengers from the Jewish Brigade viewed the campaign of vengeance and its relationship with the Haganah, which was the body representing the organized Yishuv, *The History of the Haganah* takes quite another view. Avidan and his comrades spoke of losing an opportunity to warn the world by means of their vengeance, whereas the heads of the Haganah called for wariness lest a different historic opportunity be lost in the wake of the Nokmim's full accomplishment of their plan. With all the understanding that a Jewish heart must afford to their emotions, *The History of the Haganah* says, no tears need be shed over the nonperformance of the Nokmim's plan because such clandestine vengeance served no moral or historical purpose, as Jean Améry also noted. Those unequivocal pronouncements infuriated Pasha when he read them years later.[37] *The History of the Haganah* claims further that whereas only people with nothing else to hope for would devote themselves to vengeance as a consolation, not all the avenues of life had been closed to the People of Israel, and the nation was not shouting, "Let me die with the Philistines!" The People of Israel had not yet concluded its role in history. No act of vengeance could neutralize the spilling of that innocent blood. The greatest vengeance against Hitler and his followers is the resurgence of the People of Israel, their rise out of dust and ashes, and the ascendancy of their honor through the establishment of a Jewish state in the Land of Israel. "The Haganah had the privilege of restraining that phenomenon and directing the mighty forces of spirit behind it into a more fertile channel and outlet, in a different arena of action and on the soil of the fatherland."[38] The word "historic" appears repeatedly in the writing of the book's editors, indicating their feeling that they must carry out the mission entrusted to them and nothing must impede them, not even people who have suffered indescribably.

Ben-Gurion's attitude can be assessed, but not by his words. Regarding vengeance, not one written word of his can be found—neither in his correspondence nor in his documents. At Sde Boker in the Southern Negev, where his archive is kept, the archivist explained that there are topics which he chose not to write of, especially when his position was clear and written details were unnecessary. Shabtai Tevet, his biographer, said: If Ben-Gurion had favored vengeance, then vengeance would have "taken off" and units would have been set up for the purpose. Obviously he didn't favor it, and therefore what was done was done despite and in defiance of the institutions. However, it was clear that in the long term, Jewish history could not and cannot continue without addressing this affront, and thus Adolf Eichmann, caught by the Mossad, was brought to public trial, a historic symbolic trial: In the Nuremberg trials the Jewish people was not represented, and the Holocaust was not an issue dealt with in itself. Through the Eichmann trial, held in Jerusalem, the story of the Holocaust was told in detail to the world at large, and justice was restored: one of the chief orchestrators of the mass murder was sentenced to death. And indeed Kovner felt, as he stood delivering his testimony at that trial, a deep sense that this was judgment day.[39]

Still, words and deeds from some of the officers and emissaries out of the Land of Israel form a picture more complex than what *The History of the Haganah* presents. Michael (James) Ben-Gal, one of the Jewish Brigade's commanders on behalf of the Haganah, was fully agreeable to what Moshe Shertok said about vengeance in the appropriate degree as a deed to be accomplished. The commander who preceded him, Shlomo Shamir, wrote that if he had received a serious proposal for the killing of a million Germans, he would have considered the idea of having the Jewish Brigade itself do the job. Ben-Horin, who worked hand in hand both with Avidan and with the Nokmim, agreed in retrospect with the necessity for deterrence, which underlay the idea of vengeance. In his words, even the Nuremberg operation "at its large scope"—by which apparently he means the poisoning of tens of thousands of SS veterans, a plan that was intended but did not come about— would have been no recompense at all for the murder of six million. However, vengeance did serve to express the resolute decision that "we shall not allow the spilling of Jewish blood to go unpunished." Ben-Horin uses first person plural here, like a participant, and not for the first time. Thus he implies that the decision came not only from the Nokmim but from the establishment as well. And the stand taken by Shadmi, the commander of the Haganah in Europe, requires no emphasis: in the reports that he sent back to the Yishuv, he spoke of his involvement in every stage of the Nokmim's activities, of his desire to see "Nechama" succeed, of his disappointment at the failure, and of the sin that the leadership was committing against Jewish history when it chose not to devote itself to a suitable campaign of vengeance. When he wrote to his commanders in the Land of Israel that he was in favor of "Nechama," he added that he believed they felt the same.[40] In other words, in his opinion there prevailed, even among those in the Yishuv who officially opposed vengeance, the sense of a historic sin of omission.

It can therefore be said that the desire for revenge against the Germans, and the wish for the entire German people to be punished with a weighty punishment that generations to come would remember, was shared by the entire Yishuv and its leadership. But between the thought and the deed lay a Rubicon that stayed uncrossed. The Yishuv's leadership, headed by

Ben-Gurion, decided together with the top command of the Haganah that this was not the way, although they held no formal and explicit discussions; their sense of national responsibility of the highest level was demonstrated by their decision. Their first priority, they believed, must be to take care of the survivors—because no one else would do it—and to bring the destitute remnant to Palestine. They assumed that unbridled deeds of vengeance would lessen the willingness of the international aid agencies to support the Bricha and the DPs, that the British and Americans would not stand for any harm to the POWs in general and to those they were holding in particular, that the struggle to found the state would be disrupted, and that vengeance (as Ben-Gurion told Pasha) would bring no one back to life. In order to take place, vengeance required political support, wrote Ian Buruma,[41] and there was no such support for organized Jewish vengeance on a grand scale.

KOVNER, THE NOKMIM, AND THE VISION

Until his death, Kovner remained the leader—the admired figure central to the group, with all the others gathered round him—despite the severe accusations and claims made against him. Pasha, of all people, the man who had been obliged to struggle against such great complications after Kovner left for Palestine, and to mediate between Kovner and the group, would emphasize Kovner's greatness each time he testified. Pasha deemed Kovner a "secular religious" person because in whatever Kovner did, even in purely secular activities, the religious element remained. The Jewish tradition was his life's cornerstone and his central path, the path from which all else ramified. He was productive twenty-four hours a day, never making a move to protect his public image or to secure office. On the contrary, "He remained a giant among envious little midgets," a symbol of his age in the eyes of Jews from all parties, an unchallengeable authority, and a man of boundless loyalty to his friends. "Who could oppose him?" asked Roseman, who considered him "a prophet" with a spell over his listeners—and there is no arguing with a prophet.[42]

In the 1980s, when the Nokmim began meeting together and letting their guard down, Kovner told them that he had lied "with a clear conscience" to the leaders of the Yishuv when he agreed with them that Plan B would be all.

"I don't doubt for a moment that Plan A was correct and necessary," but it went mostly unaccomplished "because we've missed the timing for restricting it to the Germans." His phrasing ignored the passage of years, as if he wished to say that he was equally sure of the plan's correctness even decades later. By then, Kovner too could afford to support the plan since the poison had been lost somewhere in the depths of the Mediterranean decades before and the plan had gone unaccomplished.[43] Was Kovner, having become a known and esteemed figure in Israel, filling a need among the Nokmim who desired justification, after the fact, for their thoughts and deeds? Or perhaps it was that, especially after living for years in Israel, the Nokmim could appreciate an overall view of his actions and behavior during and after the Holocaust, understand and value the man with his greatness and with his faults, and not isolate the revenge story from his entire life. Or perhaps the passage of time enabled them to appreciate the importance of their adventure not for what it accomplished on the ground but for what it symbolized—for the fact that a small group arose after the disaster and strove to warn the world against a new disaster to come. Kovner embodied that symbolism with the drama of his personality and with his concept of justice, a concept that impelled him and that, in his opinion, was essential for returning to the course of Jewish history and indeed of human history. And by the power of that vision, he inspired them. For all those reasons, Kovner remained their leader even after the operation that was less than achieved, and even after his death.

The leader–constituency relationship explains further difficult issues: Why Kovner untruthfully told Ben-Gal that the mission was assigned to them by the Yishuv's institutions; why he untruthfully told the Nokmim that it was Chaim Weizmann who had given Ernst David Bergman the order; why he wrote in his own handwriting, in an official letter to the archives, that he had lied to the leaders of the Yishuv. The central explanation is his relationship with his comrades. He strove to achieve legitimacy for the deed that the comrades were planning, to show the group that it had public backing and that it would be accepted as part of the Jewish-Hebrew-Zionist enterprise, flesh of its flesh, and not a band of delusionary eccentrics, driven mad by the Holocaust; not a gang challenging the authority of the Yishuv and endangering it like the breakaway IZL and Lehi, posing a risk even to the survivors in the DP camps and to the chances of receiving the world's support for the maturing plan of a Jewish state. For many years after the war, he was still haunted by the thought that "it was not an operation that deserved to have its rationale misjudged by the Jewish institutions, which could at least have helped the way certain figures who did understand wanted to." He had trouble reconciling himself to the way that with one hand the establishment drew the Nokmim closer and, with the other, stronger hand, it hobbled their steps, when aside from them "after the atrocity, there was no group considering a retaliation to equal the scale and horror of what the Nazi enemy inflicted upon us."[44]

The vision of full-scale revenge arose out of the great crisis caused by the Holocaust; beyond that, it was a sort of suicide attempt deriving from a profound feeling that the world had reached its end and the best one could do was "die with the Philistines." It was born of the inability to be reconciled with the loss of an entire universe, both personal and national. The grief it expressed was deep enough almost to tug at the heartstrings of Kovner and his comrades, alone on befouled German soil or in an isolated British prison. Only in this way is it possible to understand how he and his companions, normative youngsters who lived ordinary lives before the Holocaust and afterward, were visited by that terrible idea. Only in this way can the contradiction in Kovner's personality be understood. He was a man of vision who, while hiding in a monastery near the ghetto, realized that a systematic extermination was underway; who saw clearly what the Soviets were; who predicted the Cold War and the changes that the kibbutz movement would undergo; and who discerned the early evidence of a focus in cultural discourse, both in Western culture and in Israel, on the individual rather than on the collective. So how could he be so blind to the dire consequences that such vengeance could bring and behave during that period of his life so differently from how he behaved during the rest of it? Only in this way, too, is it possible to understand the "Battle Pages" that Kovner wrote when he was the information officer of the Givati Brigade during the 1948 War of Independence, under Shimon Avidan. The deep fear experienced by a sensitive man who is constantly attempting to read the map of the events that occur around him, and who was witness to the terrible disaster and to the uncompromising cruelty with which it was waged—such fear did not expire in the first years following the war's end, and it persisted even into the initial months of 1948.

Here was the disaster once more impending: Arab armies attacking from all around. Settlements were defeated or evacuated. The Egyptians advanced toward Tel Aviv through the territory of the Givati Brigade, which was nick-named the "Ghastly Brigade" after suffering seven hundred casualties. That fearsome situation was behind the writing of his Battle Pages that were headlined "Death to the Invaders." One of them calls explicitly for "Ven-geance. Vengeance. Vengeance!" Another states that the souls of six million who perished "cry out to us from the ground: *The great revenge must come—Israel free forever!*" and more. The Givati soldiers were urged to wage total war against the invaders, who are described in the harshest and most chill-ing of terms. In encouraging the soldiers to stand fast, Kovner draws from Haim Nachman Bialik, Nathan Alterman, and the Bible, the three canons of emerging national identity in a state still new on its feet. At the same time, it was clear to the writer and to the readers that all those words were in-tended to strengthen resilience in a time of emergency and not, heaven for-bid, to urge deadly violence anywhere off the battlefield.[45]

In the 1970s, Kovner presented the unresolved distinction between the metaphysical idea, as he called it, and the actual act:

My comrades and I did not call for the Germans to be *hated*, but rather for them to be *held responsible*, and furthermore we specifically did not wish to harm women and children. [. . .] I never emphasized vengeance, not in thought and not in deed, but rather the obligation of exacting justice. My fundamental understanding was that from the world=standing=by [here, Kovner linked the words with equal signs, which was his way of uniting words into a single term] there was no true justice to be expected, and no everyday court would take action to prove to the nations of the world that Jewish blood is not forfeit. That was the obligation resting on the surviv-ing Jews.[46]

Some ten years later, by way of contrast, he said in a long conversation with Levi Arieh Sarid:

Inside I had a burning hatred against the Germans, against Germany, and it dulled a little but essentially remains to this day, in theoretical form. It's grown into a thing [. . .] of the imagination. In my thinking, there is no innocent German. [. . .]. That nation must, for at least one generation, pay the price in order to deter the world of the future. [. . .]. I dreamed at night, when I learned that there is an atom bomb, that if I had the chance to drop it on Germany, I'd drop it. [. . .]. With my plan for vengeance, I wanted to tell the world that the remnant who remained after Auschwitz was capable of destroying the world. Take note! Next time it happens, the world perishes. [. . .] *To this day, I consider that a possibility.*[47]

There is a contradiction between those two statements of Kovner's, a contradiction that also occurs in the comparable words of Primo Levi as mentioned in this book's introduction. In the first quotation, Kovner says that he and his comrades did not preach hatred of the German people, but in the second he says that he felt a burning hatred for them, a hatred that grew into a thing of the imagination—which is to say that he went on nurturing it inside himself, or that it grew despite his wishes. In the first quotation, he says that the Nokmim had no intention of harming women and children, whereas in the second he says that if he had an atom bomb, he would drop it on Germany. Indeed, there is no solution here to the contradiction between the restraint that basic human values impose on a person's actions and the fundamental urge to avenge a terrible wrong. That contradiction exists even if the vengeance is intended to shock the world into behaving more prudently in the future, teaching it "the savage, cruel consequences that the last of the survivors will wreak. And even if only a pewful of Jews remains—Jewish blood shall not be forfeit."[48]

The unresolved contradiction is referenced in Hanoch Bartov's words as well. A neighbor and close friend of Kovner's, as a soldier he had witnessed the dispute as it erupted among the soldiers of the Jewish Brigade and felt that there was no solution, no squaring that circle. He accurately described both sides of the argument—who favored vengeance, who opposed it, and how he and his friends constantly failed in their efforts to decide. Even while clearly unable to support vengeance on the scale that he would have liked to, he concluded that

thousands of courageous young men, each one a volunteer, vowed to avenge the desecrated blood, to avenge in war and avenge in peace, against the executioners and their commanders, against those who gave applause and those who gave garlands, against those who welcomed the bloodshed and those who enjoyed the spoils, against them all. [. . .]. But [. . .] this we can never forget: We returned from the war without living that hour of great vengeance. [. . .]. We will never be able to forget that vengeance untaken, never achieve tranquility and reconciliation.[49]

In Kovner's view, vengeance was not merely a metaphysical concept but divine retribution on a cosmic, biblical scale, "an eye for an eye," six million for six million, and he himself was the instrument through which such retribution was to occur. Bartov was convinced that from childhood, Kovner had internalized for himself the role of a prophet, apostle, messenger, seer, flag bearer, and mystic.[50] Indeed, in a fable that Kovner wrote at the beginning of his book *Scrolls of Fire*, the fable of the key that sank, he was actually describing himself as a personality with a mission assigned to him as early as childhood. When the Temple went up in flames, the High Priest climbed to the roof of the burning building and threw his keys to the heavens, whereupon a hand emerged and took the keys. The fable (to be found in the Talmud, on Ta'anit 29a), one of the legends of the Temple's destruction, is told by an old man to Jewish children in a town of snow-covered roofs somewhere in the north, and that town may be equated with the one where Kovner grew up. The children then went home, "but one sad-eyed boy, as he lay in bed that night, saw a shining key fall from the sky and sink under the waters of the lake behind the town." That boy would be little Abba Kovner, receiving his mission: Only he saw where the key dropped, and only he can find it.[51] He is also the sad-eyed angel that the Yishuv's poet laureate Bialik described, whose prayer God answered by promising him that even though the Temple be destroyed, its embers will never burn out. Thus Kovner received his neverending mission, obliging him to be forever watchful: to discern what was impending and to warn of the Holocaust that was surging toward the Jerusalem of Lithuania, as he did in the manifesto that called on the city's Jews to not go like sheep to the slaughter; to light the flame of rebellion in the hearts of those locked in the ghetto and to bring them out into the forests where they could fight, and out onto the route to the Land of Israel, along which he could guide the united survivors; and—before completing the journey—to punish the perpetrators, begetters of the terrible disaster, by a punishment no less terrible. Then, once they were punished for burning down the Jerusalem of Lithuania, he would continue his mission by rebuilding the Temple in the Land of Israel and safeguarding the embers so that they will never be consumed.

For Kovner's view of a punishment decreed by heaven, the origin was his deep affinity for the Jewish sources. In his thorough familiarity with them, he was a veritable swimmer in the *Sea of Halacha*, and indeed he composed a map and a brochure by that name—presenting the history of Jewish oral and written law (halacha) and its masters over the generations—for the Museum of the Jewish people (Beit Hatfutsot) in honor of its opening. Kovner knew well the role of vengeance in these sources: He was the sad-eyed boy and angel, and Alterman, the poet laureate after Bialik, was quoted as saying, "There are four people the sight of whom is hard for me / And five whose gaze is hard for me to meet," and the first on his list was Abba Kovner.[52] And Kovner was also the divine rod sent to chastise. But a great miracle deflected Kovner and his band when the poison he was bringing from Palestine failed to reach Europe. Had it arrived and, heaven forbid, been introduced into the water systems of four or five large cities as planned, and had it brought unnatural death to some millions of people—men, women, and children—without investigation, without trial, and without distinction between the murderers of the Jewish people and those who never harmed it, what would have become of the Nokmim? And what would have become of the Jewish people as a whole? "To me belongeth vengeance and recompense," God said (Deuteronomy 32:35). To God only.

The Nokmim gave expression to the feelings of millions of people, Jewish and non-Jewish. After the war, acts of vengeance were carried out by non-Jewish Europeans on a much larger scale than was estimated until recently, and a number of new scholarly books are progressively revealing the full extent. From among the Jews, very few people, burning with the lust for revenge at the end of the war, actually killed Germans and collaborators. Those avengers included some dozens of Jewish Brigade soldiers, Avidan and the volunteers from the German Unit, Kovner's group of roughly fifty (who apparently did not cause the death of a single SS veteran in Nuremberg), the Vienna group, and a smaller assortment of individuals whose deeds are known in some cases and remain unrevealed in others. To those, we may add the Mossad operatives who continued the vengeance after the founding of the State of Israel; and the avengers in the Eastern Bloc—such as Pasha, Eliezer Lidovski, and their comrades—both immediately after liberation and in later years, when such deeds went unrecorded in the West. All told, the avengers number between 200 and 250: men and women who refused to accept the possibility that the idea of revenge would remain nothing but a sentiment and a hope. How many Germans and collaborators were killed by those men and women? It is difficult to arrive at a figure because today there is no documentation concerning the deeds of most Avengers, but it may be estimated on the basis of existing documentation, especially the testimonies and the overall context of the postwar years, that the victims did not exceed 1,000 to 1,500.

Thus most of the Jewish people voted with their feet, especially on the question of whether and how to take vengeance. There were no meetings or conventions or votes on the subject—neither in the Yishuv nor among the survivors. Rather than a decision, there was a sense, an intuitive sense, that the sweetest revenge would be to seize upon life and continue it by personal rehabilitation, by raising families, by burgeoning as a community, by achieving a thriving Jewish state and the right to defend it, by claiming the right to live among fellow Jews, and by accepting the obligation to commemorate the Holocaust in its full scope.

In the very existence of each Jew who embodies Jewish and human spiritual values, the Nazi ideology and its view of the Jews is definitively proven to be "vanity and vexation of spirit." Every Nobel Prize won by a Jew (20 percent of Nobel laureates are Jewish, although Jews amount to just two-tenths of a percent of the global population) is a manner of vengeance against those who classed Jews as *untermenschen*, subhumans. Every Israeli achievement is vengeance against those who said that a Jewish state, if established, would become a haven for criminals. And indeed the concept of vengeance, as the general Jewish public saw it following the war, did not specifically mean a physical counterattack in return for physical murder but rather struggling in different terms—building and continuity and creativity—in opposition to the dehumanization attempted by the Germans against the Jewish people:

standing erect, and maintaining Jewish identity and moral superiority over
the Germans. And the struggle in those terms bore fruit. Many survivors repeatedly mention that their holiday table, surrounded by twenty members
of the family they founded, is their very own personal revenge against Hitler and his followers; they say this even while their eyes are damp both with
pain for the previous family that they lost forever and with pride for the one
they founded.

In conclusion, the commentary on the Hebrew word for "truth," from
the introduction, is worth recalling. It obliges the researcher to seek out,
document, and analyze what occurred, from the initial letter of the alphabet
(which is also the word's first letter) through the middle letter of the alphabet (and of the word) and onward to where the alphabet (and the Hebrew
word for "truth") finishes. And in the case of this specific book, to probe the
symbolism, the ideas, and the legends that have accumulated among the Israeli and Jewish publics regarding the topic. But having made a best effort
to do so, with the help of the many sources at hand and further sources un-
earthed, what can the historian say about the saga described in these pages—
about a group of young men and women overflowing with eagerness to send
six million Germans to kingdom come in recompense for the six million
Jews the Germans murdered? And about that idea, which served as the purpose of their lives?

An acquaintance with the Nokmim—strong people, each with an individual story—inspires sympathy for them as people, as Zionists, as Jews, and
as committed family members. I came to know them, and I tried to understand their motivations in depth, but I must stress again, as has been said several times in the course of the saga's description, that there is not, and cannot be, anyone else in the world who sympathizes with the terrible idea they
conceived. So once more, I emphasize that there is no connection between a
warm and friendly feeling on the one hand for the members of the group and
an utterly negative stance, on the other hand, toward the idea of a mass murder like the one they intended, a slaughter that would certainly have extended
to myriads of innocent men, women, and children. I voiced that opinion to
them more than once, to the irritation of those among them who defend the
idea to this day. Their motivations must be understood in terms of the information currently available about the Holocaust period, information that

points up the vicissitudes, suffering, and loss that they underwent; and in terms of the realization that an entire generation of Jews growing up between the world wars had been educated in magnificent school systems established by European Jewry and in youth movements that took on the quality of a home, that made it embrace national and historical responsibility for the fate of the Jewish people and seek a way to prevent a cruel fate from recurring in future generations. Understanding the motivations of the actors, attempting to walk in the shoes of the people from the times that preceded our own, and imagining to ourselves what they felt and how they reacted to events—this is the very essence of studying history.

"To our regret, the group didn't succeed in fully accomplishing the mission that it had taken upon itself," some of the Nokmim wrote to me, "but still, in the mere founding of the group and in the mere effort to avenge and to strike at the Germans—there is great importance."[53] Even though they had no actual success in carrying out the mission they'd undertaken, they find consolation in having left a legend, a sort of myth about a group that did try and did wage the struggle, and for them that is an accomplishment of sorts. Deterrence can derive from the resolutely expressed determination that the Jewish people shall no longer be left undefended against whoever wishes to assault them, and from the knowledge, circulating through the public, that there are those intent on deterring anyone who attempts it in the future. So it is possible to agree with the letter from those Nokmim and with Vitka, who said repeatedly, both of the Warsaw Ghetto uprising and of the Nokmim: What matters most is not the result but the attempt, the ability to self-organize under dire conditions and to seek ways of resisting. And as for the results, it has been said already and will be said again: the entire Jewish people were blessed by a great miracle when the results did not come about.

Jewish sources point in two directions: both revenge and revival. Revenge was the heartfelt wish of a small, scattered, weak community, whereas revival meant a life of creativity. Thus, for example, one of the complete concordances of the Bible lists 80 appearances of "revenge" in its two Hebrew forms;[54] by comparison, "grace," "truth," and "mercy" total 260 appearances.[55] The great majority of the Jewish people took no physical vengeance against the Germans and their collaborators, and the fact is that most of them went unpunished. But most of the Jewish people did differentiate clearly between the emotion that burned inside them and the action in practice, between the natural urge to retaliate, dealing well-deserved death, and wariness of crossing the Rubicon that protects the values that forbid execution without trial. Not only the survivors, and not only the Nokmim, burned with the urge to requite the Germans as they deserved, especially for the humiliation and helplessness they'd imposed, but the Jewish public in Palestine and its leadership shared that urge. However, the thought was deliberately set aside by the Yishuv's leaders as they set their priorities. First came the survivors, who needed to be cared for and brought to Palestine, and along with them came the project of building a state. A state would serve as a response and as a deterrent. And thus the very building of the community and founding of the state became the embodiment of vengeance and prevented vengeance in a plainer form, both in the years that directly followed the war and in later years. That prioritization indicates a greatness of spirit and an affinity to life and creativity on the part of the Jews as individuals and as a collective, and it illustrates the policy of national and human responsibility that their leaders practiced in that generation.

Moshe Tabenkin

I foresee revenge
I foresee revenge.
I kiss the bombing planes' wings, my soul is a prayer for the boys,
   carrying death.
On the burning cities
I whisper a revenge blessing.

You, the city
Whose pavements
Drank rivers of my blood
Silently.

Whose balconies
Carried crowds cheering at my downfall,
Whose street lamps
Became my hanging trees.
Whose houses' walls
Witnessed the murder of my elderly;
Whose lavished gardens
Saw the hunters' schemes.

The day my last of brothers fell
Was your holiday,
And you laughed joyfully
At a baby cut off his mother's breast—
You, Sodom land!
Gamora city!
Go up,
Up in fire!
[...]
I foresee revenge.
I embrace you, my unknown brother,
A red soldier on Russian wasteland.
On the blood-drunk field of victory
My teeth crack a revenge blessing.

Moshe Tabenkin, *Poems*, Ein Harod, Hakkibutz Hameʿuchad, 1943, pp. 122–23. Translated by Yehuda Porat. Courtesy of Ofri Tabenkin-Shturman.

APPENDIXES

Chronology

1944

DECEMBER   Abba Kovner, followed by a group of comrades from Vilna, arrives in Lublin.

Ruzka Korczak arrives in the Land of Israel.

1945

FEBRUARY   Meir Yaʿari congratulates the German Unit before embarking on its revenge mission in Europe.

BEGINNING OF MARCH   Groups of Bricha activists, joined by the Avengers' leaders, move to Bucharest.

MARCH   Chaim Weizmann departs for the UK and the US.

APRIL   The German Unit leaves for Europe.

MAY 8   End of the war in Europe.

MAY 19   The Jewish Brigade arrives in Tarvisio, in Northern Italy.

JUNE   Antek Zuckerman's letter is sent from Krakow.

JULY 15   The Partisans, the Bricha, and the Hativa activists arrive in Tarvisio.

JULY 16   Kovner's speech is heard by the soldiers of the Jewish Brigade and the Holocaust survivors in Tarvisio.

JULY 27   The Jewish Brigade moves northward, via Austria and Germany, on its way to Belgium and Holland to serve as a garrison force. Kovner departs for Palestine.

BEGINNING OF AUGUST   Kovner arrives in Palestine.

AUGUST   The headquarters of the Avengers group arrives in Munich. The teams scatter and settle in various parts of Germany.

SEPTEMBER   Yehuda Ben-Horin arrives in Palestine for consultations.

SEPTEMBER 8   Rosh Hashanah (Jewish New Year) 5706; Kovner instructs his comrades in Europe to concentrate on Plan B without neglecting Plan A.

OCTOBER 27   The Avengers' HQ moves to Paris.

NOVEMBER 6   Marking a year since the assassination of Lord Moyne.

NOVEMBER 21 TO MID-DECEMBER   Kovner meets with David Ben-Gurion.

DECEMBER 14   The *Champollion*, with Kovner aboard, departs from Egypt on its way to France.

DECEMBER 18   Kovner and his colleagues are arrested and sent to jail in Cairo.

1946

JANUARY   Menashe Gewissar requests that Zuckerman and Chaika Grossman lead the Avengers.

FEBRUARY 12   Nahum Shadmi arrives in Paris.

FEBRUARY 28   Weizmann returns to Palestine after being out of the country since March 1945.

END OF FEBRUARY TO BEGINNING OF MARCH   Kovner and two of the detainees are transferred from Cairo to the Kishle Jail, in the old city of Jerusalem, and afterwards to the Russian Compound jail.

MARCH 15   Kovner and his two colleagues are freed from jail.

MARCH 15   Kovner meets with Weizmann, most likely later than this date.

THE NIGHT BETWEEN APRIL 13 AND 14   Execution of the Nuremberg operation and cancellation of the Dachau operation. Nahum Shadmi delays his visit to Palestine until after the operation.

JUNE AND JULY   The Avengers arrive in Palestine in two groups.

AUGUST 1946 TO SPRING 1947   Shimon Avidan continues revenge in Europe.

1947–1985

MARCH 1947   The Night of Division: the "second group" leaves Ein HaHoresh.

END OF 1947 TO 1950   Return of the second group to Europe to continue revenge activities.

OCTOBER 26, 1984   Kovner gives testimony to Levi Arieh Sarid.

JANUARY 25 AND 31, 1985   First reunion of the Avengers in Israel.

List of the Avengers

THE AVENGERS NUMBERED about fifty men and women, according to a list collected by Yehuda (Poldek) Maimon and published in Levi Arieh Sarid, *Ruins and Deliverance: The Pioneering Movements in Poland Throughout the Holocaust and During Its Aftermath, 1933–1949*, vol. 2, *Arising from Ashes*, Moreshet, Tel Aviv, 1997, pp. 481–82 (Hebrew).

The following lists the thirty-four members mentioned in this book, who were central activists; they gave testimonies and interviews, wrote memoirs, and were commemorated in books and brochures. These young men and women had a collective biography: they were members of youth movements; they enjoyed a Jewish and Zionist education in the best of schools; they were underground fighters in ghettos and forests; they lost most of their families and relatives; they wandered or were constantly taken from one place to another; they escaped riding trains and death marches; they fought in the 1948 war for Israel's independence; they served on a variety of secret missions; and then they started new families, each choosing his or her way, profession, and vocation, while maintaining close personal touch.

VILNA

Distel, Arie Leib (Leibke)

Galperin-Gliksman, Rachel (Rochke)

Harmatz, Yosef (Yulek), originally from Rikoshki, Lithuania

Kantarowicz-Kenet, Shlomo

Kempner-Kovner, Vitka, from Kalisz, Poland

Korczak-Marla, Reizl (Ruzka), from Bielsk, Poland

Kovner, Abba

Nissanilevich, Netanel (Senka)

Ratner, Yitzhak

Rosenberg-Amit, Zila (Cesia, Ceska)

Satz-Hammel, Helena (Lena, Lenka)

Taubes-Warchavchik, Hasya (Hashka)

Treger-Nissanilevich, Zelda, from Siemiatycze, Poland

Verbin-Shabetzky, Mira (Mirka)

Warchavchik, Jechiel (Chilik)

KRAKOW

Friedman, Yehuda (Idek)

Hammel, Yitzhak, from Przemysl, Poland

Hershderfer-Arad, Theodore (Dzhunek) Dan

Lustgarten, Shimon (Shimek)

Shutzreich-Shenar, Ze'ev (Willek)

Wasserman (Maimon), Yehuda (Poldek)

ROVNO

Goldreich, later Reichman-Avidov, Dora (Dorka), from Lodz

Kek-Michaeli, Bezalel, from Rokitno, Belarus

Lidovski, Eliezer, from Wolyn

Reichman-Avidov, Yitzhak (Pasha), from Lodz

CZESTOCHOWA

Bencelowicz–Ben-Zur, Pinchas (Yashek)

Gewirtzman–Ben-Ya'akov, Dov (Bolek)

Gliksman, Zygmunt (Zygi)

WARSAW

Gelblum, Irena

Rathajzer-Rotem, Simcha (Kazhik)

BEDZIN

Feiner–De-Nur, Yehiel (Ka-tzetnik)

L., Moshe (Manek)

LODZ

Mairanz, Ludwig (Levi Yitzhak)

BREST/LITOVSK

Rabinovich, Zeʿev (Velveleh)

Notes

SINCE THE MAJORITY OF THE SOURCES (p. 329) are in Hebrew, they are divided into sections designated by letters A–N; the notes refer the reader to the section and the number of the item. Thus, for example, endnote 1 in the introduction, which refers to Ehud Avriel's testimony to Yehuda Bauer, is E-2 (section E, Testimonies, no. 2. Avriel, Ehud, to Yehuda Bauer, May 12, 1964, Haganah, 149.3).

A Materials Entrusted by the Avengers and Their Families

B Testimonies of the Group Members and their Relatives

C Group Testimonies

D Testimonies of Survivors, Fighters, and Other Avengers

E Testimonies of Haganah Members, Jewish Brigade and German Unit Soldiers, and the Mossad for Aliyah B Activists

F Memoirs

G Collected Testimonies and Documentation

H Press Reportage

I Research Published in Hebrew

J Research Published in English and German

K Between Research and Journalism

L Literature and Poetry

M Theory and Philosophy

N Reference

PREFACE AND ACKNOWLEDGMENTS

1. I-34.

2. G-32, pp. 1068–75.

INTRODUCTION

1. E-2.

2. B-15.

3. My definition—D.P.

4. B-15i.

5. J-20.

6. J-6, p. 79.

7. J-6, p. 79.

8. J-10, pp. 14, 48–87.

9. J-6, p. 95.

10. J-21. A severely criticized account.

11. J-6, p. 94.

12. J-6, p. 76.

13. J-10, pp. 41, 174.

14. J-2, pp. 768–69; J-24, pp. 316–18.

15. Conversation with Szita Szabolcs, August 10, 2012.

16. F-24, p. 11; B-1f.

17. H-2; K-3.

18. I-36.

19. D-4; I-5, pp. 65–84.

20. F-4, pp. 69–73.

21. E-9; F-4, pp. 69–73.

22. D-3; J-15, p. 7.

23. H-21, N-6, p. 1235–36; L-4, p. 159.

24. N-1, p. 1416; N-8; N-6, p. 1077; N-3, p. 2615; N-2, p. 290; L-4, p. 371.

25. N-5, pp. 917–21; J-16.

26. G-2, p. 55; J-15, pp. 1–2.

3. H-30; I-5, pp. 40–54; I-38, pp. 35–106; I-39, pp. 126–37.

27. H-6; M-10; M-11, p. 33; J-11, p. 68.

28. L-12, p. 244; L-15, pp. 139–40.

29. L-14; J-22.

30. H-4.

31. A conversation with Wiesel, August 10, 2014; L-16. p. 233.

32. G-2, p. 55.

33. H-24.

34. J-18, pp. 73–79.

35. J-11, pp. 1–13.

36. M-3, pp. 16–17.

37. M-2, pp. 240–41.

38. J-15, pp. 14–17.

39. J-19, pp. 2–3, 24, 30–36, 55, 281–82.

40. F-21, pp. 187–88.

41. M-9, 167.

42. F-22, p. 135.

43. K-2.

44. E-7a.

45. F-37, pp. 13–17.

46. F-37, p. 26; I-40.

47. J-14.

48. M-5, pp. 22–24.

49. J-10, pp. 226–30.

50. J-15, pp. 7–14.

51. M-1, pp. 166–67.

52. M-12, p. 73–74.

CHAPTER 1

1. F-21, pp. 31, 46, 71, 108–9, 166, 173–74; D-12.

2. J-13, "Retribution," pp. 41–62; G-6, vol. 1, p. 287.

3. F-44, pp. 521, 526; D-13a.

4. B-15, 15g.

5. I-18.

6. I-11, pp. 15–37.

7. F-9, pp. 107, 113.

8. I-34, pp. 224–53.

9. B-1f.
10. C-2; G-39.
11. C-2; G-19, p. 129; I-29, p. 27.
12. B-13a.
13. B-17; B-6; B-19; B-8.
14. B-15c.
15. B-17b; B-16.
16. I-45, p. 61.
17. F-6, p. 25; G-26, pp. 39–40; D-4.
18. H-2; K-3.
19. G-19, pp. 77–78; B-11; I-22, p. 17.
20. B-8; F-32, p. 42.
21. B-15e.
22. B-1d; C-4 Avidov, C-4 Lidovski.
23. I-34, p. 369.
24. B-2.
25. G-2, p. 25.
26. Birmann's Testament at the end of chapter 6.
27. B-17b; G-26, p. 37.
28. D-4.
29. B-15c.
30. F-27, p. 68.
31. I-27, p. 215; I-29, p. 13.
32. L-11, p. 251.
33. B-15c, B-15g; G-36, pp. 415–16; D-14; G-18, pp. 312–14; I-45, p. 61.
34. B-27; D-6a; F-27, p. 79; B-30a; B-13a; D-10; B-11d.
35. I-37, p. 194.
36. M-8, pp. 30–37.
37. G-13, p. 159.
38. J-9, pp. 245–61.
39. B-15.
40. I-44; I-7; J-6, p. 115; F-9, p. 122.
41. Moreshet D.1.494 and D.2.262; J-9, p. 258; J-6, pp. 86–87; I-44; I-12, p. 49.
42. I-44; I-14, p. 300; G-35; Radio-Harmatz's diary, January 17, 1946; J-10, pp. 224–25.
43. B-15; G-15, p. 21.
44. G-10, pp. 101–3.

45. I-37, p. 194; D-12.
46. I-37, p. 211.
47. I-37, pp. 220–24; J-23, pp. 134–211.
48. I-44; I-34, pp. 171–90.
49. G-36, vol. 2, p. 412.
50. I-37, pp. 251–71.
51. G-22.
52. G-24, pp. 3–47.
53. B-15g; I-9, pp. 194–95; I-6.
54. F-9, p. 114.
55. B-15c, B-15g.
56. G-10, p. 98.
57. B-1f, 1b, 1a; C-2 Kovner.
58. I-38; B-17.
59. F-27, pp. 78, 80; B-15g.
60. F-26, p. 184; I-38.
61. F-23, pp. 190–91, 201; G-15, pp. 10–15.
62. B-15g.
63. D-11.
64. B-27.
65. F-27, p. 83; B-13c.
66. F-31, pp. 12, 17; B-15g.
67. I-44, p. 56; I-23, pp. 244–45; B-1d.
68. F-23, p. 192.
69. G-3, pp. 211, 245; I-23, p. 252; B-1a, 1b, 1d.
70. D-10.
71. D-11; I-6, pp. 27–36; I-22, pp. 21–22.
72. D-8; I-23, pp. 256–57; D-11; B-13a; D-10.
73. A list prepared and entrusted by Yashek Ben-Zur.
74. D-13, 13a; F-44, p. 488; I-17, p. 241.
75. G-3, p. 153; G-15, p. 15.
76. D-13, 13a.
77. D-13, 13b; F-44, p. 488; B-1b; E-19.
78. F-26, p. 185.
79. B-16a; D-11.
80. B-22.
81. B-1a; B-15g; F-26, pp. 184–85.
82. F-10, 193–96.
83. F-23, p. 193–96.

84. G-8, pp. 236–37; G-27, pp. 61, 71.
85. F-23, p. 193; D-11.
86. D-6a; D-10; B-11d; G-27, p. 61.
87. F-29, p. 176.

CHAPTER 2

1. B-15g; I-9, p. 195; I-38, Sarid II, pp. 63–65; D-11a; G-36, vol. 2, 415–31.
2. B-15g.
3. F-42, p. 76.
4. F-27, pp. 80–81.
5. I-43.
6. F-13, pp. 138, 140; G-41, pp. 76–77.
7. B-13a.
8. B-19, 19a.
9. G-29, pp. 177–200.
10. I-43, pp. 211–12; B-19, 19a; B-4; B-11d.
11. L-6, p. 35.
12. B-19; I-43, pp. 196–211.
13. I-43, pp. 219, 235–37; B-19a.
14. L-6, p. 38; I-43, pp. 126–36; B-19a.
15. B-19; F-16, pp. 120–30.
16. In all Yulek Harmatz's testimonies.
17. B-12; B-17a; C-2 Kek-Michaeli.
18. F-27, pp. 82–83; B-30a.
19. B-11a; G-31, p. 20; B-10.
20. B-17d; B-1b; B-3a; I-22, p. 57.
21. I-22, p. 56.
22. F-20, pp. 192, 194.
23. D-9.
24. D-5.
25. F-20, pp. 196–97; C-2 Kovner; D-9.
26. B-13b; B-6.
27. F-42, p. 75.
28. F-28, p. 138.
29. F-42, p. 76.
30. B-26; F-28, pp. 78, 138.
31. I-17, pp. 257–80.
32. B-22; I-17, p. 251; E-19.
33. I-41, vol. 1, p. 225; B-27; B-17b.
34. F-44, pp. 487, 491–93; B-22; D-6a.
35. I-44; D-6a.

36. G-24, p. 24. Emphasis Lubetkin's.
37. I-17, p. 251.
38. F-44, pp. 521, 526; D-13a; G-27, p. 72; D-6a.
39. D-13, 13a; G-41, p. 104.
40. D-13, 13a; G-38, pp. 36–38.
41. D-13; F-44, p. 488.
42. D-13.
43. D-13a; G-40, pp. 105–6; F-44, pp. 485–86, 528; E-19.
44. F-44, pp. 526–33.
45. D-7; F-14, pp. 130–31.
46. D-7; F-14, pp. 123, 145.
47. F-14, p. 143.
48. G-29; I-9, p. 65; I-11, pp. 43, 188.
49. F-23, p. 211; G-29, p. 188; I-9, p. 141: all the 1,300 swore.
50. I-22, pp. 55–56; E-31a; F-24, p. 108; I-38, Sarid II, p. 128: only the new swore; B-19; B-1g, p. 19.
51. G-39, pp. 692, 732.
52. G-29, p. 185.
53. A-6, author's translation.
54. I-22, p. 71, n. 65.
55. A-6.
56. I-22, p. 55, n. 44; B-6; B-1a.
57. F-28, pp. 138–39; B-26.
58. F-27, pp. 82–83; B-30a.
59. B-30, p. 14.
60. B-15g; F-23, pp. 223–24; F-24, pp. 112–14.
61. E-27a; B-22; B-12; B-10, 10a; F-23, p. 196; B-17c.
62. B-12; B-17c; B-29; B-14a.
63. B-7; B-8; F-11, pp. 159–63; F-40, p. 104.
64. B-9; B-15d.

65. L-6, pp. 15, 80, 84, 92.

66. I-43, pp. 258–59.

CHAPTER 3

1. F-30, p. 211; F-5.

2. G-23, p. 320.

3. I-14; G-28; I-2, pp. 173–75.

4. G-23, p. 321.

5. E-24; G-30, p. 238.

6. F-30, p. 228.

7. Churchill, September 28, 1944, on-line; G-23, p. 53; Shertok, April 29, 1945, CZA; I-14, pp. 303, 318–31.

8. I-14, pp. 318–31; I-2, pp. 173–75.

9. I-2, pp. 173–75.

10. J-25, pp. 361, 375.

11. I-24, p. 26; J-2, pp. 768–69; J-10, p. 163.

12. L-15, p. 139; J-17, pp. 80–81.

13. F-43, pp. 180–81; I have not found the German radio broadcast.

14. H-10; B-3.

15. G-16, p. 131; F-33.

16. G-23, pp. 324–27; G-16, p. 126; F-5, p. 158; G-32, pp. 1071–72.

17. G-32, pp. 1071–72; E-7; F-43, pp. 180–81; G-36, vol. 2, p. 139.

18. L-3, pp. 59–63, 116–17, 213; I-26, pp. 85–110; G-5, p. 278; G-36, vol. 2, 139–40.

19. G-16, pp. 127, 145; I-14, pp. 306–7.

20. L-3, pp. 97–124; H-10; F-43, pp. 182–85.

21. H-12; F-12, p. 205; F-43, pp. 179–82.

22. I-14, pp. 306–7; E-23, 23a; F-30, p. 229.

23. E-6; E-31; I-25, p. 140; F-5, p. 160; E-16.

24. G-32, p. 1072, as in F-5, pp. 158–61; G-36, vol. 2, p. 140, as in I-25, pp. 140–44; H-12; H-7; H-3; E-3; F-30, p. 229.

25. E-14; E-24.

67. Note in Moreshet archives, D.1.5724. Emphasis in original.

26. E-7.

27. E-7; E-23a.

28. E-7; E-31; I-25, pp. 140–41; E-12, 12b.

29. H-11; H-13; I-14, p. 327; E-18.

30. Argov's letter to Shertok, June 18, 1945, CZA, S25/6064.

31. E-31; F-5, pp. 92–106; F-3, pp. 53–59; E-21; I-25, p. 140; E-4; E-8.

32. F-3, pp. 73, 74, 77, 81; E-24; E-25.

33. E-17.

34. E-24; H-13; E-18; E-8; H-3.

35. H-11.

36. H-7; H-11; F-5, p. 160.

37. I-5, p. 37; F-30, p. 229.

38. I-31; F-5, p. 161; E-7; E-31; F-3, p. 74.

39. F-5, p. 162–63; I-25, p. 141; F-30, p. 224.

40. E-21.

41. F-3, pp. 73–74.

42. E-7.

43. G-33, p. 143; B-11a; B-14a.

44. G-33, p. 143; B-13a; F-27, pp. 84–85.

45. F-3, p. 81; G-12.

46. G-33, p. 148; F-41, pp. 4–5.

47. Full text in Moreshet, A.388; parts: G-20, pp. 35–42.

48. E-13; G-9, p. 254; G-16, p. 137.

49. G-16, p. 137.

50. E-18; B-11d; B-25.

51. Kovner's letter to the archives, May 29, 1987, Moreshet, C.61.

52. E-29.

53. E-18.

54. E-30; I-22, p. 65, n. 37.

55. Tubin's letter to his wife, Shlomit (1), July 16, 1945, Moreshet; B-15g.

56. E-31a.

57. G-7, p. 233; Tubin's letter (2), July 18, 1945, Moreshet; I-22, p. 68, nn. 31, 50.

58. G-3, p. 56; G-11, pp. 143–44; E-13; meeting summary: Haganah, 125/3.

59. E-13; F-7, pp. 92–97; G-11, pp. 143–44.

60. E-8; F-3, pp. 91–92.

61. E-7.

62. B-11a; B-22.

63. F-19.

64. C-2 Pasha; F-30, p. 230.

65. Letter to Shertok, June 4, 1945, CZA, S25/6064.

66. E-24; E-30; I-14, p. 328; F-12, pp. 207–8.

67. F-27, pp. 84–85; B-1b, 1c.

68. F-3, pp. 75, 80; G-23, pp. 329–91; I-14, pp. 357–530; N-8, "Gelber," vol. 3, p. 500; E-20.

69. G-23, p. 391.

70. H-8; G-23, pp. 322–23; L-3, pp. 55–56; H-10; M-4, pp. 26–36; I-14, p. 336.

71. I-46, p. 433.

72. I-46, pp. 435–36; poem following the epilogue.

73. F-3, p. 81; G-23, pp. 391–95; the route: I-24, p. 335, and F-30, pp. 236–38.

74. I-25, pp. 144–46; E-7; E-23a.

75. E-18; F-36, p. 117; E-20; F-43, pp. 208–9, 212.

76. H-11; E-12a; E-31a.

77. B-17c; B-7; B-14.

78. E-29; B-11a; I-22, p. 66.

79. Tubin's letter (2), July 18, 1945, Moreshet.

80. B-13; F-41, p. 6; B-17c.

81. K-2, p. 242; B-13a; Kovner's letter, May 29, 1987, Moreshet, C.61.

82. Kovner's letter, May 29, 1987, Moreshet, C.61; B-13a; B-15g; A-6 Kovner to Vitka, August 7, 1945; B-17b.

83. E-13; G-11, pp. 143–44; E-13a.

84. G-29, July 23, 1945; I-22, pp. 62, 66.

85. I-11, pp. 47, 188; G-36, pp. 424–25; G-34; G-33, p. 145.

86. B-15g.

87. E-31a.

88. B-12; B-7; B-8.

89. D-6a; B-1d, 1g.

90. B-26b; B-19a; B-10a; B-6; B-17a; B-1d; B-20.

91. G-11, p. 143; Kovner's ID in Moreshet, D.1.5546.2; A-6 Kovner to Vitka, August 7, 1945.

CHAPTER 4

1. I-28, pp. 15–22.

2. N-11, p. 43.

3. "The Future of Palestine," *The Times*, November 14, 1945.

4. N-4, pp. 206–30.

5. B-15e; I-38, Sarid II, vol. 2, p. 142; I-45, p. 46.

6. A-6 Kovner to Vitka, August 28, 1945, and early September.

7. B-15i.

8. M-8, p. 110; I-29, p. 16.

9. L-2, pp. 66–67.

10. I-29, pp. 10–12.

11. I-29, p. 27.

12. G-19, p. 96.

13. I-29, pp. 16, 27; E-8.

14. Labor Party archive, files 159, 161, September 3, 1945.

15. I-33, pp. 259–74.

16. Yehuda Tubin to Ya'ari, Givat Haviva, September 15, 1945; G-33, pp. 258–60.

17. Ya'ari to Tubin, Givat Haviva, July 24, 1945; F-44, pp. 494–98; Kovner, May 29, 1987, Moreshet C61; I-42, pp. 325–54.

18. Ya'ari to Tubin, Givat Haviva, July 24, 1945.

19. E-31a; E-30; Tubin letters, More-shet, July 1–18, 1945; B-17a; I-34, ch. 2.

20. I-19, p. 278.

21. Kovner to Gruner, Moreshet, C61.40; G-19, p. 130, letter B; I-29, p. 26.

22. G-19, p. 133, letter E.

23. G-36, p. 146; Tubin, Moreshet, D.S.404; Ya'ari to Kovner, Givat Haviva, C.61.44.

24. F-3, pp. 70, 91; E-8.

25. F-3, p. 92; Kovner, May 29, 1987, Moreshet, C61.

26. D-7; E-7; B-15g.

27. D-11.

28. Moshe Zilbertal, Givat Haviva, July 4, 1946, 43/46.

29. G-33, pp. 261, 267; I-19, pp. 281–85.

30. F-3, p. 92; E-8.

31. G-6, pp. 264, 294; D-11; B-15g.

32. F-3, p. 92.

33. Kovner, May 29, 1987, Moreshet, C61; C-2 Kovner; B-15g.

34. N-10; A-6.

35. A-6, letter 9.

36. A-6, letter 7.

37. G-19, pp. 123–26; I-29, pp. 15–16; F-18; I-8, p. 123.

38. B-15g.

39. J-12; Merav Segal, director of the Weizmann Archives, to Porat, August 12, 2012; I-8.

40. Bauer to Weizmann Archives, April 13, 1965; Segal to Porat, June 30, 1998, August 12, 2012.

41. F-35, pp. 425, 430; F-34, pp. 323, 329; C-2 Kovner, March 15; G-1, pp. 30–31, March 10.

42. E-22; Katzir, letter to Porat, August 19, 1998; C-2 Kovner.

43. E-22; F-17, p. 90.

44. C-2 Kovner; C-2 Sarid; A-6, letter 8.

45. K-2, p. 236, no sources; list in Kovner, May 29, 1987, Moreshet, C61.

46. In all Kovner's testimonies, especially B-15e.

47. K-2, p. 236; H-40.

48. C-2 Yulek.

49. E-5; C-2 Sarid, checked with Avidan and Katzir; Yulek only in 2014, F-15, pp. 90–91.

50. B-15g; G-10, pp. 98–99.

51. G-10, p. 100; D-7 and E-7: Plan B only.

52. E-28.

53. Rotbein-Korczak—they were as close as if they formed one molecule.

54. Tzur in I-45.

55. E-28.

56. G-32, pp. 1068–74.

57. G-32, p. 1070.

58. I-29, p. 27.

59. A-6, letter 7.

60. A-6, letters 10–12, 14; Ya'ari to Tubin, Givat Haviva, December 10, 1945.

61. I-29, p. 27; G-19, pp. 127–40; A-6, letters 10, 11.

62. E-15; E-6; boots: E-11.

63. Conversation with Beit-Halachmi, August 5, 1996; B-15h.

64. F-41, p. 13; F-2, p. 15; E-6.

65. B-15e, 15h; M-8, p. 111–12; G-1, pp. 30–31; H-31; G-17, p. 11; conversation with Yoram Tamir (Prisoners' Museum), November 4, 2012; Zafrir Yedidya, testimony, no details.

66. Golda's part told at Kovner's Israel Prize ceremony.

67. B-15h; F-41, pp. 17–19; F-2, p. 16; E-6; E-11, 11a, 11b.

68. F-41, pp. 17, 19, 27, 50; H-40; C-2 Kovner.

69. F-41, pp. 25–26.

70. B-15g; E-11; G-10, p. 99.
71. F-3, pp. 93, 95.
72. E-15.
73. F-41, pp. 10, 21, 36; F-2, p. 15.
74. Correspondence, Haganah archive:
December 14, 1945, January 4, 1946,
January 8, 1946; F-41, pp. 29–35; F-2,
pp. 15–16; H-40; B-11a, 11b.
75. E-15; E-26; F-2, p. 15; I-14,
pp. 575–76.
76. E-26; Haganah correspondence, February 7, 1946.
77. B-15h; E-15; E-6.
78. Committee report: Haganah,
April 9, 1946; I-15, p. 575; E-6.
79. Form: Haganah, June 21, 1984;
B-15e, 15g.
80. Kovner, Moreshet, C61, May 29,
1987; B-15e.

81. F-25, pp. 146–50; I-14, pp. 567–68;
F-5, pp. 191–97; E-12b.
82. Kovner to Gruner, Moreshet,
C.61.42; A-6, letter 15; B-13e.
83. B-1a.
84. A-6, letter 16.
85. A-6, addition to letter 16.
86. Conversation with Binyamin Cohen, undated; B-13b; G-19, p. 136;
A-6 Ruzka, January 15, 1946.
87. F-41, p. 14; G-33, pp. 267, 279–86;
A-6, letters 14–16.
88. A-6, letters probably from February
and March.
89. A-6, Kovner letters: mid-March and
March 28, 1946.
90. A-6, Yiddish, undated.
91. G-1, pp. 30–31.

CHAPTER 5

1. E-27a; G-6, pp. 271, 294.
2. G-32, pp. 1068–70.
3. F-1, p. 194.
4. Conversation with Yiska Shadmi,
Nahum's son, September 9, 2012.
5. G-32; E-27a; Yehuda Ben-David, Efal
156/37, undated.
6. F-29, p. 175; G-3, pp. 9, 29.
7. G-32, pp. 1071, 1073; poem following
chapter 6.
8. G-32, p. 1072.
9. Ben-David, Efal, 156/37; I-44; E-27a;
E-8.
10. B-13b; E-31a.
11. C-2 Pasha; G-33, pp. 200–203.
12. E-31a; B-15f; G-33, pp. 200–207.
13. B-17c; B-25; B-8.
14. B-13e.
15. B-13b; B-25; D-10; C-2 Pasha; B-15f.
16. B-13a, 13b.
17. B-2; B-18.
18. B-10a; B-18.

19. B-13d.
20. B-13b.
21. A-6, letters 10–11; G-19, pp. 127–40;
I-29, p. 27.
22. G-3, p. 57; B-1d.
23. B-19; B-1b; C-2 Pasha; B-1d, no trace
in Ben-Gurion materials.
24. C-2 Pasha.
25. B-1b.
26. G-32, p. 1073; I-44; E-27b; I-45,
p. 46.
27. C-2 Pasha; G-15 Shadmi, pp. 90–91;
E-27b.
28. Correspondence in Haganah, February 26, 1946.
29. E-27; I-14, pp. 7, 423; E-27b.
30. F-30, p. 230; I-33; Ben-Gurion, November 22, 1945, Labor Party
archive.
31. Correspondence in Haganah, February 26, 1946; Shadmi's 1946 file,
Haganah.

32. G-3, p. 27; E-27b; B-1b.
33. F-29, p. 176.
34. F-29; E-27b.
35. G-4, p. 62.
36. Conversation with Yiska Shadmi, September 9, 2012; E-27b.
37. G-32, p. 1073; F-29, p. 176; E-27b.
38. G-15 Shadmi, pp. 90–91; Shadmi's 1946 timetable, Haganah.
39. B-1b Pasha: no such plans.
40. Paul Morand, *Je Brule Moscou*, Éditions du Félin, Paris, 1925.
41. B-10; D-10.
42. B-1a; Kovner to Pasha, March 13, 1969, private.
43. B-9.
44. A continuation of the "Hebrew Resistance" 1946 union.
45. F-1, pp. 194–95; E-2; E-27b.

46. D-10; B-11b, 11d.
47. J-5.
48. F-29, pp. 177–78; G-3, p. 57 (not confirmed); E-27b.
49. B-9; F-29, p. 178; E-27b.
50. G-3, pp. 57–58; E-27b.
51. G-41, p. 105; F-44, p. 530; G-38, p. 37; D-6, 6a.
52. D-6, 6a; G-17, p. 72.
53. D-13; F-44, p. 530.
54. D-13; F-44, p. 528.
55. Poldek Maimon (in a September 4, 2013, conversation) and Vitka Kempner-Kovner (B-13)—not confirmed; B-1a; C-2 Kovner.
56. E-7; I-2, p. 173; G-3, p. 282; I-14, p. 666; G-36, vol. 2, p. 143; B-1d.

CHAPTER 6

1. B-7.
2. J-3; J-6; J-13.
3. D-11; B-29; B-30a.
4. B-7; C-2 Yulek Harmatz; B-19a; A-8; D-13; F-44, p. 527; B-17c.
5. B-29.
6. D-11; A-6, letter 11.
7. A-8, July 1945.
8. F-28, p. 139.
9. G-25, pp. 255–87; B-7; conversation on August 3, 2010; B-10A.
10. B-8; B-17a, and in every meeting.
11. A-3.
12. B-19a; A-4, in every page.
13. B-29; B-30a; Shulamit in B-10a; B-17a.
14. B-29; B-10a Shulamit; B-13d; B-8; I-5, p. 39.
15. B-30; G-31, p. 18; C-2 Yulek; B-11b; F-16, p. 130.
16. B-13d, 13b.
17. B-27.

18. D-11; B-19; F-24, pp. 101–2; B-2; I-34, p. 164.
19. B-12; B-14a; B-10a; B-30a; B-6; B-26; B-17a.
20. B-30; B-14a; B-6; B-10a.
21. B-13a; B-22; F-10, p. 92
22. B-12; A-8.
23. B-19; B-30; B-13a; C-2 Yulek; B-7.
24. B-29.
25. F-27, pp. 88–90; A-8.
26. A-8, pp. 2, 18, November 18, 1945.
27. B-1d, 1a.
28. B-17c.
29. G-31 Yulek, pp. 2, 17; F-15, p. 79.
30. F-29, p. 175; G-31 Poldek, p. 21; F-16, p. 132.
31. C-2 Pasha.
32. B-28; G-31, p. 5.
33. G-31 Yulek, p. 18, Poldek, p. 21; B-30a.
34. B-30a; B-13d, 13b; B-6; A-6 Distel; B-1b.

35. Shadmi file, final report, Haganah, October 7, 1946.
36. B-1d, 1a.
37. D-10.
38. E-27b; A-4, on October 18, 1946.
39. B-1d; B-11b; Shadmi's final report and Haganah correspondence, April 10, 1946, May 17, 1946; E-27b.
40. E-3, 3a; C-2 Pasha; Shadmi's final report; G-36, vol. 2, p. 143; B-1g; E-12b.
41. B-17c; B-30; B-13a; B-1b; B-11b; Shadmi's final report; K-4, pp. 52–56.
42. B-6.
43. B-6, p. 28; F-16, p. 85; K-4, pp. 12–13.
44. B-6, p. 29; A-4; K-4, ch. 1; I-25, p. 149; conversation with Manek, August 2017.
45. F-11, p. 167; B-8; A-2, April 29, 1946.
46. F-3, p. 92; *New York Times*, April 23, 1946, p. 20; *Sud Deutsche Zeitung*, April 24, 1946; B-1b; I-5, pp. 51–52; I-38, Sarid II, p. 161.
47. B-6; F-15, p. 87; B-1e; C-2 Pasha; Vitka—in every meeting.
48. B-13b; B-6.
49. F-3, pp. 91–92; Kovner's letter on Ben-Horin's "we," Moreshet, February 27, 1975.
50. Shadmi's reports, Haganah, October 7, 1946.
51. Summary in file arsenic poisoning, 66070, February 27, 1947, US National Archives.
52. Summary in file arsenic poisoning, 66070, February 27, 1947, US National Archives; the Sigma-Aldrich, St. Louis, Missouri, site, on arsenic.
53. Letter—courtesy of Avi Avidov.
54. US investigation files, undated or signed.
55. F-42, pp. 76–77.
56. B-26; B-1b.
57. B-11d; conversation with Porat, October 5, 2014.
58. F-42, p. 77.
59. B-7.
60. B-14a; C-2 Kenet.
61. B-10a; B-1d; B-13b, p. 62.
62. B-7; B-17c.
63. C-2 Kazhik.
64. B-19a; B-29; B-30a; B-13b, p. 62; B-8; B-17c, 17d.
65. G-3, p. 57; B-3.
66. B-13d; B-14; C-2 Pasha; B-1a, 1b; B-20.
67. C-2 Pasha.
68. B-7.
69. B-11a; Kazhik: B-26a, 26b.
70. F-23, p. 245; B-16.
71. F-23, pp. 246–53.
72. B-19; B-6, p. 26; B-17a.
73. I-37, p. 230; F-8, vol. 2, p. 31.
74. K-2, p. 252.
75. J-5.
76. F-29, pp. 175–77; B-19; B-20.
77. I-2, pp. 166–68; H-19; *Ha'aretz*, November 22, 1945; HaTzofe, October 18, 1946; Yediot Ahronot, October 1, 1946, December 16, 1945.
78. Haganah correspondence, May 17, 1946.
79. F-32, pp. 45, 67.
80. F-32, p. 45.
81. F-32, pp. 111–12.
82. F-32, p. 107.
83. F-11, p. 172; A-2, on April 16 and May 11, 1946; C-2 Yulek.
84. B-12; B-10a; B-28; B-9.
85. B-24; A-2, May 25, 1946; B-17c; G-10, pp. 99–100.
86. B-15g.
87. A-6, May 5, 1946.
88. F-32, p. 108; G-25, p. 281.
89. F-27, p. 92; B-13d Rotbein; B-26b; B-1g; F-11, p. 177; A-6, letter 16.
90. I-10, pp. 9–19; B-30; B-17c.

CONCLUSION

1. B-18; F-16, ch. 7.
2. B-1c, 1b.
3. Conversation with Poldek, August 24, 2015; B-10.
4. Kovner to Moreshet, May 29, 1987, C.61.
5. H-30.
6. C-2 Yulek Harmatz; Kovner to the group's core: March 14, 1985.
7. C-2; meeting in Yakum, July 11, 1992, recorded; Kovner to the group's core, March 14, 1985; letter to Pasha, courtesy of Avi Avidov; C-4.
8. B-26b; B-10a; L-9, p. 40.
9. F-42, p. 76; B-26.
10. F-27, p. 87.
11. F-32 Ruzka, p. 71.
12. B-27.
13. B-19.
14. B-29a.
15. C-2; conversation with Yulek, September 25, 2010.
16. B-14a, 14, p. 73.
17. B-30a.
18. A-6 Distel.
19. Conversation with Poldek, August 24, 2015.
20. B-1d.
21. L-6, p. 16.
22. B-13, 13e, 13a.
23. H-26.
24. F-14, pp. 142, 148–49.
25. F-14, p. 148.
26. F-44, p. 532.
27. D-11.
28. D-11.
29. E-27c; D-6a; D-10; F-29, p. 176.
30. H-30; I-5, pp. 86–90, no names mentioned.
31. K-4.
32. H-22.
33. G-33, pp. 280, 284–86, emphasis in original.
34. G-10, p. 102; E-1.
35. I-25, Laskov and Zorea, p. 150; E-1c; H-12 Gichon.
36. E-1c.
37. I-38 Pasha, Sarid II, pp. 172–73.
38. G-32, p. 1074.
39. Conversation with Shabtai Tevet, September 24, 1999.
40. F-3, p. 92.
41. J-6, p. 99.
42. D-11; B-1d.
43. C-2 Kovner.
44. B-15g.
45. I-34, pp. 260–79.
46. Kovner's letter in Moreshet, February 27, 1975, emphasis in original.
47. I-38, Sarid I, p. 49, emphasis in original.
48. Kovner to Moreshet, May 29, 1987, C.61.
49. L-3, pp. 108, 109, 117.
50. E-5.
51. L-7.
52. L-4, p. 395.
53. L-10.
54. Poldek and Manek, letter, November 3, 2018.
55. Etnachta.co.il; J-16.

Sources

BECAUSE OF THE ZEALOUS WISH to revive Hebrew, many of the books cited below did not carry an English or other non-Hebrew title, nor was the author's name transliterated from Hebrew into Roman characters at the time of publication. Books were sent to the National Library in Jerusalem, rather than to the Library of Congress until at least the 1970s. Therefore, most of the following translations of titles are mine. Letters and short conversations not included in this list of sources are referred to in the notes.

Material marked as "entrusted" was given to me, and sometimes to both Hava Zexer and me, courtesy of the Nokmim, researchers, and colleagues. Material for which no location is specified is in my hands.

Transliteration of names from Hebrew to non-Hebrew languages depends on personal preference: Arieh, Aryeh, and Ariye or Yitzhak, Itzhak, Izhak, and Isaac, are a matter of choice, not according to a standard rule, as are Cantorowicz or Rabinovitch. While the reader may find what seems to be an inconsistency in transliteration, it in fact honors each individual's wishes.

ARCHIVES CONSULTED
- The Ben-Gurion Heritage Institute archive at Sde Boker
- The Central Zionist Archives, Jerusalem (hereafter CZA)
- The Ghetto Fighters' House
- The Gnazim Archive of the Hebrew Writers Association in Israel, Tel Aviv
- The Haganah Historical Archives, Tel Aviv (hereafter Haganah)

- The Hanoch Bartov archive at the Kipp Center for Hebrew Literature and Culture, Tel Aviv University
- The IDF (Israeli Defense Forces) Archive, Kiryat Ono
- The Inter-University Project for the Study of the Haʿapalah, Tel Aviv University
- The Israel Galili Defense Forces Archive, Yad Tabenkin, Efal (hereafter Efal)
- The Israel State Archives, Jerusalem
- The Jewish Legion Museum at Avichail
- The Kibbutz Ein-HaHoresh archive
- The Kovner family archive at Givat Haviva
- The Labor Party archive, Beit Berl, Kfar Saba
- The Lavon Institute for the Study of the Labor Movement, Tel Aviv
- The Massuah Institute, Tel Yitzhak
- The Moreshet archives and the Hashomer Hatzair Yaʿari archives at Givat Haviva
- The Oral History Archives, Institute of Contemporary Jewry, Hebrew University, Jerusalem (hereafter Oral HU)
- The Palmach House Archive in Tel Aviv
- The US National Archives, College Park, Maryland
- The Weizmann Archives at the Weizmann Institute, Rehovot
- The Yad Vashem archive
- The YIVO Archives, New York

A – MATERIALS ENTRUSTED BY THE AVENGERS AND THEIR FAMILIES

1. Avidov (Reichman), Yitzhak (Pasha), material entrusted by his son Avi Avidov.
2. Galperin-Gliksman, Rachel, written diary in Yiddish and Hebrew.
3. Hammel, Yitzhak, notes written in Polish to Lena Satz.
4. Harmatz, Yosef (Yulek), a diary written in Lithuanian.
5. Kenet (Kantarowicz), Shlomo, material gathered at Beit Zera (his kibbutz), entrusted by his family.
6. Kovner, Abba, the *Nakam* ("revenge") File, entrusted by his widow, Vitka Kempner-Kovner.
7. Mairanz, Ludwig, a forged *oleh* (immigrant) certificate, entrusted by his widow Paulette.
8. Satz-Hammel, Helena (Lena), a diary written in Polish.
- Testimonies given at the Massuah Institute and printed in booklets for family members.
- Booklets written and printed for family only.
- Clips from the American and German press of 1946, kept by a number of the Nokmim.
- Recordings of the group's meetings.

B – TESTIMONIES OF THE GROUP MEMBERS AND THEIR RELATIVES

1. Avidov (Reichman), Yitzhak (Pasha): 1a—to Yehuda Bauer and Aharon Keidar, January 10, 1966, Moreshet, C.61/45; 1b—to Yehuda Ben-David and Naftali

Sagi, January 19, 1989, Efal, file 157; 1c—to Natan Beirak and Anita Tarsi, July 30, 1989, *Massuah*, no. 75; 1d—to Dina Porat, September 19, 1995; 1e—testimonies to Zexer, September 2000; 1f—undated, Moreshet, A.1587.02; 1g—to his grandson, undated.

2. Avidov, Avi, son of Avidov (Reichman), Yitzhak (Pasha), a conversation with Zexer and Porat, July 2008 and June 5, 2009.

3. Ben-Ya'akov (Gewirtzman), Dov (Bolek), undated, Moreshet A.587.1 and A.587.2; 3a—to Levi Arieh Sarid (hereafter Sarid), February 21, 1984.

4. Ben-Zur (Bencelowicz), Pinchas (Yashek), to Zexer and Porat, December 24, 2009.

5. De-Nur (Feiner), Yehiel (Ka-tzetnik), to Zvika Dror, May 16, 1990, entrusted by Dror.

6. Distel, Arie (Leibke), *Days of Life*, a printing of his testimony at Massuah, September 7, 1984, A.11701.

7. Friedman, Yehuda (Idek), to Porat and Zexer, April 14, 2010.

8. Galperin-Gliksman, Rachel, to Zexer and Porat, October 24, 2009.

9. Gliksman, Zygmunt (Zygi), to Levi Arieh Sarid (hereafter Sarid), August 12, 1992, printed for his family.

10. Hammel (Satz), Helena (Lena), to Zexer, January 7, 1997; 10a—with Shulamit Wodislawski to Zexer and Porat, January 29, 2010, and July 7, 2020.

11. Harmatz, Yosef (Yulek), to Porat, May 5, 1994; 11a—July 16, 1996; 11b—July 20, 2009; 11c—to the BBC, July 4, 1998; 11d—to Zexer, April 27, 1999.

12. Hershderfer, Theodore (Dzhunek), later Dan Arad, to Beirak, June 16, 1994, Massuah 272.

13. Kempner-Kovner, Vitka, to Naftali Sagi, December 21, 1988, Efal, file 157; 13a—to Porat for Yad Vashem, July 10 and 17, 2001, tape VT.3236; 13b—to Avraham Atzili, 1989, Moreshet, A.1742; 13c—to Danny Siton, November 8, 1995; 13d—with Yonat Rotbein to Porat, April 23, 2009; 13e—to Porat, last conversation, August 13, 2009; 13f—speaking on Holocaust Memorial Day, April 2000.

14. Kenet (Kantarowicz) to Ayala Weiss of Ein Harod Meuchad, January 1998; 14a—to Beirak, undated, *Massuah*, A.1767, printed under "Life Story."

15. Kovner, Abba, to Haim Gouri, February 1, 1978, 5832/33, and tapes 408 and 413, in the Inter-University Project for the Study of the Ha'apalah, Tel Aviv University; 15a—to Shlomo Kless (1), October 27, 1982, the Kovner family archive; 15b—to Kless (2), December 17, 1982, Oral HU, 36(170); 15c—to Anita Shapira (1), at Tel Aviv University, November 22, 1982; 15d—to Shapira (2), June 25, 1985, Moreshet A. 1262/61; 15e—to Sarid, October 26, 1984; 15f—Kovner and Kempner with L. Weintraub and Y. Sela, June 10, 1986, Moreshet A. 1258; 15g—to Bauer, March 5, 1962, May 10, 1964, June 16, 1964, the Kovner family archive; 15h—to Zili Brendstater, September 18, 1983, Efal, 25/159/30; 15i—at the Hashomer Hatzair secretariat, August 16 and 23, 1945, and September 22, 1945, Givat Haviva (6)5.10–5.

16. Lidovski, Eliezer, to Beirak and Tarsi, *Massuah*, undated, no. 119; 16a—to Sarid, August 22, 1983.

17. Maimon (Wasserman), Yehuda (Poldek), to Sarid, November 21, 1985; 17a—to Beirak in *Massuah*, an undated booklet; 17b—to Porat and Zexer, March 18, 2009; 17c—with Yashek Ben-Zur to Porat and Zexer, December 24, 2009; 17d—with Galperin-Gliksman to Porat and Zexer, November 30, 2010.

18. Mairanz, Paulette, to Zexer and Porat, July 1, 2010.

19. L., Manek (did not release his full name), to Porat, July 10, 2010; 19a—May 21, 2014.

20. Michaeli-Kek, Bezalel, to Yarin Kimor, November 30, 1995, video.

21. Nakdimon, Shlomo, interviews with two unidentified Avengers, recorded for a report in *Yedioth Ahronoth*, April 10, 1966, entrusted to Porat.

22. Nissanilevich, Netanel (Senka), to Porat, June 20, 1996.

23. Orchan, Esther, conversation with Porat, August 10, 1993.

24. Rabinovich, Ze'ev (Velveleh), to Sarid, May 16, 1990.

25. Ratner, Yitzhak, to Kovner, June 24, 1984, Nakam File.

26. Rotem (Rathajzer), Simcha (Kazhik), to Beirak and Tarsi, March 24, 1994, Massuah; 26a—to Zexer, July 25, 1995, March 12, 1997; 26b—to Porat, December 27, 1995, September 16, 2009.

27. Schedlitz (Sedlis), Gavriel (Gabi), to Porat, January 1996.

28. Shenar, Leah (Lucia), widow of Ze'ev Willek Shenar, to Porat, February 16, 2010.

29. Taubes (Warchavchik), Hasya, to Porat and Zexer, September 5, 2009; 29a—July 23, 2012.

30. Verbin-Shabetzky, Mira (Mirka), *Mira's Story*, a printing of her testimony at Moreshet, A.1702; 30a—to Zexer and Porat, November 6, 2009.

C – GROUP TESTIMONIES

1. Nokmim meeting at Porat's home, August 5, 2010.

2. Nokmim meetings on January 21 and 31, 1985. The ninety deciphered pages were entrusted by Sarid in a meeting with him, September 5, 1995. Also in Moreshet, (4)95-61-27.

3. Sarid copybooks: Testimonies given to Sarid by the group members in the mid-1980s, unnumbered, in the Ghetto Fighters' House Archive.

4. Video testimonies at Massuah. Interviews—Natan Beirak and Anita Tarsi with Yitzhak (Pasha) Avidov (58319), Simcha (Kazhik) Rotem (58428), Eliezer Lidovski (58839), Arie (Leibke) Distel (59301), Mira Verbin-Shabetzky (59461), and Dov (Bolek) Ben-Ya'akov, not numbered.

D – TESTIMONIES OF SURVIVORS, FIGHTERS, AND OTHER AVENGERS

1. Averbuch, Israel, February 20, 1956, Haganah, 148.9 (4227).

2. Blatt, Leon, January 30, 1993, Massuah, 129.

3. Chanoch, Uri, to Beirak and Tarsi, undated, Massuah, 334.

4. Diamant, Manos, to Beirak and Levanah Frank, July 22, 1993, Massuah, 100; 4a—to Beirak and Tarsi, January 30, 1993, Massuah, 129.

5. Eichenwald, Israel, to Yehuda Bauer, July 5, 1964, Moreshet, A.1548.

6. Gewissar, Menashe, to Sarid, March 1986, Moreshet, A.1587.18; 6a—to Zexer, March 31, 1997, August 12, 1997.

7. Grossman, Chaika, to Naftali Sagi, July 6, 1989, Efal, 157.

8. Kless, Shlomo, to Porat, January 1995.

9. Lazar, Haim, to Porat, July 16, 1996.

10. Meiri, Ben, to Sarid, August 17–23, 1984.

11. Roseman, Mordechai, to Porat, June 24, 1997, July 30, 2010; 11a—to Bauer, June 23, 1964, Oral HU, (38)4.

12. Urman, Menachem, to Zexer, August 14, 1998.

13. Zuckerman, Yitzhak (Antek), to Aharon Keidar, February 6, 1964, Oral HU, tape 542; 13a—to Zvika Dror, undated, entrusted by Dror; 13b—tapes 34–35, Ghetto Fighters' House 35431.20, entrusted by Itzik Nir.

14. Unidentified avenger to Zvika Dror, entrusted by Dror.

E – TESTIMONIES OF HAGANAH MEMBERS, JEWISH BRIGADE AND GERMAN UNIT SOLDIERS, AND THE MOSSAD FOR ALIYAH B ACTIVISTS

1. Avidan, Shimon, to Uri Brenner, May 5, 1953, Efal, 1/105/45; 1a—to Haya Ironi, May 5, 1953, Haganah, 150.89; 1b—to Bauer, September 13, 1957, Efal, 150.91;1c—to Avraham Zohar, December 20, 1982, Efal, 45/105/1.

2. Avriel, Ehud, to Yehuda Bauer, May 12, 1964, Haganah, 149.3.

3. Baharav (Rabinovitch), Yehezkel, to Porat, April 3, 1996; 3a—conversation with his daughter Yael Baharav, November 10, 2014.

4. Bar-Tikva (Pasternak), Mondek (Moshe), August 23, 1966, Haganah, 102.11, interviewer not mentioned.

5. Bartov, Hanoch, to Porat, April 26, 1996; 5a—to Porat and Dan Laor, December 23, 1991.

6. Barzilai (Eisen), Moshe, to Yigal Wilfand, August 1990, Moreshet, A.1556.

7. Ben-Gal (Rabinovitch), Michael (James), to Aharon Keidar and Nana Nosinov, December 13, 1967, Oral HU 95(4); 7a—Ben-Asher, Haim, letter, July 30, 1945, CZA, A292/24.

8. Ben-Horin, Yehuda, December 13, 1966, Efal, 15-24/7/5, interviewer not mentioned.

9. Ben-Natan, Asher, to Zexer, April 3, 1997.

10. Ben-Zvi, Issar, to Haya Cohen-Tenenbaum, November 2, 1960, Haganah, 9.28

11. Carmeli (Rabinovitch), Moshe, to Ezra Greenbaum, October 1987, Palmach House Archive, testimonies, tape 2; 11a—March 16, 1963, Haganah, 124.3, interviewer not mentioned; 11b—to Sarid, October 27, 1993.

12. Carmi, Israel, report, Efal, 36/14/4; 12a—report, Haganah, 18.34, undated; 12b—interview to Ezra Greenbaum, August 1991, the Yigal Alon House.

13. Davidson, Meir (Meirke), to Ayala Dan, August 22, 1955, Haganah, 97.34 (4308); 13a—March 30, 1967, Haganah, 80/158/3, interviewer not mentioned; 13b—to Porat, February 10, 1995.

14. Giladi, Shalom, Haganah, 4758 (150.4).

15. Grudjinski, Zeʿev, April 16, 1951, Haganah, 193.9.

16. Gur (Grossman), Dov (Robert), to Haya Ironi, December 29, 1953, Haganah, 12.36.

17. Gur Aryeh (Mirkis), Nachman, to Zippi Dagan, November 6, 2002, Haganah, 220.3.

18. Hadash, Mordechai (Motke), to Aharon Keidar, undated, Moreshet, A.1546.

19. Hellman, Yehuda (Yudke), to Sarid, October 9, 1990 (?—handwriting illegible).

20. Hoter-Ishay, Aharon, to Bauer and Keidar, 1965 (date missing), Oral HU, 22 (4).

21. Kahana, Haim, to Dan, November 20, 1967, Haganah, 138.28.

22. Katzir, Ephraim, to Porat, June 3, 1998.

23. Kitt, Kalman, February 16, 1950, Haganah, 48.42; 23a—March 31, 1959, Haganah, 19.17. No interviewers mentioned.

24. Laskov, Haim, to Dan, December 27, 1963, Haganah, 192.13.

25. Miller, Haim, September 2, 1988, Efal, 12-3/1/8; 25a—to Porat, June 2, 2013, and November 10, 2014.

26. Ron (Singer), Shalom, report, Haganah 176, undated.

27. Shadmi (Kremer), Nahum, to Adir Cohen, September 9, 1959, Haganah 165.39; 27a—to Yehuda Ben-David, August 1, 1966, Haganah 37.33; 27b—to Ben-David, November 7, 1985, Efal 15-24/7/8; 27c—the Shadmi file, Haganah 165.39; 27d—Shadmi, Issachar (Yiska, Nahum's son), to Porat, September 9, 2012.

28. Sneh, Moshe, to Yehuda Ben-David, March 30, 1967, Haganah 80/158/3.

29. Surkis, Mordechai, to Naftali Sagi, December 19, 1988, Efal, 156/23; 29a—March 13, 1986, Efal, 156, interviewer not mentioned.

30. Tubin, Yehuda, to Porat, January 24, 1995.

31. Weinberg, Yeshayahu (Shaike), to Aharon Keidar, November 14, 1967, Oral HU, 106(4); 31a—to Porat, July 16, 1996.

32. Zafrir, Yedidia, testimony found in the Clandestine Immigration and Naval Museum, undated and unnumbered.

F – MEMOIRS
All in Hebrew, except 16 and 39.

1. Avriel, Ehud, *Open the Gates*, Tel Aviv, Maariv Books, 1976.

2. Barzilai, Moshe, *From Hashomer Hatzair in Brooklyn to Ein Hashofet*, Bichtav, Ein Hashofet, 2006.

3. Ben-Horin (Brieger), Yehuda, *My Life*, Moreshet and Sifriat Poalim, Tel Aviv, 1975.

4. Ben-Natan, Asher, *Memoirs*, Israel Ministry of Defense Publishing House (hereafter MOD Books), Tel Aviv, 2002.

5. Carmi, Israel, *On the Fighters' Road*, Maʿarachot, Tel Aviv, 1960.

6. Davidson, Gusta, *Justina's Diary*, Ghetto Fighters' House and Hakibbutz Hameuchad, 1978.

7. Davidson, Meir, *Villa Fezana*, Maʿarachot, Tel Aviv, 1969.

8. Ehrenburg, Ilya, *People, Years, Life*, vols. 1–2, Sifriat Poalim, Merhavia, 1961–1962.

9. Eichenwald, Israel, *On Roads and Borders*, Moreshet and Sifriat Poalim, Tel Aviv, 1989.

10. Fried-Budenstein, Dina, *An Unforgettable Testimony*, Moreshet, Givat Haviva, 2008.

11. Galperin-Gliksman, *Meidale, Don't Cry*, Holon Municipality, Holon, 2011; 11a— Galperin-Gliksman, *Smile, Meidale, Smile*, Holon Municipality, Holon, 2015.

12. Gichon, Mordechai, *Mordechai's Rod*, Efi Meltzer Ltd., Tel Aviv, 2008.

13. Greenspan-Frimer, Pnina, *Our Days Were the Nights*, Ghetto Fighters' House and Hakibbutz Hameuchad, Tel Aviv, 1984.

14. Grossman, Chaika, "Almost a Confession," *Yalkut Moreshet* 69, May 2000, pp. 95–149.

15. Harmatz, Yosef (Yulek), *Life Story: Never Say This Is My Last Road*, Docustory, Ra'anana, 2014.

16. ———, *From the Wings: A Long Journey, 1940–1960*, The Book Guild, Sussex, UK, 1998.

17. Katzir, Ephraim, *A Life's Tale*, Carmel, Jerusalem, 2008.

18. Korczak, Ruzka, "My Meeting with Weizmann After the Holocaust," *Me'asef* 16, 1986, pp. 151–53.

19. Kovner, Vitka, "A Junction of Roads and Lives," *Yalkut Moreshet* 43–44, August 1987, pp. 171–76.

20. Lazar-Litai, Haim, *Chapters of Escape*, Jabotinsky House, Tel Aviv, 1986.

21. Levi, Primo, *The Truce: A Survivor's Journey Home from Auschwitz*, Am Oved, Tel Aviv, 2002.

22. ———, *The Drowned and the Saved*, Am Oved, Tel Aviv, 1991.

23. Lidovski, Eliezer, *And the Spark Hasn't Been Extinguished*, the Partisans' Association, Tel Aviv, 1986.

24. ———, *Reaching 80: A Message from One Generation to Another*, Brit Rishonim, Tel Aviv, 1990.

25. Merdor, Meir (Munya), *On a Secret Mission*, Ma'arachot, Tel Aviv, 1957.

26. Reznik, Nisan, *Budding from the Ashes: The Story of a HaNoar HaZioni Youth in the Vilna Ghetto*, Massuah and Yad Vashem, Jerusalem, 2003.

27. Rosenberg-Amit, Zila (Cesia), *Not to Lose the Human Face*, Moreshet, Ghetto Fighters' House and Hakibbutz Hameuchad, Tel Aviv, 1990.

28. Rotem (Rathajzer), Simcha (Kazhik), *The Past Is Inside Me: In the Fighting Jewish Organization*, Ghetto Fighters' House and Hakibbutz Hameuchad, Tel Aviv, 1984.

29. Shadmi, Nahum, *Memoirs*, MOD Books, Tel Aviv, 1995.

30. Shamir, Shlomo, *Divine Intervention and a Jewish Flag in the British Army*, Tel Aviv, 2014.

31. Taubes-Warchavchik, Hasya, *Writing to Giora*, private printing, Ramat Gan, 1978.

32. Treger-Nissanilevich, Zelda, *Zelda: The Partisan*, Moreshet and Sifriat Poalim, Tel Aviv, 1989.

33. Viernik, Ya'akov, *A Year in Treblinka*, the Histadrut, Tel Aviv, 1944.

34. Weizmann, Chaim, *Chapters of Life*, the Zionist Library, Jerusalem, 1964.

35. ———, *Trial and Error*, Schocken Books, Jerusalem, 1953.

36. Wierzberg, Benni, *From the Killing Field to Sha'ar HaGai*, Carmel, Jerusalem, 2008.

37. Wiesenthal, Simon, *The Sunflower: On the Possibilities and Limits of Forgiveness*, Human Fraternity, Ashdot Ya'akov, 2009.

38. ———, *Justice, Not Revenge*, Maariv Books, Tel Aviv, 1991.

39. Wodislawski, Shulamit and Henryk (Yechiel), *Errinerung an den Holocaust*, private printing, no details.

40. Wodzislawski, Ya'acov, *My Revenge*, Yad Vashem and Azrieli Fund, Jerusalem, 2008.

41. Yaron, Jacquo, *With Concern and Fear: With Abba Kovner and a Palmach Group on the Way to Europe*, Kibbutz Hatzor, 1995.

42. Sened, Yonat, *Kazhik*, Hakibbutz Hameuchad, Tel Aviv, 2008.

43. Zilbertal, Moshe (Miyetek), *Roads and Encounters*, Sifriat Poalim, Merhavia, 1947.

44. Zuckerman, Yitzhak (Antek), *Those Seven Years, 1939–1946*, Ghetto Fighters' House and Hakibbutz Hameuchad, Tel Aviv, 1990.

G – COLLECTED TESTIMONIES AND DOCUMENTATION

All in Hebrew except 35.

1. Ashbel, Michael, *On Barricades: The Prison Diary of Michael Ashbel*, Hadar, Tel Aviv, 1976.

2. Bacharach, Walter Zwi (ed.), *Last Letters from the Shoah*, Yad Vashem, Jerusalem, 2003.

3. Ben-David, Yehuda, *The Haganah in Europe*, Tag Publications, Israel, 1995.

4. ———, *Sword in a Foreign Land, Some "Hagana" Actions in Europe, 1945–1948*, MOD Books, Tel Aviv, 1978.

5. Ben-Dor, Israel, *The First Regiment's Book*, Efi Meltzer Ltd., Tel Aviv, 2000.

6. Ben-Gurion, David, *Visits in the Valley of Death: Ben-Gurion's Journeys to Bulgaria, Sweden and the Displaced Persons Camps in Germany*, vols. 1–2, ed. Tuvia Friling, the Ben-Gurion Institute, Beersheba, 2014.

7. Ben-Zion, Israeli, *Writings and Speeches of Ben-Zion Israeli of Kinneret*, ed. Shlomo Yavne'eli, Am Oved and Kvutzat Kinneret, Tel Aviv, 1956.

8. Burger, Adolf, *The Devil's Workshop: A Memoir of the Nazi Counterfeiting Operation*, Contento de Semrik, Tel Aviv, 2009.

9. Dagan, Shaul, *The Jewish Brigade: The Third Regiment*, Veterans Association, Tel Aviv, 1996.

10. Dagan, Shaul, and Yakir, Eliyahu, *Shimon Avidan Givati: The Man Who Became a Brigade*, Yad Ya'ari, Dalya, 1995.

11. Davidson, Meir, *A General in Dispute (On Eliyahu Ben-Hur)*, Tel Aviv, 1990.

12. ———, "We Are the Saving Remnant," *Yalkut Moreshet* 43–44, August 1987, pp. 165–69.

13. Gefen, M., et al. (eds.), *The Jewish Partisans Book*, vols. 1–2, Sifriat Poalim, Merhavia, 1958.

14. Golomb, Eliahu, *The Secret Strength*, Ayanot, Tel Aviv, 1954.

15. Grayek, Stephen Shalom, *Struggling to Go On: Polish Jews in 1945–1949*, Am Oved, Tel Aviv, 1989.

16. Hadash, Mordechai, *Motke, Sent by His Heart, On and By Motke Hadash*, Tel Aviv, 1987.

17. Hagai [Avriel], *Chapters of Life*, Kibbutz Mashabei Sade, 1973.

18. Korczak, Reizl (Ruzka), *Flames in the Ashes*, 3rd enlarged ed., Moreshet and Sifriat Poalim, Merhavia, 1965.

19. Korczak-Marle, Ruzka, *The Personality and Philosophy of the Life of a Fighter*, ed. Y. Tubin, L. Dror, and Y. Rab, Moreshet and Sifriat Poalim, Tel Aviv, 1988.

20. Kovner, Abba, "The Mission of the Last," *Yalkut Moreshet* 16, April 1973, pp. 35–42.

21. ———, "On the Beginnings of the 'Bricha' as a Mass Movement," *Yalkut Moreshet* 37, June 1984, pp. 7–31, 38, December 1984, pp. 133–46.

22. ———, *A Missive to Hashomer Hatzair Partisans*, Moreshet, Tel Aviv, 2002.

23. Lipschitz, Ya'acov, *The Jewish Brigade Book: History of the Fighting and Survivors Rescuing Brigade*, Yavne, Tel Aviv, 1947.

24. Lubetkin, Zivia, *The Last on the Wall: Testimony at Kibbutz Yagur, June 8, 1946*, the Yagur Fourteenth Conference Book, June 1946.

25. Lustgarten, Shimon, *Shimek: A Mensch, a Friend, a Fighter*, private family printing, no details.

26. Maimon, Yehuda, et al. (eds.), *The Fighting Pioneer, The Jewish Pioneer Youth Journal in The Cracow Underground*, Ghetto Fighters' House and Hakibbutz Hameuchad, Tel Aviv, 1984.

27. *Menashe Gewissar, 1916–1999*, private printing, no details.

28. Naor, Mordechay, *A Living Bridge*, MOD Books, Tel Aviv, 1993.

29. Porat, Dina, "The East European Survivors Brigade: Its Protocols of April 4– July 23, 1945," *Locks of Silence: The Survivors and the Land of Israel*, Massuah yearbook 28, 2000, pp. 177–200.

30. Rupin, Rapha'el, *The Unmatched Second Regiment*, MOD Books, Tel Aviv, 2000.

31. Shenar, Ze'ev, *A Man of the Water Canals: From the Vistula Shores to the Mediterranean Beaches*, family printing, 2001.

32. Slutzki, Yehuda (ed.), *The History of the Haganah: From Resistance to War*, vol. 3, pt. 2, Am Oved, Tel Aviv, 1973.

33. Tubin, Yehuda, *From the Senio to the Bunker in 18 Mila Street*, Moreshet and Sifriat Poalim, Tel Aviv, 1987.

34. ———, "The Jewish Brigade Soldiers' Encounter with the First Survivors," *Yalkut Moreshet* 39, May 1985, pp. 15–54.

SOURCES

35. *West Germany Prepares War of Revenge: Facts on the Rebirth of German Militarism in the Bonn State*, the Committee for German Unity, New York, 1954, the YIVO Archives.
36. Ya'ari, Meir, and Ya'acov Hazan (eds.), *The Hashomer Hatzair Book*, vol. 1: *1913–1945* (1956); vol. 2: *1939–1945* (1961), both by Sifriat Poalim, Merhavia.
37. Zilbertal, Moshe (Miyetek), "Summing up a Mission," Hashomer Hatzair Newsletter, July 4, 1946, Givat Haviva, 43/46.
38. Zuckerman, Yitzhak, *Exodus out of Poland*, Ghetto Fighters' House and Hakibbutz Hameuchad, Tel Aviv, 1988.
39. Zuckerman, Yitzhak, and Moshe Bassok (eds.), *The Book of the Ghettos' Wars: Inside the Walls, Camps, and Forests*, 3rd ed., Ghetto Fighters' House and Hakibbutz Hameuchad, Tel Aviv, 1956.
40. Dror, Zvika (ed.), *Pages of Testimony: 96 Members of The Ghetto Fighters' Kibbutz Speak*, Ghetto Fighters' House and Hakibbutz Hameuchad, Tel Aviv, 1984.
41. ———, *They Were There: With the Survivors*, Hakibbutz Hameuchad, Tel Aviv, 1992.

H – PRESS REPORTAGE
All in Hebrew.

1. "The Authors' Committee," *Davar*, November 26, 1942.
2. Abramov, Eti, "Mother, Father, Killing," *Yedioth Ahronoth*, January 27, 2012, Saturday supplement.
3. Aderet, Ofer, "Revenge on the Germans," obituary for Johanan (Yanush) Peltz (1917–2014), *Ha'aretz*, July 3, 2014.
4. ———, "How Different Is This Night," *Ha'aretz*, Galeria, April 28, 2016.
5. ———, Obituary for Mordechai Gichon (1922–2016), *Ha'aretz*, September 30, 2016.
6. Appelfeld, Aharon, in *An Eye for an Eye*, a Yarin Kimor and Benny Uri documentary, March 10, 1996, a Mabat Sheni broadcast.
7. Arif, Ora, "A Revenge Satan Never Created," *Yedioth Ahronoth*, February 25, 1996.
8. *BaMa'avak* ("In Struggle," the Jewish Brigade journal) 3, July 1945, IDF Archives.
9. Baronovsky, Yoram, *Ha'aretz*, March 15, 1996.
10. Bartov, Hanoch, "Our Indifference to the Holocaust Is a Libel," *Iton 77*, January–February 1999, pp. 144–45.
11. Ben-Horin, Yitzhak, "The Avengers," *Maariv*, Saturday supplement, May 29, 1987.
12. Bergman, Ronen, "In the Name of the People," *Yedioth Ahronoth*, Seven Days, September 17, 2010.
13. Capra, Michal, "I Shot, Strangled and Killed and Have No Remorse," *Maariv*, Saturday supplement, November 26, 1993.
14. Carlebach, Ezriel, "To Me Belongeth Vengeance and Recompence; Their Foot Shall Slide in Due Time," *HaTzofe*, January 16, 1942.

15. Fichman, Ya'akov, "For the Avengers' Fist Gathers Strength Day and Night," *Davar*, November 13, 1942.

16. Giladi, Shalom, "The Hunters," *HaOlam HaZeh*, March 29, 1961.

17. Gilboa-Nachshon, Nachman, "The Last Avengers," *The Green Page*, June 25, 2009.

18. Goldberg, Leah (as Ada Grant), "Plagues of Egypt," *Mishmar* 4, January 21, 1944.

19. Gotthelf, Yehuda, "Small and Big Crimes," *Davar*, October 19, 1945.

20. ———, "Justice or Revenge," *Davar*, October 7, 1942.

21. Gringer, Matan, "An Eye for an Eye = Money," *Makor Rishon*, December 17, 2012.

22. Hadar, Roni, "The Suspicion: Murdering S.S. Officers," *Tel Aviv*, March 3, 2000.

23. Hartglas, Apolinary, "Ways of Reaction and Rescue," *HaOlam*, December 17, 1942.

24. Heilperin, Falk, "There Will Be No Revenge," *Davar*, June 18, 1942.

25. Katzenelson-Shazar, Rachel, "Poems of Our Time," *Dvar HaPoelet* 106, July 13, 1944.

26. Kempner-Kovner, Vitka, in *Etzleinu* (the Ein HaHoresh journal) 18, May 12, 2000.

27. Kleinman, Moshe, "The Problem of Revenge," *HaOlam*, December 31, 1942.

28. Laski, Harold, "What Should Be Done to Germany?" *Davar*, October 10, 1944.

29. *Masa'ot uMa'asim* (the Jewish Brigade 462 Transport Unit journal), February 1943, Haganah 86/200.

30. Nakdimon, Shlomo, "The Avengers," *Yedioth Ahronoth*, April 10, 1966.

31. Porat, Elisha, "How I Restored the Lost Honor of Abba Kovner and His Two Comrades," *The Green Time*, January 17, 2013.

32. Schoffman, Gershom, "Two or Three Lines," *Davar*, November 27, 1942.

33. Segev, Tom, "The Revenge of the Last Jews" (A), *Ha'aretz*, September 13, 1992; "Abba Kovner's Revenge" (B), September 20, 1991; "Abba Kovner's Revenge" (C), October 4, 1991; "Abba Kovner's Revenge" (D), October 25, 1991.

34. ———, "The Avengers Are out of the Closet," *Ha'aretz*, June 26, 1992.

35. Shelach, Menachem, "We Were the Address for Operations Best Left Unspoken," *Hotam*, an Al Hamishmar supplement, June 5, 1966.

36. Shlonsky, Avraham, Light Emphasis column, *Davar*, February 12, 1943.

37. Vansittart, Robert, "What Should be Done to Germany?" *Davar*, October 12, 1944.

38. Weiss, Yehuda, "When the Survivors Started Out," documents and testimonies, *Hedim* 60, January 1959.

39. Weltch, Robert, "The Trial Started," *Ha'aretz*, December 12, 1945.

40. Wilfand, Yigal, "Revenge," *The Green Page* 342, March 3, 1992.

41. ———, "An Unaccomplished Revenge," *Bemachaneh Nahal* 10, December 1990.

42. Unidentified letter to editors of *Eshnav* (the Haganah journal), December 7, 1942.

43. Unidentified letter to editors of *HaOlam*, December 31, 1942.

I – RESEARCH PUBLISHED IN HEBREW

All in Hebrew.

1. Avizohar, Meir, "Ben-Gurion's Visit to the D.P. Camps and His National Perception at the End of WWII," in Binyamin Pinkus (ed.), *East European Jewry Between Holocaust and Resurrection 1944–1948*, Sde Boker, Ben-Gurion University of the Negev, 1987, pp. 253–70.

2. Barzel, Neima, "The Demand in the Yishuv to Punish Germany, 1944–1947," *Cathedra* 73, September 1994, pp. 158–81.

3. ———, "Honor, Hate and Memory in the German Reparations and Compensations Debate," *Yad Vashem Studies* 24, 1995, pp. 203–25.

4. ———, *Sacrificed Unredeemed, The Encounter Between the Leaders of the Ghetto Fighters and the Israeli Society*, the Zionist Library and Yad Ya'ari, Jerusalem, 1998.

5. Bar-Zohar, Michael, *The Avengers*, Levin-Epstein, Tel Aviv, 1969 (2nd ed.: *Revenge Day: Jewish Revenge on the Nazis*, Teper-Magal, Tel Aviv, 1991).

6. Bauer, Yehuda, *Flight and Rescue: Bricha*, Moreshet and Sifriat Poalim, Tel Aviv, 1974 (1st ed.: Random House, New York, 1970).

7. Bender, Sarah, *In Enemy Land: The Jews of Kielce and the Region, 1939–1946*, Yad Vashem, Jerusalem, 2012.

8. Ben-Nahum, Yizhar, *The Dreamer and Accomplisher: The Life Story of Mordechai Shenhavi*, vol. 2, Moreshet and Sifriat Poalim, Tel Aviv, 2011.

9. Cohen, Yohanan, *Operation "Bricha": Poland 1945–1946*, Zmora/Bitan and Massuah, Tel Aviv, 1995.

10. Eldad, Meir, *The Sea Voyage of the Biria Passengers*, private printing, Jerusalem, February 2003.

11. Engel, David, *Between Liberation and Flight: Holocaust Survivors in Poland and the Struggle for Leadership, 1944–1946*, Am Oved and Tel Aviv University, Tel Aviv, 1996.

12. ———, "Patterns of Anti-Jewish Violence in Poland, 1944–1946," *Yad Vashem Studies* 26, 1998, pp. 35–70.

13. Freilich, Miri, *The Partisan: Vitka Kovner's Life*, Resling, Tel Aviv, 2013.

14. Gelber, Yo'av, *Jewish Palestinian Volunteering in the British Army During the Second World War*, vol. 3, Yad Yitzhak Ben-Zvi, Jerusalem, 1983.

15. ———, *The History of Israeli Intelligence: Roots of the Fleur-de-Lis*, vol. 2, MOD Books, Tel Aviv, 1992.

16. Golan, Ze'ev, *Underground in Prison: History of the Jerusalem Prison Under the British Mandate 1917–1948*, Yair, Jerusalem, 2014.

17. Gutterman, Bella, *The One Zivia: The Life of Zivia Lubetkin*, Yad Vashem and Hakibbutz Hameuchad, Tel Aviv, 2011.

18. Gutman, Israel, "Jews in Poland After the War," *Yalkut Moreshet* 33, June 1982, pp. 62–102 and 34, December 1982, pp. 121–50.

19. Halamish, Aviva, *Meir Ya'ari, A Collective Biography: The First Fifty Years, 1897–1947*, Am Oved and Yad Ya'ari, Tel Aviv, 2009.

20. Halperin, Hagit, *The Maestro: The Life and Works of Avraham Shlonsky*, Tel Aviv University Press, Tel Aviv, 2011.

21. Hausner, Gideon, "Intellectuals in the Service of Extermination," *Massuah* 10, April 1982, pp. 19–22.

22. Kless, Shlomo, *On an Unpaved Path: The History of the Bricha, 1944–1948*, Moreshet, Dalya, 1994.

23. ———, "The Branches of the Vilna Center Meet Again in Lublin," *Yalkut Moreshet* 43–44, August 1987, pp. 231–62.

24. Margalit, Gilad, *Guilt, Suffering, and Memory: Germany Remembers Its Dead of the Second World War*, Haifa University Press, Jerusalem, 2007.

25. Naor, Mordechay, *Laskov*, Keter and MOD Books, Tel Aviv, 1988.

26. Ben-Dov, Nitza, *Lives in War: On the Army, Revenge, Grief and the Consciousness of War in Israeli Fiction*, Schocken Books, Tel Aviv, 2016.

27. Pagis, Ada, *Days of Darkness, Moments of Grace: Chapters from Israel Gutman's Life*, Yad Vashem and Hakibbutz Hameuchad, Jerusalem, 2008.

28. Porat, Dina, *An Entangled Leadership: The Yishuv and the Holocaust, 1942–1945*, Am Oved and Tel Aviv University Press, Tel Aviv, 1986 (*The Blue and the Yellow Stars of David*, Harvard University Press, Cambridge, MA, 1990).

29. ———, "With Forgiveness and Grace: The Encounter Between Ruzka Korczak, the Yishuv, and Its Leaders, 1944–1946," *Yalkut Moreshet* 52, April 1992, pp. 9–33.

30. ———, "'Al-Domi': Palestinian Intellectuals and the Holocaust, 1943–1945," *HaZionut* 8, 1983, pp. 240–70.

31. ———, "A Jewish Triangle in Italy: The Encounter of Italian Jews with the Survivors and the Jewish Brigade Soldiers, 1944–1946," *Yalkut Moreshet* 50, April 1991, pp. 91–111.

32. ———, *The Smoke-Smelling Morning Coffee: The Encounter of the Yishuv and Israeli Society with the Holocaust and Its Survivors*, Am Oved and Yad Vashem, Jerusalem, 2011.

33. ———, "The Role of European Jewry in the Plans of the Zionist Movement During and After WWII," in *She'erit Hapletah, 1944–1948: Rehabilitation and Political Struggle*, Yad Vashem, Jerusalem, 1990, pp. 259–74.

34. ———, *Beyond the Reaches of Our Souls: The Life and Times of Abba Kovner*, Am Oved and Yad Vashem, Tel Aviv, 2000 (translated into English as *The Fall of a Sparrow*, Stanford University Press, Stanford, CA, 2010).

35. Preis, Aryeh, "The Reactions of the Eretz-Israeli Undergrounds to the Annihilation of European Jewry," *Massuah* 8, April 1980, pp. 51–82.

36. Ronen, Avihu, "Alex Gatmon, a Fighter," *Massuah* 19, 1991, pp. 22–62.

37. Rubenstein, Joshua, *Tangled Loyalties: The Life and Times of Ilya Ehrenburg*, Mossad Bialik, Jerusalem, 2010.

38. Sarid, Levi Arieh, "The 'Nakam' Organization, Its History, Image and Deeds," *Yalkut Moreshet* 52, April 1992, pp. 35–106; Sarid II, *Ruin and Deliverance: The Pioneer Movements in Poland Throughout the Holocaust and During Its*

Aftermath, 1939–1949, vol. 2, *Arising from Ashes*, Moreshet, Tel Aviv, 1997, pp. 114–78.

39. Segev, Tom, *The Seventh Million: The Israelis and the Holocaust*, Keter, Jerusalem, 1991.

40. ———, *Simon Wiesenthal: The Biography*, Keter, Jerusalem, 2010.

41. Shalev, Ziva, *Chaika*, Moreshet, Tel Aviv, 2005.

42. Shapira, Anita, *Visions in Conflict*, Ofakim/Am Oved, Tel Aviv, 1988.

43. Szeintuch, Yechiel, *Salamandra: Myth and History in Katzetnik's Writings*, Carmel, Jerusalem, 2009.

44. *The Haganah in Europe, Researchers' Conference*, November 8, 1988, Efal, 157/23.

45. Weiss, Ayala, *Post-Holocaust Jewish Revenge Groups: Ambitions and Reality*, matriculation paper, Ein Harod Meuchad ORT School, January 1998.

46. Werdyger-Stepak, Raquel, "The Hebrew Writers' Community in Eretz Israel and Its Response to the Holocaust, 1939–1945," PhD diss., Tel Aviv University, 2011.

47. Zexer, Hava, "Post-Holocaust Vengeance," master's thesis, Tel Aviv University, November 1997.

J – RESEARCH PUBLISHED IN ENGLISH AND GERMAN

1. Beckman, Morris, *The Jewish Brigade: An Army with Two Masters, 1944–1945*, Spellmount, UK, 1998.

2. Beevor, Antony, *The Second World War*, Little, Brown and Company, New York, 2012.

3. Bessel, Richard, *Germany 1945: From War to Peace*, Simon and Schuster, New York, 2009.

4. Blum, Howard, *The Brigade, An Epic Story of Vengeance, Salvation and World War Two*, Simon and Schuster, New York, 2001.

5. Bower, Tom, *Blind Eye to Murder: Britain, America and the Purging of Nazi Germany: A Pledge Betrayed*, Andre Deutsch Limited, Great Britain, 1981.

6. Buruma, Ian, *Year Zero: A History of 1945*, Penguin, New York, 2013.

7. Esrati, Stephen G., *Comrades, Avenge Us*, Xlibris Corp, USA, 2000.

8. Goertemaker, Manfred, and Christoph Safferling, *Die Akte Rosenburg. Das Bundesministerium und die NS-Zeit*, C. H. Beck Verlag, Munich, 2016.

9. Gross, Jan T., *Fear: Anti-Semitism in Poland After Auschwitz*, Random House, New York, 2006.

10. Grossmann, Atina, *Jews, Germans, and Allies: Close Encounters in Occupied Germany*, Princeton University Press, Princeton, NJ, 2007.

11. Jacoby, Susan, *Wild Justice: The Evolution of Revenge*, Harper & Row, New York, 1983.

12. Jensen, William B., Henry Fenishel, and Milton Orchin, *Scientist in the Service of Israel: The Life and Times of Ernst David Bergmann (1903–1975)*, Magnes, Jerusalem, 2011.

13. Judt, Tony, *Postwar: A History of Europe Since 1945*, Penguin, New York, 2005.

14. Kraft, Andreas, "Narratives of Jewish Revenge After the Holocaust," in *Revenge, Retribution, Reconciliation: Justice and Emotions Between Conflict and Mediation: A Cross-Disciplinary Anthology*, ed. L. Jockush, A. Kraft, and K. Wünschmann, Magnes, Jerusalem, 2016, pp. 91–110.

15. Lang, Berel, "Holocaust Memory and Revenge: The Presence of the Past," *Jewish Social Studies* 3, 1996, 1–20.

16. Peels, Hendrik G. L., *The Vengeance of God*, E. J. Brill, Leiden, 1995.

17. Roseman, Mark, "'. . . But of Revenge Not a Sign': Germans' Fears of Jewish Revenge After WWII," *Jahrbuch fuer Antisemitismusforschung*, vol. 22, 2013, pp. 79–95.

18. ———, "'No, Herr Führer!': Jewish Revenge After the Holocaust: Between Fantasy and Reality," in *Revenge, Retribution, Reconciliation: Justice and Emotions Between Conflict and Mediation: A Cross-Disciplinary Anthology*, ed. L. Jockush, A. Kraft, and K. Wünschmann, Magnes, Jerusalem, 2016, pp. 69–90.

19. Rosenbaum, Thane, *Payback: The Case for Revenge*, University of Chicago Press, Chicago, 2013.

20. Rosenfeld, Alvin H., *The End of the Holocaust*, Indiana University Press, Bloomington, 2011.

21. Sack, John, *An Eye for an Eye: The Untold Story of Jewish Revenge Against Germans in 1945*, Basic Books, New York, 1993.

22. Seidman, Naomi, "Elie Wiesel and the Scandal of Jewish Rage," *Jewish Social Studies* 3/1, 1996, pp. 1–19.

23. Shneer, David, *Through Soviet Jewish Eyes: Photography, War, and the Holocaust*, Rutgers University Press, New Brunswick, NJ, 2011.

24. Snyder, Timothy, *Bloodlands: Europe Between Hitler and Stalin*, Basic Books, New York, 2010.

25. Zimmermann, Volker, *Die Sudetendeutschen im NS-Staat: Politik und Stimmung der Bevoelkerung in Reichsgau Sudetenland (1938–1945)*, Klartext Verlag, Essen, 1999.

K – BETWEEN RESEARCH AND JOURNALISM

1. Cohen, Rich, *The Avengers, a Jewish War Story*, Alfred A. Knopf, New York, 2000.

2. Elkins, Michael, *Forged in Fury*, Ballantine Books, New York, 1971.

3. Lavee, Simon, *Jewish Hit Squad: Armja Krajowa Jewish Raid Unit Partisans*, Gefen, Jerusalem, 2014. (H)

4. Tobias, Jim G., and Peter Zinke, *Nakam: Juedische Rache an NS-Taetern*, Konkret Literatur Verlag, Hamburg, 2000. (G)

L – LITERATURE AND POETRY

All in Hebrew except 11 and 12.

1. Alterman, Nathan, *Plague Poems*, 6th ed., Mahbarot Lesifrut, Tel Aviv, 1960.

2. ———, *Joy of the Poor: Poems*, Mahbarot Lesifrut, Tel Aviv, 1959.

3. Bartov, Hanoch, *The Brigade*, 5th ed., Am Oved, Tel Aviv, 1972 (*The Brigade*, Holt, Rinehart & Winston, New York, 1968).
4. Bialik, Haim Nachman, *All Poems*, Dvir, Tel Aviv, 1960.
5. Broides, Avraham, "Avenge and Avenge Again," *Moznaim* 15/5, February 1943.
6. Ka-tzetnik, *Revenge*, Tarmil, Tel Aviv, 1981.
7. Kovner, Abba, *Scrolls of Fire*, Keter, Jerusalem, 1981.
8. ———, *Sloan-Kettering*, Hakibbutz Hameuchad, Tel Aviv, 2002.
9. ———, *My Little Sister*, Sifriat Poalim, Merhavia, 1970.
10. Orland, Ya'akov, *27 Poems: Nathan Said*, Hakibbutz Hameuchad, Tel Aviv, 1985.
11. Oz, Amos, *A Tale of Love and Darkness*, Keter, Jerusalem, 2002.
12. Wiesel, Elie, *Un' die Welt Hot Geshweigen*, Buenos Aires, 1956. (Y)
13. ———, *La Nuit: Temoingnage*, Les Éditions de Minuit, Paris, 1958. (F)
14. ———, *Night*, trans. Haim Gouri, Yedioth Ahronoth, Tel Aviv, 1964.
15. ———, *All Rivers Run to the Sea*, Yedioth Ahronoth and Hemed, Tel Aviv, 2005.
16. ———, *Legends of Our Time*, Bard Books (Avon), New York, 1968.

M – THEORY AND PHILOSOPHY
1. Améry, Jean, *Beyond Guilt and Expiation: The Attempts of a Defeated Man to Overcome Defeat*, Am Oved, Tel Aviv, 2000.
2. Arendt, Hannah, *The Human Condition*, 2nd ed., University of Chicago Press, Chicago, 1998.
3. Bacon, Sir Francis, *The Essays or Counsels, Civill and Morall*, ed. Michael Kieman, Oxford, Clarendon Press, 1985.
4. Bartov, Hanoch, *I Am Not the Mythological Sabra*, Am Oved, Tel Aviv, 1995. (H)
5. Fackenheim, Emil L., *The Jewish Return into History*, Schocken Books, Jerusalem, 1978.
6. Ginzberg, Shlomo, "Peace Without Revenge?" *Moznaim* 16, July–September 1943, pp. 273–82. (H)
7. Kovner, Abba, "Representing the Honorary Doctorate Recipients," *Tel Aviv University Magazine*, June 1980.
8. ———, *On the Narrow Bridge: Essays*, Sifriat Poalim, Tel Aviv, 1981. (H)
9. Levi, Primo, *The Periodic Table*, Hakibbutz Hameuchad, Tel Aviv, 2000. (H)
10. Neria, Moshe-Zvi, "In Terrible Days," *Zeraim*, February 1944. (H)
11. ———, *A Land of Heritage: Written and Oral Essays*, Kfar Haro'eh, 1994. (H)
12. Nietzsche, Friedrich, *On the Genealogy of Morals*, ed. Walter Kaufmann, Vintage Books, New York, 1989.

N – REFERENCE
1. *Cassell's Spanish-English, English-Spanish Dictionary*, Cassell, London.
2. *Der Grosse Brockhaus Enzyklopaedie*, vol. 9, F. A. Brockhaus, Wiesbaden, 1980.
3. *Dictionnaire de Théologie Catholique*, vol. 4, J. M. Alfred Vacant, 1899–1950, Editions Letouzey & Ané, Paris.

4. Stern, Eliyahu (ed.), *The History of the New Jewish Yishuv in the Land of Israel, 1936–1947: A Chronology*, Yad Ben-Zvi, Jerusalem, 1974. (H)

5. *Encyclopaedia Biblica*, vol. 5, Mossad Bialik, Jerusalem, 1968. (H)

6. Even Shoshan, *Dictionary*, vol. 4, New Dictionary Inc., Tel Aviv, 2006.

7. *Funk & Wagnalls Standard Dictionary*, Hill & Wang, New York, 1996.

8. Gutman, Israel (ed.), *Encyclopedia of the Holocaust*, Yad Vashem and Sifriat Poalim, Tel Aviv, 1990. (H)

9. Merriam-Webster, an Encyclopedia Britannica Company, online.

10. Rivlin, Gershon and Aliza (eds.), *A Stranger Will Not Understand, The Code Names Book, Secret Code Names in the Jewish Yishuv in the Land of Israel*, Efal, 1988.

11. Shifris, Amos, "Israel Galilee: Ideology, Policy, and Political Action, 1935–1967," PhD diss., Hebrew University, 2000.

Index

Illustrations are indexed by figure number, for example *fig. 1*. Persons with multiple names are listed under the name most commonly used for them in the text.

"About the *Nakam*" (Kovner), 278

Agami (Auerbach), Moshe, 67, 78, 95, 152

Agasi, Grushka, *fig. 7*

Akiva movement, 39, 43, 76, 78

Aliyah B, x, 34, 93, 97, 127, 146, 148, 183, 184, 200, 217, 219

Aliyah D, 186, 189

Alon, Azaria, v

Alterman, Nathan, 150–51, 194, 297

Améry, Jean, 25, 292

Anglo-American Committee, 147

antisemitism, postwar resurgence of, 47–52, 82, 97, 147, 213

Appelfeld, Aharon, 14, 16, 17

Arad, Dan (Theodore [Dzhunek] Hershderfer), 76, 93, 138, 235, 237, 268, *fig. 31*

Arazi, Tuvia, 209–19

Arazi, Yehuda (Alon), 68, 93, 94, 189, 209–10, 268

Arendt, Hannah, 19, 22

Argov, Levy (Kopelevich), 267

Argov, Meir (Grabovsky), 113, 162

Armia Krajova (AK), 48–49

Armia Ludowa, 83

arrest and imprisonment of Kovner (December 1945–March 1946), 175–93; committee of inquiry on, 187–89; correspondence with Nokmim, 189–91, 200, 203, 205, 235–36; departure from Palestine and arrest, 175, 177–80; in Egypt, 178–79, 191; escape proposals, 184–85; in Jerusalem, 179, 191; Plan A, loss of poison and cancellation of, 241; Plan A, possible change of heart regarding, 191–93; poison, dumping of, 179, 180–82;

arrest and imprisonment of Kovner
  (*continued*)
  poison, smuggling of, 178–79; reasons for, 182–87; release from prison,
  167, 179–80; Chaim Weizmann,
  Kovner's meeting with, 167
arsenic, 200–201, 218, 246, 248–49,
  254
"Asians" (Jewish returnees from Central
  Asia), 57, 58, 61–62, 71, 83, 157, 244
atropine, 200
Auschwitz, 8, 14, 15, 21, 32, 74–75, 110,
  200, 231, 263, 266, 298
Auschwitz death march, 37, 76, 81
Auschwitz group, in Bucharest, 72–75,
  76
Avatihi, Arye, v
Avidan (Koch), Shimon: after German
  operations, 275, 276; Jewish Brigade and, 113; Kovner in Palestine/
  in prison and, 163, 171–72, 182, 189,
  191; in Lublin, 56; Nokmim and vengeance, views on, 289–91; Paris,
  Nokmim in, 203, 204; in War of Independence, 296
Avidov, Avi, 235
Avidov (Reichman), Dorka, 59, 71, 117,
  201, 235, 245, 268, *fig. 10*
Avidov (Reichman), Yitzhak "Pasha": after German operations, 277, 279;
  Améry's comment, reaction to, 292;
  arrest/imprisonment of Kovner
  and, 180, 189–90, 235–36; assistance
  sought by, 243–44; Bricha and, 65;
  Bucharest, relocation to, 71; Dachau
  operation and, 257–60; deterrence,
  on vengeance as, 56; Eastern Bloc,
  vengeance in, 301; Germany, Nokmim in, 229, 232, 234–35, 238, 243–
  44; on Hativa, 88; Jewish Brigade and, 117, 126, 128, 176; Kovner,
  view of, 294; Kovner in Palestine
  and, 139–40, 149, 159, 161, 164, 171;

Lublin, meeting with Kovner in, 35,
  59, 60–61; migration of Nokmim to
  Palestine, after German operations,
  266–70; motivations of, 42; Nuremberg operation and, 243–44, 245,
  255; Nuremberg trial defendants, efforts to assassinate, 264; organization of Nokmim and, 64, 77, 78; in
  Paris, 198–206, 211–16, 222; photo
  of, *fig. 11*; Plan A and, 243, 282; as
  successor to Kovner, 203–4, 222,
  294; urging author to write about
  Nokmim, ix
Avigur (Meirov), Shaul: arrest/impris-
  onment of Kovner and, 187; Pasha
  Avidov sent to Poland by, after German operations, 277; description of
  Nokmim by, x; Ruzka Korczak and,
  151–55; Kovner in Palestine and, 146,
  148–49, 159, 162, 171, 174; migration of Nokmim to Palestine, after
  German operations, 269; Nokmim
  in Paris and, 205, 206, 214, 216, 218;
  Nuremberg operation and, 245; Plan
  A, awareness of, 171
Avriel, Ehud, 216–18

Bacharach, Walter Zvi, 13, 16, 17, 43
Bacon, Sir Francis, 18, 19
Baharav (Rabinovich), Yehezkel, 132,
  214, 245, 246, 258
Bamivhan, v
Bar-Zohar, Michael, 287–88
Bartov, Hanoch, 105, 107–8, 170–71,
  298–99
"Baruch of Mainz" (Tchernichovsky),
  197, 224
"Battle Pages" (Kovner), 296, 297
Bauer, Yehuda, 45, 165
Będzin, 263–64
Beevor, Antony, 7, 104
Beirak, Natan, 39
Beitar, 78–79, 287

Beit-Halachmi, Benjamin, 178, 185
Belgium and Holland, Jewish Brigade/
    Nokmim moving to, 124–33, 155,
    199, 216
Bełżec, 240
Ben-Asher, Haim, 22
Ben-David, Yehuda, 197, 207, 211–12, 219,
    259, 287
Ben-Ephraim, Yitzhak (Mano), 78
Ben-Gal (Rabinovitch), James (Michael):
    Jewish Brigade and, 106, 111–12, 115–
    16, 124–26, 132, 134, 137; Kovner in
    Palestine/in prison and, 171, 176,
    295; Paris, meeting with Shertok in,
    222–23; on vengeance, 293
Ben-Gurion, David: DP camp survivors,
    meeting with, 195–96, 210; Jewish
    Brigade and, 113, 125, 129, 133; Jew-
    ish Resistance Movement and, 217;
    Kovner in Palestine and, 146, 161–
    62, 170; on Nokmim and vengeance,
    292–93, 294; Paris, Nokmim in, 195,
    196, 203, 205–6, 209, 218
Ben-Gurion, Paula, 205
Ben-Haim, Paul, 277
Ben-Horin (Brieger), Yehuda: arrest/im-
    prisonment of Kovner and, 182–83,
    186, 190; Hacker replacing at head of
    German Unit, 211; Jewish Brigade in
    Italy and, 114, 115, 123–24; Kovner
    in Palestine and, 158–61, 163, 171,
    209; on Nuremberg operation, 251–
    52; Paris, Nokmim in, 198, 203, 204,
    205, 217, 218; Plan A, knowledge of,
    218, 252; on vengeance and the Nok-
    mim, 293
Ben Hur (Cohen), Eliyahu, 122, 134, 135
Ben Meiri, 47, 61, 62, 67–68, 211, 218,
    244, 266, 287
Ben-Natan, Asher, 8–9
Ben-Ya'akov, Bolek (Dov Gewirzman),
    62, 78, 92, 94, 105, 138, 200, 237, 262,
    263, fig. 13

Ben-Zur, Yashek (Pinchas Bencelowicz),
    62, 94, 132, 134, 229, 245, 248, 249,
    253, 255, 277, fig. 7, fig. 12
Benes, Edvard, 6
Benjamin, Levi (Ernest Frank), 100, 111,
    128–29
Bergen-Belsen, 290
Bergmann, Ernst David, 165, 166, 169,
    170, 295
Bet-Zuri, Eliyahu, 186
Bevin, Ernest, 147, 188
Bialik, Chaim Nachman, 11, 22, 297, 299
Biblical and spiritual warrant for ven-
    geance, 2–3, 10–12, 297, 299, 303. See
    also specific texts
Biltmore Program, 196
Biria (ship), 271
Birmann, Zippora, 43, 272–73
Bloodlands (Snyder), 7
The Book of Hashomer Hatzair, 159
The Book of the Ghettos' Wars, 36, 98, 273
Bowilski, David, fig. 7
Bozikowski, Tuvia, 62
bread, poisoning. See Dachau operation;
    Nuremberg operation
Bricha: in Bucharest, 68, 78, 81, 93; fund-
    ing operations of, 66, 67, 93–94;
    Germany, Nokmim in, 228; Haga-
    nah and, 195; Hativa and, 55, 57; Is-
    rael, leadership passing to represen-
    tatives from, 93; Italy, relocation
    from Bucharest to, 92–97; Jewish
    Brigade in Italy and, 117, 125; Kovner
    and, 65, 88, 97, 157, 193; Zivia Lubet-
    kin and, 81, 89; in Lublin, 33–34, 54,
    55, 57, 58, 64–68; migration of Nok-
    mim to Palestine, after German op-
    erations, 266, 267, 268; Nokmim, as
    cover for, 57, 65, 88; Nokmim, dis-
    tancing from, 137, 138–39, 216; or-
    ganization and headquarters, 65;
    Pakhakh and, 88; Paris as headquar-
    ters of, 199; postwar formation of, to

Bricha (*continued*)
help Jews leave Europe, 33–34, 54, 55, 57, 64; prioritization of mission of, 173–74, 291, 294; success of, 136–37; vengeance taken by, 8–9; Antek Zuckerman on, 83
The Brigade (Bartov), 107–8
Brigg, Emil, 8
Britain/British: Anglo-American Committee, 147; Beitar's desire to attack, 79; British occupied zone in Germany, 50, 86; clandestine immigration, efforts to arrest, 146, 147; migration to Israel, limitations placed on, x, 186, 271; Lord Moyne, assassination of, 185–86, 187; Palestinian Mandate of, x, 1, 141, 145, 146, 164; *saison* in Israel/Palestine and, 146–47; SIB (Special Investigation Branch), British Army, 110. *See also* arrest and imprisonment of Kovner; Jewish Brigade
Broklyn, Julien, 253
Bucharest (March-June 1945), 71–97; Bricha in, 68, 78, 81, 93; first post-Holocaust Passover gathering in, 73–74; "fundamentals" (goals and methods of action) of Nokmim, defining, 89–92; Chaika Grossman's refusal to join Nokmim, 85–86; Hativa, formal founding of, 86–89; Italy, relocation of Bricha, Hativa, and Nokmim to, 92–97; Jewish Brigade, contact with, 72; Ka-Tzetnik and Auschwitz group in, 72–75; kibbutzim, division of Jewish survivors into, 73; Lublin, relocation from, 68–69; meeting with representatives from Israel in, 72; migration to Israel from, 71–72, 75, 80; organization of Nokmim in, 75–80; Warsaw Uprising survivors Antek and Zivia not joining Nokmim, 80–85

Buchenwald, 238, 239
Bulawko, Henry, 200
Buruma, Ian, 5, 6, 7

Carmi, Israel, 110, 112, 114–16, 120, 122, 132, 198, 237
Champollion (ship), 178, *fig. 5*
Chanukah, v, 148
Chelmno, 47, 64
Chernyakhovsky, Ivan, 46
Churchill, Winston, 102–3, 104, 136
Cohen, Binyamin, 190
collaborators, and Jewish Brigade in Italy, 109
communists and communism: Ben-Horin, former communism of, 114, 159; Holocaust discrediting, 34, 45, 60, 157; *I Burn Paris* (Jasieński), as communist response to *I Burn Moscow*, 215; Komsomol, 40, 203; Kovner, anti-Sovietism of, 52, 83, 120, 157; MAKI (Israeli Communist Party), 173; Nokmim and, 40, 56, 60, 63, 121, 159, 203, 244, 266; in Paris, 200, 201, 215; in Poland, 6, 48, 58, 63, 68–69, 83, 233; Zionism and, 203. *See also* Soviets
Cyganeria café, Krakow, Jewish underground attack on German officers at, 76
Czechoslovakia: liberation parade in (May 9, 1946), 267; Nokmim in Germany migrating to Palestine through, 266–67, 268, 271; vengeance in, 6
Częstochowa/Częstochowa group, 49, 57, 62, 76, 78, 95, 105, 202, 314

Dachau, 6, 97, 290
Dachau operation and its cancellation, 225, 226, 238, 243, 244, 246, 248, 256–61, 280

Davar, 16, 265

Davidson, Meirke, 119, 122–23, 133–35, 217

Derez, Machush (Michael), *fig. 7*

Deuteronomy 32:35, 300

Diamant, Manos, 8–9, 23, 39–40, 43

Diaspora Center, Milan, 91, 94, 125, 135, 262

Diaspora Jews, Lidovski on, 90

displaced person (DP) camps in Germany, 132, 136, 147, 162, 195–96, 210, 218, 243, 291, 294, 295

Distel, Leibke (Arie Leib): after German operations, 277; Dachau operation and, 263–64, 288; in Germany, 235, 242, 245, 247–49, 253, 255, 263–64; Jewish Brigade in Italy and, 140; in Lublin, 37; photos of, *fig. 7, fig. 17*; on Plan A, 282

Doctors' Plot, 53

Draenger, Gusta and Shimshon (Szymek), 39

Dror, Zvika, 83, 84, 85

Dror movement, 43, 61, 63, 64, 69, 71, 78, 84, 89, 155

The Drowned and the Saved (Levi), 21

Dushia, *fig. 7*

East European Survivors' Brigade. *See* Hativa

Ehrenburg, Ilya, 50, 51–52, 264, *fig. 1*

Eichmann, Adolf, 25, 72, 292–93

Ein HaHoresh, 275, 276

Eisen, Moshe (Barzilai), 178–79, 180, 181, 183–85, 187, 188

Eišiškės, Lithuania, postwar antisemitism in, 48

Eliav, Lyova, 187, 188, 189

Elkins, Michael, 21–22, 134, 169, 170, 191, 265

emigration. *See* migration to Palestine/Israel

England. *See* Britain/British

Eshbal, Michael, 179, 192

Exodus 21:24, 3, 10

expropriation, 66–67

An Eye for an Eye, 6

Ezekiel 25:15, 129

Fackenheim, Emil, 23–24

Faust (Goethe), 148

Feldschuh, Reuven, 64, 65

The Fighting Pioneer, 43

fishing kibbutz near Marseilles, 269–70

Flames In Ashes (Korczak), 152, 153

forgiveness versus vengeance, 19

FPO Underground (United Partisan Organization), Vilna, 35, 77, 247

France: fishing kibbutz near Marseilles, 269–70; Limoges, Nokmim in Germany moved to, 258, 261; migration of Nokmim to Palestine through, after German operations, 260, 268, 269, 270, 271. *See also* Paris, Nokmim in

Freier, Recha, 135

Freier, Shalhevet, 135

Friedman, Ruth, 225–26

Friedman, Yehuda (Idek), 76, 94, 132–33, 138, 225–26, 229, 231, 239, 256–61, 277, *fig. 32*

"From That Fire" (Gouri), 142

funding operations, 66–69, 91, 94, 123, 138–39, 165–66, 168–69, 199, 202–3, 232–33, 236–37

Galili, Yisrael, 146, 148, 160, 162–63, 165, 171, 175, 181, 208, 210, 242, 266

Galperin-Gliksman, Rachel, 37–38, 41, 94–95, 140, 231, 249–50, 270, *fig. 15*

Gatmon, Alex, 8, 9, 23

Gelblum, Irena, 123, 238, 239, 256–59, 261, *fig. 14*

Genesis: 4:15, 11; 9:6, 11

Genia, *fig. 7*

German prisoners: Jewish Brigade and, 101–2, 105–8, 109–10, 128, *fig. 4*; Nokmim uncovering information on whereabouts of, 199. *See also* Dachau operation; Nuremberg operation; Plan B

German Unit, 113–14, 116, 158–60, 191, 211, 214, 220, 223, 245, 251, 275, 287, 300

Germany: collective guilt of, 265; DP camps in, 132, 136, 147, 162, 195–96, 210, 218, 243, 291, 294, 295; Jewish Brigade attitude toward, 102–3; Jewish Brigade in, 127–32; poisoning of water supply in (*See* Plan A); rehabilitation of, 227–28; removal of Jewish survivors from, after Nokmim vengeance, plans for, 218–19; reparations by, 25, 227; vengeance, expectations of, 103–5, 213. *See also* Nazis/ Nazi Germany

Germany, Nokmim in (August 1945– June 1946), 225–71; Berlin and Frankfurt, in ruins, 236, 238; Dachau operation and its cancellation, 225, 226, 238, 243, 244, 246, 248, 256–61, 280; difficulties of life in Germany, 227–35; friendships and love matches between, 229, 231, 232; Göring and others, attempts to assassinate, 261–65; Hamburg operation, discarded, 225, 238, 239; Jewish Brigade assisting entry into, 124–27, 132–33, 138–39; Kovner, concerns about absence of, 204; migration to Israel/Palestine, immediately following operations, 219, 245, 258, 265–71, *figs. 7–8*; migration to Israel/ Palestine, postponement of, 229–30; Munich, as logistical headquarters, 236–37, 267; Nuremberg trials, 261– 65; Plan A and its cancellation, 235,

239–44, 248, 256; poison, obtaining, 228, 240, 241, 245–46, 257–58, 260, 284; relatives, separation from/rediscovery of, 230–31, 232, 235; target sites, searching for, 235–39; teams, division into, 237–39; Weimar area operation, abandoned, 238–39. *See also* Nuremberg operation

Gewissar, Menashe, 46, 67, 68–69, 139, 219–22, 287

ghetto fighters: *The Book of the Ghettos' Wars*, 36, 98, 273; *History of the Haganah* failing to mention, 174; Nokmim members as, 36–37, 41; in Vilna ghetto, 37–38, 41, 44, 46–47, 49–50, 52, 59, 77; Warsaw Ghetto uprising and survivors, 33, 53, 57, 58, 62–64, 72–73, 257, 259, 283. *See also specific individuals by name*

Gichon, Mordechai, 114, 290

Gilboa, Amir, 130

Givati Brigade, 56, 296–97

Gliksman, Zygmunt (Zygi), 94, 95, 200, 215, 229, 267, 277, *fig. 16*

Goethe's *Faust*, 148

Göring, Hermann, 262–65

Gouri, Haim, 15, 48, 49, 50, 142

Grajek, Stephen, 63, 65

Greek refugees, Jews hoping to pass as, 69, 95

Greenspan-Frimer, Pnina, 72

Gropius, Walter, 236

Gross, Jan, 48

Grossman, Chaika, 85–86, 219, 221, 284–85, 286

Grossman, Robert (Dov Gur), 110

Grossmann, Atina, 24

Grudjinski, Ze'ev, 183

Gruner, Pinchas, 157, 189, 190

Guilt, Suffering, and Memory (Margalit), 104

Günthergrube, 37

Gutkind, Arie, 239
Gutman, Israel, 16, 45, 288
Gutterman, Bella, 82

Habimah, 148
Hacker (Givon), Shmuel (Uli), 211
Hadash, Motke, 105, 107–8, 119–20, 139, 199
Hadash, Shmulik, 105
Hadassah (code name for vengeance), 164, 189
Haganah: arrest/imprisonment of Kovner and, 177–78, 180, 182–84; Pasha Avidov and, 141; Ben-Horin and, 159; breakaway militias and, 146–47, 155, 187; communications equipment smuggled by, 93; defined, x; *History of the Haganah*, x, 106, 174–75, 197, 279, 291–92, 293; IZL and, 146–47; Jewish Brigade and, 100, 106, 110, 111, 112, 122, 123, 125; Jewish people, claiming representation of, 207, 209; Jewish Resistance Movement and, 217; Kovner in Palestine and, 134–35, 140, 146, 148, 155, 161, 163, 165, 169, 171; Kovner's order from, 175–76, 182–84; migration of Nokmim to Palestine, after German operations, 268; Nokmim in Paris and, 195–98, 199, 204, 211, 212; Nuremberg operation and, 245, 252–53; Plan A, awareness of, 139, 163, 171; poison acquired by Kovner, knowledge of, 169; on postwar anti-semitism, 50, 51; Shadmi and, 68, 195–98; vengeance, perspective on, 261, 291–92
Haganah (ship), 271
Hakim, Eliyahu, 186
Hamburg operation, 225, 238, 239
Hamlet (Shakespeare), 19
Hammel, Yitzhak, 76, 140, 229, 231, 237–38, 268, 277, *fig. 19*

Hanoar Hatzioni, 65, 78
Hanokem, 41
Harmatz, Yulek (Yosef): in Bucharest, 75–76, 78; communist past of, 203; Dachau operation and, 260; in Germany, 230, 232, 233, 234, 237, 238, 239, 287; Jewish Brigade in Italy and, 117, 119, 125; on Kovner, 170–71; in Lublin, 40, 41, 46, 59, 65; migration of Nokmim to Palestine, after German operations, 267; as Mossad agent, 276; Nuremberg operation and, 239–41, 244, 246–50, 255, 258; photos of, *fig. 7, fig. 23*; on Plan A, 281; on Shadmi, 218
Hashomer Hatzair: arrest/imprisonment of Kovner and, 190, 191; Pasha Avidov seeking help from member of, 244; Ben-Horin and, 159; *The Book of Hashomer Hatzair*, 159; in Bucharest, 78, 81, 85, 94, 95; Hativa and, 121; Jewish Brigade and, 116, 121–22, 123; Kovner in Palestine and, 35, 133, 154, 155, 156, 157, 160, 162, 176; in Lublin, 35, 40, 53, 61, 63; in Paris, 199, 200; *Yalkut Moreshet* sponsored by, 191, 279–280190; Antek Zuckerman's criticism of, 85
Hativa: in Bucharest, 74, 81, 82, 86–89; continuing loyalty of Nokmim to, 190; disbanding of, 135–36; founding of, 86–89, 173; Israel, representative from Land of, 89; Italy, relocation to, 92–97; Jewish Brigade in Italy and, 117, 121–22, 130; Ka-Tetznik and, 96; Kovner in Palestine and, 136, 149, 154, 155, 156–57, 176; Zivia Lubetkin and, 88, 89; in Lublin, 54–55, 57, 61, 62, 63, 65; manifesto sent to Potsdam Conference, 136; migration to Israel and, 87; oath and swearing-in ceremony, 87–88; Antek Zuckerman on, 83

Hazan, Ya'akov, 116, 121, 160, 161, 183–84, 190, 191

Ha'aretz, 27

HeHalutz, 220, 221, 222

Heilperin, Falk, 16, 17

Hellman, Yudke, 64

Herald Tribune, 250

Histadrut, 105, 146, 156, 180

History of the Haganah, x, 106, 174–75, 197, 279, 291–92, 293

Hitler, Adolf, 23, 24, 25, 49, 74, 79, 100, 130, 262, 292

Holland and Belgium, Jewish Brigade/Nokmim moving to, 124–33, 155, 199, 216

Holocaust: academic studies of vengeance for, 13–26; defined and described, 3–5; Chaika Grossman on, 285; humiliation produced by, 4–5; identity and, 173; ideologies discredited by, 34; Jewish Brigade and, 100–101, 103, 105, 108, 110–11, 115–16, 132; Jewish people, representation of, 206–7; in Lithuania, 152–53; as motivation for vengeance, 42 (See also vengeance); Nokmim, definition and purpose of, 2–3; non-Jews, vengeance by, 5–7, 10, 300; scope of, 44–45; uniqueness of, in genocidal events, 4; Yishuv's understanding of, 123, 148, 154, 173, 197, 208, 278

Holocaust Memorial Day, 226

Hoter-Ishay, Aharon, 119

The Human Condition (Arendt), 19

L'humanité, 215

I Burn Moscow, 215

I Burn Paris (Jasieński), 215

immigration. See migration to Palestine/Israel

Israel, Land of: Arab world, struggles with, 25; breakaway militias in, 146–47, 155, 187; Bricha group ordered to cease activities by, 9; Bricha leadership taken over by representatives of, 93; British Mandate in, x, 1, 141, 145, 146, 164; Bucharest, Nokmim and representatives of Israel meeting in, 72, 78, 79; Hativa and, 89; Holocaust, understanding of, 123, 148, 154, 173, 197, 208, 278; Jewish Brigade in Italy and Yishuv, 100, 101, 103, 105, 106, 108, 113, 123; Nokmim, view of Yishuv leadership on, 291–94; Nokmim assigned to Kovner by Yishuv, 1; Nuremberg trials and Yishuv leadership, 265; partisans, views on, 154–55, 173–75; reparations, debate over, 25; Soviets, Yishuv's admiration of, 120, 139, 154–55; state of Yishuv in 1945, 145–48; vengeance, establishment of state of Israel as, 304; vengeance, Yishuv's position on, 145, 148, 149, 158–61, 171–75, 261, 291–94; War of Independence in, 8, 56, 172, 276, 296–97. See also Haganah; Jewish Brigade; Kovner in Palestine; migration to Palestine/Israel; Mossad

Israeli, Ben-Zion, 122

Italy: bombing of Tel Aviv and Haifa, during WWII, 151; Diaspora Center, Milan, 91, 94, 125, 135, 262; Levi's return to, 21, 32; migration of Nokmim to Palestine through, after German operations, 269, 271; relocation of Bricha, Hativa, and Nokmim to, 92–97. See also Jewish Brigade in Italy

Itka, fig. 7

IZL, 79, 106, 146–47, 174, 179, 187, 295

Jacoby, Susan, 18–19, 20

Jasieński, Bruno, 215

Jewish Agency, 94, 99, 146, 178, 182, 207, 217

Jewish Anti-Fascist Committee, Soviet Union, 52, 53

Jewish Brigade: Bar-Zohar on, 287; Dachau operation and, 258, 259; disbanding of (July 10, 1946), 223, 268; flag of, 99–100; in Germany, 127–32; Nokmim assisted in entering Germany by, 124–27, 132–33, 138–39, *fig. 3*; Nokmim assisted in leaving Germany by, 267, 268, 269; Nokmim in Paris and, 199, 203, 204, 216; Nokmim's continuing relationships with, 176, 236; Nuremberg operation and, 245, 249, 251–52; recruitment poster, *fig. 2*; return to Palestine, 160; Shadmi sent to head Haganah in Europe and, 196; Thirteen Commandments for Jewish soldiers in Germany, 128–29, 130

Jewish Brigade in Italy (July–August 1945), 99–141; arrest of Kovner and, 178; Belgium and Holland, move to, 124–33, 155; Berlin, desire to march as army through, 103; breakaway militias in Israel/Palestine, association of Nokmim with, 106, 146–47, 155; Bricha movement and, 34; British military and, 100, 108, 109, 110, 112, 113, 125; Bucharest, contact with Jews in, 72; collaborators and, 109; defined and described, 10, 100–101; Diaspora Center set up in Milan by, 91, 94; general strike, fast day in response to, 147; German captured soldiers and, 101–2, 105–8, 109–10, 128, *fig. 4*; German Unit and, 113–14, 158; Holocaust and, 100–101, 103, 105, 108, 110–11, 115–16, 132; Italy, relocation of Bricha and Hativa to, 94, 95–96; Ka-Tzetnik with, 75, 96; Kovner and Nokmim, meeting with, 97, 116–24, 137, 210; Kovner in Palestine and, 150, 153–54, 161, 162; Plan A,

awareness of, 123, 137–38, 139, 171; postwar killings of Jews by Nazi groups and, 50; procedures as army of conquest, decisions about, 101–8; survivors, assisting, 101, 102, 108, 110, 111, 115–16, 119, 127–28, 132; Tarvisio, complex ethnicities and politics in, 108–10; vengeance and, 9, 22, 99–108, 111–13, 116, 119–20, 122, 124, 127, 129–32, 161; vengeance squad within, 110–15, 197, 300; Yishuv and, 100, 101, 103, 105, 106, 108, 113, 123, 125–26, 140

Jewish Combat Organization, 83

Jewish National Council, 146

Jewish people: Nuremberg trials, not represented in, 261–65, 292; representatives of, 207–9, 211; on vengeance, 300–304

Jewish Resistance Movement/United Resistance Movement/Meri, 147, 216–17

Joint Distribution Committee (JDC), 66, 71, 77, 137–38, 237, 262

Josiah Wedgwood (ship), 271

Joy of the Poor (Alterman), 151, 194

Judt, Tony, 32

Justice, Not Vengeance (Wiesenthal), 23

Kafkafi, Yitzhak, v

Kagan, Aharon and Dinka, 232–33

Kaminetzky, Hadassah, 164, 179, 191

Ka-Tzetnik (Yehiel Feiner, later De-Nur), 72–75, 96, 283, *fig. 37*

Katzir (Katchalsky), Ephraim and Aharon, 165, 167–68, 170, 178, 193

Katznelson, Itzhak, 70

Kaufmann, Dalia (Daicha), 237

Kazhik. *See* Rathajzer, Kazhik

Kek-Michaeli, Bezalel: in Bucharest, 78; Dachau operation and, 260; in Germany, 201, 236, 243–44; Jewish Brigade in Italy and, 117; Kovner in

Kek-Michaeli, Bezalel (*continued*)
Palestine and, 140, 149, 164; in Lublin, 59, 60, 61, 65; in Paris, 201, 211; photo of, *fig. 38*

Kempner-Kovner, Vitka: after German operations, 276, 277; arrest/imprisonment of Abba Kovner and, 177, 180, 181, 189–91, 235–36; in Bucharest, 71, 76, 80; on Dachau operation, 257, 259, 260; Leibke Distel and, 247; Germany, Nokmim in, 229–30, 234, 237, 242, 244, 245; Jewish Brigade in Italy and, 117, 126; Ruzka Korczak and, 153, 177, 205; Abba Kovner's trip to Palestine and, 134, 135, 139, 141, 149, 161, 164, 168, 175, 176, 177; in Lublin, 37, 39, 45–47; migration of Nokmim to Palestine, after German operations, 266, 269, 270; on Nuremberg operation, 251; papers given to author by, x; parachuting into Berlin with Red Army, opposition to, 39, 45–46; in Paris, 198–99, 201–5, 209, 213, 222; photos of, *fig. 1, fig. 35*; on Plan A, 242, 283–84

Kenet (Kantarowicz), Shlomo, 94, 117, 235, 236, 245, 257–59, 277, 281–82, *fig. 36*

Kielce pogrom (1946), 49

Kishleh (prison), Jerusalem, 179, 191

Kitt, Kalman, 112, 131–32

Klarsfeld, Beate and Serge, 25

Kless, Shlomo, 40, 51, 61, 62, 71, 91, 117

Kliger (Eliav), Ruth, 217

Knesset Israel, 148

Komsomol, 40, 203

Korczak-Marla, Ruzka: after German operations, 276; arrest/imprisonment of Kovner and, 189–91; Vitka Kempner-Kovner and, 153, 177, 205; Kovner in Palestine and, 151–55, 156, 157, 158, 161, 167, 170, 175, 176–77, 205; love affair with Kovner, rumors

of, 205; parachuting into Berlin with Red Army, opposition to, 39, 45–46; photos of, *fig. 1, fig. 34*; on Plan A, 281; summoned to Palestine, 134, 151–52; traits of Nokmim members and, 37, 39, 40; on vengeance, 153, 158; Chaim Weizmann and, 165, 166

Kovner, Abba: after German operations, 276–80; on antisemitism's postwar resurgence, 48–54, 82, 97, 118; Ehud Avriel on, 217; Beitar members, exclusion of, 79, 80; Belgium and Holland, departure of Jewish Brigade for, 124–27; biography of, ix, x; Bricha and, 65, 88; Bucharest, relocation to, 68, 71, 72; on duty of vengeance, 37; at Eichman trial, 293; Elkins and, 21; final illness and death of, 277, 278, 279, 294; formation of Nokmim around, in Lublin, 59; on "fundamentals" (goals and action plans) for Nokmim, 89–92; funding operations and, 67; Germany, Nokmim in, 229–30, 234, 235; Chaika Grossman and, 85–86, 285; Hativa, disbanding of, 136; Hativa, founding of, 87–88; on Holocaust, 3, 4; Israel, organizing postwar Jewish migration to, 35; Italy, relocating to, 93; Jewish Brigade and, 101, 116–24, 137; on Jewish Central Committee in Lublin, 58; Ka-Tzetnik and Auschwitz group, 74, 75; leadership abilities of, 35, 40, 41, 59; Zivia Lubetkin compared, 82; Lublin, postwar flight to, 33, 68; migration of Nokmim to Palestine, after German operations, 268–70; motivations of, 42, 43–44; organization of Nokmim by, 2, 64–65, 76, 77, 79, 80; photos of, *fig. 1, fig. 5, fig. 33*; Plan A and, 191–93, 235–36, 241, 242, 269, 294–95; pseudonyms of, 135, 141, 164, 178, 179,

185; on Shadmi's claims about Nokmim plans to attack Paris, 216; silence about operations, breaking, 278, 279–80; successors to, 203–4, 219–22; Sutzkever and, 52; on traits of Nokmim members, 36, 37, 38; vengeance, consequences of dedication to, 135–37; vengeance, vision of, 294–300; in War of Independence, 296–97; Warsaw Ghetto uprising survivors and, 62–64; Antek Zuckerman's criticism of, 84–85. *See also* arrest and imprisonment of Kovner; Kovner in Palestine

Kovner, Michael (brother), 52, 120
Kovner, Michael (son), 42
Kovner, Vitka. *See* Kempner-Kovner, Vitka
Kovner in Palestine (August–December 1945), 145–80; breakaway militias in Israel/Palestine, association of Nokmim with, 146–47, 155; coded correspondence with Nokmim during, 163–64; consolidation of Yishuv's position on vengeance and, 145, 148, 149, 158–61, 171–75; departure for Palestine, 133–36, 141; departure from Palestine, 175, 177–80; effects on Hativa, Bricha, and Nokmim, 138–41, 175–77, 284; Ruzka Korczak and, 151–55, 156, 157, 158, 161, 167, 170, 175, 176–77, 205; love affair with Ruzka Korczak, rumors of, 205; meetings and activities, 148–51, 161–65; poison, acquisition of, 162–63, 165–71, 175; purpose of, 148; state of Yishuv in 1945, 145–48; Meir Ya'ari and, 155–61. *See also* arrest and imprisonment of Kovner

Kristallnacht, anniversary of, 104

Lamdan, Yitzhak, 230
Landsberg/Kaufering camp, 9, 97
Lang, Berel, 13, 19–20, 24–25

Laskov, Haim, 110, 111, 112, 114, 290
Lavee, Shimon, 40
Lazar, Haim, 78–80, 88, 117, 125, 287
Lazar, Haya, 117
Lehi, 106, 146, 147, 156, 174, 179, 186, 187, 295
Leibowitz, Yeshayahu, 11, 12
Lena. *See* Satz-Hammel, Lena
Levi, Primo, 21, 22, 31–32, 298
Levin, Baruch, 88
Lidovski, Avraham, 59
Lidovski, Eliezer: Bricha and, 65; in Bucharest, 68, 71, 78; on compartmentalization of Nokmim, 65; on Diaspora Jews, 90; Eastern Bloc, vengeance in, 301; on funding operations, 67; Germany, Nokmim in, 235, 243; Hativa, founding of, 88; Lublin, meetings in, 59, 60–61; on Nuremberg trials, and attempt to assassinate Göring, 262–63; organization and allocation of responsibilities for Nokmim, 64; photos of, *fig. 7, fig. 25*
Lidovski, Rachel, 71
Lidovski, Vita, 59
Liebermann, Aviva, 231
Limoges, France, Nokmim in Germany moved to, 258, 261
Lipschitz, Ya'akov, 100–101, 102
Lithuania: Holocaust in, Ruzka Korczak on, 152–53; Jews of, 7, 45, 48, 57, 58, 73, 97, 152; postwar antisemitism in, 48
London Times, 250
Lost Writings (Katznelson), 70
Lubetkin, Zivia: on antisemitism's postwar resurgence, 53–54, 82; Bricha and, 81, 89; in Bucharest, 71, 73, 76, 78, 80–85; Dachau operation's cancellation and, 259; decision not to join Nokmim and attitudes toward vengeance, 80–85, 220; Hativa and, 88, 89; Kovner compared, 82; in Lublin, 53–54, 62, 64; Antek Zuckerman

Lubetkin, Zivia (*continued*)
approached to lead Nokmim and,
220
Lublin (Jan–March 1945), 31–69; antisemitism, postwar resurgence of,
47–54; Bricha movement in, 33–34,
54, 55, 57, 58, 64–68; Bucharest, relocation to, 68–69; camps and killing
fields, visiting, 45–47; consolidation
of concept, 55–57; funding operations, 66–68; Hativa (East European Survivors' Brigade) and, 54–55,
57, 61, 62, 63; Jewish Central Committee in, 58, 68; meetings of Jewish
survivor groups in, and formation of
Nokmim, 57–66; motivations and
reasons for considering vengeance,
42–54; organization, recruitment,
and ideological foundation, 64–65;
postwar movement of Jewish survivors to/through, 33–35, 54, 57; post-
WWII chaos, shifting to Lublin in,
31–35; traits of Nokmim members
and, 36–42
Lukawiecki, Anna and Mundek, 40
Lustgarten, Shimek (Shimon), 76, 231,
236, 238, 258, 277, *fig. 7, fig. 24*

Maimon, Poldek (Yehuda Wasserman):
after German operations, 278; in Bucharest, 76, 81, 94; on Dachau operation, 259; in Germany, 231, 232, 235,
237, 241–42; Göring, Lidovski's attempt to assassinate, 262–63; Jewish Brigade in Italy and, 132, 135, 140,
fig. 7; in Lublin, 37; migration of
Nokmim to Palestine, after German
operations, 266, 268; in Paris, 200,
201, 202, 219–20, 222; photos of,
fig. 3, fig. 7, fig. 27; on Plan A, 282
Mairanz, Ludwig (Levi Yitzhak), 202,
276, *fig. 26*
Mairanz, Paulette Rabinovich, 202

Majdanek, 46–47, 73, 77, 118, 152
MAKI, 173
Maklef, Mordechai, 125
Manek (Moshe) L.: after German op-
erations, 277; Auschwitz group, as
part of, 73; in Bucharest, 73, 74, 75;
in Germany, 229, 230–31, 233, 234,
238, 239; on Kovner's trip to Pales-
tine, 140; in Lublin, 37, 68; Nurem-
berg operation and, 248, 249, 253,
255; Nuremberg trial defendants, at-
tempt to assassinate, 263–64; photos
of, *fig. 7, fig. 28*; on Plan A, 281
Mapai, 120, 122, 133, 146, 162
Maquis, 201, 215
Mardor, Munya, 189
Margalit, Gilad, 104
Marla, Avi, 276
Marshall, George, and Marshall Plan,
227
Masada, v, 230
"Masada" (Lamdan), 230
Masaryk, Jan, 137
Mauriac, François, 14
Mauthausen, 115–16, 237
Meir, Golda, 103, 179–80
Meri/Jewish Resistance Movement/
United Resistance Movement, 147,
216–17
migration to Palestine/Israel: age and or-
igins of migrants, in 1945, 145; Ali-
yah D, 186, 189; Anglo-American
Committee on, 147; arrest/impris-
onment of Kovner and, 189; from
Bucharest, 71–72, 75, 80; clandes-
tine immigration, 146, 147; Ha-
tiva on, 87; Jewish Brigade and, 118;
Kovner involved in migration efforts, 35; from Lublin, 34–35, 54;
Mossad for Aliyah B, x, 34, 93, 97,
127, 146, 148, 183, 184, 200, 217, 219;
of Nokmim, after German operations, 219, 245, 258, 265–71, *figs. 7–8*;

Polish and Soviet Jewish remnants, 277; postponement of, for Nokmim in Germany, 229–30; Soviets on, 34–35; success of Bricha and, 136–37. *See also* Bricha

Mira/Mirka. *See* Verbin-Shabetsky, Mira

Mishmar, 159

"Missive to Hashomer Hatzair Partisans" (Kovner), 53

Moller, Hans, 165–66, 169

Morewski, Avrom (Silva), 201

Morgenthau, Henry, and Morgenthau Plan, 6, 227

Mossad: acts of vengeance by, 301; Eichman captured by, 292; Nokmim recruited by, 276, 277

Mossad for Aliyah B, x, 34, 93, 97, 127, 146, 148, 183, 184, 200, 217, 219

Moyne, Lord, assassination of, 185–86, 187

Mussolini, Benito, 100

Nakam (Ka-Tzetnik), 283

Nakdimon, Shlomo, 279, 287

Nasza Grupa, 8–9

Nativ, 277

Nazis/Nazi Germany: academic studies of vengeance and, 16; Americas and Europe, disappearance of former Nazis into, 265; bombings of, in WWII, 131; Cyganeria café, Krakow, Jewish underground attack on German officers at, 76; expropriation of funds of, 67; Holocaust perpetrated by, 4; *judenrein* aspirations, countering, 24; legislation of, 3; as motivation for vengeance, 42 (*See also* vengeance); Nuremberg trials, 261–65; postwar killing of Jews by gangs of Nazis, 50; postwar Nazi underground, document about, 212–13; retrospective views on moving into/taking vengeance in, 68–69;

Slavs, treatment of/revenge by, 5–6; SS prisoners in, actions against (*See* Dachau operation; Germany, Nokmim in; Nuremberg operation; Plan B); Wiesenthal and, 23; Meir Ya'ari on, 158–59

Nechama (code name for vengeance), 208–10, 211, 245, 252, 278

Neria, Moshe-Zvi, 14, 17

New York Times, 250

Nietzsche, Friedrich, 26

Night (Wiesel), 14–16, 17

Nissanilevich, Senka (Netanel), 65, 71, 81, 93, 125, 237, 277, *fig. 30*

NKVD, 120

Nokmim, ix–xi, 1–26, 275–304: academic studies of vengeance for Holocaust and, 13–26; after German operations, 275–77; breakaway militias in Israel/Palestine, association with, 146–47, 155; Bricha as cover for, 57, 65, 88; chrononology, 309–11; compartmentalization of membership, 41, 65; conception of, in Lublin (Jan–March 1945), 31–69 (*See also* Lublin); criticism of/support for, 284–91; definition, etymology, and purpose of, 2–5, 10; definition of vengeance and, 10–13; documentary films about, 278; "fundamentals" (goals and methods of action), defining, 89–92; funding operations of, 66–69, 91, 94, 123, 138–39; in Germany (August 1945–June 1946), 225–71 (*See also* Germany, Nokmim in); interviews with, xiv; Italy, relocation to, 96–97; Jewish Brigade and (July–August 1945), 99–141 (*See also* Jewish Brigade); Jewish vengeance against Nazis, non-Nokmim, 7–10, 14, 300–301; on Kovner's trip to Palestine, 138–41, 175–77, 284 (*See also* arrest and imprisonment of Kovner;

Nokmim (*continued*)
Kovner in Palestine); list of members, 313–15; non-Jewish vengeance against Nazis and, 5–7, 10, 300; number of members, 213, 300; in Paris (February–June 1846), 195–223 (*See also* Paris, Nokmim in); preparation for, in Bucharest (March–June 1945), 71–97 (*See also* Bucharest); reassembly of (1985), and speaking out, 36, 279–80; "the second group," 275, 276; Shadmi on need to disband, 209–10, 211, 219, 268; silence about operations, 277–79, 284; traits of members, 36–42; Yishuv leadership's view of, 291–94; Antek Zuckerman on, 81–82, 84–85

Numbers 31:2, 2

Nuremberg operation, 244–56; attribution of responsibility for, 252, 253, 255, 256; Ben-Horin on, 293; concentration of efforts on Munich and, 239; Dachau operation and, 256–57, 258, 260; migration of Nokmim to Palestine after, 267; number of persons affected in, 250–51, 252, 255, 300; Plan A and its cancellation, 239–44, 252, 258; Plan B (poisoning the bread) at, 243, 244–49; poison used in, 245–47, 248–49, 250, 254–55; results of, 249–56; teams, positioning of, 239–40, 247–48; Yehuda Tubin and, 289; US army and, 240, *fig. 6*; Mira Verbin-Shabetsky's lodgings and, 233–34, 246, 248; water system at Nuremberg, 240–41

Nuremberg trials, 261–65, 292

"Of Revenge" (Bacon), 18
"On the Slaughter" (Bialik), 11
Orland, Ya'akov, 130
Ossia, Shmuel, 135
Oz, Amos, 45

Pages of Testimony, 83
Pakhakh, 88, 98
Palestine. *See* Israel, Land of; Kovner in Palestine; migration to Palestine/Israel
Palgi (Nussbacher), Yoel, 156
Palmach, 113, 119, 146, 153, 178, 184, 220, 223, 269–70, 276
Palyam, 178, 182
Paris, Nokmim in (February–June 1946), 195–223; headquarters of, 198–206; Jewish people, claims to representation of, 207–9, 211; Nokmim in Germany migrating to Palestine through, 268; plans of Nokmim reported by Shadmi, 214–16; poison obtained in, 200–201; reasons for moving to, 199; Résistance/Maquis, contacts with, 201, 215; Shadmi, appointed as had of Haganah in Europe, 195–98; Shadmi, first contact with and views on vengeance of, 206–10; Shadmi, on need to disband Nokmim, 209–10, 211, 219; Shadmi's meetings with Nokmim, 211–19; Antek Zuckerman approached to lead vengeance operations, 219–22
partisans: "Missive to Hashomer Hatzair Partisans" (Kovner), 53; Nokmim members viewed as, 36–37; Résistance/Maquis, Paris, 201, 215; United Partisan Organization (FPO underground), Vilna, 35, 77, 247; Yishuv's views on, 154–55, 173–75
Partizanka, 35
Pasha. *See* Avidov, Yitzhak "Pasha"
Passover, 73–74, 267
Pasternak, Mondek (Moshe Bar-Tikva), 114
Payback (Rosenbaum), 20
Peltz, Johanan, 110–11
Perchik, Avraham, 65, 236, 237
The Periodic Table (Levi), 21

Philistines, 38, 129, 192, 289, 292, 296
Phoenix over the Galilee (*Nakam*;
Ka-Tzetnik), 96
Plan A (to poison German water
sources): cancellation of, 239–44,
248, 256, 280–84, 285; Gliksman in
Belgium and, 216; Jewish Brigade,
Nokmim with, 123, 137–38, 139, 171;
Kovner in Palestine and, 149, 160,
162–64, 169–72; Kovner's feelings
about, 191–93, 235–36, 241, 242, 269,
294–95; Kovner's postponement of,
235–36, 241; Lublin and Bucharest,
first bruited in, 64, 90; Nokmim interviewees on, 280–84; Nuremberg
operation and, 239–44, 252, 258; on-
site planning for, 25–236; Shadmi
and, 212, 218; Tubin and, 289; Yishuv
leadership's opposition to, 209, 218.
See also poison
Plan B (actions against SS prisoners
in Germany): Allied treatment of,
Nokmim's concerns about, 218, 256,
265; Avidan on, 290; Bucharest, development of Plan in, 91; at Dachau,
256, 260; Gliksman in Belgium and,
216; Jewish Brigade, Nokmim with,
138; Kovner in Palestine and change
of focus to, 160, 163, 164, 165, 167,
169, 170, 171, 176, 182, 193; at Nuremberg, 243, 244–49, 252; Paris, Nokmim in, 206, 218; Plan A prevented
by, 252; removal of Jewish survivors
from Germany after execution of,
plans for, 218–19; Yishuv leadership's
support for, 209–10, 222–23, 245. *See
also* poison
Plan C (actions against individual Germans), 216, 269
Płaszów, 226
poison: for Dachau operation, 257–58,
260; dumping of, due to Kovner's
arrest, 179, 180–82; German teams

waiting for, 228, 240, 241, 257, 284;
Ruzka Korczak seeking to replace,
190; Kovner's acquisition of, 162–63,
165–71, 175; for Nuremberg operation, 245–47, 248–49, 250, 254–55;
Paris, obtained by Nokmim in, 200–
201, 206, 245; Plan A, loss of poison
and cancellation of, 241; Shadmi on
poisoning SS prisoners, 218; smuggling into Germany, 206, 245–46;
smuggling out of Palestine, 178–79.
See also Plan A; Plan B; *specific types*
Poland: Communist regime in, 6, 48, 58,
63, 68–69, 83, 233; Cyganeria café,
Krakow, Jewish underground attack
on German officers at, 76; migration of Polish remnant to Israel, 277;
postwar antisemitism in, 48–50; retrospective views on moving into/
taking vengeance in, 68–69; vengeance against Nazis by, 6, 7, 8. *See
also* Lublin
Poldek. *See* Maimon, Poldek
Ponar, killing fields of, 45, 47, 49, 118,
201
Postwar (Judt), 32
Potsdam Conference (1945), 136
"Prayer for Revenge" (Alterman), 151,
194

Rabinovich (Czeczja), Leah, 202
Rabinovich, Velveleh, 202, 267, 268,
fig. 39
Rabinovitch (Carmeli), Moshe, 179,
180–81, 185, 187, 189
Rabinow, Baruch, 171
Rathajzer, Kazhik (Simcha Rotem): after German operations, 277; in Bucharest, 80–81, 91–92; Dachau operation and, 256–61, 280; in Germany,
230, 235, 238–39, 244, 246, 256–61;
Jewish Brigade in Italy and, 91–92,
140–41; migration to Palestine/

Rathajzer, Kazhik (*continued*)
  Israel, 270; photo of, *fig. 41*; on
  Plan A, 280
Ratner, Yitzhak, 119, 165, 200–201, 206,
  246, 254, *fig. 7*, *fig. 42*
Red Army. *See* Soviets
Red Cross, 31, 65, 69, 91, 201
reparations, 25, 227
Résistance, Paris, 201, 215
Reznik, Nisan, 65, 88
Roseman, Mark, 16–17
Roseman, Mordechai, 61, 62, 65, 67, 93–
  95, 160, 228, 234, 286–87, 294
Rosenbaum, Thane, 20
Rosenberg-Amit, Cesia (Zila Roseberg),
  44, 46, 58, 59, 77, 92, 117, 204, 238,
  277, 281, *fig. 40*
Rosh Hashanah, 164
Rotbein-Marla, Yonat, 192, 270, 283
Rotem, Simcha. *See* Rathajzer, Kazhik
Rovno Jews, v, 7, 42, 57, 59–60, 314
*Rowno, a Memorial to the Jewish Com-
  munity o Rowno, Wolyn* (ed. Ava-
  tihi), v
Russia. *See* Soviets
Ruzka. *See* Korczak-Marla, Ruzka

Sachsenhausen-Oranienburg, 238
Sadeh, Yitzhak, 135, 146, 150, 153, 171
saison, 146–47
"Salamandra" (Ka-Tzetnik), 75, 96
Sarid, Levi Arieh, 41, 60–61, 188, 279,
  297
Sarig, Nahum, v
Satz-Hammel, Lena: after German operations, 278, 280; Dachau operation and, 256, 258; in Germany, 229,
  230, 231, 232–33, 235, 236, 237, 238–
  39; Jewish Brigade in Italy and, 93–
  94, 140; in Paris, 204, 215; photos of,
  fig. 9, *fig. 18*
Schenkel, Dov, 214, 245–46, 248, 254–55
Schneider, Ruvke, *fig. 7*

Schwartz, Joseph, 66, 137
Scrolls of Fire (Kovner), 299
Sea of Halacha (Kovner), 300
"the second group," 275, 276
The Second World War (Beevor), 7
Sedlis, Gabi (Gavriel Schedlitz), 46, 58,
  71, 234, 281
Sened, Yonat, 72, 80
Shadmi, Yiska (Issachar), 196, 213
Shadmi (Kremer), Nahum: communist
  past of Pasha Avidov and, 203; on
  Dachau operation, 258, 259; first contact with Nokmim, and views on
  vengeance, 206–10, 293; Menashe
  Gewissar/Antek Zuckerman and,
  220–21; Haganah in Europe, as head
  of, 68, 93, 195–98, 217; meetings with
  Nokmim in Paris, 211–19; migration
  of Nokmim to Palestine, after German operations, 266, 268; on need to
  disband Nokmim, 209–10, 211, 219,
  268; Nokmim, later appreciation of,
  287; Nokmim's lack of awareness of
  reports of, 279; Nuremberg operation and, 244–45, 246–47, 252–53;
  Nuremberg trial defendants, efforts
  to assassinate, 264; Plan A and, 212,
  218, 242–43, 252
Shakespeare, William, 19
Shamir (Rabinovich), Shlomo: Jewish Brigade and, 100, 102, 106, 111,
  112, 115–16, 126–27, 134, 163; on vengeance and the Nokmim, 209, 293
Shapira, Anita, 43
Shazar, Zalman, 170
Shenar, Leah (Lucia), 241
Shenar, Willek (Ze'ev Shutzreich), 76,
  240–42, 248, 256, 258, 277, *fig. 7*,
  fig. 43
Shenhavi, Mordechai, 165, 166
Shertok, Moshe, 99–100, 103, 113, 125,
  209–10, 220, 222–23, 245, 293
Shertok, Yaakov (Kobi), 113

Shklar, Israel (Srulik), 94
Shlonsky, Avraham, 27
Shnot Hamahanot Ha'olim, v
Sieff, Daniel, 168
Singer (Ron), Shalom, 186
Sneh, Moshe, 146, 148, 160, 162–63, 165, 171–75, 198, 208, 245
Snyder, Timothy, 7
Soviets: antisemitism of, 48–49, 51–53, 83, 120, 162; Berlin, unit of Red Army parachuting into (1944), 39, 45–46; border controls of, 91–92, 95; camps and killing fields visited by, 47; Germany, "Russian babies" in, 227; Greek refugees, Nokmim hoping to pass as, 69; I Burn Paris (Jasieński) calling for solidarity with, 215; Israel, Jewish postwar migration to, 34–35; Jewish Anti-Fascist Committee, 52, 53; Jewish soldiers in Red Army, 41; Kovner, anti-Sovietism of, 52, 83, 120, 157; Lublin, power in, 58; migration of Jewish survivors to Israel, Red Army assistance with, 137; migration of Soviet Jews to Israel, 277; in post-WWII chaos, 32; rubles, smuggling, 66; vengeance taken by, 5–6, 7, 51–52; Yishuv's admiration of, 120, 139, 154–55. See also communists and communism
Special Investigation Branch (SIB), British Army, 110
SS prisoners, actions against. See Dachau operation; Germany, Nokmim in; Nuremberg operation; Plan B
Stalin, Joseph, 52, 53, 136
Stern, Yair, and Sternists, 188
strychnine, 200
Süddeutsche Zeitung, 250
suicide, 39, 55, 100, 136, 151, 191, 265, 296
Surkis, Mordechai, 120, 125, 133, 162, 199

Sutzkever, Abraham, 52, 264
Szenes, Hannah, 156

Tabenkin, Moshe, 305
Talmud, Ta'anit 29a, 299
Tashkenters (Jewish returnees from Central Asia). See "Asians"
Taubes-Warchavchik, Hasya, 94, 228, 232, 235, 238, 268, 277, 281, fig. 21
Tchernichovsky, Shaul, 197, 224
"A Testament" (Birmann), 272–73
Tevet, Shabtai, 292
Thirteen Commandments for Jewish soldiers in Germany, 128–29, 130
Tito, Josip Broz, 114
Tobias, Jim G., 288
Tour de France (ship), 179, 185
Transport Company 462, 122, 135
Treblinka, 47, 48, 56, 64, 82, 105, 110, 118
Treger-Nissanilevich, Zelda, 41, 65, 71, 266, 277, fig. 29
The Truce/The Reawakening (Levi), 21, 31–32
Truman, Harry, 136
truth, Hebrew word for, 2, 302
Tubin, Shlomit, 116, 232, 289
Tubin, Yehuda, 116, 120, 121, 127, 133, 134, 155, 156, 160, 198, 232, 236, 244, 288–89
Tzur, Muki, 173

United Kingdom. See Britain/British
United Nations Relief and Rehabilitation Administration (UNRRA), 66, 72, 147, 212, 236
United Partisan Organization (FPO underground), Vilna, 35, 77, 247
United Resistance Movement/Jewish Resistance Movement/Meri, 147, 216–17
United States: Anglo-American Committee, 147; disappearance of former

United States (*continued*)
  Nazis into, 265; US occupied zone in
  Germany, 86, 227; vengeance in, 6
United States Army: Dachau operation
  and, 259, 260; Jews serving in, 100,
  138, 213, 237, 251, 260, 264; Nurem-
  berg operation and, 240, 242, 243,
  244, 247, 249–55, *fig. 6*; Palestine/
  Israel, assistance with migration to,
  137
"Until No Light" (Kovner), 192
Uzi (weapon), 277

vengeance: academic studies of Holocaust vengeance, 13–26; Allied division of Germany as, 25; antisemitism, postwar resurgence of, 47–54,
  213; Biblical and spiritual warrant
  for, 2–3, 10–12, 297, 299; criticism
  of/support for Nokmim regarding,
  284–91; defined, 10–13; as deterrence, 56; displacement of, 23–25; as
  duty, 37; establishment of state of Israel as, 304; forgiveness versus, 19;
  German expectations of, 103–5, 213;
  Chaika Grossman on, 85–86; as Hadassah, 164, 189; Haganah's perspective on, 261, 291–92; Hativa, disbanding of, 136; for Holocaust, 2–5;
  Jewish Brigade and, 9, 22, 99–108,
  111–13, 116, 119–20, 122, 124, 127,
  129–32, 161; Jewish mentality and,
  14–18; Jewish people on, 300–304;
  by Jews outside of Nokmim, 7–10,
  14, 300–301; Ka-Tzetnik on, 96;
  Ruzka Korczak on, 153, 158; Kovner's
  dedication to, consequences of, 135–
  37; Kovner's trip to Palestine and,
  134–35; Kovner's vision of, 294–300;
  legal concept of punishment versus,
  18–23; motivations of Jewish survivors for, 42–54; as Nechama, 208–
  10, 211, 245, 252, 278; by non-Jews,

5–7, 10, 300; Shadmi's appointment
  as head of Haganah in Europe and,
  195–98; Shadmi's views on, 206–10;
  Warsaw Uprising survivors Antek
  and Zivia on, 80–85; Meir Ya'ari on,
  158–59; Yishuv leadership's position
  on, 145, 148, 149, 158–61, 171–75, 261,
  291–94; Antek Zuckerman on, 80–
  85, 286. *See also* Nokmim
Verbin-Shabetsky, Mira (Mirka): after
  German operations, 277; in Bucharest, 77, 92; in Germany, 228, 232–
  34, 236, 241, 246, 248, 258, 259; in
  Lublin, 46; in Paris, 204; photo of,
  fig. 20; on Plan A, 282
Vilna ghetto: Beitar members from, 78–
  79; death of Kovner's girlfriend in,
  191; fighters/underground in, 37–
  38, 41, 44, 46–47, 49–50, 52, 59, 77,
  fig. 1; Ruzka Korczak's account of,
  151–53; Kovner's meditation on, in
  prison, 191, 192; Kovner's prewar activism in, 35; liberation of (1944), 39,
  45, 49; list of members of Nokmim
  from, 314; Lublin, survivors in, 33,
  59, 60; Nuremberg trials, Sutzkever
  testifying at, 264; United Partisan
  Organization (FPO underground),
  35, 77
Vitka. *See* Kempner-Kovner, Vitka
Vlasov, Andrey, 108

Wacksler, Max, *fig. 7*
Wagner, Richard, 25
Walish, Otto, *fig. 2*
War of Independence in Israel, 8, 56, 172,
  276, 296–97
Warchavchik, Yehiel (Hilik), 229, 238,
  fig. 22
Warsaw Ghetto uprising and survi-
  vors, 33, 53, 57, 58, 62–64, 72–73, 257,
  259, 283. *See also* Lubetkin, Zivia;
  Zuckerman, Antek

water supply, poisoning: at Dachau, 256; in Germany (*See* Plan A); at Nuremberg, 240–41; of SS prisoners in Germany, 218
Weimar area operation, 238–39
Weinberg, Shaike (Yeshyahu): Pasha Avidov asking for assistance from, 244; Jewish Brigade and, 110, 112, 114, 115, 120–22, 123, 132, 134, 138, 139; Kovner in Palestine and, 157, 160; Nokmim in Germany and, 236; Paris, Nokmim in, 198–200
Weitz, Yehiam, 167
Weizmann, Chaim, 146, 165–71, 295
Welner, Lipa, 253
Werewolf unit, 50
Wiesel, Elie, 14–16, 17, 104
Wiesenthal, Simon, 23, 25
Wild Justice (Jacoby), 18
Williams, Samuel T., 255
"Willy," in Toulon, 183, 184
Wingate, Orde, 108
Wodzisławski, Heniek, 202–3, 267
Wolf, Joseph, 76
World Zionist Organization, 99, 146, 165, 170

Ya'ari, Meir, 116, 121, 133, 155–61, 166, 171, 176, 190–92
Yahil (Hoffmann), Chaim, 212
Yalkut Moreshet, 279–80
Yaron, Ya'akov "Jacquo," 134, 178, 180, 181, 183–84, 191
A Year in Treblinka, 105, 132
Year Zero (Buruma), 5
Yishuv. *See* Israel, Land of

Yom Kippur, 2–3, 157
Youth Aliyah, 135
youth movement, Nokmim members' involvement in, 41, 126
Yulek. *See* Harmatz, Yulek

Zertal, Miyetek (Moshe Zilbertal), 120, 160
Zexer, Hava, 225, 226
Zhukov, Georgy K., 5
Zinke, Peter, 288
Zionism: communism and, 203; Kovner fleeing Vilna to escape Soviet charges of, 33; on Nokmim, 276; post-Holocaust Jewish interest in, 34; of Rovno and Vilna Jews in Lublin, 60–61; vengeance in Europe and, 56; World Zionist Organization, 99, 146, 165, 170
Zionist Congress, 155
Zohar-Vilozni, Yitzhak, 198, 229
Zorea, Meir, 110, 112, 114, 290
Zuckerman, Antek (Yitzhak): approached to lead Nokmim during Kovner's imprisonment, 219–22, 286; Dachau operation's cancellation and, 259; decision not to join Nokmim and attitudes toward vengeance, 80–85, 286; disagreement with Kovner in Lublin and move to Warsaw, 33, 62–64, 69, 71; Dror movement and, 63, 69, 71, 78, 84, 89; Kovner in Palestine and, 155–56, 188–89
żydokomuna, 48
Zyklon B, 47

STANFORD STUDIES IN JEWISH HISTORY AND CULTURE

David Biale and Sarah Abrevaya Stein, Editors

This series features novel approaches to examining the Jewish past in the form of innovative work that brings the field into productive dialogue with the newest scholarly concepts and methods. Open to a range of disciplinary and interdisciplinary approaches, from history to cultural studies, this series publishes exceptional scholarship balanced by an accessible tone, illustrating histories of difference and addressing issues of current urgency. Books in this list push the boundaries of Jewish Studies and speak compellingly to a wide audience of scholars and students.

Christian Bailey, *German Jews in Love: A History*

2022

Matthias B. Lehmann, *The Baron: Maurice de Hirsch and the Jewish Nineteenth Century*

2022

Liora R. Halperin, *The Oldest Guard: Forging the Zionist Settler Past*

2021

Samuel J. Spinner, *Jewish Primitivism*

2021

Sonia Gollance, *It Could Lead to Dancing: Mixed-Sex Dancing and Jewish Modernity*

2021

Julia Elsky, *Writing Occupation: Jewish Émigré Voices in Wartime France*

2020

Alma Rachel Heckman, *The Sultan's Communists:*
Moroccan Jews and the Politics of Belonging

2020

Golan Y. Moskowitz, *Queer Jewish Sendak: A Wild Visionary in Context*

2020

Devi Mays, *Forging Ties, Forging Passports: Migration and the Modern Sephardi Diaspora*

2020

Clémence Boulouque, *Another Modernity: Elia Benamozegh's Jewish Universalism*

2020

Dalia Kandiyoti, *The Converso's Return: Conversion and Sephardi*
History in Contemporary Literature and Culture

2020

Natan M. Meir, *Stepchildren of the Shtetl: The Destitute, Disabled, and Mad of Jewish Eastern Europe, 1800–1939*
2020

Marc Volovici, *German as a Jewish Problem: The Language Politics of Jewish Nationalism*
2020

Dina Danon, *The Jews of Ottoman Izmir: A Modern History*
2019

Omri Asscher, *Reading Israel, Reading America: The Politics of Translation Between Jews*
2019

Yael Zerubavel, *Desert in the Promised Land*
2018

Sunny S. Yudkoff, *Tubercular Capital: Illness and the Conditions of Modern Jewish Writing*
2018

Sarah Wobick-Segev, *Homes Away from Home: Jewish Belonging in Twentieth-Century Paris, Berlin, and St. Petersburg*
2018

Eddy Portnoy, *Bad Rabbi: And Other Strange but True Stories from the Yiddish Press*
2017

Jeffrey Shandler, *Holocaust Memory in the Digital Age: Survivors' Stories and New Media Practices*
2017

Joshua Schreier, *The Merchants of Oran: A Jewish Port at the Dawn of Empire*
2017

Alan Mintz, *Ancestral Tales: Reading the Buczacz Stories of S. Y. Agnon*
2017

Ellie R. Schainker, *Confessions of the Shtetl: Converts from Judaism in Imperial Russia, 1817–1906*
2016

For a complete listing of titles in this series, visit the Stanford University Press website, www.sup.org.

For a complete listing of titles in this series, visit the Stanford University Press website, www.sup.org.